HOMER RODEHEAVER
AND THE RISE OF THE GOSPEL MUSIC INDUSTRY

MUSIC IN AMERICAN LIFE

A list of books in the series appears at the end of this book.

HOMER RODEHEAVER

AND THE RISE OF THE GOSPEL MUSIC INDUSTRY

KEVIN MUNGONS
& DOUGLAS YEO

UNIVERSITY OF ILLINOIS PRESS
Urbana, Chicago, and Springfield

© 2021 by Kevin Mungons and Douglas Yeo
All rights reserved
1 2 3 4 5 C P 5 4 3 2 1
♾ This book is printed on acid-free paper.

Library of Congress Cataloging-in-Publication Data
Names: Mungons, Kevin, 1963– author. | Yeo, Douglas, author.
Title: Homer Rodeheaver and the rise of the gospel music industry
  / Kevin Mungons & Douglas Yeo.
Description: Urbana: University of Illinois Press, 2021. | Series:
  Music in American Life | Includes bibliographical references
  and index.
Identifiers: LCCN 2021006510 (print) | LCCN 2021006511 (ebook) |
  ISBN 9780252043840 (cloth) | ISBN 9780252085833 (paperback)
  | ISBN 9780252052743 (ebook)
Subjects: LCSH: Rodeheaver, Homer A. (Homer Alvan), 1880–1955.
  | Music publishers—United States—Biography. | Musicians—
  United States—Biography. | Trombonists—United States—
  Biography. | Evangelists—United States—Biography. | Gospel
  music—History and criticism.
Classification: LCC ML429.R63 M86 2021 (print) | LCC ML429.R63
  (ebook) | DDC 782.25/4092 [B]—dc23
LC record available at https://lccn.loc.gov/2021006510
LC ebook record available at https://lccn.loc.gov/2021006511

CONTENTS

Introduction 1

1 Prologue 13
2 Southern Roots and Early Years 38
3 Gospel Songs and Urban Revivalism 58
4 Commercial Gospel Music 91
5 New Technology to Promote an Old Story 113
6 The Mission of Rainbow Records 142
7 Spirituals and Minstrelsy 165
8 Jim Crow Revivalism Meets the Klan 190
9 Preserving and Exporting the Gospel Songs 210
10 Falling Out of Step at the Close of an Era 230
11 Epilogue: "It's Up to You, Rody, to Free Them" 251

Acknowledgments 257
Notes 261
Index 313

HOMER RODEHEAVER
AND THE RISE OF THE GOSPEL MUSIC INDUSTRY

INTRODUCTION

Just before the start of World War I, Homer Rodeheaver reached the pinnacle of his national fame—but not as a politician, athlete, or Hollywood celebrity. Instead, Homer Rodeheaver played the trombone and led mass singing for the revivalist Billy Sunday, a gig that vaulted both men to national prominence. In an era when music styles emerged as marketable genres, Rodeheaver created a brand of gospel song that cast an enormous influence on American vernacular music. And when the era of tabernacle revivalism inevitably declined, Rodeheaver adroitly shifted

FIGURE 0.1. Homer Rodeheaver and Billy Sunday in Winona Lake, 1931. Courtesy of Rodeheaver Collection, Grace College, Winona Lake.

to other ventures. He started the first gospel record label in 1920, established the largest gospel music publishing company, flirted with a film career, and then shifted to radio, where his programs ran on three national networks. At his death in 1955, no one had to ask "Who was Homer Rodeheaver?"

Thirty years later, however, the question lingered in the air as a dumpster lid clanked shut in Winona Lake, Indiana. Workers had just thrown away the last fragments of Rodeheaver's musical empire, adding one more stanza to the sad lament sung by archivists and researchers. Rodeheaver Music closed its offices in 1987 after several corporate shuffles by its parent company, Word Music of Waco, Texas. And from a corporate standpoint, Word Music kept the one asset it knew was valuable—copyright records for Rodeheaver's famous song catalog. But this sort of information fit in a few filing cabinets. The rest of the stuff seemed to lack present value: early recordings, scrapbooks, correspondence, and original manuscripts from important gospel songwriters. The dumpster seemed to win out, for now.

"It's a major mystery," says Bill Darr nearly thirty years later, having retired from a long career as library director at Grace College and Seminary, just up the road from the Rodeheaver offices in Winona Lake.[1] He looks back on the dumpster incident with lingering frustration. "Did Rodeheaver's life really end up in a landfill?" he asks, voice trailing off, question unanswered.

Back in the 1970s, Darr was part of the team that dug through boxes of papers in Billy Sunday's attic, assembling a research trove at Grace's Morgan Library. The collection continues to fuel a steady stream of projects about a key figure in evangelical Protestantism. As one indication, Billy Sunday became the subject of at least fifteen biographies, many of which credited Rodeheaver for contributing to Sunday's fame.

"Rodeheaver is a man of immense value. Whatever he gets for his services, he is worth it," a *New York Times* reporter claimed in 1917. "A man with his mixing ability and his capacity for molding a crowd into just the right state of mind for Sunday's arrival would be worth a fortune to a political leader."[2]

If Rodeheaver's value—and fame—were unquestioned during his era, one could rightly ask about his relative obscurity today. The clank of the dumpster lid was more than a rude benediction to Rodeheaver's life; it also signaled emerging trends in gospel music research—trends that paid scant attention to Rodeheaver's branch of gospel music. By this point the genre had developed its own historiography, a standardized account with two streams of research: Black gospel and southern gospel. But Rodeheaver's music did not fit neatly into either category, perhaps the real reason that he seemed neglected. In light of this, our brief introduction will place Rodeheaver in the context of ongoing research, which proves to be a difficult task, given the conflicting ideas that have been suggested about gospel music's origin.

Rodeheaver and his contemporaries called their music *gospel songs*, a term rooted in Protestant congregational singing but broad enough to include solo and ensemble performances.[3] He positioned himself in a long progression of vernacular church music: first the New England singing schools, then Lowell Mason's philosophies of "better" church music, then the Sunday School songs of William Bradbury, and the early gospel hymns of Ira D. Sankey.

"The gospel song is to bring to the people God's plan of salvation, with its warnings, promises, hopes, and comforts," Rodeheaver said, providing his own definition.[4] He viewed his gospel songs as a different genre than traditional church hymns but wasted little time debating their relative merits ("we need both," he insisted). Rodeheaver's conception of gospel songs drew from his biblical understanding of *gospel* as a direct reference to the death, burial, and resurrection of Jesus Christ. For Rodeheaver, *gospel* always included the doctrine of substitutionary atonement, a key aspect of the evangelical theology he embraced.

Rodeheaver also believed his gospel songs could communicate "the entire scale of human emotions" to individuals who would readily understand their proper response: "urging repentance, warning of the consequences of sin and the judgment, sympathizing in trouble, offering assurance of God's care and comfort, urging young people to show the joy of their salvation, and to be happy in the service of the King." Most importantly, Rodeheaver described his brand of gospel music as "a popular appeal to the masses." As originally conceived, he meant the masses of people who sang together at revival events, 10,000 or more at a time. When the era of tabernacle revivalism ended after World War I, he continued his appeal through mass communication—forays into radio, recordings, and film. All of these would play a part in his expanding idea of gospel music.

Having defined his gospel songs in ideological terms, Rodeheaver gave comparatively few descriptions of their musical style. He commissioned songs with "a bit of lilt, melody, and rhythm," but immediately tempered his enthusiasm by saying "it is very easy to go to the extreme and have too much rhythm of a certain kind."[5] His rhythmic songs were first accused of being ragtime, then jazz—accusations that Rodeheaver vociferously denied. Still, his stylistic choices were famously eclectic. His hymnals and record label did not fit neatly into emerging regional or racial categories that researchers preferred to use.

For anyone wishing to understand the ongoing historiography, look no further than the successive editions of *Grove's Dictionary of Music and Musicians*. The subject of "Gospel Hymns" is skipped over in the first (1879) and second (1904) editions, finally appearing in the American Supplement of 1920, full of snarky judgments ("the whole movement is to be condemned") and a pointed omission of the most famous gospel musician of that era, Rodeheaver himself.[6] The supplement presented a half-hearted summary of "Negro Music," and virtually nothing about the southern tradition.

When the *New Grove Dictionary of Music and Musicians* was released in 1980, the subject of "Gospel Music" was subdivided into two racial categories, "white gospel" and "Black gospel," with the "white" category providing a cursory summary of Sankey's successors in the north, followed by a more thorough examination of the southern tradition. Then editors of the 2012 edition gingerly stepped around the color line by creating categories of "northern urban gospel," "southern gospel," "gospel music in the African American community," plus the leftover category of "country and bluegrass gospel."[7] And—no surprise—the category of northern gospel was now half the length of the other sections. Wherever Rodeheaver was supposed to fit, the implications were clear: our potential readers would need to understand the ongoing tension in gospel music research.

Southern gospel emerged as a yet-unnamed genre at roughly the same time Rodeheaver was working the northern revival circuit.[8] The birth of southern gospel is often traced to 1910, when James D. Vaughan formed his first vocal quartet as a way of plugging songbooks at the community songfests known as All-Day Singings. By the late 1940s these events morphed into All-Night Sings, a concert format organized by Wally Fowler. The original idea of communal singing quickly disappeared as audiences sat and listened to the quartet performances. Southern gospel concerts and radio performances now boosted the sale of records rather than hymnals. Many described the period after World War II as a golden era of southern gospel—a golden era of performance music. Audiences had changed from music creators to music consumers.

Black gospel emerged in the 1920s, roughly the same time Rodeheaver was starting his record company. The gospel music of African Americans began as an eclectic blend of congregational song styles, anchored by the 1921 publication of *Gospel Pearls*.[9] Now remembered as the first African American hymnal with *gospel* in the title, the book included songs written by Black composers, traditional spirituals, and some songs that seemed better suited for soloists or ensembles. Black gospel, like southern gospel, was expanding from communal song to performance music: choirs, quartets, and female vocalists who used concerts and live radio shows to promote their recordings.

Whatever names it would eventually inherit, gospel music started in the church and became a marketing category. Names for gospel music preserved the "race" and "hillbilly" categories of the 1920s. When the terms *Black gospel* and *southern gospel* became prevalent in the 1960s, they reflected tension that was present from the beginning. At the very least, the terms reflected the "separate-but-equal ethos" of the Jim Crow South. The idea of Black and white gospel music seemed like parallel train tracks, headed in the same direction but never connecting.

As we struggled to fit Rodeheaver into one of the existing categories, other researchers were reevaluating the milestones, the "fathers," and the golden eras. For instance, why choose 1910 to mark the rise of southern gospel? Important elements of the southern tradition were in place before 1910—oblong tunebooks such as *The Sacred Harp*, the shape note hymnody of Aldine Kieffer and Ephraim Ruebush, and the folk-song tradition exemplified by "Amazing Grace."[10] Though later gospel music (after World War I) could be studied as (essentially) a performance idiom, key elements of earlier gospel music deserved more study.

For the reader who wants to jump right into the story, perhaps this seems like too much background. We include it here for the gospel music insiders, as a way to frame a common thread that stands out in the existing research: whatever the branch, everyone cites Homer Rodeheaver, at least in passing, for his influence.

* * *

Homer Rodeheaver's life was a shotgun blast—or a trombone blast—that left notes and fragments of his story all over American life. If the primary documents of his life were no longer available in the company archives, researchers could reconstruct the story by gathering the notes and fragments. As it turned out, there were a lot left to find.

During his career, Rodeheaver appeared in more than 20,000 news articles, plus news magazines, trade publications, and the evangelical press. We used this first draft of Rodeheaver's history as a guide when searching for his correspondence, now scattered in at least 20 libraries. Many of his personal effects had been rescued at auction by a retired employee of Rodeheaver Music who knew they would eventually be of interest. And Rodeheaver's seminal recordings were stashed in various public and private collections, waiting for a discographer to show how they connected to the broader stream of American music.

Of all the resources waiting for study, the songs themselves were the most important. Rodeheaver's own song output was limited (he wrote or cowrote about 30 songs). But his Rodeheaver Music Company owned the copyrights to a significant body of gospel songs, snapshots of American popular religion that could be studied on their merits (or lack of merit, as critics charged). Fifty years after the heyday of urban revivalism, Elvis Presley was still singing "The Old Rugged Cross" and "In the Garden." Country and bluegrass singers adopted "Will the Circle Be Unbroken." Black gospel divas cranked out "His Eye Is on the Sparrow" in dozens of versions. Nearly every music genre borrowed from the Rodeheaver song catalog. And though the data might have been invisible to researchers, the popularity of Rodeheaver's songs could be observed every Sunday morning, still sung by thousands of Protestant congregations.

As we searched for Rodeheaver, we found each other—the two authors were introduced by an archivist who noticed that we were looking at the same materials and asking the same questions. *Kevin Mungons* is a Chicago-based editor and freelance author. As an ordained Baptist minister and church musician, he grew up singing from Rodeheaver hymnals. *Douglas Yeo* was bass trombonist of the Boston Symphony Orchestra (1985–2012), then professor of trombone at Arizona State University, and now teaches trombone at Wheaton College, his undergraduate alma mater. Years ago he met Homer Rodeheaver as a life-size cardboard cutout in Wheaton College's Billy Graham Center Museum of Evangelism. With arms stretched wide, trombone in one hand and hymnal in the other, the cardboard Rodeheaver was hard to miss.

Both authors benefited from the assistance of David N. Lewis, the discographer who spent the better part of a decade researching Rodeheaver's early recordings. More of the story is told in the Acknowledgments, where we express gratitude to the librarians and archivists and others who helped us find a mountain of undiscovered Rodeheaver sources. Having worried about lost opportunities, we discovered the opposite. An exhaustive treatment would overwhelm the reader, so we narrowed our research scope to a shorter list of topics that seem to define Rodeheaver's life and times.

* * *

"Call me Reverend Trombone," Rodeheaver would tell news reporters at the start of an interview. Rodeheaver understood the developing celebrity culture of his era and was one of the first religious figures to harness its power. He hired a press agent and news clipping service and then developed stock stories that tantalized readers with details of his personal life. If newspapers were looking for entertaining feature articles about sports heroes and Hollywood starlets, Rodeheaver figured they would extend the same coverage to religious personalities. And they did.

Rodeheaver's publicity machine generated a good deal of myth-making—nostalgic stories that merit a measure of skepticism. Rodeheaver hyped his role as "Billy Sunday's trombone-playing songleader," treating his trombone as a personal brand. But despite his widespread musical fame, he possessed the skills of only a decent high school trombonist. He stuck to a limited repertoire that provided few technical challenges, playing the same five or six songs (for decades) with consistent showmanship. Then there's the story of the tabernacle fire in Toledo, where Rodeheaver supposedly calmed the escaping mob with a trombone serenade, averting a riot.[11] Or maybe it was Kansas? Rodeheaver had a storyteller's approach to factual details—but a good biographer must also be a tireless debunker, alert to his subject's embellishment. For starters, "Reverend Trombone" had never attended seminary or been ordained. But everyone loved Rody and wanted his stories to be true—they were so fitting, so perfectly descriptive of his carefully cultivated public persona. Told and retold, the sources grew fuzzy as one author cited another in succession.[12] At the very least, today's reader can understand Rodeheaver through the personal memories he wanted to preserve. He tells some great stories and provides a fascinating glimpse into an era of remarkable change.

Valuable as they are, such accounts pose challenges to the contemporary biographer. Rodeheaver's life was in danger of becoming another sentimental hymn story, like the mythic tales he told on the revival circuit to demonstrate what he called "the power of gospel music." If we were not careful, we could easily preserve Rodeheaver as a flat cardboard personality smiling from a museum display. Instead, we move past his entertaining persona and ask deeper questions about interpretation and context.

Our research took place while scholars were rethinking many of the larger issues that touched Rodeheaver's life and work. Several of these developments have influenced our interpretation and context of Rodeheaver's era.

THE INFLUENCE OF TECHNOLOGY Rodeheaver encouraged churches to install a phonograph player in their sanctuaries, where his Rainbow Records would teach congregations the "proper" singing of gospel songs. Rodeheaver's technological innovations would excite churchgoers and vex the denominational gatekeepers who questioned the value of Rodeheaver's ideas. Our approach draws from several writers who have recently studied the influences of recorded music on American life, extending their interpretations to include the phonograph's effect on American popular religion.[13]

THE EXPANSION OF COMMERCIAL MUSIC By 1917 Rodeheaver was the largest gospel music publisher in the country, using a marketing model that came straight from Tin Pan Alley. The evangelical church had its own vaudeville circuit—revivalism—led by an army of song pluggers who created an audience for the new music. Rodeheaver grew his company by exploiting his copyright catalog, finding new revenue streams in live performance, recording, and publishing.[14] The gospel publishers in Chicago created a market for music typesetters, printers, artists, advertising agencies, recording studios, law offices, and retail stores. After rapid expansion between 1900 and 1920, gospel music dominated Chicago's music publishing industry.[15] The commercial music revolution transformed every category—classical, folk, sacred, popular.

THE SEARCH FOR AUTHENTICITY   Soon after Rodeheaver started his record label, folklorists began searching for music that was elemental and pure and, above all, authentically American. Using new recording technology to collect songs from the oral tradition, they shaped a new definition of folk music, curating a style that they thought was untrammeled by the commercial world. In the process, a trio of "authentic" southern genres—blues, folk, and country—became enshrined as "roots" music to preserve in their purest form. Later researchers would challenge these definitions and whether purity actually existed.[16] Did these genres really describe the whole of southern music, or did they tell us more about the attitudes and interests of the folklorists who curated the categories?

Rodeheaver was skeptical of these emerging categories, filling his own catalog with happy incongruities. His Rainbow label featured Perry Kim and Einar Nyland, a guitar and mandolin duo whose old-timey sound would please anyone searching for southern authenticity.[17] Produced a few years before Victor's "first" country sessions, the Kim and Nyland recordings could be regarded as early country music. But wait. Kim and Nyland were construction workers who lived on the south side of Chicago. Both were immigrants—Holland and Norway. Their eclectic musical roots will frustrate anyone who confines them to a traditional category.

The strict categories assigned to southern roots music led to similar categories in gospel music, explained as distinctions of region and race. For a time, the search for authentic gospel music suffered from the rhetorical canard known as the "No True Scotsman" argument. If a writer dared to suggest that gospel music may be a broader genre than its conventional northern, southern, or racial boundaries, critics could merely respond, "Ah, but that's not *true* gospel music."

We raise the "Scotsman" idea with some irony, given that George Pullen Jackson once argued that Black spirituals originated from, yes, the highlands of Scotland. His claim would polarize the research community, but the issue had been lingering near the surface for some time. As distinct musical categories emerged in the 1920s, it was impossible to discuss American music without addressing its racial context.

THE IMPACT OF RACIAL SEGREGATION   At the height of Jim Crow attitudes in the 1920s, record executives created consumer audiences with classifications like "race" music and "hillbilly" music. The new separate-but-equal color line influenced music marketing, and it also shaped music's formal study. George Pullen Jackson searched for authentic American music in the white folk songs sung in camp meetings and revivals. He suggested in 1932 that African American spirituals sprang from the singing of southern whites, which in turn hearkened to original folk songs in Great Britain.[18] Reaction was swift. Whatever point Jackson was trying to make about common musical sources, he seemed to argue that white spirituals were inherently superior to Black spirituals. Not only did he marginalize Black music, his use of the "white spiritual" label irked Blacks who felt Jackson had wrongly appropriated the term.

Then Rodeheaver wandered into the fray. He had opinions—influenced by his experiences growing up in rural Tennessee, and rekindled on the revival circuit as he met various Black performers. When urban revivalism declined, Rodeheaver used his Rainbow Records label to record African American groups singing spirituals—and he often sang with them, early examples of interracial recording sessions.

Having grown up with both folk styles, Rodeheaver vastly preferred the spirituals over hillbilly music. His championing of Black music could be seen as progressive for his era, though sometimes interrupted by society's inability—and his own inability—to overcome lingering prejudice. Later in life, Rodeheaver filmed a respectful tribute to the spirituals but thought nothing about narrating his account in blackface. At one point the Klan hijacked his copyrighted songs, with "The Old Rugged Cross" becoming "The Bright Fiery Cross." All of these contradictory incidents must be explored in order to understand Rodeheaver's life.

While Rodeheaver continued with his own gospel music agenda, ethnographers and folklorists searched for the true southern roots of American music. Each discovery seemed to fit into a standard narrative where each style moved "from social isolation to contact, from pure musical styles to compounds, from music made outside the commercial market to music that is deeply integrated into it."[19] This approach, now widely critiqued, treated *commercialism* as an evil, the direct antonym of *pure* and *authentic*. As a result, these constructed narratives placed a heavy emphasis on the origin of a style but tended to ignore the changing ways a variety of people may have used the style.

Here we arrive at a key to understanding Rodeheaver's contribution to American music. What follows is not another gospel music origin story or a new definition of "true" gospel music. Rodeheaver's approach to gospel music was defined by the influences he absorbed, which were many. Black, white, southern, classical, folk, popular—pick a category, any category, and you'll find Rodeheaver, who was generally mystified by the imposed boundaries. He viewed gospel music as a congregational idiom, not merely a performance idiom. The gospel music

Rodeheaver championed had a broad appeal because it functioned as a congregational testimony forged from diverse American musical influences.

THE GOSPEL IN GOSPEL MUSIC   A final interpretive idea may seem obvious in a gospel music biography. In writing about Rodeheaver as a religious leader, we need to address his theological beliefs and devotional practices. Being aware of the inherent perils, we offer a straightforward analysis, beginning with the charitable assumption that Rodeheaver's religious beliefs were transformative *for him*. When exploring sensitive topics such as racial attitudes, we tried to avoid presentism (making moral judgments that reflect our present world more than the subject's own times), but we did ask if he lived up to his own stated religious ideals.

As we study Rodeheaver, we enter the realm of American popular religion and its long history of conflicting approaches too numerous to list here. Some readers will notice that we do not describe Rodeheaver and Billy Sunday as *fundamentalists*—for a reason. The era of tabernacle revivalism somewhat predates American fundamentalism as a religious movement. After World War I, some of Rodeheaver's constituency embraced the *fundamentalist* label and some eventually adopted *evangelical*. Both groups would function as two overlapping communities with similar views during much of Rodeheaver's life. When we use the word *evangelical* to describe Rodeheaver's community, we do so as a broad reference to their conservative Protestant self-identity (which they described in theological terms, not sociological, political, or economic).[20] Having said this, some readers may be interested in our speculative opinion: Had Billy Sunday lived longer, we believe he would have embraced the *fundamentalist* label. And Rodeheaver would have chosen *evangelical*. The fact that they worked together for twenty years attests to the murky distinctions of their own time and our hesitancy to describe their era with modern labels.

* * *

The story of Homer Rodeheaver is a story about gospel music and hymnals and pioneer recordings and religious devotion. Throw in some money and celebrity gossip. And trombones, lots of trombones. From the standpoint of the biographer, one would never imagine all of those words to appear in the same paragraph, describing the same life, but this is the Rodeheaver we discovered. As a result, his varied interests become something of an interdisciplinary challenge. We responded with a focus on Rodeheaver's contributions to American music, his relationship to urban revivalism, his "early adopter" attitude toward technological change, his resulting wealth and philanthropy, his status as a trombone player and cultural icon, and his influential role in defending gospel music as a congregational idiom. The biography that emerged was not strictly chronological; we aimed for topical chapters that readers could understand as stand-alone essays.[21] We hope readers will arrive from a particular discipline, start with the chapter that interests them most, and then allow themselves to be drawn into a fascinating life that touches many related disciplines. In essence, this is how the authors met; we would be happy if our readers met each other in the same way. Some will check every footnote, others will skip the wonky bits. Please do so with our blessing.

Everyone who reads about music will eventually encounter the same obstacle: Our understanding remains limited until we sing, play, and listen to the music itself. "Serious study of African American music requires getting to know the music, which means listening to it and, if possible, performing it," Eileen Southern wrote.[22] We agree, and perhaps we could add one more suggestion for readers who wish to grasp the ideas of Rodeheaver's life: *Sing*. And sing together!

Rodeheaver's phenomenon of mass communal singing cannot be understood by reading an essay—it must be experienced, even in some limited way. Sing together with a crowd of one hundred people, and then imagine how a crowd of one thousand would sound. No, we're not talking about the halfhearted mumble of sports fans, hands stuffed in pockets, waiting for the national anthem to finish. Perhaps fleeting glimpses of Rodeheaver's idea could be felt after the 9/11 tragedy, when civic mourning was assuaged by the spontaneous singing of "God Bless America." But then the mumbling starts again, halfway through the second line, when nearly everyone under the age of fifty forgets the words. Communal singing seems to have disappeared from civic settings. Rodeheaver's idea, a prolonged concert of communal singing, can barely be imagined today. Think of it this way—when reading *about* orchestral music, we still have a fair chance to hear an orchestra play. We may even perform *with* an orchestra as a way of further understanding the music. In contrast, Rodeheaver's favorite performing ensemble—a crowd of ten thousand singers in a wooden revival tabernacle—no longer exists.

Rodeheaver's ideas about the power of music were directly related to these astonishing communal performances. He struggled to articulate the special, ineffable quality that moves humanity toward a common goal by singing together. He never successfully explained it, but absolutely believed in the power of music. "It wasn't I, Homer Rodeheaver, who was going to do this thing," he wrote. "It was music, itself. The music that was here in my trombone, that was waiting in the throats of the choir massed on the platform waiting for my signal; above all, the music that was waiting in the hearts of all those men and women before me, and that I had somehow, only to release."[23]

This power of communal singing helped Rodeheaver ride a wave of early-twentieth-century religious fervor, living on the front page of newspapers, hobnobbing with the celebrities of his day. For a time, he could do no wrong—attendance and offerings grew with each subsequent revival campaign. Rodeheaver thought anyone could borrow the same power by using "practical, modern methods which cannot fail when intelligently applied."[24]

If this were true, Rodeheaver should have enjoyed uniformly successful meetings throughout his career, guaranteed by his modern methods and the power of music. But the revival meetings peaked around 1917, followed by a steep decline that Rodeheaver understood much more quickly than Billy Sunday. The opening chapter of this book examines the moment when Rodeheaver began to eclipse his boss: their 1917 Atlanta revival meetings. By exploring a key moment in Rodeheaver's life, we can also reexamine a cross section of conflicting American ideals.

1

PROLOGUE

ATLANTA 1917

Fifteen thousand singers filled the revival tabernacle with an old hymn, waves of sound pouring from a proud sea of African American voices. As the verses were lifted up, each stronger than the last, Homer Rodeheaver gestured from the platform with broad, sweeping motions. Everyone—*everyone*—sang.[1]

FIGURE 1.1. Billy Sunday and Homer Rodeheaver in Los Angeles in 1917, just before the Atlanta revivals. Courtesy of Morgan Library, Grace College, Winona Lake.

CHAPTER 1

Was it his impish good looks or the freshly pressed linen suit? Perhaps the infectious chorus he blew from his gold-plated trombone? Or was Rodeheaver's theory correct, that something more basic commanded this attention—the power of gospel music to unite the most diverse audiences? Rodeheaver had been anticipating this particular Atlanta meeting as a way to test his ideas about the universal appeal of gospel songs, those congregational testimonies that were forged from diverse American musical influences. While later generations would speak of Black gospel or white gospel or southern gospel, Rodeheaver didn't live in such categories. To his way of thinking, a good gospel song would unite any audience, even audiences fragmented by racial tension.

He started the service on common ground, leading everyone in "My Country, 'Tis of Thee," which he added to the tabernacle repertoire after World War I broke out in April. The construction crew had draped the Atlanta platform with flags, and Billy Sunday would spike his sermon with slam-bang attacks on the godless Kaiser and Huns. Like politicians throwing out easy applause lines, the revivalists knew how to provoke a chorus of Amens. Rodeheaver's motivation for choosing a patriotic song seemed pretty obvious. A thousand African American soldiers were sitting tall in their khaki uniforms, right in front of him, visiting from nearby Camp Gordon.

By the time the audience reached the end of the first stanza, a group of late-arriving journalists hurried to the row of desks reserved at the front. Rodeheaver was starting the service a half-hour early again. The tabernacle filled up quickly, just like the first ten days of meetings when organizers enforced a whites-only attendance policy. Thanks to Sunday's friendly attitude toward reporters, the *Atlanta Constitution* had been running Billy Sunday news on the front page, right next to its war coverage. One reporter took shorthand during the sermon, which was transcribed and printed verbatim by the next morning. Another *Constitution* reporter—usually assigned to theater and vaudeville—covered the tabernacle music just like a concert review. Every other local paper sent reporters, too, along with the *Atlanta Independent*, a Black-owned paper that had fearlessly called the segregated meetings a religious affirmation of Jim Crow.

Professionally jaded but smart enough to ride a populist trend, the reporters ended up writing positive stories, lots of stories. But now, just when they thought their nightly revival beat was becoming routine, something new drew the journalists back to their seats. Rodeheaver had started the service with the same patriotic song the reporters had heard from the white audiences. Now the Black congregation was singing the same words with a different meaning, warming up to a full roar on the final line: "Let freedom ring!"

Not waiting for the echo to die down, Rodeheaver waved his accompanists into a familiar hymn. He had arranged two grand pianos in front of the platform and pulled the lids off for maximum volume. George Ashley Brewster and Bob

Matthews sat side by side, dueling pianists who could be heard above any crowd. The news reporters, accustomed to staid church music played on a pump organ, didn't quite know how to describe what they saw.

"Brewster literally fights the keys, bringing out the harmony in great thunderous chords, while Matthews's hands run up and down the keyboard of the other piano in ragtime accompaniment," said Ned McIntosh, the arts reporter. But another reporter for the *Constitution* claimed just the opposite: "They struck up 'Come, Thou Fount of Every Blessing,' and romped off toward the home plate. Brewster played the ragtime version, and Matthews injected the classical technique."[2]

Perhaps one of the players was trying to fuse traditional church music with ragtime? Maybe, but no one could tell for sure. No one had heard anything like it.

"I've seen Toscanini direct an army of musicians without a score; I've seen Damrosch do his doggonedest; I've listened to jazz bands and have heard Irving Berlin's wildest creations," claimed McIntosh. "But when Ashley Brewster and Bob Matthews begin to fight the ivory out at Billy Sunday's big meetin', I wouldn't swap my seat for a ticket to anything I ever heard of. And did it sound sacrilegious? Not on your life. It was thrilling, contagious, infectious.

"It compelled you to sing."[3]

* * *

By this point, Sunday and Rodeheaver had been traveling the revival meeting circuit for eight years. Reporters gave Rodeheaver a good deal of credit for Sunday's success. Both of them had adopted stage personas that seemed close to their own personalities: Sunday was a rough-hewn former baseball player with a flair for slang-filled oratory, a hellfire-and-brimstone theatrical force who could hold a crowd's attention even if the sermon stretched to two hours. Rodeheaver was the suave, joke-cracking sidekick, a one-man vaudeville show who was happy to provide the opening act. On any given night, Sunday and Rodeheaver offered the best show in town—and free.

Offstage, Sunday struck many as introverted, even aloof, but he could turn on the charm when surrounded by reporters or celebrities. Rodeheaver never worried about turning on the charm—he *was* charming, a larger-than-life personality who lit up the tabernacle as soon as he mounted the platform steps. Just before dinner he would change from his day clothes into a custom-tailored business suit with a contrasting vest; a white, round-collared shirt; and a silk four-in-hand tie. His pants were hemmed fashionably high, revealing calfskin shoes covered by gray spats. Billy Sunday dressed the same way. Neither one looked like a preacher; both tried to project the image of successful, stylish businessmen.

CHAPTER 1

At thirty-seven, Rodeheaver was an eligible bachelor, five feet, eight and one-half inches tall, barrel-chested, with wavy brown hair and brown eyes. He would have been a fine catch for a chorus girl or a preacher's daughter. But after suffering a public breakup with Georgia Jay in 1914 (she sued him for $50,000), Rodeheaver seemed unlikely to take the plunge anytime soon. He flirted from the podium and otherwise seemed achingly inaccessible. A few days earlier, the *Atlanta Constitution* had reported how Rodeheaver created "quite a fluttering among the feminine hearts" when he deliberately leaked a few personal details to his audience.

"I have a wife and two children to support," he said, expertly waiting a beat for the soft sighs before continuing with his explanation.[4] The wife and two children were not his—they were the wife and children of his late father. Rodeheaver used the tease as a way of introducing his stepmother, Bettie Rodeheaver, who had traveled from Roanoke, Virginia, for the evening service. And behind the scenes, Homer Rodeheaver did exactly what he claimed, sending support checks and eventually moving his stepfamily to Winona Lake, Indiana, his home base.

As affable as Rodeheaver seemed onstage, nothing was quite as effortless as it appeared from the pine benches that lined the sawdust trail. Rodeheaver had tamed his Tennessee twang through voice and diction lessons, had played trombone in an army band, and had studied choral conducting. After honing his platform presence through years of Chautauqua appearances, he aggressively tested a revival format programmed to bring spiritual results. He recruited the best musicians—Sunday paid them as much as Sousa paid his band members. And Rodeheaver's publishing company cultivated the best gospel songwriters. Given his personal drive and effervescent personality, Rodeheaver would have succeeded on the vaudeville stage, had he been so inclined.

And yes, the critics quickly made that connection. A few months earlier, a group of liberal Boston clerics had attacked Sunday as the "vaudeville revivalist," but nearly everyone understood who, exactly, was creating the vaudeville atmosphere.[5] Fueled with an endless supply of songs, magic tricks, and stand-up comedy, Rodeheaver's warm-up act was getting great reviews. Theater ticket sales plunged as audiences flocked to the revival tabernacle instead. One victim was Al Jolson, who tried to counter sagging attendance by adding another act to his vaudeville lineup, a wicked parody of Billy Sunday and revivalism. "When Sunday comes to town, I hear that he'll save women, free," sang Jolson, clowning and mimicking Sunday before landing the punch line: "I hope he saves a blonde for me!"[6]

Jolson even planted a group of costumed chorus girls at the back of the revival tabernacle, irreverently instructing them to go forward when Billy Sunday called for sinners to hit the sawdust trail. Jolson figured that if he poked at Sunday a few times, his Broadway troupe might earn a public condemnation, money in the bank for any entertainer.

But Jolson was no match for Rodeheaver when it came to publicity stunts. When Jolson's chorus girls had an afternoon off, Rodeheaver upped the ante by inviting them to sing at the Boston tabernacle. Of course they said yes (Rodeheaver hadn't lost his touch), leading to the spectacle of "Don't Leave Me, Daddy" one night and "Brighten the Corner" the next afternoon. Jolson loved it—the resulting flap gave his musical revue a fresh blast of publicity, and his ticket sales recovered.

Rodeheaver was never worried. By sharing the spotlight, he had primed Jolson for a quiet visit the next morning. Mr. Sunday would be grateful if you stopped mentioning him in your fine show, Rodeheaver suggested, ever unctuous. Jolson immediately agreed.

Homer Rodeheaver had become more than a warm-up act. Everything he did was calculated to generate publicity, following a careful sequence to create audience participation. Any audience.

* * *

"Not before in the history of the South, perhaps, have so many Negroes been gathered together for a meeting of any sort," reported the *Atlanta Constitution*. "Through a natural inclination and the urgings of Rody, no such harmony has ever been heard in the south, or probably in any other man's neck of the woods."[7]

But all this talk of "harmony" from white journalists obscured the controversy of the 1917 Atlanta revival. Until now, Sunday and Rodeheaver's fame had been limited to northern cities. After a string of successes in New York, Boston, and Philadelphia, their Atlanta invitation came with a huge condition from the local ministerial association: the meetings would be segregated. Billy Sunday wanted the Atlanta meetings badly enough that he accepted the ground rules. To his way of thinking, his mission was to preach the gospel, even if that required an affirmation of southern status quo. Like most of Atlanta's leadership, the white ministers saw themselves as progressive, believing Atlanta to be a model city in the New South. Black pastors were less convinced. They wanted the Sunday meetings, too, but they were weary of the imposed social order. The ongoing tension would severely test Sunday and Rodeheaver's loose coalition of Protestants.

When fire swept through Atlanta five months earlier, it was no respecter of persons, destroying 300 blocks of Black and white neighborhoods, including churches of every denomination. Firefighters finally contained the blaze by dynamiting a row of old-money mansions; even the rich suffered loss. But recovery efforts were less democratic. By the time the Sunday party rolled into town that November, Atlanta was selectively rebuilding white neighborhoods, using the tragedy as another excuse to isolate Blacks into the Old Fourth Ward.

The U.S. Army opened Camp Gordon in July, planning a boot camp where blacks and whites would train together before marching on to war. Then the

Commission on Training Camp Activities segregated all recreational activities, resulting in precious little social territory for the African American troops. A deeper problem emerged as the local draft board registered every eligible male, feigning equality, but turned around and granted exceptions to 85 percent of Atlanta's whites. Meanwhile, only three percent of Blacks were excused. The New South looked suspiciously like the old.[8]

During preparations for the Atlanta meetings, Billy Sunday freely admitted that he had not spent much time in the South, nor had he spent much time around Blacks. In fact, his sermon on November 19 would be the first time he had preached to a large crowd of African Americans. Rodeheaver, on the other hand, grew up in the racially mixed environment of eastern Tennessee. He absorbed the Black musical tradition more directly.

"The songs of my earliest recollection were the songs the Negro boys sang to my mother in the mountains of East Tennessee," he later wrote. "I not only grew up in the atmosphere of the Negro spiritual but their songs were part of my life. Then too the Negro boys would sing spirituals to me while I, in turn, would sing to them the gospel songs." Rodeheaver absorbed the southern tradition, the whole complicated lot of it, including the folk songs of rural whites. "I sang the mountain ballads and won many a prize for singing them at picnics, playing the harmonica from an improvised holder while I picked the melody on the guitar," he recalled, but he still expressed preference for the spirituals.[9]

Right from the start, Rodeheaver's music would defy easy categorization. Surrounded by a wide variety of influences early in life, he never wasted much energy trying to sort them out. All of this music, whatever its source, belonged to his broad definition of gospel music.

For two weeks prior to that night's meeting, Rodeheaver had spent his mornings visiting Atlanta's Black colleges—Clark, Morehouse, Morris Brown, and Spelman—persuading them to combine their choirs for a spectacular tabernacle concert. To this core he added the best choirs from Atlanta's Black churches. On the evening of the Sunday meeting, the choir arrived early for a single rehearsal. In spite of their limited preparation, the hastily assembled choir performed without printed music. These songs were rarely written down—perhaps *couldn't* be written down in any way that would capture their full glory. The singers knew them by heart.

Rodeheaver's plan to showcase African American music was by no means new. First Congregational Church began hosting the Atlanta Colored Music Festival in 1910, an annual event that featured college choirs, solos by Harry T. Burleigh, and spirituals sung by the Fisk Jubilee Singers.[10] When Rev. Henry Hugh Proctor became pastor of First Church in 1894, he had just finished his thesis at Yale Divinity School, writing the first formal study on the theology of southern slave songs.[11] Proctor was known as a zealous preservationist; he quickly threw his influence behind Rodeheaver's plan for a mass choir.[12]

As the local ministerial association began looking for a suitable location to build Billy Sunday's temporary tabernacle, a conspicuous irony developed. Though the revival organizers had mandated segregated meetings, the best tabernacle site happened to be in the heart of the Old Fourth Ward. An open block of land (bordered by Jackson Street, Auburn Avenue, Boulevard, and Irwin Street) was available and was serviced by public transportation. Traveling circuses often pitched their tents here—everyone called it the circus grounds.

Reporters wrote about the ongoing tabernacle construction but never mentioned the obvious. Whites would have their segregated meetings, but they would have to travel into a Black neighborhood in order to attend. Billy Sunday would cultivate the support of white churches, but the churches surrounding his tabernacle were Black. A further irony would not become evident until decades later. The circus grounds would become sacred land for all Americans, consecrated by tragedies yet to come.

The closest church—an odd, low-slung building with a flat roof—sat a block south. Here an African American congregation was in the middle of a pay-as-you-go construction project. After laying a cornerstone in 1914, they finished and roofed the basement, waiting to finish until the close of World War I.[13] Their pastor, Rev. Adam D. Williams, had taken a church with thirteen members and grown it into a vibrant congregation. Just that morning the *Constitution* had called Williams "one of the real leaders of his race in the city, and in the state of Georgia he is recognized as one of the leading forces of the denomination."[14]

Though he bristled over the segregation policy, Williams agreed to join Proctor in supporting the revival meetings. Both men were convinced that Billy Sunday would help their churches and their neighborhoods. As much as they hated Jim Crow, they didn't expect Billy Sunday to single-handedly change the system. "It was tacitly agreed between the practical workers of both races in the city that we should refrain from putting upon these meetings the burden of the solution of this great problem," Proctor explained after the meetings concluded. "It was felt that for Black and white penitents to come down together would be an impossible undertaking under the circumstances."[15]

When discussing political and social strategy, Atlanta's Black clergy hovered somewhere between the ideological positions of Booker T. Washington and W. E. B. Du Bois—a range of complex feelings, full of nuances that prove difficult for historians to summarize. When Washington addressed the Atlanta Cotton States and International Exposition in 1895, his speech created an instant sensation. Calling for improved social and economic relations between the races, Washington pressed for white support of Black educational efforts, especially vocational training. Later critics tagged Washington's speech as "The Atlanta Compromise," a short and damning title that summarized Washington's tolerance of racial separation. His speech was followed by twenty years of uncomfortable status quo and increasing criticism from progressive Blacks. Now Du Bois charted a different course, advocating a liberal arts education for a "talented tenth" of the Black population.

The Atlanta pastors leaned charitably toward at least some of Washington's views, perhaps believing they had pressed the issue as far as could be hoped, given the abysmal conditions of the era. Two factors influenced their loyalty. When northern donors supported Washington's push for vocational training, the money came from church groups. Vocational funding was accompanied by additional support for seminaries and Bible schools, especially helpful to the rising generation of Atlanta pastors who directly benefited from the ministerial training. Washington's "Atlanta Compromise" campaign financed their seminary education. A second factor, subtler than the first, sprang from the pastors' cool relationship with Du Bois himself. Though he lived in Atlanta for 15 years and wrote many of his influential essays while in their midst, Du Bois never joined any of their churches. Eyebrows were raised; questions were asked.

At any rate, the segregated Billy Sunday meetings seemed like another "Atlanta Compromise," where no one was completely happy with the plan but willing to accept it, temporarily, if it furthered their own agenda.

Despite the gracious endorsement of most Black clergy, Billy Sunday seemed oblivious to their actual situation. On the morning of November 19, the day of the long-anticipated meeting for Blacks, Sunday and Rodeheaver had gone in separate directions. Rodeheaver had lunch with some of the Black ministers sponsoring the event. Billy Sunday, on the other hand, celebrated his fifty-fifth birthday with Samuel Hoyt Venable, founding member of the Ku Klux Klan and co-owner of Stone Mountain.

The mountain's famous quarry had petered out by this point, having supplied material for the U.S. Capitol and the Panama Canal. Venable had recently donated land to the United Daughters of the Confederacy, who hired Gutzon Borglum to carve a stupefying memorial on the mountain's north face.[16] But Venable's most dubious accomplishment was on Thanksgiving Day, 1915, when he hosted William J. Simmons and a handful of friends who were trying to resurrect the Ku Klux Klan. Simmons installed himself as Imperial Wizard, lit a makeshift cross, and declared Atlanta the "Imperial City of the Invisible Empire." Venable would grant the Klan a permanent easement on his property, with formal permission to continue burning crosses on Stone Mountain whenever they wished.

It would take ten years for Protestants to recognize the Klan for its inherent racism and corruption. When Imperial Wizard David C. Stephenson, Indiana's Klan leader, was arrested for the 1925 rape and murder of a young woman, the

Klan was eventually exposed for its drunken orgies, financial corruption, political bribes, and moral excess.[17] But in the meantime, the Klan was covering itself with a veneer of family values and Christian theology, dusting off their Bibles and hijacking Christian hymns. For a few years, Sunday and Rodeheaver would allow themselves to be hijacked, too. Not only had Venable cooked up this birthday party stunt, he invited reporters, who ran glowing stories about Sunday's mountaintop experience.

A month later the Klan got another burst of publicity when Ned McIntosh wrote a notoriously fawning review of *The Birth of a Nation*, D. W. Griffith's racist film with a cross-burning scene.[18] Now the same reporter sat at the front table in Billy Sunday's segregated tabernacle, preparing to write a glowing review of the African American choirs and soloists. The Black ministers gathering for the evening service could not have been impressed. And whatever affinity the ministers had for Sunday's gospel message, they would never connect with him on a personal level, at least not the way they did with Rodeheaver. Billy Sunday seemed tone deaf to the difficult life of Atlanta Blacks living under Jim Crow.

* * *

Rodeheaver kept the service moving quickly that night. After leading everyone in "America" and unleashing his dueling pianists on "Come, Thou Fount of Every Blessing," he proceeded to sing every stanza. Tonight's audience knew "Come, Thou Fount" as a Dr. Watts hymn, a generic name for traditional songs that bridged the gap between Black and white traditions. The oldest members of the audience, the ones freed by Lincoln's Emancipation Proclamation, learned this song as preachers lined it out one phrase at a time in the "hush harbors" and makeshift buildings that became their refuge.

The song's ecumenical words could be embraced by any Protestant denomination, though a few of the lyrics were obscure. When singing "Come, Thou Fount" with northern crowds, Rodeheaver usually stopped to explain the metaphor in stanza two: "Here I raise my Ebenezer, hither by thy help I've come." But tonight no clarification was necessary, for right in front of him sat the entire congregation from Ebenezer Baptist, the church Adam Williams pastored across the street. Like the prophet Samuel, the Ebenezer church was already raising their stone monument of divine help—on a block that would be remembered for its monuments.

After their ten-minute opening flurry, Brewster and Matthews stopped playing, canny enough to use silence as an ally. Rodeheaver turned to the mass choir and asked for "one of your real southern Negro songs." A soprano soloist from Clark University stepped forward with the haunting melody of "Swing Low, Sweet Chariot." The classic call-and-response was answered by a choir of one thousand voices singing pianissimo, carried along by an undulating current of rhythm and sweetness. One immediately understood why W. E. B. Du Bois had described these spirituals as "the one true expression of a people's sorrow, despair, and hope."[19]

Ned McIntosh was still sitting at the news table, but he stopped taking notes, unashamed to weep in front of his journalist friends. When the massive chorus stopped singing, he jotted one brief note: "It was beyond description—that's all."

Rodeheaver reached into his suit jacket for a pocket-size notebook where he kept notes for the service—he had a long list of introductions and he did not want to leave anyone out. Though Atlanta's segregated meetings posed special problems, they still leaned heavily on a well-developed system of grassroots organization. Billy Sunday didn't like to hold a citywide revival unless all of the Protestant churches agreed to participate. Once committed, Sunday would dispatch event planners to help the churches organize under committees and subcommittees, a structure that local business leaders understood and supported. In addition to the churches, advance workers also visited factories and shops during lunch hour. Children's workers visited schools. Women's workers organized teas and lectures. Each night Rodeheaver would introduce leaders of the various delegations, spreading attention to popular local figures.

Having organized this particular meeting with the help of Black clergy, Rodeheaver made certain he mentioned each by name. He invited H. H. Proctor to stand, followed by his prominent congregation from First Church. Then Rodeheaver called on Adam Williams and a dozen other pastors, representing congregations large and small. Tonight's audience drew from a broad cross section, including many who came to the service straight from work or had asked off early. "Atlanta's white folks cooked their own suppers Monday night," was the crass description from the *Atlanta Georgian*, a newspaper known for fanning racial flames.[20]

Rodeheaver had another use for his pocket notebook. He made friends faster than Sunday ever would, and his new Atlanta relationships would help him in ways he did not yet know. Frederick Douglass Hall sat in the tenor section that night, a freshman in the Morehouse College choir. He had grown up in Atlanta and knew most of the local pastors. As a boy soprano, Hall sang as guest soloist in their churches. After graduating from Morehouse, he would teach music at Jackson State College, immersing himself in research about the spirituals and recording them with Rodeheaver. Later Rodeheaver would hire Hall as an editor for the Rodeheaver Music Company.

Alberta Williams, the daughter of Rev. Adam Williams, was allowed to sing with the sopranos even though she was only thirteen. Musically precocious, she was already taking organ lessons. She would continue working across the street for the rest of her life, serving at Ebenezer Baptist as organist and choir director. But at the time of the revival meetings, she had not yet met the young seminary student who would become her husband, Michael Lewis King. They would marry in 1926, and then live upstairs at the family home a few blocks east on Auburn Avenue.

Michael Lewis King became pastor of Ebenezer Baptist after Adam Williams passed in 1931. Then after traveling to Europe's Reformation sites in 1934, Rev. King changed his name to Martin Luther King Sr. His son, only five at the time, took the name Martin Luther King Jr., though his family continued to call him Mike. After the revivals were over, after workers tore down the tabernacle and sold the lumber, the site became a vacant lot and then a makeshift baseball field where Mike King and his friends played after school.

Such details are more than an anecdotal aside. Alberta Williams King represents gospel music's essential diversity. She would play from various editions of the *National Baptist Hymnal* and *Gospel Pearls* for the rest of her life—hymnals that featured a mix of Dr. Watts hymns, Rodeheaver's gospel songs, Black gospel, and spirituals. When evaluated in the context of congregational practice, Rodeheaver's deliberately loose definition accurately describes what was happening in local congregations. Gospel music has always been a synthesis of many influences, a point borne out by another young man who sang in Rodeheaver's Atlanta choir.

Tom "Barrel House" Dorsey, a pianist, visited the Atlanta revival service out of curiosity, joining the makeshift choir at the last minute. He had returned home from Chicago to visit his parents, who were not pleased with his recent career direction. While growing up in Atlanta, Dorsey had found work as a water boy, hanging out at the same circus grounds where Sunday's tabernacle now sat. At fourteen he had picked up enough piano to play for dances at the Odd Fellows auditorium a few blocks west. Then came the theater jobs and bordello gigs. The tension at home could have been predicted—his father had been a rural Baptist pastor, his mother a church organist—so no one was surprised when Dorsey left for Chicago at 16.[21] The northern migration was in full swing, but Dorsey's piano career hadn't risen above the low-paying gigs at South Side sporting houses. His fusion of rural and urban blues seemed passé to Chicago audiences expecting to hear the new jazz music.[22]

Dorsey's initial attraction to the revival meeting might have come from news coverage given to the pianists, Matthews and Brewster, who had been featured in front-page photos a few days earlier. Whatever Dorsey's motivation for attending that night, he wasn't among the trail hitters. Unrepentant, he returned to Chicago, rebranded himself as "Georgia Tom," and continued his blues career. Four years later he would be converted at a church convention while the congregation sang "I Do, Don't You?" from *Gospel Pearls*.

Thomas A. Dorsey later become known as the composer of "Take My Hand, Precious Lord," and was called "the father of gospel music" while serving as music director at Chicago's Pilgrim Baptist Church. Though the Billy Sunday revivals did not play a direct role in his conversion, Dorsey would fondly remember Rodeheaver's "sweet trombone" in later interviews.[23] More importantly, the two would become fast friends when they lived in Chicago, yet another relationship of many that were born in the Atlanta meetings.

* * *

Rodeheaver finished his introductions by gesturing to a white-haired gentleman in the front row, Charles Gabriel, who stood and waved. Despite his distinctive walrus moustache, Gabriel wasn't the sort of person you'd recognize on the street, though everyone recognized his music. Generally acknowledged by his peers as the greatest living gospel song composer, Gabriel worked in the Chicago office of Rodeheaver Music Company. Born on an Iowa farm and educated in the singing school tradition, Gabriel had spent six years conducting singing schools in the South, including some in Atlanta. In the process he taught groups of whites, Blacks, Native Americans, and even Texas cowboys; his developing musical vocabulary would draw from all of these sources.

Some of the pastors knew the real reason for Gabriel's appearance in Atlanta and the reason for the sheaf of blank score paper tucked under his arm. Gabriel had been visiting area churches, transcribing old spirituals as sung by the Atlanta congregations. Rodeheaver intended to publish a new songbook based on the spirituals he heard as a child and was hearing from the Atlanta choirs.

Everyone could agree that the African American musical experience needed to be preserved and nurtured. But how to preserve it—and who should preserve it—became a matter of great controversy that spilled over into church music. Younger Blacks, educated in the liberal arts and now successful in their careers, expected a high-toned church service with organ music and choral anthems. They appreciated the spirituals as their cultural heritage but questioned whether they were appropriate for public worship. While their congregations might sing them spontaneously at informal gatherings, they were not planned for Sunday morning services or yet codified by a denominational hymnal.

At the same time Gabriel was transcribing the southern spirituals for publication to Rodeheaver's northern (primarily white) customer base, his own gospel songs were being absorbed into the Black church tradition, despite their white, northern roots. Favorites included "Higher Ground," "Since Jesus Came into My Heart," "He Lifted Me," and the big hit of the Sunday revivals, "Brighten the Corner Where You Are." All of these would be incorporated into *Gospel Pearls*, where Gabriel's songs ran right next to songs from Black composers like Dorsey.[24] Gabriel's greatest crossover tune, "His Eye Is on the Sparrow," became a beloved diva anthem, later recorded by Sister Rosetta Tharpe, Mahalia Jackson, Ethel Waters, Carmen McRae, and many others during the golden age of gospel soloists.

FIGURE 1.2. Rodeheaver's edition of the spiritual "Heab'n," from *Plantation Melodies*, 1918.

Not every Black leader agreed that this mixture of regional and racial sources was a positive development. W. E. B. Du Bois, a friend and Fisk classmate of H. H. Proctor's, would sometimes criticize choirs for singing the spirituals in refined four-part harmony. The Fisk singers could pull this off in artful ways, but Fisk imitators often missed the mark. Du Bois felt these performances lacked authenticity, having been transformed by the European classical tradition. Perhaps these choral interpretations conformed to the expectations of white audiences (many gave generously to support Black educational efforts), but the songs were not pure renditions of the spirituals, Du Bois charged.

When Charles Gabriel visited the Atlanta congregations, he did not hear the "original" versions of the spirituals. What he heard had already been transformed (critics would say polluted) by thirty years of the Fisk sound. Was that a problem? Not for Rodeheaver, who was mostly interested in publishing the spirituals for use in congregational singing and worship services. He searched for functional church music, not authenticity.

This discussion—the search for authenticity—would continue for decades. Gatekeepers continued to define gospel music by excluding groups they deemed less pure. In the first three editions of *Blues and Gospel Records*, vaunted as "the bible" of early Black recordings, the authors deliberately omitted the Fisk Jubilee Singers because they sang for white audiences and had "little authentic gospel quality."[25] The snub was eventually corrected, but its influential viewpoint swayed research for several decades. The argument about "authentic gospel quality" made sense for anyone who viewed gospel music as primarily *music*. In such cases, emerging definitions of gospel could be surprisingly narrow. But if gospel music was also studied as a functional art (devotional songs connected to a worship service), the field of understanding would inevitably broaden.

W. E. B. Du Bois evaluated the Black church (and its music) as a sociological phenomenon, paying scant attention to theology and devotional practices. In *The Souls of Black Folk*, he critiqued southern Methodists and Baptists for presenting "the religion of poor whites" as a "plain copy of Negro thought and methods." This led to his opinion that the northern gospel songs were also derivative: "The mass of 'gospel' hymns which has swept through American churches and well-nigh ruined our sense of song consists largely of debased imitations of Negro melodies made by ears that caught the jingle but not the music, the body but not the soul, of the Jubilee songs," he wrote.[26]

Du Bois delivered a stern critique, but his advice on church music was widely ignored. For as much as the Atlanta pastors loved their own heritage of African American music, they also embraced "the mass of gospel hymns," essentially rejecting the musical "purity" appeal as summarized by Du Bois. The pastors were wary of his unstated subtext, his emphasis on the music but not the devotional texts. Du Bois was very familiar to the local clergy, having taught at Atlanta University from 1897 to 1910. On a civic level, the Atlanta pastors partnered with Du Bois to form the NAACP. But they also voiced quiet questions about his faith, which soon blew into a controversy. Atlanta University's administration delayed the appointment of Du Bois to department chair because he refused to open his meetings with an invocation prayer. With the matter out in the open, Du Bois unapologetically described himself as an agnostic. This was a serious breach for the private religious university, which was founded and funded by the American Missionary Association. For anyone who tried to lead Atlanta's Blacks without attending church, the path chosen by Du Bois was a tough row to hoe.[27]

If one viewed the spirituals—"Negro melodies," as Du Bois described them—as primarily a musical resource and a cultural heritage, one would be tempted to preserve the "melodies" in their purest form, precisely the point Du Bois was trying to make. But if one also viewed the spirituals as a theological and even liturgical resource (the theme of Proctor's dissertation), more complex attitudes would emerge. The spirituals were more than "Negro melodies"; they had specific lyrical intention. In the context of religious life, these songs of personal testimony merged and mingled with other "gospel" streams, finding a home in any church that viewed public testimony as an important mission of the gathered church.

Rodeheaver was discovering that his broad definition of gospel song had the most affinity (or bluntly put, sold the best) in Methodist, Holiness, and Baptist churches, along with a growing mix of nondenominational and Pentecostal groups. Within Protestantism, these churches were the most likely to feature extemporaneous expressions of testimony during worship services. Collectively known as the free church tradition, these church groups were "free" in the sense that they were not bound by a denominational hierarchy or liturgical mandate—and consequently had the flexibility to encourage spontaneous testimony, both spoken and sung.

Rodeheaver considered himself well read, and he understood the range of opinions that Blacks were voicing about the spirituals. He and Gabriel were wading into a complicated issue, two white northerners armed with their high school educations and a lifetime of diverse musical experiences. They were also wading into complex transcription issues. While Gabriel worked within the constraints of standard music notation, these rules could be a blunt-force tool when approaching melodies performed in unusual scales or songs lacking a clear meter. The nuances that made the spirituals beautiful were impossible to write down.

A dozen years would pass before the first trained ethnographers began making field recordings to preserve the actual sounds of southern folk songs. Or certain kinds of songs, at least. Full of zeal and eager to curate authentic folk life, the ethnographers wielded firm control of the song selection. The "authentic" recordings they preserved are now understood as a reflection of the collector's own views—an interesting slice of Americana, yes, but only a slice.[28] In the meantime, Rodeheaver found himself pulled into issues that would interest him for the rest of his life, culminating in his own recordings of African American musicians, a research tour to Africa, and publication of his book, *Singing Black*.

* * *

The Rodeheaver Co., by all estimations, had become a publishing juggernaut, enough to raise public suspicion about Homer Rodeheaver's growing wealth. Reporters knew that Billy Sunday was paying Rodeheaver more than any other team member, but more importantly, Sunday had also granted Rodeheaver permission to run the tabernacle's bookstall as a private enterprise.

Many of the products catered to souvenir shoppers. Guests would snap up photos and postcards of the revival team, pamphlets of Sunday's famous booze sermon, three different Sunday biographies, and Rodeheaver's *Song Stories of the Sawdust Trail*, containing his personal anecdotes about the power of gospel music. But the real money came from hymnal sales. The Rodeheaver Co. produced a new volume of gospel songs every two years or so, having purchased the songs outright from various gospel music composers. Just prior to the Atlanta campaign, Rodeheaver had updated an earlier book and given it a new name, *Awakening Songs*. Some of these hymnals were branded as a Special Tabernacle Edition, complete with a special 16-page section about the Sunday party, including photos and autographs. Available in three bindings for as low as 25 cents, the book made another fine souvenir for guests when they exited the tabernacle. In preparation for his southern foray, Rodeheaver had created a shape-note version of *Awakening Songs*, his first shape-note hymnal and a concession to southern custom.

Rodeheaver and other gospel song publishers were changing the way hymns were introduced to congregations. In previous eras, various Christian denominations appointed music committees to sort through new submissions, a winnowing process that resulted in a new denominational hymnal every twenty years or so. The denominational committees viewed their role as commending (and controlling) the worship music of local congregations. Rodeheaver's privately owned company bypassed these denominational structures, marketing its songbooks directly to churches and individual purchasers. His methods were wildly successful, spawning dozens of imitators and countless critics. And everyone wanted to know about the money.

A generation earlier, Dwight L. Moody and Ira Sankey faced the same question when their seminal *Gospel Songs* hymnal sold surprisingly well. Shocked by the unexpected windfall, Moody and Sankey recruited a group of trustees to distribute the money to various ministries, including a new building for their Chicago church (destroyed in the 1871 Chicago fire). At the time of Sankey's death, the *New York Times* said he never accumulated personal profits—though they sold 50 million copies.[29]

Rodeheaver and several other second-generation gospel publishers were venturing into new territory when their companies generated significant sales. The average person could understand when a church denomination distributed hymnal profits for altruistic purposes—but what about these new hymnal profiteers who kept the money for themselves? Could ideas about Christian altruism apply to a for-profit business model?

Rodeheaver's marketing methods—identical to Tin Pan Alley's song-plugging model—would provoke questions as well. Rodeheaver recruited the hottest writers, purchased and published his favorite new gospel songs, and then plugged them relentlessly during his personal appearances at revival meetings. He further plugged the songs in recordings, piano rolls, sheet music, and magic lantern slides. For every outlet that Tin Pan Alley could conceive, Rodeheaver created commercial-sounding Christian music in eclectic styles.

Rattled by Rodeheaver's growing influence, denominational leaders struck back with stern critiques about the money, marketing techniques, and musical styles. Rodeheaver found himself in the middle of a full-blown controversy that we will explore. He preached the power of gospel music, but the power of money could not be ignored.

As the Atlanta revivals were winding down, Rodeheaver and his pianists presented a sacred music recital at a popular downtown record store on Peachtree Avenue.[30] The concert featured the same songs and recitations from the tabernacle meetings. Bolstered by the idea of "recording artists," a new industry was now in full swing. The Atlanta dealership remodeled its limited space to create the Edison Concert Hall, impressively named but closer to a cramped jazz club, just a small platform surrounded by tea tables. After a few live songs in the Concert Hall, Rodeheaver sang along to his recordings of "Mother's Prayers Have Followed Me," "If Your Heart Keeps Right," and other hits. The demonstration was successful, at least from the standpoint of publicity; yet another article appeared in the *Atlanta Constitution*.[31]

Various record companies had been slugging it out for years over the best technology and format, resulting in phonograph cylinders and discs in various sizes and recording speeds. Having recorded for several companies on various discs and cylinders, Rodeheaver was agnostic about the recording industry's format wars. But he was downright evangelistic when talking about the power of gospel song recordings. He told the record store crowd a story about a blind woman who could not attend the Atlanta tabernacle meetings, and yet purchased some of his gospel recordings and played them for her friends. The result, according to Rodeheaver, was three more conversions, all the proof he needed.

Ever tactful, Rodeheaver did not air his brewing complaint with the new recording industry and his irritation with their truncated concept of gospel music. The industry gatekeepers had already carved music into marketing genres and coded names that mystified Rodeheaver. In addition to his irritation about the narrowly defined definition of gospel music, Rodeheaver worried that record executives didn't understand what "the gospel" even meant. In the case of the Edison discs, each release was still approved by the old man, the inventor himself, whose personal beliefs (a generic deism) left little room for intensely devotional performances.

CHAPTER 1

With the press coverage that Matthews and Brewster were getting, why weren't they featured on a major label, demonstrating the new gospel style? Or old-guard gospel vocalists like E. O. Excell and Charles Gabriel? Why not a rural-sounding guitar and mandolin duet, or an African American vocal quartet? And what if Rodeheaver wanted to sing *with* the Black groups? What category was *that*?

For Rodeheaver, the unifying factor was not race or region or stylistic genre. All of these were subsumed in his larger ideas about gospel music. He would spend a few more years asking hard questions of various industry executives, but he was already considering a better option—start his own record label, one without categories.

* * *

Halfway through the song service, Billy Sunday's driver pulled up to a side door outside, allowing Sunday to slip into the tabernacle with as little commotion as possible. Rodeheaver had just played a verse of "Brighten the Corner" on his trombone, and now he was moving into one of his stunts. The trombone became a conductor's baton for a few seconds, and then Rodeheaver parked it in the crook of his elbow while he waved with both arms.

Though a player of modest ability, Rodeheaver was one of the most famous trombonists in the country. Virtuosos like Arthur Pryor and Simone Mantia elicited awe from audiences, but Rodeheaver captured the public's imagination with his accessible style. For a while, Rodeheaver's influence was so strong that evangelical churches actively recruited trombone players to lead their worship services (yes, trombone players), similar to a trend in the late twentieth century when churches recruited guitar players. Rodeheaver's trombone became a personal brand. The trombone-wielding songleader became an evangelical trope.

Of all the songs he published and promoted, "Brighten the Corner" earned him the most criticism, which he constantly deflected. He claimed it was not intended for a formal church service but was "designed and used as a stepping-stone from the popular songs of the day to the great Hymns of worship." In addition to the irreligious, his tabernacle audience included many who "have trouble, and heart aches, and sadness, and discouragement; where things have been going hard for them ... and their hearts are heavy."[32] Songs like "Brighten the Corner" helped Rodeheaver sell the "practical, cheerful side" of religion; his boss would provide the fire and brimstone.

As Billy Sunday took a seat in the front section reserved for local preachers, Rodeheaver called out to various sections of the auditorium, assigning parts. "All of the soldiers, you'll sing the first line just like this," he shouted to the delegation from Camp Gordon, demonstrating the opening bars of "Brighten the Corner."

"Then everyone in the last ten rows will sing the second line, the choir will sing the third, and the final line will come from this fine group up front." Rodeheaver knew his audience, and he knew how to program a grand finale. Looking down at the rows of ministers in their go-to-meeting suits, he nodded. "The preachers will sing the last."

While each group was singing, Ned McIntosh tallied the results. On the final line, the preachers "made the rafters shiver," singing with such verve that Rodeheaver called on them to stand and sing the entire song again, punctuated by a thunder of Amens and much shouting.[33] Rodeheaver was carefully building toward an unexpected climax.

While most of the evening program featured the mass choir with Black soloists, Rodeheaver injected a few surprises. Mrs. Virginia Asher, who directed Billy Sunday's outreach to women, joined him at the podium. A graduate of Moody Bible Institute, Asher possessed a powerful alto voice that matched well with Rodeheaver's baritone, though she was ten years older. Brewster and Matthews hit the opening chords of a rhythmic introduction, and then Rodeheaver and Asher sang "Heab'n," one of the spirituals his childhood friends taught him in Tennessee.[34] On the surface his song choice seems gutsy or naive, white performers singing Black material to a Black audience, but it also indicates Rodeheaver's close relationship with a crowd he helped organize.

FIGURE 1.3. Rodeheaver with longtime duet partner Virginia Asher. Courtesy of Rodeheaver Collection, Grace College, Winona Lake.

African Americans were zealous to preserve their own musical heritage, even if they could not agree on whether the spirituals were appropriate for formal church services. But the matter of *who* should do this preserving was even more complicated. Did Blacks need the help of a famous white man to preserve their own cherished songs? And some would argue that Rodeheaver wasn't "preserving" the spirituals in their purest form. He was dressing up the original *a cappella* melody with a formal piano accompaniment, a transition that sounded European, even in the hands of Matthews and Brewster. Composer H. T. Burleigh would not produce his noted piano accompaniment to "Heav'n, Heav'n" for another five years. And purists never liked the Burleigh version any better than they had liked Rodeheaver's.

Lyrics written in Black dialect posed another challenge. Writers like Paul Laurence Dunbar and James Weldon Johnson (friends of Du Bois and Proctor) were at the height of their old-school popularity, but younger Blacks soon tired of their approach. Was this an early form of African American Vernacular English? Maybe, but it was difficult to parse the difference between an artful use of the vernacular and pure minstrelsy. Even more complicated was the matter of *whites* singing the spirituals in dialect, even if done with respectful intentions.

But in the meantime, two white singers were finishing up a cherished spiritual for their audience of fifteen thousand Blacks, accompanied by two more white pianists whose favorite style was—what? The great melting pot of American music was being stirred again.

"And they got away with it with such faithfulness that the last verse wound up in a thunder of Amens from the parsons' corner, and a big tribute of applause from all over the audience," Ned McIntosh wrote the next morning.[35] One wonders how much McIntosh knew about "faithful" renditions of the spirituals—but his report of the crowd's reaction is interesting.

Brewster and Matthews kicked into the next song, hitting a slow groove just like Rodeheaver wanted it. He always felt whites sang the spirituals—and most gospel songs, for that matter—too fast. Tonight's audience would recognize the sturdy, reverent pulse, a tempo that left room for plenty of vocal ornamentation. As soon as the crowd heard the call of the opening line, "I'm a gonna walk on the streets of glory," they knew their response: "I'm a gonna walk on the streets of glory, some of these days, hallelujah!"

Amid the shouting and falling out, Ned McIntosh offered this play-by-play: "The Negroes recognized their singing as a real work of art. One could feel the rhythm of it, and everybody was keyed to the melody and harmony of the song. Suddenly Rody swept his arm over the audience and the choir and shouted: 'Come on, everybody!'"

"It was like unleashing a pack of hounds on a hot trail. The promptness and unanimity with which at least 5,000 Negroes grabbed that chorus was not short of a psychological phenomenon."[36]

A hundred years later, one scours the contemporary accounts with a bit of skepticism, wondering if any of the reporters offered a more cautious opinion. Apparently not. In the papers the next day, every writer mentioned this moment as the high point of the meeting. In Black terms, Homer Rodeheaver had wrecked the house.

* * *

During the final chorus, Billy Sunday pulled out an enormous gold watch on a heavy gold chain. Each night he would fidget while the singing reached its climax; at 8:00 he would subtly remind Rodeheaver that it was his turn to preach. Rodeheaver would then repeat the same announcement he made in every service: Please refrain from talking to your neighbor. If you must cough, please step out of the auditorium. The ushers will be happy to assist mothers of crying babies.

Somehow, Rodeheaver sounded friendly and helpful, not at all scolding. He was motivated by practical concerns. In an era before electronic amplification, the rustle and shuffle of fifteen thousand whispers could become loud enough to drown out any preacher, even a leather-lung shouter like Billy Sunday. Audiences were becoming used to this sort of admonition—fine-suited vaudeville ushers were now passing engraved cards to unruly patrons, asking them to stop talking.

As vaudeville became a codified performance genre, supplanted with magic lantern slides and silent films, urban audiences were transformed into passive spectators. Ever sensitive to crowd dynamics and shifting cultural expectations, Rodeheaver presented a vaudeville lineup of acts that moved on and off the platform in quick succession. His revival audience learned to respond with the same genteel applause expected at Chautauqua and other stage performances.

The briskly moving program was not his first priority, however. "The greatest part of our effort is to try to get the whole congregation to sing, every man, woman and child in it," Rodeheaver had explained a few years earlier. "We spend more time trying to do that than trying to get the wonderful and artistic effect from our service."[37]

Homer Rodeheaver would stay with Billy Sunday for another dozen years after the Atlanta meetings ended, continuing his front-page role as the nation's songleader. The idea of urban revival meetings was tied to the same arc as vaudeville—hot trends that cooled after World War I, drifting into nostalgia as a younger generation embraced new media. The decline was already evident in Atlanta, if anyone cared to look closely. Offerings were down. Some thought that local

YMCA campaigns had drawn away potential supporters; others suggested that Atlanta was tapped out by the great fire a few months earlier. Either way, the meetings would barely break even, so Helen Sunday, Billy's wife and campaign organizer, suggested a few judicious staff cuts before the coming meetings in Washington, DC.

Almost twenty years younger than his boss and with a good deal of his life ahead of him, Rodeheaver adroitly shifted his business ventures but continued to apply his ideas about group singing. When he started a record company, he suggested that church congregations would sing along with the Victrola. Experimenting with broadcasting, he gathered groups to sing around the radio. And when he produced films, Rodeheaver would wave his arms on-screen as theater audiences sang along to the scrolling lyrics. In Rodeheaver's estimation, the idea of group singing was strong enough to survive the era of technological change.

Tonight's event would be remembered for highlighting the contributions of Black musicians in the wider spectrum of American culture. When H. H. Proctor wrote to the *Atlanta Constitution* a few weeks later, he offered a positive review. If the only accomplishment was "the revelation of the wealth of musical power that lay within the colored race, it was worth the cost of the campaign," he said.[38]

Proctor articulated the essence of the Harlem Renaissance, a rising movement that encouraged racial harmony through artistic achievement, not politics or protest. At the time, Sunday and Rodeheaver's Atlanta meetings were viewed with this attitude. Despite tensions that demanded segregated meetings, the meetings served as a showcase for the African American musical experience. At the very end of the campaign, Rodeheaver invited the Black choirs to sing for a whites-only service and invited their preachers to sit in the front rows. Jim Crow was not dead yet, but Blacks of the era viewed the Sunday meetings as progress in their entrenched struggle.

"It is true that Mr. Sunday has brought us into closer touch with our white friends, who really did not know us," said Lulu R. Rhodes in a letter to the *Atlanta Constitution*. "But, thank God, the Thursday night we sang for the white people a change was made, and I never shook hands with so many white men and women, who congratulated us on our singing and told us they were proud of us."[39]

The talking point was racial progress, a beginning rather than a final resolution. H. H. Proctor concluded in the *Atlanta Constitution*, "No man who ever came to Atlanta has done so much good in so short a time in creating a better feeling between white and colored races as Mr. Sunday."[40]

Billy Sunday was not off the hook, however. As successful as the Atlanta meetings seemed, Sunday was squandering the one power he had, the power of the pulpit. He fearlessly addressed nearly every form of vice. He singled out the corrupt liquor trade for special venom, despite pressure from the local business owners and politicians. But if Billy Sunday was against sin, why was he silent about Jim Crow?

"For all Sunday's denouncing of sins, he never mentioned rotten, stinking, hell-born race prejudice," said Rev. Francis Grimké a few months after the Atlanta campaign was finished. "It is pitiable when we think of the thousands of white men in this country, claiming to be ministers of the gospel . . . sitting down quietly in the midst of this spreading leprosy of race prejudice."[41]

Grimké's criticism stung on several levels. As the influential pastor of a large Presbyterian church in Washington, DC, Grimké was an early leader with Du Bois in the NAACP. But unlike Du Bois, Grimké still embraced conservative theological views that were quite compatible with Sunday's. When launched from a common doctrinal perspective, Grimké's pointed barb hit Sunday where he was most vulnerable. Was Billy Sunday following his own evangelical ideals?

* * *

Though society was changing rapidly, and though Atlanta viewed the 1917 revivals as racial progress, the forward motion stalled sooner than anyone cared to admit. Atlanta became a regional center for commercial music, but a musical color

FIGURE 1.4. Homer Rodeheaver, about the time of the 1917 New York revival meetings. Courtesy of Library of Congress.

line remained in full force, influencing the way musical genres were perceived and studied.[42] Consumer audiences were carved into categories of race music and hillbilly music, subtly suggesting that the two styles had little to do with each other. Folklorists descended from the North to preserve a pure "folk" music while winnowing out the music they deemed less pure. The southern music produced in (supposed) social isolation was prized for its authenticity and deemed worthy of preservation. The folklorists worked with great urgency to rescue what they viewed as an endangered idiom, believing that urban influences (especially the northern migration) would inevitably bring the taint of commercialism.

But this is not what Rodeheaver discovered in Atlanta. He met Black and white musicians who were already hearing and experiencing music in eclectic ways, certainly not isolated from other musical environments. Those imposed racial categories existed in the crisply printed record catalogs and academic papers—but in real life, the lines had always been murky. Wherever the styles might have originated, each idiom was quickly adopted by a variety of people who used the style in diverse ways. Whites were singing Black spirituals. Blacks adopted northern gospel songs.

Rodeheaver's combination of traditional hymns, northern gospel songs, and jubilee-style spirituals would become a model that Atlanta churches followed for many years. The songs that he plugged during his 1917 tour would become enormously influential in gospel music of every type.

Ebenezer Baptist serves as a fine example. After succeeding his father-in-law as pastor, Martin Luther King Sr. would explain his own approach to congregational worship by saying, "Our song books should contain classes of songs: The old standard Hymns, the current gospel songs, and an assortment of attractive new pieces."[43] In the context of Ebenezer's ministry, "the current gospel songs" meant Rodeheaver's style of northern gospel, as learned during the Atlanta revivals. They were sung side by side with "attractive new pieces" written by Thomas A. Dorsey and other Black composers.

"A new song with meaning carries a wonderful force, it arrests attention," King Sr. said, sounding a lot like Rodeheaver. "The people will sing a new song at home, on the street, about their work. Singing makes our burdens lighter, soothes our tired and weary souls, drives away the sorrows and heals our broken hearts. It lifts us and gives us new courage."[44]

In the context of a church service, Black gospel and white gospel had the same liturgical function: a congregational testimony that "drives away the sorrows and heals our broken hearts." The comments help explain the diverse mix that *Gospel Pearls* offered. Rodeheaver and King Sr. were saying the same thing about gospel music—whether northern or southern, Black or white, the genre was unified by its emphasis on congregational testimony. *Gospel Pearls* included songs from several

PROLOGUE

contemporary Black composers (Charles A. Tindley, Charles Price Jones, Thomas A. Dorsey, Carrie Booker Person, Lucie Campbell), cementing its importance to Black gospel music. This will be explored more fully in the chapters to come.

Though Black and white church musicians were clearly learning from each other, the effects of Jim Crow lingered, a point that would later be made clear by the son of Alberta Williams King and Martin Luther King Sr.

Having played on the circus grounds as a child and having learned the eclectic mix of songs his mother played from *Gospel Pearls*, Martin Luther King Jr. saw little improvement to the segregation problem. "At 11:00 on Sunday morning when we stand and sing 'Christ has no east or west,' we stand at the most segregated hour in this nation. This is tragic," King said.[45] But he revealed something else about his own religious experience: the diverse mental hymnal that nurtured his spiritual life. He made his famous point by ironically quoting a hymn from the white church, "In Christ There Is No East or West" by John Oxenham.

At the close of his Lincoln Memorial "I Have a Dream" speech four months earlier, King drew on this same mental hymnal, quoting the same line Rodeheaver had sung in the revival tabernacle: "Let freedom ring...." To make sure everyone got the point, King added a specific reference to describe the ongoing problem: "Let freedom ring from Stone Mountain of Georgia," a phrase with echoes of the Klan and Atlanta's slow progress toward a New South.

King would die from an assassin's bullet and was honored with a national holiday, but his mother's tragic death is lesser known. In 1974, a gunman interrupted Ebenezer Baptist during a worship service, shooting Alberta Williams King while she played the organ.[46] The last thing she saw was her beloved *Gospel Pearls*, opened to "The Lord's Prayer." Then Atlanta raised its Ebenezer, a stone monument on the same land where Billy Sunday's revival tabernacle once sat, directly across the street from the original site of Ebenezer Baptist Church.

* * *

When Homer Rodeheaver visited Atlanta in 1917, he crossed paths with many people and ideas. For a few brief moments the revival tabernacle seemed to represent Atlanta's future hopes and dreams, stirred by communal music, then marred by future tragedy. Yet in these brief moments we can see all of the themes that would later characterize Rodeheaver's life: his contributions to American popular music, his relationship to urban revivalism, his "early adopter" attitude toward technological change, his resulting wealth and philanthropy, and his influential role in defending gospel music as a congregational idiom. All of these complicated themes were rolled into a lifetime of song, one that started in rural Tennessee in the aftermath of the Civil War.

2

SOUTHERN ROOTS AND EARLY YEARS

"SOMETHING IN OUR HOME THAT MADE US VERY RICH"

On July 4, 1890, a crowd gathered in Jellico, Tennessee, waiting for the annual parade to start.[1] Independence Day fell on a Friday, giving a long weekend to the men of Campbell County, where coal mines and timber mills provided most of the jobs. On a day devoted to national unity, most everyone was celebrating the twenty-fifth anniversary of the Civil War's end—in these parts, a conflicted event. Though Tennessee had fought for the Confederacy, Jellico and the northwestern part of the state had voted overwhelmingly against secession. Slaves had been few in Campbell County before the war, and while African Americans made up only four percent of the county's population in 1890, they generally lived harmoniously among whites in Jellico. On this day of celebration, no one could foresee the racial tensions that would explode only a few years later.

By noon, a parade was forming at the railway yard, where the Louisville & Nashville Railroad met tracks of the Knoxville & Ohio Railroad, making Jellico a hub for transporting coal and lumber to the industrial north. From there it was an easy walk to Main Street and just a few feet from the Kentucky state line. Fully a third of Jellico's 758 residents prepared to take part in the parade. Whites and Blacks mingled together, and many women sported umbrellas to shield themselves from the sun. Two bands tuned up, one in uniform and the other smartly dressed in Sunday-go-to-meeting clothes.

The thirteen members of the Jellico town band were joined by an eight-member band from the Rodeheaver Manufacturing Company in Newcomb, three miles

FIGURE 2.1. Jellico, Tennessee, on July 4, 1890—Homer Rodeheaver (bottom left) next to the bass drum. Courtesy of Thompson Photograph Collection, McClung Historical Collection, Knoxville.

to the south. The Jellico band was grateful for the reinforcements, given that Rodeheaver's band had something the town band didn't have—drummers—and its leader, Yumbert Rodeheaver, was a skilled musician who, fifteen years later, would open Jellico's first music store.

The youngest member of the Rodeheaver band was nine-year-old Homer Rodeheaver. Determined to play the bass drum but too small to carry it himself, Homer walked alongside and kept the beat while an older boy carried the drum. As the parade stepped off, nobody would have imagined that little Homer, running to keep up with his drum, would become one of the world's most well-known and influential musicians.

Many years later, Homer Rodeheaver looked back on his early life and found themes of family, faith, music, and race:

> In our home, as well as in church under Uncle John's leadership, we sang the sonorous hymns dear to all followers of John and Charles Wesley. We sang, too, out of a battered songbook that had come over the mountains from West Virginia. We children who ran barefoot over every inch of mountain side and

knew everybody Black and white within a radius of ten miles, added to our repertoire the songs we heard the Negroes singing in their cabins and corn patches. The first I heard the spirituals was when the Negro railroad section gangs came to sing for my mother.[2]

FAMILY ORIGINS

Rodeheaver's romanticized childhood memories introduce a complex family history, rooted in the American South and fraught with conflict and tragedy. Four generations earlier, Hans David Rothenhoeffer emigrated to America in 1740 by way of Philadelphia and settled as a farmer in the Shenandoah Valley of Virginia.[3]

In 1807, one of Rothenhoeffer's grandsons, John F. Rodeheaver, moved his family from Woodstock, Virginia, north to Preston County.[4] Sharing its northeastern border with Pennsylvania and Maryland, Preston had one of the lowest percentages of slave ownership in Virginia.[5] Yet by 1820, "Saddler John"—so named because of his work as a saddle maker in addition to his farming over 360 acres—owned two slaves and by 1830 owned four. After Virginia seceded from the Union in April 1861, Preston County was one of thirty-eight northwestern counties that split from Virginia over the slavery issue, leading to the establishment of West Virginia.[6] John Rodeheaver's son George did not own slaves after he inherited his father's estate in 1838. From this point forward the Rodeheavers joined the abolitionist cause, igniting the family's long interest in African American life and culture. Two of George Rodeheaver's sons, John Jenkins Rodeheaver (1838–1908) and Thurman Hall Rodeheaver (1841–1912), mustered with the Third Regiment, Company H, West Virginia Infantry Volunteers in May 1861; Thurman suffered a gunshot injury at the second battle of Bull Run (August 29, 1862).[7] "This we endured for love of freedom," he wrote in his diary, "and for the sake of the government that our forefathers established."[8]

The Rodeheavers had close ties with other Preston County families, in particular the family of George Rodeheaver's wife, Lourana Jenkins, and that of their neighbors, Isaiah and Elizabeth Armstrong, who also owned a prosperous farm. The Armstrongs left West Virginia in 1861 for Hocking County, Ohio, and settled two miles southwest from Union Furnace.[9] The land was rich in coal and iron ore, and the hilly and rugged terrain was also suitable for farming, especially growing peach trees and grazing of sheep and cattle. The Armstrongs also established a strong presence in the McKendree Centre Chapel Methodist Episcopal Church near their home.[10]

Following his discharge from the Union Army in 1864, Thurman Rodeheaver followed the Armstrongs to Hocking County for the love of a girl. He married his childhood sweetheart, Francis C. "Fannie" Armstrong, in November 1865.[11]

SOUTHERN ROOTS AND EARLY YEARS

Homer Rodeheaver liked to boast that his mother's family was descended from a Captain John Armstrong who came to America on the *Mayflower*. But that story, like so many that Homer liked to tell throughout his life, was more than a little embellished; no John Armstrong was on the *Mayflower* passenger list.[12] Thurman and his older brother, John, purchased a 186-acre parcel of land about five miles south of Union Furnace and there, on the bank of a small stream that fed into Raccoon Creek that locals called Simco Creek, the brothers built homes for their families, not far from Thurman's in-laws.[13] John and Thurman shared the land, working together as farmers and also in the timber and lumber business.[14] Here another part of Rodeheaver's life narrative begins to unravel. The historical record contradicts the dramatic rags-to-riches version Homer preferred to tell, in which he even described his birth as occurring in a one-room log hut. In reality, Homer and his brothers were born in a stylish, two-story frame dwelling with front and back porches. After building the house, Thurman Rodeheaver further developed the property with barns and other outbuildings.[15] Land ownership such as this became the single most important—and lucrative—investment that the Rodeheaver family made over many generations. Though he often spoke of his own "humble beginnings,"[16] Homer Rodeheaver, in truth, was born into a family that enjoyed prosperity and success for many generations as farmers, lumbermen, and property owners.[17]

Homer remembered his Uncle John leading singing in church, "A fine, upstanding figure, muscular—full black whiskers—kindly eyes—splendid voice, throwing back his head as he sang 'Beulah Land.'"[18] These memories also point to a

FIGURE 2.2. Rodeheaver's birthplace in Simco Hollow, Ohio, where the family lived until 1882. Courtesy of Rodeheaver Collection, Grace College, Winona Lake.

major musical influence in Rodeheaver's early life, the gospel hymnals introduced by Ira D. Sankey and others during the early 1870s.[19] Just before Homer's 1880 birth, a new style of church music had taken hold in many Protestant denominations—Presbyterian, Baptist, and especially Methodist. The songs flourished in the north, influenced by recurring revival meetings, the abolitionist and temperance movements, and new ideas about music education.

The gospel song (or at least the term itself) is often traced to the evangelist D. L. Moody and his musical partner, Ira D. Sankey. Of course, the full story is more complicated and includes the contributions of William Bradbury, Philip Phillips, Philip P. Bliss, Daniel B. Towner, and James McGranahan. All of them were recruited by Moody for his evangelistic efforts, but they shared another thing in common. All had connections to Lowell Mason (1792–1872), the Boston publisher who advocated communal singing and "Better Music" for churches and schools.[20] When Uncle John Rodeheaver opened his hymnal and led his small Methodist congregation, he introduced these new gospel songs to Joseph, Yumbert, and Homer Rodeheaver, who embraced them and became part of the next generation of gospel song publishers. Their ideas about gospel hymnody would draw heavily on the traditions they inherited from Lowell Mason.

TENNESSEE YEARS

Uncle John Rodeheaver lived a peripatetic life, traveling back and forth between Ohio and Tennessee in a number of business ventures. His wanderlust ignited frequent moves until a midlife stroke confined him to a wheelchair. Thurman, on the other hand, put down roots in the woods near Union Furnace, where he and Fannie had four children, all born in the house on the creek: Yumbert Parks (1868–1950), Isaiah (1871–1872), Joseph Newton (1873–1946), and Homer Alvan (1880–1955).[21] Homer sometimes mentioned that his mother had hoped for a daughter when he was born, but the rest of the story he never told in public.[22] He never knew and never talked about his brother Isaiah, who lived only four months. The three surviving brothers developed very close relationships. In 1921, Homer looked back and recalled that, "there has not arisen a single serious misunderstanding between either of my brothers and myself, or between us and our father; neither do I recall a single unkind word having passed between us."[23] It would be easy to dismiss this as sentimental revisionism, but later chapters will show how Homer Rodeheaver, despite serious disagreements with a number of coworkers and business partners, never had significant discord with members of his own family.

Until Homer was born in 1880, Thurman Rodeheaver engaged in logging and milling of oak, maple, poplar, and hickory around Union Furnace until the forests were depleted. Shortly after Homer's birth, the Louisville & Nashville Railroad completed an extension to Jellico, Tennessee, where it met with the Knoxville & Ohio Railroad (later called the Southern Railroad). The discovery of high-quality coal in the Jellico area led to economic and population growth that extended into the early twentieth century. With his lumbering fortunes in Ohio dwindling and the railroad providing a new and efficient means of transporting goods, Thurman moved his family and sawmill business south to Newcomb, Tennessee, where the rich oak, maple, and walnut forests of the Cumberland Mountains had not yet been exploited. Thurman and Fannie purchased a Newcomb house in 1882, and with Uncle John, they established the Inter-State Manufacturing Company, later named the Rodeheaver Manufacturing Company.[24] John and Thurman Rodeheaver jointly owned the company, with each of them taking charge of operations at various times due to John's frequent trips back to Ohio to manage his concurrent coal mining operations. The brothers were joined in the business by their younger brother, Hamon, who drowned at age 29 in Elk Fork Creek on June 26, 1885, while inspecting damage caused to the company factory after a fire. Thurman nearly drowned in a failed rescue effort. The factory was rebuilt and in time, Thurman's three sons worked at the factory in various roles.[25]

FIGURE 2.3. Thurman Hall and Fannie Rodeheaver. Courtesy of Rodeheaver Collection, Grace College, Winona Lake.

CHAPTER 2

The family retained ties to Ohio, renting rather than selling their properties, visiting family, and shipping lumber north on the newly completed railroad. Homer's mother took her children to the Lancaster Camp Ground in Ohio, a spiritual community and the site of evangelistic meetings since 1872, where Homer converted to the Christian faith in 1888.[26] He would return to Lancaster many years later to lead singing at the camp and give programs of classical and sacred music; it remained a place with fond memories of his mother.[27]

Fannie Rodeheaver died in 1889 after struggling with a long illness. She addressed her last words to her son Joseph: "Take care of Homer."[28] She was 43 years old. Homer, eight years old at the time, later spoke of his loss:

> I have a clear memory of my brother Yumbert coming and waking me in the early dawn and taking me into her room to say goodbye to her. I remember her voice charging my older brother particularly to look after me . . . With my mother's going, something had gone out of our home.[29]

Homer rarely talked about the death of his mother, but his affection for and connection to her was evident during his entire life—later seen in the music he published and recorded.

While Homer would wistfully recall how "something had gone out of our home" with the death of his mother, he also remembered there was "something in our home that made us very rich"—their music.[30] Yumbert Rodeheaver described his parents as not being musical in the technical sense, but interested in providing lessons for their children. "On the old farm where I was born my father bought a small cottage organ and employed a young lady to live with us and teach my brother Joe and I to play it," Yumbert said. Thurman Rodeheaver also bought a second-hand organ for the Sunday School he had organized. When the regular organist moved away, the family looked to Yumbert. "There being no one else, I was made the 'goat' and forced to preside at the organ," he said, "although knowing almost nothing about playing it." His mother bought a mail-order instruction book and assigned a few songs per week, which Yumbert then played at the Sunday services. "That is about all the help and instruction I ever received in music, and had that necessity not arisen in my life, I doubt if any of us would ever have become musically inclined," Yumbert said.[31]

He may have felt forced into the organ duties, but Yumbert had a long fascination with brass bands. Teaching himself cornet, he organized a band at the Rodeheaver factory and instructed his little brother on how to play the bass drum. Dressed in jackets and ties that would later give way to uniforms, the band played at political rallies, town events and parades, growing to as many as fourteen members who played cornet, tenor horn, euphonium, tuba, and drums.[32]

OHIO WESLEYAN UNIVERSITY

The three Rodeheaver brothers somehow sensed that education would provide the path to a better future. Thurman Rodeheaver wasn't fully convinced of this; his own business acumen came without formal schooling. Yumbert recalled, "my parents were not enthusiastic over an extensive education. Their environments did not demand or require it."[33] Even so, they did allow their sons to attend school, and all three Rodeheaver boys attended Ohio Wesleyan University in Delaware, Ohio. The university was officially nonsectarian, but with loose Methodist affiliations.

Joseph Rodeheaver began studies at Ohio Wesleyan University in 1893 at the age of 20. Like that of his brothers, his enrollment at Ohio Wesleyan was intermittent. He stayed in Ohio as long as his money held up, and he returned to Tennessee to work when funds were low. He began as a special student in the university's preparatory department, designed for students who were not yet ready for university classes, particularly those who attended classes part-time or irregularly due to the need to work.[34] Joseph was the only member of the family to graduate from Ohio Wesleyan, earning a Bachelor of Science degree in 1901 and a Master of Arts in 1902. In 1907, he earned a PhD at Boston University.

Five years older than Joseph, Yumbert Rodeheaver arrived at Ohio Wesleyan University in 1895 and stayed for only one year; his brief time at the university was undistinguished. It was Homer, however, who would make the strongest impressions upon OWU campus life.

As a young boy, Homer attended school in Newcomb, where the school year ran for only three months so children could work on family farms and businesses. His brother Joe, still following his mother's charge to take care of Homer, encouraged him to enroll in 1896 as a special student in OWU's preparatory division. Homer later described the shock of his first day:

> I was fifteen and hardened to a man's work out of doors. When I got to Delaware and was examined by the school principal and assigned to a place in the sixth grade with little boys and girls who didn't know which was the kicking end of a mule, it seemed more than I could endure.[35]

Homer Rodeheaver stayed in the preparatory department for most of his years at Ohio Wesleyan; he was officially a "special student" until he left school in 1905, apart from one year of college credit, 1900–1901. He excelled at English and elocution but received a grade of 75 in voice lessons; there is no record of him taking lessons on any musical instrument.[36] Like his brother Joe, he was constantly in and out of school, traveling home to earn money, and then back to school when he had made enough to afford tuition.[37]

Once on campus, Rodeheaver first achieved notice as a public speaker. In 1903, he took first prize in the State Prohibition Oratorical Contest. The campus newspaper raved about his speech, saying "his personality was attractive, his gestures appropriate, and his audience seemed to hear his eloquent words rather than to see the speaker."[38]

Rodeheaver's effervescent, outgoing personality also landed him a role as director and lead actor in the university's 1903 and 1904 minstrel show, "Delaware's Dandy Darkies," where he performed in blackface for the largely white student body. Throughout his life, he voiced his affection for African Americans, championed the spirituals, and collaborated with Black singing groups in concerts and recordings. But like many whites, his views on race were shaped by the complex attitudes of his own era, and as we discuss more fully in chapters 7 and 8, the situation remained complicated.

The fitful starts and stops of racial progress can be illustrated by Rodeheaver's friend and fellow student, the president of the OWU Athletic Association, which sponsored the annual "Dandy Darkies" minstrel show. History remembers Branch Rickey for his later role as general manager of the Brooklyn Dodgers—the same Branch Rickey who hired Jackie Robinson in 1945, famously breaking the color line in Major League baseball. Rickey would become a staunch civil rights activist; yet, in 1903, Rickey and Rodeheaver produced a blackface minstrel show where Rodeheaver received critical acclaim as a singer and trombone soloist.

FIGURE 2.4. Rodeheaver (second row, seated, fourth from right) with the Ohio Wesleyan University Cadet Band, 1903. Courtesy of Ohio Wesleyan University Historical Collection, Delaware.

Rodeheaver's college activities were interrupted when the battleship *Maine* exploded and sank in Havana harbor on February 15, 1898, ushering in the Spanish-American War. The short-lived conflict ended quickly after the Spanish fleet was destroyed, followed by an armistice on August 12. The brevity of the conflict, however, did not prevent volunteers in many states from enlisting in the army. Yumbert and Homer Rodeheaver enlisted in Tennessee's Fourth Volunteer Regiment Band on November 18, 1898, playing cornet and trombone respectively.[39] The brothers arrived in Trinidad, Cuba, just before the Treaty of Paris formally ended the war on December 10. After a few months of garrison duty, they were discharged on May 6, 1899. "All the enemies we had to fight," Yumbert later said, "were the Cuban flies and tarantulas."[40]

After the war Homer continued to alternate between Ohio Wesleyan and periods of employment back home. At some point he also connected with Ohio's largest publisher of gospel hymnals, the Fillmore Brothers of Cincinnati. James Henry Fillmore recruited Rodeheaver for a summer job, asking him to play his trombone and sell hymnals on a revival tour of the upper Midwest. Rodeheaver was assisted by Henry Fillmore, the son of J. H. and apparent heir to the family hymnal business, except that Henry was quickly tiring of traditional church music. Henry also played trombone and would soon become known as the composer of marches such as "Americans We." He also became famous for "Lassus Trombone," one in a series of trombone solos he called "niggah smears" (for their use of slide glissandi).[41] But for now, before either became famous, they were just two college students playing trombones and selling hymnals.[42]

The summer tour with Fillmore seems to be the first documented instance of Rodeheaver using his trombone to lead singing at evangelistic meetings. "In those days there were no loudspeakers or microphones," Roger Butterfield would later write. "Rody found that neither his voice nor the piano was loud enough to carry all the way through the crowds and he looked around for something more powerful."[43] Later, after both men were famous, Henry Fillmore wrote a march in tribute to tabernacle revivalism, "Billy Sunday's Successful Songs," a medley of gospel songs with copyrights owned by Rodeheaver.

RODEHEAVER AND THE TROMBONE

While a student at Ohio Wesleyan, Homer Rodeheaver began an obsession with the slide trombone, something that would define him for the rest of his life. His initial interest in owning a trombone had been thwarted by a lack of money, but he heard of a student who needed quick cash and wanted to sell his instrument.[44] "I wanted that slide trombone as I'd never wanted anything before," Rodeheaver said, "but when I looked inside my lean wallet, the purchase price—four and a half dollars—looked as far beyond my means as if it had been twenty times that sum."[45] In his telling of the story, Rodeheaver reasoned that he might never have such a chance again:

> What it amounted to was that I had to choose, as Life makes us choose again and again. I had to weigh the comfort of three meals a day for a couple of months minus the trombone against the joy of having the trombone and living for that length of time on one meal and a miserly breakfast a day.
> The trombone won.[46]

The trombone had not only won, but Rodeheaver's "little old trombone of the Lord" became his personal brand, a focal point for his leading singing in evangelistic meetings.[47] Without ever having received any formal training on the instrument, he played in the OWU Cadet Band, made a splash playing trombone solos on campus, performed with numerous traveling evangelists, and, later, gave concerts on the Chautauqua circuit. By the time he began leading music at meetings with Billy Sunday, "the glorious Rodeheaver trombone was," in one writer's

FIGURE 2.5. Rodeheaver promotional postcard.

account, "a weapon of the Lord, marshaling the troops in song... Rody lugs the trombone around the stages as if it were glued to him; he points it, twirls it, tucks it under his arm, and, at last, plays it."[48]

In the 1920s, Rodeheaver's fame as a trombonist was so significant that C. G. Conn Ltd. featured his endorsement in their musical instrument catalogs. "Accept my sincere congratulations on your unusually fine trombone," Rodeheaver gushed. "I am using it in our great tabernacle meetings and everyone speaks of the beauty of its tone. I like it better every day."[49] His words appeared alongside those of some of the finest trombonists of the time, including Arthur Pryor, the undisputed Paganini of the trombone; Simone Mantia of Sousa's Band and the Metropolitan Opera Orchestra; Leroy S. Kenfield, bass trombonist of the Boston Symphony; and Gardell Simons of Patrick Conway's Band and the Philadelphia Orchestra. During his career, Rodeheaver played for over 100 million people—a staggering number—and used trombones by Conn, Lyon & Healy, Rudolph Wurlitzer (which he also endorsed), and York.

But while Rodeheaver was counted among the artists in Conn's pantheon of notable players, the advertisements ignored an uncomfortable truth: Homer's trombone playing wasn't very good. In fact, he wasn't much better than the school-age players in Conn's target market. While Rodeheaver was playing "My Old Kentucky Home" and solos that were full of "big, round, sustained notes, followed by tender, mezzo tones that resembled a fain echo,"[50] Arthur Pryor was performing solos like his "Blue Bells of Scotland" with a blistering, virtuosic technique.

Rodeheaver's own publicity machine reported that "few trombone soloists have appeared before the American public under any auspices equipped with a clearer tone and finer technique than Mr. Rodeheaver possesses."[51] By contrast, astute commentators periodically mentioned the deficiencies in his playing, as when the *Chicago Tribune* suggested "that Rodey, in the interest of humanity's ears, trade his trombone for a shoe horn."[52] His friends were more generous. "It didn't make any difference whether he played in tune or sang in tune. We were still inspired," one said. "This is a trait that, of course, cannot be taught, but somewhere along the line he learned how to do this."[53]

Rodeheaver took his trombone everywhere. To France in 1917 when he entertained troops at the front under the auspices of the YMCA during the waning days of World War I, on his world tour of 1923–24, to the Holy Land (where he played trombone while floating in the Dead Sea), and to Africa in 1936 (a *Time* magazine correspondent reported that villagers gave Rodeheaver the name "White Song Man" but "for the trombone they could think of no descriptive word.").[54] His goal was communication of the gospel, not technical expertise. "I play to reach people, and so I don't play over their heads," he said in a 1943 interview. "There's such a thing as being too sweet and low. You've got to attract people before you can convert them. One good blast is worth a dozen soft toots."[55]

Whether or not Rodeheaver knew (we don't know) of the work of Rev. Wilson Carlile, the founder of England's Church Army (1882) who played the trombone in streets, pubs, and from his pulpit in an effort to gain converts, Homer's high-profile trombone playing spawned the genre of the trombone-playing evangelist.[56] Beginning in the early twentieth century, acolytes from Rodeheaver's trombone tree fell like apples at harvest time. These included Harold Fremont Holbrook, Horace Erwin, Ted Ness, Burton [B.B.] Bosworth, Walter J. Bateman, Joe Talley, Sam Saltar, and Marcy Tigner, who was best known as the bizarrely unsettling ventriloquist voice behind her children's puppet "Little Marcy."[57] All of these, though, paled against the work of Billy Graham's trombone-playing song leader, Cliff Barrows (discussed in chapter 10). Even today, the trombone remains closely associated with Christian evangelism.

Having heard Rodeheaver at the tabernacle revivals and the Winona Lake Chautauquas, pundit Will Rogers summarized the contemporary view of Homer's trombone playing when he claimed that "Rody has slip-horned more sinners into the Kingdom of Heaven than any of the old timers with their trumpets." Rogers was not alone in attributing more than a little of Rodeheaver's success to the trombone—or the popularity of the trombone to Rodeheaver—when he quipped, "Rody sure gave that old instrument a Holy standing, and any revised edition of the Bible has sure got to give Rody and his Slip Horn a chapter."[58]

AFRICAN AMERICAN INFLUENCE

Some of Homer Rodeheaver's earliest musical memories came from African American farm hands and railway workers who sang spirituals. "I was just a kid," Rodeheaver said, "but I learned something from them that has influenced my entire life."[59] His early contact with Blacks and their spirituals—discussed in depth in chapter 7—shaped his music making, and these songs formed a core part of his concert and revival meeting repertoire for all of his adult life:

> Many of those songs were the 'spirituals' that today are recognized as some of the greatest folk music in the world.
>
> In those days nobody thought very much about them. They were just 'nigger songs.' But even as a child, they had great emotional appeal for me. And what a treasure of music they are! You only have to listen to their minor cadences to know all the longing and the heartache song can hold.
>
> Negro spirituals are popular everywhere now—one rarely sees a program of classic songs without at least one spiritual represented. I was singing these

songs in my evangelistic campaigns with Billy Sunday, and in my recitals long before music critics had pronounced them the song heritage of our nation. They are still the most popular part of my concert repertory.[60]

Homer Rodeheaver's fond memories and good personal relations with African Americans notwithstanding, times grew difficult for Blacks in eastern Tennessee. In Jellico, the next town north of Newcomb, three Black men were lynched by mobs in 1892 and 1893. The Jellico lynchings were typical of thousands of similar extra-judicial sentences carried out by whites against Blacks throughout the South.[61]

As Campbell County's Black population slowly grew—from four percent of the population in 1870 to six percent by 1910—the unrest continued, culminating in a 1908 incident where a Black woman and five children were burned in their cabin near Jellico. Some local whites began stirring up trouble when the Kings Mountain Coal Company had assigned Blacks and whites to work side-by-side in Jellico-area mines. Next came the warning notes pinned on trees and cabins: Leave in three days, or else.[62] Then an arsonist killed a family of six, presumably because they didn't move out fast enough.[63] Blacks living in Campbell County got the message, and the number of African Americans declined precipitously for the next century.[64]

Rodeheaver never spoke directly of the Jellico race incidents, but their memory proved indelible. "When you know the colored people and know something of their struggles," he later wrote, "you will realize how these songs were born amidst the trials and tribulations of this race and how they typify their thought and life."[65]

FAMILY TRAGEDY

In 1891, another fire at the Rodeheaver Co. factory destroyed the family business; there was no insurance. Rather than rebuild, Thurman Rodeheaver sold the company to new owners who renamed it the Newcomb Manufacturing Company. Thurman and his brother John started another lumber company, Rodeheaver Brothers Lumber Company, located near Jellico's railway yards, and in February 1901, Thurman moved his family from Newcomb to a home on Main Street in neighboring Jellico.[66] Yet, tragedy continued to follow him. As Yumbert Rodeheaver related, "fire once more completely destroyed our plant, leaving us stranded—from the shock of which my father never wholly recovered."[67] The family business started over one more time as Thurman, Yumbert, Homer, and two other local friends put up $15,000 to form the Kimberly Lumber Company.[68] Yumbert also opened a Jellico music store in 1904 or 1905, and various sources credit him as the first teacher of the celebrated opera singer Grace Moore, although her autobiography makes no mention of the influence of any Rodeheavers in her life.[69] Likely provoked by Thurman's poor health, Homer moved his father and family to Colorado in 1908, followed by another convalescent move to Winona Lake, Indiana, where Thurman died in 1912. At age 71, Civil War veteran Thurman Rodeheaver's long life of family, church, prosperity, and tragedy came to an end.

REVIVAL SONGLEADER

Homer's approach to education was less focused than that of his brother Joe; his developing musical interests did not fit neatly into any academic program. During his last two years on the OWU campus, his name frequently appeared in the *Ohio Wesleyan Transcript*, but not for any scholastic achievement. An issue from May 1904 featured Homer Rodeheaver on nearly every page.

His concert with the quartet-choir from William Street Methodist Episcopal Church received notice for its high-toned art music. For the special event the group sang "The Forty-Sixth Psalm," advertised as "perhaps the greatest masterpiece of all the works written by Dudley Buck."[70] In the ongoing church music squabble between the cultivated and vernacular traditions, Rodeheaver's church had positioned itself squarely in the cultivated camp, where a paid double quartet rendered a high standard of musical performance.

Two nights before singing in the Dudley Buck concert, Rodeheaver had also volunteered as yell leader at OWU's oratorical contest, a peculiar collegiate spectator sport that enjoyed a brief popularity in the early 1900s. Teams from Indiana University and Ohio State sent their best speakers to Gray Chapel, accompanied by cheering sections. Each team brought yell leaders who warmed up their constituents with cheers and group songs, followed by the orations. "Nothing stirs a speaker like the use of pennants, the radiant faces, and the enthusiastic support of his fellow students," the campus paper declared. "It's up to all of us to pull together and the victory is ours."[71]

If the gap between high church music and college yell leader wasn't enough, a third article in the same paper reported Rodeheaver's previously mentioned role in "Dandy Darkies."[72] Casual observers might conclude—quite rightly, and a full decade before Rodeheaver achieved worldwide fame—that he could not be pigeon-holed into any one category of music. Cultivated or vernacular? Rodeheaver would spend his entire life answering that basic question with a "Yes."

Rodeheaver found a way to reconcile these diverse musical activities in February 1903, when the OWU music faculty received an urgent visit from Robert A. Walton (1857–1911). The Presbyterian minister scheduled a series of meetings in Mount Gilead, about 25 miles by rail from the OWU campus. When his planned songleader canceled at the last minute, Walton contacted the college for possible replacements. Rodeheaver, everyone's best suggestion, accepted the two-week job. Little is known about the Mount Gilead meetings, other than Rodeheaver's lifelong references to them as his first songleading efforts.[73] Rodeheaver always attributed his songleading skill to his experiences as a college yell leader.

"At the football games and oratorical exercises in my college someone was needed to lead the crowds in singing and in the delivery of the college yells," he would typically tell reporters. "The work fell to me and the experience I got in that way has helped me more than a little since, in leading great congregations in the singing of devotional songs."[74]

The idea of a congregational songleader was relatively new, and a direct outgrowth of Ira Sankey's gospel song performances. Sankey sang from a small reed organ that sat near D. L. Moody's pulpit. Positioned so he faced the audience, Sankey could accompany his solo singing on the stanzas of each song, then invite the congregation to join him.

Sankey eventually retired from touring and settled in Brooklyn. Moody found a new partner at an 1884 Sunday School convention, where Daniel Towner led the congregational singing with a conductor's baton while his wife played the organ. Impressed, Moody offered Towner a job, one that quickly expanded when Moody opened his Chicago training school, now known as Moody Bible Institute. Towner developed a music curriculum and began propagating the idea of a gospel *songleader*, a chorister who used conducting gestures to lead the congregation in singing. His idea would dominate evangelical worship services for the next century and strongly influence the community song movement of the 1920s.

TOURS WITH W. E. BIEDERWOLF

When the Mount Gilead meetings were over, Rodeheaver finished the spring semester at Ohio Wesleyan and spent the summer working and saving money for the next year of school. His decision to drop out after the 1905 spring semester surprised no one. After a few semesters of college courses, he was better educated than 98 percent of American adults. He returned to Jellico to work at the Kimberly Lumber Company, but the venture lost money—a problem, since Rodeheaver had borrowed money to secure his stake. He took a job in the coal mines to dig himself out of his personal financial hole, a grimy job that made any other offer more attractive. An unexpected letter from William E. Biederwolf proved to be especially interesting. The noted evangelist planned a series of meetings in Springfield, Missouri, and needed a last-minute songleading replacement. Two weeks of work—and maybe more.

Biederwolf's offer could not be ignored. He was considered the equal of R. A. Torrey (1856–1928) and J. Wilbur Chapman (1859–1918), top-tier speakers who could go into any city and draw a crowd night after night. All three could attract and pay the best musicians, and traveled with a growing entourage of personal assistants, public relations specialists, Bible study leaders, and logistics coordinators.[75] A second tier of lesser-known evangelists found work in smaller towns as the local demand increased for revival meetings, leading to problems. For a time, the informal network of preachers remained tight enough to police itself. Then, somewhat like a startup company that grew too fast, the revivalists found their own reputations besmirched by inferior preaching and financial impropriety.

Biederwolf grew concerned enough about quality control that he founded the Interdenominational Association of Evangelists in 1904, ostensibly as a training and networking organization, but also as a watchdog agency. The IAE held annual summer meetings in Winona Lake, Indiana, where Biederwolf and Chapman had summer homes. The sessions ran concurrently with the Winona Lake Bible Conference, but the general public was not allowed to attend IAE meetings.[76] The group would be important to Rodeheaver for two reasons. First, he started at the top, working for a leader in revivalism rather than moving up the ranks in a succession of lesser-known positions. Second, the IAE would later adjudicate a public scandal involving Rodeheaver and his girlfriend. The revival circuit was approaching its heyday and needed a dose of regulation.

Rodeheaver accepted Biederwolf's offer in October 1905, arriving in Springfield, Missouri, without his trombone and no plans after the two-week campaign. Biederwolf took an immediate liking to Rodeheaver and hired him for the rest of the 1905–6 season. Homer sent for his trombone, marking his first full-time job as revival songleader, and leading to an unbroken string of twenty-five years where he traveled constantly.

Little is known about these earliest Biederwolf-Rodeheaver meetings, other than Rodeheaver's later report about spending four months in Ohio, Illinois, Tennessee, Kentucky, and Missouri.[77] Rodeheaver played trombone, sang vocal solos, and directed the choirs—none of which overshadowed his primary responsibility to lead congregational singing. For their first meetings together, Rodeheaver used *Hymns for His Praise*, which Biederwolf and James McGranahan had edited together. Beiderwolf invited Rodeheaver to collaborate on a successor book, what would become *Hymns for His Praise No. 2*, Rodeheaver's first publishing credit.

While compiling the song list, Rodeheaver purchased two songs and registered his first copyrights. He bought the lyrics to "Prepare Ye the Way of the Lord" from the Presbyterian minister A. J. Arrick, a friend of Biederwolf's, and then composed a tune. He also acquired lyrics to "Hail to the King" from Biederwolf's tenor soloist, Paul J. Gilbert.[78] The songwriting credit was shared by Myrtle Henderson and Homer Rodeheaver—a story in itself.

Myrtle Henderson enrolled at Ohio Wesleyan University in the fall of 1904, Rodeheaver's last year on campus.[79] Perhaps they dated on campus, perhaps not. Rodeheaver never mentioned it, though it seems likely that they had some sort of relationship while Rodeheaver was touring with Biederwolf. Then came a 1908 notice in the *Reading Times* "Matrimonial" column: "Announcement has been made of the marriage of Homer Rodeheaver to Miss Myrtle Henderson, a California woman who happened to be visiting in Reading, Pennsylvania, during the Biederwolf campaign." The article also mentioned that the couple had been writing songs together.[80]

Most of the story, however, was false—they were not married, not even engaged. Though the newspaper never issued a retraction, the article didn't garner much attention, either. Rodeheaver was not yet famous enough to receive the celebrity gossip treatment from national wire services. Five years later, when touring with Billy Sunday, he would not enjoy such anonymity. His status as an eligible bachelor eventually provoked much speculation, accompanied by additional conjecture about his growing wealth. He would not dodge this bullet twice—from now on, his dating life would be everyone's business.

Though not a musician himself, Biederwolf showed a strong sense for what sort of songs worked with revival congregations. *Hymns for His Praise No. 2* was helped immeasurably by major contributions from three Chicago songwriters. Of the 152 selections, twenty-two were written or composed by Charles Gabriel. Eight were contributed by James McGranahan, and twenty-four were written or owned by E. O. Excell.[81] In addition to their Chicago connection, all three were devotees of Lowell Mason's Better Music ideas, grandchildren (so to speak) who traced their teaching lineage directly to him. All three knew Moody and Sankey, all three contributed to Sankey's *Gospel Hymns 1–6*, and all three had previously traveled with Biederwolf.

Rodeheaver met another key figure when he and Biederwolf stopped at Monmouth College, a Presbyterian school in Monmouth, Illinois. Music professor John B. Herbert was well-known among church musicians, though his career started on a different track. Growing up near Monmouth, he followed his father's wishes by earning a medical degree in Chicago and then returning home to open a local practice. Successful by any measure, Herbert then pursued his real passion, music, and eventually abandoned his first career. In the years to come, Herbert would collaborate with Rodeheaver on many projects, especially temperance songs and male quartet music.

For all of the connections that Rodeheaver made during the 1905–6 revival season, he did not cross paths with the premier stars of the circuit, R. A. Torrey and Charles Alexander. Now famous enough that they did not need the support of the evangelistic network, the Torrey-Alexander team became their own whirlwind with their own team and their own hymnal. The pairing seemed perfect. Torrey exuded the restrained air of a theology professor or a college president (he was both). And Alexander served as the ideal antithesis and prototypical sidekick. A few days later, the same reporter suggested that people went to the Torrey-Alexander meetings to hear the singing more than Torrey's preaching.[82] Probably true, and a commentary on the growing importance of communal singing at the meetings.

When the 1905–6 revival season drew to a close, Biederwolf planned to spend the summer in Winona Lake, where he had a growing leadership role. Rodeheaver had already accepted an offer from James Ely to spend the summer in Philadelphia, where the Presbyterian Evangelistic Committee held tent meetings at Lemon Hill, a bluff overlooking the Schuylkill River. Now in its fifth summer, the event enjoyed renewed popularity stemming from the just-concluded Torrey-Alexander revival. Rodeheaver planned to lead the children's meetings, but his responsibilities expanded quickly to include trombone solos and songleading.

While summering in Winona Lake, Biederwolf agreed to join J. Wilbur Chapman's fall schedule of "Simultaneous Campaigns" for 1906–7, a plan that drew inspiration from Moody's citywide meetings in Chicago during the 1893 World's Fair. A large team of traveling evangelists held a coordinated series of meetings at various venues all over the host city, a Simultaneous Campaign. Chapman tested his decentralized model for the first time in 1904, dividing Pittsburgh into nine zones, each with its own preaching and music teams. From there, Chapman would scale his model upward, eventually organizing cities into twenty or more zones of simultaneous meetings.[83]

Chapman's big idea—even bigger than pushing a simultaneous model—was his plan to connect his Presbyterian organization to the broader efforts of conservative Protestants. He coordinated his teams through the Presbyterian assembly's committee on evangelistic work, but invited the participation of Baptist, Methodist, and other evangelical churches.

Chapman's efforts kept Biederwolf and Rodeheaver busy through the spring of 1907. When the revival season wound down, Rodeheaver agreed to a second summer at the Lemon Hill conference. Enjoying a bump from the recent Simultaneous Campaign, organizers splurged on a new canvas tent to accommodate larger crowds. They also convened a reunion of "the famous Torrey-Alexander choir" from 1906, asking Rodeheaver to lead in Alexander's place.[84] Some sort of movement was afoot, yet unnamed, where common ideas about gospel song evangelism were passed from one practitioner to another. And no one was surprised when the same singers would reconvene in 1915 for the epic Billy Sunday Philadelphia campaign.

The 1908 Philadelphia meetings were also notable as the only time Alexander and Rodeheaver worked together. One would surmise that they could have been friends. They shared common roots in East Tennessee. Alexander had even attended Maryville College for a year with Homer's brother, Joseph.[85] Both songleaders were masters of crowd dynamics, and both had similar ideas about the importance of congregational singing in revivals. But after 1908, Rodeheaver would lean heavily on the fraternity of gospel song publishers in Chicago—a tight knit group that collectively distanced themselves from Alexander, despite his ability to plug hymnals. Alexander would return to England and fade from memory, to the point where his influence is sometimes forgotten. Rodeheaver, on the other hand, was stepping into the spotlight of national celebrity.

3

GOSPEL SONGS AND URBAN REVIVALISM
"A TORNADO WITH MUSIC AT ITS CORE"

When Ira D. Sankey died in 1908, Homer Rodeheaver and a host of second-generation successors were busy with their own revival meetings—too busy to attend the funeral. Instead, they planned to end the year with a New Year's Eve tribute, where everyone returned to Chicago for a signature event. Making no small plans, Daniel Towner rented out the Chicago Coliseum, the city's largest venue, which had just hosted the notorious First Ward Ball. Some adjustments were necessary—a crew of workers cleaned up the shattered beer bottles and slop and then arranged the 10,000 seats in church-like rows for the gospel song event. They also built a choir loft to seat 2,000 choir singers, who had been rehearsing for two months at assigned Protestant churches in each Chicago neighborhood.

All revivalists of note wrapped up their December meetings and traveled back to Chicago, Biederwolf and Rodeheaver included. Towner hosted a three-day training symposium at Moody Bible Institute, issued membership cards to the choir members, printed a new hymnal, and contacted all of the newspapers. His event name telegraphed his real intentions. Not just a one-time tribute, this was the Gospel Song Evangelistic Movement.[1]

So at the stroke of midnight on New Year's Eve 1908, the event culminated with twelve thousand revelers joining hands and reciting the Lord's Prayer. Then they sang a roof-rattling version of "Praise God from Whom All Blessings Flow," and the party broke up. The next morning, the *Tribune* contrasted two December events with a pointed headline: "Gospel Meeting Crowds Coliseum; Wipes Out

FIGURE 3.1. Rodeheaver and chorus at Lancaster, Ohio, camp meetings, 1911. Courtesy of Rodeheaver Collection, Grace College, Winona Lake.

Stain of Ball." The reporter noted how the two events had filled the Coliseum to capacity, "but there the resemblance stopped. Hymns took the place of two-steps; sermons and prayers were heard where maudlin oaths resounded, and money that changed hands, instead of paying for wine and beer, went to promote the work of the movement."[2]

In addition to marshaling a capacity crowd, the event planners had succeeded in a broader goal—positioning gospel songs as a rising movement that worked as an equal partner with preaching to produce personal revival. "Through all of the addresses ran a note of optimism concerning the rapid strides being made in various parts of the country by the gospel song movement," the *Inter Ocean* concluded.[3] D. L. Moody's successors were teaching a brand of revivalism with two primary methods. "The aim is to win souls to Christ by means of gospel singing and evangelistic address," organizers said.[4]

During Sankey's memorial service, John M. Hitchcock had called him "the father of gospel songs and also the father of a new generation of gospel songsters." The *Chicago Tribune* quoted this tribute and described Sankey as the "father of gospel harmonies."[5] Later, when gospel music branched into regional and racial genres, Sankey's status as "the father" seemed tenuous. But for the Chicago successors, such claims were unassailably true. Homer Rodeheaver, leader of the "new generation of gospel songsters," would absorb all of this ideology before pushing gospel songs into the mainstream of American popular music.

CHAPTER 3

MEETING BILLY SUNDAY

A few months later, Homer Rodeheaver met Billy Sunday in Winfield, Kansas, where both had been scheduled to appear at a summer Chautauqua meeting on July 15, 1909.[6] Though the event marked the first time the two appeared together, they may have previously crossed paths, given the tight-knit associations of the revival evangelists. After spending the past five summers at Philadelphia's Lemon Hill, Rodeheaver scheduled two full months on the summer Chautauqua circuit. Protestant evangelists were discovering that the Chautauqua pace was less strenuous, the pay was good, and the tour was valuable for making enough personal connections to fill the next nine-month season of revival meetings. Or in Rodeheaver's case, new audiences for his hymnal ventures.

The year before Billy Sunday arrived in Winfield, the town built a permanent tabernacle with 3,500 seats, nearly large enough for every adult in town.[7] Inviting Billy Sunday made good financial sense—he drew as much as $1,000 in gate receipts.[8] At the 1909 event, Sunday out-drew all the other speakers, including Gov. Frank Hanley of Indiana.

Sunday immediately noticed two things about Rodeheaver. First, he had the unteachable gift of connecting to people. The conference organizers had planned a diverse program, including acts like Pamahasika's Pets, a circus juggler, and a troupe of Swiss bell ringers. When Rodeheaver arrived in Winfield, he enhanced the planned program by scouting out local talent to help him during the meetings: soloists, a children's choir, the town band, even a group of gymnasts who were willing to perform a few stunts after Sunday spoke. Rodeheaver applied all of the crowd-building lessons he learned during his travels with Biederwolf. And the whole town turned out, packing the new tabernacle and singing up a storm before Sunday began his lecture. One more fact became immediately obvious: Homer Rodeheaver was a better songleader than Fred Fischer, Sunday's current assistant.

When Sunday and Rodeheaver parted ways at the conclusion of the Winfield Chautauqua, Rodeheaver stayed in Kansas. Biederwolf planned to saturate the state with the Kansas Forward Movement, a full year of Chapman-style simultaneous campaigns held by cooperating evangelists. Billy Sunday, however, did not cooperate. Ever the loner, Sunday followed D. L. Moody's original model of a single, centrally located tabernacle or tent. As much as Billy Sunday valued the support of every Protestant church in town, he did not share his pulpit with other ministers. Sunday was the featured speaker, period. And though he counted on the local network of churches for financial support and general publicity, Sunday also reached past them. He appealed directly to the community for his financial support, and he bolstered attendance by encouraging delegations from every organization in town. So far, Sunday's methods showed every sign of earthly success. Each meeting seemed to be in a successively larger town, coupled with more publicity, more conversions, and bigger offerings.

Billy Sunday didn't take many vacations. He stayed on the road after Thanksgiving Day, even though Biederwolf had already returned to Winona Lake for a year-end break. This gave Rodeheaver a few open weeks in his schedule, so he joined Sunday for year-end meetings in Joplin, Missouri. Rodeheaver played his trombone and led children's meetings while Fred Fischer continued as Sunday's music director and songleader.[9] Did Fischer feel threatened by Rodeheaver's presence? Maybe. For their last meeting in Joplin, Fischer organized a farewell concert featuring everyone on the Sunday team. When Billy Sunday picked up the newspaper the next morning, he read wall-to-wall coverage of Rodeheaver's trombone solos, his instrumental duet, and his vocal trio. Then he read about Rodeheaver's magic tricks, his humorous story about a stammering boy, and two more recitations—six name checks in one article. And if Sunday was keeping track (he always kept track), he would have noted that his usual songleader and traveling partner netted a single mention, one "Fred Fischer" near the end of the article.[10]

Fischer ran smack into Rodeheaver's natural gift for media coverage. Much later, after the revival team employed a full-time press agent, one would expect this saturation coverage. But in the early days, before their calculated attempts to manipulate news reporters, Rodeheaver seemed to attract coverage without trying. "Mr. Rodeheaver is better known among local clergy than many of the singing revivalists as his work has been heralded by religious publications and press all over the country," a Davenport, Iowa, reporter had said.[11] One is naturally tempted to discount the breathless tone of these early news accounts, but the reporter's comment stands out for a different reason. He was writing in 1906, barely six months after Biederwolf hired Rodeheaver, and already noticing a media presence "all over the country."

From Billy Sunday's perspective, the Joplin experiment went well enough that he invited Rodeheaver to help with the January campaign in Youngstown, Ohio. Rodeheaver could at least participate for the first few weeks before resuming his February commitment with Biederwolf in Monmouth, Illinois.

REPLACING FRED G. FISCHER

Fred G. Fischer had been traveling with Billy Sunday since their 1900 meetings in Bedford, Iowa. Back then, before the entourage grew, it was just Sunday and Fischer, traveling from one small town to another. They grew close—probably closer than Sunday ever was to Rodeheaver. And though biographers would characterize Sunday as aloof and intensely private offstage, these descriptions seem less accurate for his pre-fame years. Or perhaps Sunday's natural introversion took over when the crowds grew out of hand. At any rate, Sunday described Fischer in effusive terms, calling him "the best in the world" and repeated similar comments in every town they visited.[12] Until Sunday met Rodeheaver, that is.

Fred G. Fischer aspired to a music publishing career, having been born into gospel publishing royalty.[13] His uncles, George and Peter P. Bilhorn, owned the Bilhorn Brothers Music Company of Chicago, famous for their gospel hymnals and their Folding Organ, a portable reed organ that collapsed into a suitcase. They had also worked with Billy Sunday during his early days at the Chicago YMCA. So when Sunday needed a full-time songleader, the Bilhorns recommended their nephew, Fred.

Perhaps their recommendation was entirely altruistic, but the marketing potential could not be ignored. Having a nephew on the revival circuit allowed the Bilhorns to produce and plug more hymnals. Fischer set to work, compiling a collection that soon became the official Billy Sunday hymnal, *Hymns of His Grace No. 1*, named as if they anticipated a second volume.[14] But no sequel would be produced, owing to stiff competition from three similar projects: the Torrey-Alexander *Revival Hymns* (1905), Biederwolf and Rodeheaver's *Hymns for His Praise No. 2* (1906), and Towner and Excell's *Famous Hymns* (1907). In retrospect, the Bilhorn-Fischer project sold poorly because they cut too many corners. Unwilling to pay Alexander, Towner, or Excell a slice of the royalties, the Bilhorn-Fischer book did not include the most popular songs. Then the Panic of 1907 created a survival-of-the-fittest scenario for the oversaturated Chicago hymnal market, with Fischer's book the loser.

The Chicago gospel publishing fraternity could be brutal for unprepared upstarts, but they essentially viewed themselves as colleagues who could share slices of a very big pie. When Homer Rodeheaver floated the idea of starting his own company in 1910, the publishers welcomed him to the fold. Rodeheaver's new enterprise, discussed at length in the next chapter, earned their respect. Rodeheaver cut deals with Excell and Gabriel, and he paid his bills on time.

Fred G. Fischer could not have been happy. The newly named Rodeheaver-Ackley Co. featured Bentley DeForest Ackley as co-owner, effectively preempting Fischer's idea for his own Ackley partnership. And when Billy Sunday invited Rodeheaver to join the team for a few weeks, it felt more like a tryout. Though Fischer did not yet know it, Billy Sunday used the Youngstown meetings to float a quiet offer to Rodeheaver.

After spending six weeks with Billy Sunday, Rodeheaver rejoined the Biederwolf team in Monmouth, Illinois. Billy Sunday traveled on to Danville, Illinois, but immediately wrote to "Prof. Homer Rodeheaver" on March 1, 1910, extending a job offer as music director. "My time is all filled from Sept. 25 to June 15. I only rest about one week between towns," Sunday said, promising Rodeheaver a full schedule and $75 a week.[15] In practical terms, Rodeheaver would have the annual income of an accountant or business executive. More importantly, Sunday added another detail that might close the deal: "You can use your own book and have all you can make from the sale of the same."[16]

Throughout their years of working together, Sunday and Rodeheaver never signed a contract for services. Many of the top-tier revivalists were using formal agreements to spell out the length of tour, responsibilities, weekly pay, and the newly important issue of music rights. Sunday would soon raise Rodeheaver's weekly pay to $100, but he never felt a contract was necessary. Neither man would ever complain about their relationship or fight over money—the informal agreement remained in place for at least twenty years.

Sunday did have one concern about the proposed arrangement—Rodeheaver was still under contract with Biederwolf, Billy Sunday's respected friend. They both had been mentored by Chapman, they owned homes near each other in Winona Lake, they were members of the Interdenominational Association of Evangelists. Sunday did not want to jeopardize his Biederwolf friendship, he told Rodeheaver in a later letter. "I don't want to do anything that will prejudice his mind against us."[17] So after Sunday's careful wooing, Biederwolf gave his blessing to the transition. Rodeheaver and Biederwolf would continue to work together as their schedules allowed, including a world tour in 1923–24.

After accepting Sunday's offer for the next season, Rodeheaver stayed in Monmouth with Biederwolf, continuing plans for his new company. His first order of business was to develop a new hymnal to replace *Hymns for His Praise No. 2*, now nearly four years old. He enlisted Biederwolf to help compile new songs and worked closely with J. B. Herbert, still living in Monmouth. Rodeheaver's sudden shift to Sunday's team posed no problems for his business ventures. Biederwolf agreed to continue helping with the project even though Rodeheaver was leaving. From Rodeheaver's standpoint, endorsements from Biederwolf and Sunday would virtually assure his success.

A NOT-SO-NEW STRATEGY

Billy Sunday and Homer Rodeheaver understood the history of their own movement and absorbed the most effective strategies from a variety of sources. Their mastery of the revival format was so complete that they often received credit for ideas that came from their predecessors.

When Billy Sunday learned that Perry, Iowa, had no large auditoriums, he arranged for a specially constructed tabernacle to be built for his 1901 meetings.

CHAPTER 3

FIGURE 3.2. Rodeheaver caricature from the *Los Angeles Morning Tribune*, 1917.

Some Sunday biographers claimed it was the first; others suggested he built a tabernacle in 1900 for the Elgin, Illinois, meetings.[18] Sunday became famous for constructing these temporary tabernacles, some of which seated 15,000–20,000 people. But he was by no means the first to do so—a point acknowledged by Homer Rodeheaver in his later correspondence with Milan B. Williams, the relatively obscure revivalist who originated the practice.[19]

Billy Sunday also popularized the "sawdust trail" metaphor, inviting tabernacle guests to respond at the end of his sermons by walking forward on the sawdust-covered aisles. As the story goes, "hitting the sawdust trail" was first used by news reporters covering the 1910 meetings in Bellingham, Washington.[20] Perhaps so, but revivalists had been spreading sawdust on the aisles to cut down on sound reverberation since at least 1858, when Edwin M. Long suggested the practice in *The Union Tabernacle; Or, Movable Tent Church*.[21] What Sunday really contributed was a catchphrase.

Homer Rodeheaver's role as revival soloist was invented by P. P. Bliss, C. M. Wyman, Philip Phillips, and Ira Sankey—singers from D. L. Moody's era. Likewise, Rodeheaver's quickly moving program with three-minute features came from Moody's noon prayer meetings. The expanded role of a choir (and the huge front-and-center choir loft) came from Daniel Towner. The flamboyant songleading personality and "master of ceremonies" approach came from Charles Alexander. And the idea of a custom-produced hymnal came from, well, everyone.

If one were to ask Billy Sunday about the source of his platform persona and sermons, he would happily acknowledge his debt to Chapman and Biederwolf's masculine Christianity. More particularly, Chapman gave Sunday a supply of texts and sermon outlines when Sunday started out on his own.[22] So what did Sunday and Rodeheaver invent? Nothing, really. But they assembled the entire package, did it on a larger scale, and did it better than anyone else had ever done.

TOLEDO CAMPAIGN

Billy Sunday had been planning a 1911 campaign in Toledo, Ohio, a shipping and rail center with a growing population of 150,000 and his largest city to date. Several factors made the Toledo meetings memorable. Sunday had his eye on a prime downtown location, a baseball field known as Armory Park. A year earlier, the Toledo Mud Hens moved to a new ballpark, leaving Armory Park empty and available. The old stadium seated only 4,500, so Sunday arranged to demolish it and build a temporary tabernacle of gargantuan proportions, his largest to date, with room for 10,000 guests. Tabernacle builder Albert P. Gill drew up the plans according to his prevailing theory, that choir lofts should equal 10 percent of the audience seating, but this meant the loft should seat 1,000 singers—a wild figure that created doubt for some of the planners. In retrospect, after the meetings were over, Gill and Rodeheaver agreed that the size of the loft was a mistake. Way too small—1,500 singers attended the local rehearsals, forcing Rodeheaver to divide the performing choir into groups and sing in shifts.

On the opening night of the campaign, Sunday swung for the fences. "Toledo is the wickedest city I've ever campaigned in," he said in his sermon. "You who run the gambling halls, I say to you, come on! I defy you in the name of God and the Christian people of Toledo!"[23] Earlier that night, 10,000 people arrived early to the tabernacle—plus the overflowing choir loft. Could Sunday sustain these numbers for six weeks? Given his penchant for flamboyant, headline-grabbing stunts, maybe. And then Sunday was aided by one more event that would give him a final burst of publicity.

CHAPTER 3

Five days into the campaign, Addie Joss died from a sudden bout of tubercular meningitis. He was only 31 and the star pitcher for the Cleveland Naps (today the Cleveland Indians). Early in his career, Joss had played for the Mud Hens, right there at the Armory Park stadium, and he made Toledo his home in the off-season. The funeral grew into a media event when the Naps canceled their opening day game with the Detroit Tigers. Both teams attended the Toledo funeral, along with 15,000 grieving fans. And who better to preach than Billy Sunday?

"Joss tried hard to strike out death," Billy began, leading off with a baseball metaphor. "The great manager of the Universe took the star Nap twirler out of the box and sent him to the clubhouse." The great Cy Young sat with the rest of Cleveland team, crying, while Sunday exhorted the players to "leave the minor leagues of this world and play the game in God's Big League forever."[24] No one remembers if any of the players hit the sawdust trail after the funeral, but the resulting publicity guaranteed Sunday a successful campaign.

When the meetings were over, the *Toledo Blade* reported a cumulative attendance of 800,000 people, 7865 converts, and a final offering of $15,423.58. "The Toledo Campaign has resulted in [the] most conversions and largest offerings in history of Mr. Sunday's Evangelistic Work," the paper said.[25] Whatever dim thoughts Billy Sunday may have had about Toledo's sin, he ended by boasting of "the greatest campaign I have held during the 14 years of my evangelistic career, and perhaps the greatest revival ever held in any city in this country."[26]

Rodeheaver celebrated his own milestone. He arrived at the Toledo tabernacle with crates and crates of a new hymnal, *Great Revival Hymns*, bearing the imprint of the new Rodeheaver-Ackley Company in Chicago. He and Ackley shared their editorial credit with Biederwolf, who had gotten the project rolling before Rodeheaver left to work with Sunday. Both teams planned on using the hymnal, which Rodeheaver immediately advertised in periodicals like the *Record of Christian Work* and the *Sunday School Times*. Many of the ads prominently featured Billy Sunday's endorsement: "I consider GREAT REVIVAL HYMNS the best Gospel song book that has been published for years. It is the only one I have ever endorsed with a written statement."[27]

On the first night of the Toledo meetings, a choir of 1,000 singers opened their new hymnals with the red embossed cover. Rodeheaver led them in a demonstration of the new songs and then taught the tabernacle crowd to join in on the chorus. "The people of Toledo have become infatuated with the gospel songs," the *Toledo Blade* said, three weeks later. "Wherever one goes . . . at almost any hour of the day or night, one sees men and women carrying what is becoming a familiar burden—the red-covered hymnal of Rodeheaver and Ackley."[28]

Rodeheaver discovered he did not need overt salesmanship to create a market. Charles Alexander, known for blatant hymnal commercials from the pulpit, found himself in hot water with R. A. Torrey over the issue.[29] In contrast, Rodeheaver believed that his music would speak for itself. "It surges with the power that makes men and women more willing to work for the souls of human kind," his advertising claimed.[30] If so, infomercials before the sermon would not be necessary. Billy Sunday would later receive a good deal of criticism for his book stands at the back of his tabernacles. But profit margins were never as important as message control. If Sunday didn't market his own ideas, someone else would open a stand across the street, and Sunday would have no way to regulate the content.

Charles Gabriel traveled from Chicago to visit the Toledo meetings. He wanted to see the new hymnal in action and wanted to introduce Rodeheaver to an old friend, Ina Duley Ogdon.[31] Gabriel had been using her poems since 1892, paying her the going rate of $3.00 to $5.00 per song. She still lived in Toledo, and Gabriel was in the market for new song lyrics. On March 28, 1911, just a few days before the Toledo meetings opened, Gabriel had signed a one-year contract with the Rodeheaver-Ackley Company, agreeing to edit all song manuscripts that the new company would publish. In turn, Rodeheaver agreed to pay Gabriel $75.00 for new songs, and also agreed to pay for any lyrics that Gabriel wanted to purchase from other writers like Ogdon.[32] Rodeheaver and Gabriel were looking for a specific style of writing—something that could bridge the gap between the popular song and traditional hymnody. Perhaps Ogdon would be willing to work on some ideas, maybe something with potential to be a tabernacle theme song, something Rodeheaver lacked.

WINONA LAKE

The 1911 Toledo meetings marked a turning point for both Sunday and Rodeheaver. Measured by any statistic—attendance, offerings, hymnal sales, spiritual decisions—their campaign was the biggest ever. For the next seven years, Sunday and Rodeheaver would hold meetings in the largest cities—Boston, New York, Chicago, Philadelphia, Atlanta—and capture the public imagination like no revivalists before or since. Their public lives would never be the same, and their private lives would soon become public.

In 1911, Rodeheaver also expanded his publishing business. Yumbert moved to Chicago to run the growing hymnal venture, having liquidated most of the family's business interests in Jellico. Now Rodeheaver rented an office at Chicago's Methodist Book Concern, sharing space with editor Charles Gabriel. And though Homer was the youngest of the three brothers, he took a greater role in caring for the extended family, mostly because he could. The hymnal business had given him financial security.

CHAPTER 3

FIGURE 3.3. Rodeheaver purchased a Winona Lake home for his stepmother, Bettie, in 1911. Left to right: Yumbert, Joseph, Homer, Bettie, Jack, Ruth. Courtesy of Rodeheaver Collection, Grace College, Winona Lake.

Rodeheaver bought a home in Winona Lake and moved his father's family from Colorado. The generous gesture helped his father escape a speculative land venture that never quite worked. After Frances Rodeheaver died, Thurman Rodeheaver had married his secretary, Bettie, and then moved to Colorado in 1908. He purchased mining rights at a site that didn't pan out. And now Thurman, 70 and quite ill, could no longer work. Bettie, who was 31 years younger, spent her days caring for their children, Ruth, 13, and Jack, 7. No one had time to homestead, so Homer's Winona Lake plan proved to be the best solution.

Earlier in 1911, Billy Sunday had built a new house on a bluff overlooking Winona Lake. News reporters habitually described it as a mansion funded by revival offerings, the sort of description that sounded plausible to people who never visited. Locals called Sunday's home a well-appointed cottage, which it was. Rodeheaver's new house, the Hillside, was actually larger than Sunday's, sufficient for the blended family and plenty of guests.[33] A few years later, Rodeheaver would also purchase The Franconia, just five houses away from Sunday's.[34] Jack Rodeheaver could play with Billy Sunday Jr. (b. 1901) and Paul Sunday (b. 1907). The move allowed Rodeheaver to care for his extended family, and it also gave Bettie a source of income. She would operate the properties as summer hotels for many years.

Rodeheaver's eventful year closed on a sour note. Sunday and Rodeheaver finished the year with a six-week campaign in Wichita, Kansas. After their last meeting on Christmas Eve, the Sunday party took the overnight train to Chicago.

Rodeheaver planned to spend Christmas Day with Georgia Jay, a young typist he had been quietly dating. Their planned gift exchange led to awkward moments. She bought him a bathrobe, a surprisingly personal gift. Rodeheaver presented her with a set of fine furs. Pricey, yes, but Georgia Jay expected a ring. And she had already told her friends and her mother that they were planning to marry, a point that apparently had escaped Rodeheaver's notice. She would later claim that he had formally proposed just before leaving for the Toledo meetings in April—arguably, the sort of event he would have remembered.

Though he was famous for his diplomacy, Rodeheaver was also exhausted from touring and short on patience. A long argument ensued where Rodeheaver, feeling unromantic, managed to call her "an unusually good friend."[35] Already feeling rebuffed, Jay did herself no favors when she asked how much money she could have per week. Then she asked about children. Rodeheaver closed the conversation with a clarifying word: No. There would be no wedding. Georgia Jay stormed out, grabbing the furs, and the next time they saw each other was in a Chicago courtroom.

"BRIGHTEN THE CORNER"

A year after the Toledo campaign was over, Ogdon wrote lyrics to "Brighten the Corner Where You Are" and mailed them to Charles Gabriel, who composed the now-famous tune. Rodeheaver liked it and immediately introduced it at the 1913 Columbus, Ohio, meetings.[36] Ina Duley Ogdon traveled from Toledo to hear it sung, noting its immediate popularity in her growing scrapbook.[37] Having searched for five years, Rodeheaver finally had his theme song.

The idea started at the 1908 Gospel Song Evangelistic Movement, when organizers introduced "O That Will Be Glory," written by Charles Gabriel and published by E. O. Excell.[38] The song came alive in large groups, possessing some ineffable quality that Rodeheaver could not explain. When Charles Alexander first saw the music, on paper, his impression was negative. "In looking over a new song-book, I just glanced at it, and said, 'That man has wasted a page, for I do not believe that song will be sung much,'" Alexander recalled. But a few months later, Alexander heard it sung by a large audience and completely changed his opinion. "It took such a hold of me . . . I dreamed about it, and awoke to the rhythm of it," he said, adding that "I began to teach it to large audiences."[39]

Alexander voiced a basic tenet of the revival songleaders, that certain gospel songs were ideally suited for large group singing, that certain songs came alive when sung together by mass groups in a wooden tabernacle. Gabriel and Ackley believed they could summon this power with their compositional techniques. "Often I need to change only a message or a few words to get a rhythm and

CHAPTER 3

FIGURE 3.4. Hymnal version of Rodeheaver's campaign theme song.

harmony which the people in our meeting will sing," Ackley said. "Sometimes my arrangement may not be as good as that of the composer, but the crowds will sing mine—and a song sung is better than a better song they won't sing, or can't sing."[40] As Rodeheaver searched for a theme song, he reached beyond the usual church crowd to find songs that everyone in the community could sing. In his next hymnal with Gabriel and Ackley, he included "Brighten" and other songs like it. "We have been collecting and trying out new songs. Each one has been tested on the anvil of experience in practical religious work," he said in the Preface to *Great Revival Hymns No. 2*.[41] Though only two years had passed between the first and second edition, Rodeheaver dropped 123 songs and added 158; half the book was new.

Rodeheaver introduced *Great Revival Hymns No. 2* at the 1913 Billy Sunday meetings in Wilkes-Barre, Pennsylvania. Just as he had experienced in Columbus, crowds especially loved the new "Brighten" song, already a hit. Five years later, Charles Gabriel would claim, "Probably no song has ever found its way around the world in so short a period of time as 'Brighten the Corner Where You Are.' It is sung in the war trenches and on foreign mission fields; in the Sunday School and prayer meeting; it is played by brass bands, orchestras and on phonographs, hummed in camps and whistled on the street."[42]

Like a Tin Pan Alley hit, the song's popularity sprang directly from Rodeheaver's incessant song plugging. He printed it in numerous forms (more than 12 million copies by 1925) and recorded it numerous times, starting in 1915 (discussed in chapter 5). Rodeheaver claimed the song "has been sung and played more times during the past ten years than any other song, sacred, secular or patriotic."[43] Despite these successes in commodified formats, Rodeheaver believed its popularity came from its essential singability. "It has been said that one can plug any song and make it popular. This is not true," he said. "If a song does not have melody, the sublime gift of hymn writers, no amount of plugging will make the song popular."[44]

According to Rodeheaver, "Brighten the Corner," became a favorite because "the chorus is so simple in its musical construction, that any crowd can learn it after just hearing it over a couple of times. Possibly its greatest value is because of its simplicity, and because it presents such a tremendously important truth in such simple and compact form."[45] He also attributed its popularity to stunts: "because of the stunts it made possible . . . we used this antiphonal idea effectively with many other songs, but none were as universally popular as 'Brighten the Corner Where You Are.'"[46] As Alexander had discovered with "The Glory Song," Rodeheaver felt that "Brighten the Corner" worked especially well when the tabernacle was filled.[47]

Rodeheaver had always programmed what he called "warm-up songs" for his tabernacle audience, specifically intended to get the crowd singing together.[48] Crowds tended to arrive early—Billy Sunday never sold tickets—so Rodeheaver began his songs whenever the tabernacle looked full. Most of the time he started the warm-up song by singing the stanzas solo and then teaching the chorus to the congregation. For Rodeheaver, the perfect warm-up song had a simple melody, a relatively narrow range, and a chorus with repeating lyrics.

Anyone who looked closely at *Great Revival Hymns No. 2* (or paid attention to the revival meetings) could see how Rodeheaver's ideas about gospel songs were expanding. He still published and programed songs from the Sankey era, along with some newly written songs that sounded like Sankey. He also included traditional Protestant church hymns, always a staple of his repertoire. Now he added a new kind of gospel music that drew more closely from popular idioms and featured positive, feel-good lyrics. In addition to "Brighten," Rodeheaver introduced "If Your Heart Keeps Right" ("Every cloud will wear a rainbow if your heart keeps right")[49] and "In the Service of the King" ("I am happy in the service of the King, I am happy, Oh, so happy").[50] All three songs quickly grew in popularity and would soon be recorded by several artists. A Philadelphia newspaper called them "cheer-up songs," referencing the term that musicians were using to describe a certain genre of popular music.[51] Compared to their earlier cousins, Rodeheaver's new gospel songs could be identified in four ways: 1) they had lyrics with positive, feel-good themes and comparatively little doctrine; 2) the music drew from popular idioms; 3) the songs were crafted for the unique needs of a tabernacle service; and 4) they were planned as temporary, populist expressions and replaced quickly with similar songs.

Several other songs in *Great Revival Hymns No. 2* exhibit the same characteristics, though they never grew as popular: "Help Somebody Today,"[52] "Is the World Any Better?"[53] and "A Glad Way Home,"[54] plus an ingratiating children's ditty, "Song of the Sunbeams."[55] Despite their happy themes—and despite Rodeheaver's plugging—some just never caught on. Rodeheaver and Gabriel responded by ruthlessly pruning their own catalog, happy to drop a low-performing song and replace it with a new hit. Rodeheaver also voiced what many had suspected, that the influx of new songs was part of a deliberate strategy. "In the musical part of our service it is our aim always to make it as cheery and bright and sunshiny as we can, at the same time not losing sight of the reverential, devotional power of gospel song," he explained to a group of church music students. "If we can show the sunshine in our own faces it will recommend our religion to other folks more than anything else we can do."[56]

GOSPEL SONG CONTROVERSY

The ensuing controversy over Rodeheaver's new songs serves as an archetype for all future critiques of gospel music, a two-front war where sacred theologians attack them as bad theology and secular critics attack them as bad art.

The Presbyterian theologian J. Gresham Machen preached at Winona Lake in 1915 and then reported to his mother: "My criticism of Winona is that the 'rough house' element is overdone. I do not object to a little of it, or even a good deal of it, but it does seem to me to be a pity that it should almost crowd everything else out."[57] The conference used *Great Revival Hymns No. 2*, including many songs that did not impress Machen. "Practically every lecture, on whatever subject, was begun by the singing of some of the popular jingles, often accompanied by the blowing of enormous horns or other weird instruments of music," he told his mother. He did not mention anyone by name, but the "the blowing of enormous horns" seems clear enough. If Rodeheaver's plan was to attract an audience with "cheery and bright and sunshiny" music, Machen admitted he could tolerate "a little of it," but now he feared that it was overdone.

On another front, *Musical America* weighed into the controversy as "the voice of the performing arts industry." After a music critic heard "Brighten the Corner" at a Billy Sunday meeting, the magazine snidely suggested the lyrics were "written by a Sapolio pressagent," referring to a popular brand of soap that was famous for its advertising jingles.[58] *Musical America* lumped Rodeheaver's song into the same general category as ragtime, cakewalks, hillbilly, and jazz—all were enemies of true American music.

As the controversy continued, Rodeheaver conceded one obvious point. The "Brighten" lyrics did not actually speak of the death, burial, and resurrection of Jesus Christ, the traditional Protestant declaration of the gospel that gave gospel songs their name. "I suppose, if you should analyze it, you would not find much theology in it," Rodeheaver admitted to students at Moody Bible Institute.[59] But even if it did not have a clear declaration of the gospel, Charles Gabriel still defended its biblical outlook. "Each line in each stanza of that hymn is supported by a Scripture text, and the fact that the song has found its way into almost every corner of the Christian world proves that it has a message," Gabriel said.[60]

The controversy over Rodeheaver's new gospel songs continued as theologians and music critics fanned the flames with new attacks. Soon Rodeheaver would need to address the accusations about musical style, but not before his ex-girlfriend presented accusations of a different sort.

GEORGIA JAY SCANDAL

Georgia Jay grew up in Dakota City, Nebraska, a town of 500 people. She had just turned twenty when Biederwolf and Rodeheaver began their 1909 meetings in nearby Sioux City, Iowa. She sang in the chorus, dated Rodeheaver for five weeks during the meetings, and then he left for the next town. They would write back and forth during the next year but saw each other only intermittently. The couple spent more time together during Billy Sunday's Waterloo, Iowa, meetings in 1910. Jay arranged to room in Waterloo for six weeks so she could sing in the chorus again. Then immediately after the meetings, Georgia Jay and her mother moved to Chicago, expecting an impending engagement.

Another full year would pass, followed by their 1911 Christmas fight and breakup. On the next day, Laura Jay started to bombard Billy Sunday with letters, complaining of her daughter's treatment. Once Georgia Jay realized that she would now have to work for a living, she took a position as a stenographer in January 1912 and—according to her later report—suffered a nervous breakdown on her first day of work. "That day in the office made me ill," she said. "I looked at the desk in the corner, the telephone, and the waste basket and said: 'This is your future.'"[61] Her brief foray into office work provoked a spasm; she had to be carried home. Weary of the drama, and wary of Jay's meddling mother, Rodeheaver fired off a cold response: "Better to suffer a little now than to suffer a whole life long."[62]

But Rodeheaver did not yet have the last word. At the end of the Fargo, North Dakota, revivals in May 1912, Rodeheaver returned to Chicago for a few days, long enough to be served with a heart balm suit, which would consume his spare time for more than two years. Now an obscure legal footnote, heart balm suits were at the peak of their popularity in the 1910s. The "breach of promise" idea was intended as legal protection for a woman's presumed loss of social standing. If a planned wedding did not occur, the law presumed that a woman might never get a second opportunity for marriage (or more accurately, a *lucrative* marriage). In practice, the suits were waged against the rich and famous, creating ready-made fodder for news reporters. Savvy lawyers could generate enough publicity to force a fast settlement from men who could not afford a public scandal. The idea of

FIGURE 3.5. Georgia Jay, who sued Rodeheaver in 1914. Courtesy of *Sun-Times/Chicago Daily News* Collection, Chicago History Museum.

FIGURE 3.6. Rodeheaver during the Georgia Jay court case. Courtesy of Library of Congress.

heart balm suits eventually fell into disrepute, something like legal blackmail, and Rodeheaver's home state of Indiana would outlaw them entirely in 1935.[63] None of this helped Rodeheaver; right now he had a mess on his hands.

The *Chicago Daily News* and *Chicago Tribune* reported the story on the front page, of course, with headlines about the Chicago girl who wanted $50,000 in compensation from Billy Sunday's star singer. "My lawyers tell me there never has been a case in Chicago in which a girl was more entitled to damages," Jay said.[64] But her case would be difficult to prove. If Rodeheaver had actually proposed in April 1911, where was her ring? What sort of evidence did she have, other than her own wishful thinking?

Georgia Jay's case used the same tactics as most heart balm suits. Put the plaintiff on the stand, ask a lot of embarrassing questions, and make sure the newspaper reporters are there to record the answers. When the case went to trial in June 1914, Jay's lawyers immediately fished for lurid details. "Did you kiss or caress Miss Jay when at Waterloo?" they asked.

"No gentleman ever tells whether he kissed or embraced a girl," Rodeheaver replied, but Jay's lawyers demanded a real answer, which the judge forced.

"Yes," Rodeheaver admitted.

"This was in the first five weeks of your acquaintance?"

"Yes."

"You took these liberties knowing marriage was not feasible for you?"

"Yes, but I thought this might ripen into marriage later. My intentions were honorable."

The resulting news story seemed to write itself—all a reporter needed to do was print the court transcript, and then add a rowdy subhead: "Rodeheaver Admits Caressing Miss Jay with Honorable Intentions."[65]

More than a century later, the incident seems quaint, a humorous reminder of antiquated attitudes. But for the Sunday party, the court action posed a serious threat. By 1915, the revival preachers had survived their share of local scandals, which motivated them to organize the Interdenominational Association of Evangelists. The most famous revivalists—Chapman, Biederwolf, and Sunday—wanted a watchdog agency to purge the movement of disreputable characters. If someone successfully tagged Sunday's songleader with a verified scandal, it would discredit the entire movement. Every time Georgia Jay's lawyers made a public statement, it was quoted by local papers in every town that had ever hosted a Biederwolf or Sunday campaign. By the time the court proceedings were over, more than 100 different newspapers had covered the story. Even the teeniest newspapers in far-away towns like Bryan, Texas, weighed in with pointed editorials: "The cause of Jesus Christ is being put to open shame in these latter days of sensationalism and gospel grafting."[66] The situation was serious enough that W. E. Biederwolf

CHAPTER 3

returned to Chicago to hear the court testimony for himself. Biederwolf would need to make a report at the summer IAE meetings, his friendship with Sunday and Rodeheaver notwithstanding.[67]

But after two years of investigation, after fishing for the most embarrassing material possible, Georgia Jay's lawyers didn't have much on Rodeheaver. Some hugging. Hand-holding. And kissing "in the first five weeks of your acquaintance."

At the close of the four-day trial, Judge Lockwood Honore looked past the tawdry testimony and isolated a key question. Did Rodeheaver propose to Georgia Jay on April 3, 1911? The jury spent the better part of an afternoon in deliberations, then found Rodeheaver guilty. Though Georgia Jay had asked for $50,000, the jury awarded her $20,000, not what she expected but still a headline-grabbing sum. And though she won the suit, Jay managed to sound petulant in her post-trial interviews. The *Chicago Tribune* ran her comments with a cynical headline: "Doesn't Mention Love. Had Looked Forward to Life of Ease as Mrs. Homer Rodeheaver."[68] As public opinion shifted, a new trope emerged, that of a conniving country girl who comes to the city with the naked ambition to marry well and spend money.

Georgia Jay and her mother enjoyed their court victory for a few days until Rodeheaver went off script. Most heart balm suits ended with the plaintiff quietly paying up, if for no other reason than to extinguish the media spotlight. But now it was Rodeheaver's turn to play the part of a wronged suitor. He knew he hadn't proposed to Georgia Jay, he knew her mother was lying, and now he was going to fight with an appeal. His risky approach could backfire, if for no other reason than extending the out-of-control news coverage. But a week later, his lawyers successfully petitioned the judge to consider the appeal. By the time Rodeheaver and Sunday left for their Colorado Springs campaign, the tide had turned against Georgia Jay.

While waiting for the verdict to be set aside, Rodeheaver didn't act particularly anxious about the petition. When supporters asked him for the down-and-dirty details, Rodeheaver put the blame squarely on Laura Jay. "The whole trouble lies with the mother of this girl, who tried to force an engagement between us and she was so sure she would succeed that she had told some of her friends that we were engaged," he wrote to a friend in Kansas. "When she tried to force me definitely to it and failed, she thought she would have to make this play in order to make her statement to her friends seem right."[69]

On July 17, 1914, Rodeheaver received the news he had hoped to hear. Judge Lockwood Honore had thrown out the jury's decision. Georgia Jay lost her chance for $20,000—her lawyers could ask for a private settlement, but her negotiating position had evaporated.

PHILADELPHIA MEETINGS

Though Rodeheaver's six-year relationship with Georgia Jay caused him a great deal of public pain, the years were also marked by unprecedented growth for the Sunday-Rodeheaver revivals, which now stopped in the nation's largest cities. When their remarkable run drew to a close in 1930, Rodeheaver reported the team's consensus opinion: "We all felt that the greatest single meeting was the Philadelphia campaign in 1915."[70] His recollection is interesting, given that the 1915 meetings began and ended with embarrassing scandals.

Scheduled to begin on January 3, 1915, the Philadelphia campaign was upstaged once again by Georgia Jay. Two days earlier, the lawyers forged a private agreement—which someone immediately leaked to the press. Both parties agreed not to disclose the settlement amount, but newspapers reported $10,000, disclosed by someone close to the story. If the newspapers correctly reported the amount, Georgia Jay had just settled for a fifth of her original request. The actual settlement was probably even less. Two years later the flap had died down and the figure was reported as $5,000.[71] Whoever had leaked the figure of $10,000 had reasons for inflating the number, probably someone close to Jay or her mother. Considering the typical 1915 salary of a typist or stenographer (about $600), Georgia Jay could live for quite a while on the $5,000.[72] But her dreams of a carefree life of travel and luxury were over.[73] And so were Rodeheaver's dreams of privacy.

During the Philadelphia meetings, Rodeheaver responded to one more question, the last time he would speak of the matter. Six full years had passed since he met Georgia Jay, during which he had become wealthy and nationally famous. The same newspapers that helped him fill the revival tabernacles had also brought him public shame. "Do a favor to the girl, myself, and Christianity by not mentioning the affair," he begged reporters. "I am through with the women."[74] As it turned out, he was not quite through with the women, but for the rest of his time with Billy Sunday he avoided dating anyone he met at the tabernacle.

Philadelphia was known to be friendly to recurring Protestant revivals, having played host to the Prayer Revival (1858–59), Moody-Sankey campaign (1875–76), the Lemon Hill summer conference (1902–12), the Torrey-Alexander campaign (1906), and the Chapman-Alexander Simultaneous Campaign (1908). These previous meetings created certain expectations for Sunday and Rodeheaver, and also provided an existing network of support. Philadelphia's Protestant mainstream was symbolized by the Main Line railroad leading to Philadelphia's elite northwestern suburbs, threading through various Protestant communities and giving rise to a new term, *mainline denominations*. Then, as now, the term hinted at upper-crust, old-money, socialite implications. The mainline churches would gradually distance themselves from Sunday's brand of revivalism, a fracture that would be hastened by the onset of World War I. But for now, Philadelphia's Protestants enjoyed one final moment of unity, or something close to it.[75]

Rodeheaver inherited a ready-made chorus, the same basic group who sang for the 1906 Torrey-Alexander meetings and then with Rodeheaver at Lemon Hill. When the former singers started recruiting additional voices, Rodeheaver found himself with 5,000 singers and a loft that seated 2,000, leading to another system of singing in shifts. Organizers planned a tabernacle dedication service for December 31, 1914, with a program that felt a lot like the New Year's Eve watch-night service for the Gospel Song Evangelistic Movement in 1908. The choir sang, Rodeheaver led the crowd in familiar hymns, and then he taught them a few of the new gospel songs. Governor-elect Martin Brumbaugh sat on the platform, as did Philadelphia's mayor, Rudolph Blankenburg. A Progressive reformer known as "The Dutch Cleanser," Blankenburg retired from a successful business career to become active in politics. "I shall never forget the Moody-Sankey revival 40 years ago," Blankenburg told the first-night guests. "But it was a mere sideshow compared with this great uprising."[76]

THE DELEGATION SYSTEM

Tabernacle attendance grew by cultivating delegations from shops, factories, lodges, church societies, service clubs, and organizations of various kinds, which Rodeheaver called "a most valuable asset in the promotion of a Billy Sunday campaign."[77] During morning and noontime events throughout the city, Sunday's associates would make personal appearances, speak briefly, and conclude with an invitation to attend a tabernacle meeting as a group. Sunday's associates also promised each delegation a section of reserved seats in the tabernacle, plus Rodeheaver's public recognition during the service. The delegation system took on a life of its own and came to include formal processions into the tabernacle, performances by company bands, special songs sung by each group, and cheers from college groups. "The purpose of this was to give each individual in the delegation an opportunity to participate, even in a small way, in the service. You gain their interest when you give them a part of it," Rodeheaver said.[78]

Billy Sunday's publicity machine became a rising tide that floats all boats. In addition to Rodeheaver acknowledging delegations at the start of the tabernacle service, B. D. Ackley typed up a nightly press release that listed each delegation for local reporters—leading to publicity for everyone in the morning papers. For large or influential delegations, Rodeheaver promised to introduce important leaders by name from the platform, asking them to stand for recognition. The leaders would inevitably present gifts in return—fine china, engraved silver, or products from their factory (a lifetime supply of Stetson hats, Hanes underwear, wool blankets). Sunday collected stacks of baseball mitts; Rodeheaver received more trombones than he could ever play.

Sunday and Rodeheaver welcomed all groups, a policy that extended to fraternal orders, including service organizations (Rotary International, Knights of Columbus, Kiwanis, Lions), agricultural clubs (4H, Grange), and the so-called secret societies (various groups of Freemasons, Odd Fellows, Elks). Lampooned today as societies of funny hats and secret handshakes, these fraternal groups played a large and sometimes forgotten part of American life in the early 1900s.[79] During the heyday of the tabernacle delegation system, virtually all of the meetings featured at least one fraternal delegation, with Rodeheaver often inviting them to stand and sing their group's song. Rodeheaver joined as many fraternal orders as he could, including the Rotary International, Knights of Pythias, Masons, and Shriners. Rodeheaver's masonic affiliations were not a secret—he spoke of his membership from the tabernacle platform, and newspapers regularly covered his attendance at masonic events.[80] Billy Sunday, on the other hand, welcomed fraternal orders to his tabernacle meetings but never joined any himself.[81] Prior to World War I, evangelicals had mixed opinions about fraternal membership, which eventually turned to consensus opposition. In the meantime, as awkward as it seemed, the system worked. At the close of the Philadelphia meetings, Rodeheaver said there were still enough unfilled reservations from various delegations that they could have continued another three months.[82]

In a few years, the system also developed problems. Sunday and Rodeheaver accepted all requests—they were never known to have said "No" to a proposed delegation visit, whether saints or sinners. Critics asked if this posed a conflict of interest, for instance, when a contingent of saloon owners came to hear the famous "Booze Sermon."[83] And if the saloon owners should put a wad of cash in the nightly collection, shouldn't Sunday give back the ill-gotten gain? Billy Sunday's stock answer—perhaps apocryphal—was "The devil has had that money long enough." Their policy of accepting all comers and asking no questions would be challenged in just a few years, when white-robed and hooded Klan members visited their meetings and expected the usual unctuous welcome.

For now, the nightly tabernacle attendance soared on the success of the delegation system, which was sustained in turn by the local organizing committee and Sunday's growing team of salaried deputies.[84] He aggressively recruited the best assistants, favoring those with experience on other revival teams and often graduates of Moody Bible Institute. The nine-month revival season demanded physical health and unusual stamina. Sunday hired people who could work long days without much rest. A typical day during the Philadelphia revivals might start with Helen Sunday addressing a local church meeting, Mr. and Mrs. F. R. Stover meeting workers at a shoe factory, Rose Federolff and Jean Lamont leading a girls' Bible study at a local high school, Rodeheaver leading a similar study for boys, and Virginia Asher and Frances Miller attending a YMCA committee meeting.[85] After lunch Grace Saxe could fill the tabernacle with her daily Bible class, which would clear out in time for Rodeheaver to start Sunday's afternoon service. No matter what the event, they all ended the same way, with Sunday's paid assistants inviting everyone to attend a tabernacle service. Bring your whole group—dress in your uniforms—carry the company banner—sing us your theme song. We'll make a special announcement from the platform and put a notice in the papers.

The system worked. On the first day of meetings, Sunday and Rodeheaver filled the 20,000-seat tabernacle three times—morning, afternoon, and evening. By the end, after 122 meetings, 2.3 million people had attended a tabernacle service, and another million attended daytime meetings all over the city. Even the harshest critics had to acknowledge Sunday's whirlwind effect, and Rodeheaver's key contribution of communal singing. Looking back years later, a news reporter would call it "A Tornado with Music at Its Core."[86] Considering the results, one begins to understand why Sunday and Rodeheaver believed the Philadelphia campaign was their greatest ever. Self-inflicted wounds, however, would continue after the final attendance was announced.

B. D. ACKLEY SCANDAL

At the close of the 1914–15 season, Bentley D. Ackley resigned from the Sunday team after making scandalous charges to the Philadelphia newspapers. Ackley complained about his pay ($75 a week) and complained about George Sunday, Billy's 23-year-old son and business manager. Ackley also grumbled about selling his gospel songs for only $10 each, outright, while Rodeheaver profited immensely from hymnal royalties. "Rody promised me a share of the proceeds, but I never got a penny," Ackley said. "He gave me a few presents. That was all."[87] The kicker came when Ackley accused Sunday of plagiarizing sermons from other revivalists.[88] "I'm not attacking anybody, however. It's only the system I have in mind," Ackley said, hinting that his real target was the entire revival industry.[89]

If Ackley missed out on hymnal profits, the reason seemed straightforward. The Rodeheaver-Ackley Music Company began in 1910 as a 50/50 partnership with Ackley, where Rodeheaver contributed the capital investment (Ackley had no cash), and where Ackley agreed to write and edit songs for the partnership. After impatiently waiting for the profits to roll in, Ackley sold his half-ownership stake back to Rodeheaver and netted a short-term cash gain.[90] Yumbert Rodeheaver became office manager and Ackley's name dropped off the letterhead. When the reorganized company turned a profit (according to his Philadelphia critics,

FIGURE 3.7. Rodeheaver with pianist B. D. Ackley, about 1913. Courtesy of Rodeheaver Collection, Grace College, Winona Lake.

exorbitant profits) Ackley expressed regret. Then Rodeheaver signed a contract with Charles Gabriel, a marquee name that brought with it a substantial catalog of well-known gospel song copyrights. Perhaps Ackley felt pushed to the side. Or perhaps he suspected Rodeheaver would pay Gabriel more per song (which was true, though Gabriel's contract hid this fact with nondisclosure clauses).

Newspapers gave the incident nationwide coverage, including the vigorous denials of Sunday and Rodeheaver.[91] The situation took a turn when Ackley issued a full retraction on June 22, 1915. "I have never had any disagreement with Mr. Sunday or dissatisfaction with him, growing out of money matters: never offered nor suggested any agreement with reference to my musical publications," Ackley said, and further clarified that he was no longer accusing Sunday of plagiarism. Ackley confessed that "in unguarded and almost unconscious weakness and under very peculiar circumstances I may have said things which have been distorted with statements for which I disclaim responsibility."[92] Many read Ackley's retraction as thinly veiled code words.

CHAPTER 3

William McLoughlin floated a gossipy explanation in his acclaimed Sunday biography, attributing the incident to Ackley's "depression resulting from chronic alcoholism."[93] Many years later, Bob Jones Jr. offered a different reason, that Ackley had an unhappy marriage.[94] The full story will probably never be known, one more case of journalists recording the scandal but giving scant coverage to its resolution. The truth? A New Jersey bar owner confessed to fabricating the entire story. A supposed friend of Ackley's, William H. Fenley, "boasted of his cleverness in picking out a weak member of the party, getting him under his personal influence and finally taking advantage of his weakness to print allegations that something was wrong with the Sunday organization."[95]

Fenley, the vice president of the New Jersey Liquor Dealers Association, kept a typewriter in the back room of his bar, where he manufactured press releases and mischief. In feeding the Ackley story to willing reporters, Fenley hid his role as a liquor-industry lobbyist and lied about having a long-standing friendship with Ackley (they only met once, when Fenley cold-called at the Sunday office in Philadelphia). Once Fenley wormed his way inside, and once the story had done its damage, he bragged openly about his deception.

"I worked the same thing on the suffragists here," Fenley said, adding insult to injury by revealing a previous stunt he pulled with the *Camden Post-Telegram*.[96] Given the level of Fenley's duplicity, it is hard to know if his story contained any truth at all. Even the best papers like the *New York Times* had taken the bait, tolerating loose attributions from "friends of Ackley," and bolstering their lack of reporting with weasel words like "it has been learned," "it is said," and even "it is rumored." No Pulitzers for this one.

While researching this book we raised this incident with Bruce Howe, a coworker and close friend of Ackley and Rodeheaver. Howe gave a taciturn response, calling the Philadelphia incident "a private matter" between the two men. According to Howe, Ackley remained on warm personal terms with Billy Sunday but never again worked on his team. Whatever happened in 1915, Howe pointed out that Ackley moved to Winona Lake, purchased a house near Rodeheaver's, and remained his primary accompanist for summer concerts and recordings.[97] Rodeheaver's will left Ackley a generous sum, and Ackley continued working as a Rodeheaver Co. editor until his 1958 death.

PHILADELPHIA CRITICS

Criticism came to Rodeheaver and Sunday in many ways: sometimes mild satire, sometimes overt censure. A New York publisher whipped up sheet music for "When Billy Sunday Comes to Town," a frothy and forgettable Tin Pan Alley song that lampooned Sunday.[98] Vendors sold the sheet music on the sidewalks leading to the tabernacle (Rodeheaver refused to sell it in the official tabernacle book stall). No one would argue this was high art—just a souvenir that took advantage of Sunday's fame.

A friendly critic offered a mild pastoral rebuke in the *Atlantic Monthly*. The Rev. Dr. Joseph H. Odell, who backed Sunday in the 1914 Scranton campaign, became increasingly uneasy about the mechanics of modern revivalism.[99] He found "a mercenary side" to the gospel hymnal business, mentioning Rodeheaver by name. Odell worried about commercialism and singled out the rapid increase in Sunday's personal offerings. "The commercial aspects and activities of their campaigns are bringing, not only their office, but the whole cause of religion, into disrepute," Odell said.[100] But he gave Sunday high marks for preaching a pure gospel, "the grace and power of Jesus Christ getting into the heart and will of men and producing results in character and conduct."[101] Odell voiced what many clergy were thinking: Sunday and Rodeheaver deserved their continued support, but they also needed a mid-course correction.

Part of the problem stemmed from Sunday's financial model. During his early years, the local pastors devoted a single "free will" offering to Sunday, who was paying his personal expenses and two-thirds of the team salaries. None of this attracted much attention until the 1911 Toledo campaign, when his one-night offering totaled $15,000 (in current dollars, $350,000).[102] To his credit, Sunday had introduced financial transparency to the revivalists, who rarely disclosed financial information about their ministries. Sunday also advocated grassroots funding appeals, rather than relying on the support of wealthy patrons. But everything was bigger now. When the Philadelphia officials announced an offering of $51,136.85 (equivalent to $1.2 million today), Sunday could no longer escape public scrutiny. Sunday's offerings for the 1914–15 revival season totaled $109,136 ($2.6 million today).[103] Even after subtracting his growing expenses (his team had doubled in size), Sunday was wealthy, no question. And Rodeheaver? His music company remained a private family venture; he saw no reason to emulate Sunday's financial transparency. Sales were up, way up, but the actual figures remained a mystery. Some Philadelphia papers estimated hymnal sales at $5,000; others reported $30,000 for the ten-week campaign. No one had a clear idea, so Odell's questions seemed appropriate.

More pointed criticism came from writers, artists, and poets who aggressively denounced Sunday's revival methods and his ties to big business. The literati framed their concerns as social criticism, but their evident anger came from a much deeper resentment. One might say righteous indignation, except in this case their indignation was avowedly unrighteous. When organizers announced plans for the Philadelphia meetings, New York's *Metropolitan* magazine commissioned John Reed to write a behind-the-scenes exposé. His initial interview request stalled when it reached Helen Sunday, who had a knack for recognizing trouble. Reed described himself as an atheist, socialist, and free love advocate—not a friendly journalist for Billy Sunday, but too important to be ignored.

CHAPTER 3

Reed's article justified all of Helen Sunday's fears and became the mother of all future criticism.[104] Reed accused Sunday and Rodeheaver of brokering populist support from the working-class proletariat while simultaneously cultivating help from Reed's archenemy, the bourgeoisie business leaders. Politics aside, Reed also demonstrated a masterly eye for narrative moments and a knack for quick character sketches. Negative character sketches, mostly. Rodeheaver became "a short, stocky man with a deep, sanctimonious voice, suspicious eyes, and the kind of clammy hand that won't let yours go." Helen Sunday and the rest of the team fared no better.

Reed attacked Sunday's waffling position on Jim Crow segregation policies, and oddly accused him of using "the methods of a negro camp meeting exhorter."

FIGURE 3.8. "The Sawdust Trail," illustration by George Bellows for a 1915 magazine article.

Rodeheaver's performance of "Brighten the Corner" fell under the same critique: "one of those good old revival hymns with an almost negro swing to it." In context, the reader can't quite tell if Reed's comments on the Black experience are supposed to be good or bad. Coded insults?

Reed's article was accompanied by two pen-and-ink illustrations from George Bellows, an artist famous for his urban realism and radical politics. Bellows depicted Billy Sunday on the edge of the platform, reaching out to shake the hands with trail hitters who were slobbering and fainting in the aisles. Helen Sunday hovers behind her husband, hand on a bentwood chair, looking like a stern gatekeeper (her punishment for obstructing Reed and Bellows when they asked for an interview). Standing to the side with arms outstretched, Rodeheaver resembles a choir director, but Bellows deliberately poses him as a well-dressed crucifix.

Toward the end of the Philadelphia revival, Carl Sandburg published his poem "To Billy Sunday" in two radical literary magazines.[105] Perhaps Sandburg was participating in some sort of coordinated leftist attack—the Reed article, the Bellows illustrations, and the Sandburg poem—three friends plotting a takedown of Sunday and Rodeheaver. Too convenient to be a coincidence? At any rate, Sandburg pulled no punches in his pulpit-pounding poem, pointedly turning Sunday's fire-and-brimstone delivery against him:

> *You came along—tearing your shirt—yelling about Jesus.*
> *I want to know what the hell you know about Jesus?*

Having enjoyed enormously positive free publicity during their early years, Sunday and Rodeheaver would never again get a free pass. Their actions were scrutinized and their failures magnified. Their harshest critics played hardball, and at times went to unethical lengths to discredit the Sunday party. Reed squandered his own journalistic credibility, claiming that "the papers" reported Sunday's personal offering as $100,000.[106] But the actual report was $51,136.85, a fantastic amount, but only half of what Reed claimed. He further accused Rodeheaver of selling hymnals "a thousand a day at $1 apiece."[107] The truth was less spectacular. Rodeheaver sold *Great Revival Hymns No. 2* at 35 cents each for deluxe hardcover and 20 cents for paperback. Reed's casual regard for facts never rises above muckraking; the overall effect of his article becomes more important than the veracity of its details.

In the ensuing years, people remembered Reed's allegations of fraud and profiteering. Few remembered his main point, the root of his defiant tone. He and his coterie of friends positioned themselves as leftists, but also as atheists who had no interest in Sunday's message of spiritual deliverance. They attributed Sunday and Rodeheaver's popularity to business and political connections and attributed their financial success to graft and corruption. Reed and Bellows did not explore the possibility that Rodeheaver and Sunday actually believed the gospel they preached, nor did they acknowledge how American popular religion, however crude, was also transformative for its adherents. In his magazine article, Reed preached a message of assurance for those who did not believe. He concluded his article by saying "We left yet unconverted," which in retrospect should be seen as his essential point.[108] Sunday and Rodeheaver's younger critics did not yet have a name, but soon would call themselves a Lost Generation.

THE VAUDEVILLE REVIVALIST

Immediately after the Philadelphia revivals, the Sunday team ran into a new round of criticism, this time from the Unitarians. They plotted a series of competing revivals at local churches in Paterson, New Jersey, but news reporters pounced on "Unitarian revivals" as a funny oxymoron and the plan fizzled.[109] The Unitarians plotted another stunt for the 1916 Boston meetings, where they tagged Billy Sunday as "this vaudeville revivalist." As was typical, their critique tried to piggyback on Sunday's publicity in order to hawk their competing theological ideas. Their scheme collapsed again, but Sunday was stuck with the "vaudeville revivalist" nickname. In truth, Sunday's warm-up act deserved much of the blame. In the eyes of a critic, Rodeheaver's platform persona came straight from vaudeville, as did his variety show of quickly moving entertainments.

For someone searching for connections between vaudeville and tabernacle revivalism, parallels abound. As one example, vaudeville managers of 1915 consulted a how-to manual filled with rules that seemed suspiciously close to tabernacle revivalism:

1. Must have a "corker" of an act, a big name (like Billy Sunday);
2. Aim for variety—no two acts alike (Rodeheaver's vocal solos, trombone solos, magic tricks, recitations);
3. Must not place two "single" acts next to each other (Rodeheaver's mix of solos, duets, quartets, choirs);
4. Never place two "quiet" acts together (Rodeheaver skipped these altogether); and
5. Use a good man-and-woman singing act to "settle the audience and prepare it for the show" (Rodeheaver and Asher's vocal duets).[110]

Having mastered the format, Rodeheaver's tabernacle programs competed directly with local theaters, which struggled to stay open when a revival came to town. As early as 1905, when Biederwolf and Rodeheaver visited New Brunswick, New Jersey, the local vaudeville group complained about losing its audience and defaulting on their theater rental—but not because the new converts had forsaken theater attendance. No, the vaudeville group went bankrupt because Rodeheaver was more entertaining.[111] And free.

If Rodeheaver emulated vaudeville, a similar observation could be made of the theaters, which were strongly influenced by the revivalists. Once known for tawdry, adults-only fare, the vaudeville houses had clearly shifted to cleaner material, with some disgruntled critics calling it "the Sunday School circuit."[112] Theater managers posted lists of banned words ("Liar, Slob, Son-of-A-Gun, Devil, Sucker, Damn, and all other words unfit for the ears of ladies and children"). One observer claimed that vaudeville theaters had cleaned up to the point where "godliness has proved so profitable" for "the wholesome middle classes."[113]

Given all of the convenient parallels, did Sunday and Rodeheaver deliberately cultivate a Protestant vaudeville atmosphere to build crowds at their meetings? Some historians played up the connection, such as Bernard Weisberger's 1958 summary: "Revivalism had been born in the marriage of Calvinism and the American frontier, introduced to the city by Finney, and nourished to gigantic growth by Moody. Now it was about to put on the trappings of vaudeville."[114] Such theories seem plausible, in a surface sort of way, though other reasons may be cited for the apparent similarities. For instance, Rodeheaver's formula of fast-moving acts followed the same model D. L. Moody used in the 1870s, which predated vaudeville. If anything, a critic could claim the vaudeville rules drew on patterns that had already been worked out by the revivalists. The same could be said for Sunday's unique preaching style. His critics claimed he preached like a vaudeville performer, but they struggled to actually name the theatrical performers Sunday supposedly copied. After George M. Cohan wrote *Hit-the-Trail Holliday* as a Billy Sunday parody, the opposite seemed more likely—vaudeville was borrowing from the revivalists. And the real Billy Sunday got better reviews, according to the *New York Tribune*: "All in all, we believe that Sunday has more of the dramatic instinct than Cohan."[115]

END OF THE ROAD

Nonstop travel took its toll. Rodeheaver's curly brown hair began to recede, and with it, his status as a revival heartthrob. In fact, after living out of a suitcase and eating restaurant food for a full decade, Rodeheaver gained quite a bit of weight. A *New York Times* reporter noticed the obvious and called him "a fat, dark man in frock coat and white vest."[116] But Rodeheaver never lost his essential magnetism. Even the *Times* acknowledged how he won over 20,000 cynical New Yorkers before Sunday got up to preach. After Rodeheaver's perfect set-up, the crowd cheered Billy Sunday "from the first moment when it saw his head over the platform as he came in with his wife; it was with him in advance, and it handed over its heart to him from the first moment when he appeared beside the pulpit."[117] Sunday and Rodeheaver conquered New York as American revivalism reached its peak. There was nowhere to go but down.

Urban revivalism and vaudeville followed the same arc of popularity, rising in the 1880s, falling into steep decline after World War I, and disappearing entirely in the early 1930s. The simultaneous deaths of vaudeville and revivalism can be traced to the same economic and cultural forces. A new generation emerged from WWI with different expectations for entertainment. When movie tickets became cheap enough for the average wage earner, the days of live vaudeville were numbered. Soon after, when radio sets became affordable and when radio stations began broadcasts of a vast array of free content, vaudeville died—and with it, revivalism.

For the performers and preachers caught in transition, the future offered plenty of opportunity, but only for those who could navigate the era of technological change. As revival audiences dwindled, Rodeheaver spent less of his time with Sunday, sometimes planning other trips and missing several months of the revival season. Rodeheaver's first absence came during his trip to France at the close of WWI. Then he agreed to a world tour with Biederwolf and missed Sunday's entire 1923–24 season. The absences only confirmed what had become obvious: Having been an equal contributor to Sunday's fame during the glory years, Rodeheaver was now propping up his boss's dwindling popularity.

When Sunday was forced to use a substitute songleader in Rodeheaver's absence, attendance immediately dropped off. As Sunday arrived in Niagara Falls for his 1923 campaign, Rodeheaver was onboard the *Tenyo Maru* and steaming toward Japan. "I hope your organization will work together so perfectly and efficiently that you will find it even better without me," Rodeheaver wrote to Sunday, offering encouragement for a successful revival.[118] But on opening night, Sunday had found himself preaching to a half-empty tabernacle.[119] Rodeheaver's absence was keenly felt, and to a large extent Sunday would never recover.

Rodeheaver seemed aware of the societal changes that led to revivalism's decline and was perhaps more willing than Sunday to accept the different paradigm. He viewed Sunday as increasingly aloof and unwilling to change—and had been telling him so in a series of tactful letters.[120] The existence of this formal correspondence bears witness to their changed relationship. During the height of the revival era, they had worked and ministered in close quarters—formal letters were unnecessary. But now, though their Winona Lake houses were still a five-minute walk from each other, they were rarely home at the same time. Sunday seemed increasingly unavailable to his coworkers, often shielded by Helen—a gatekeeper who now shut out his own staff.

Rodeheaver felt a change in 1925, having noted Sunday's "extreme nervousness" during the dwindling tabernacle meetings. "Mr. Sunday has shown a spirit of dissatisfaction and irritation on the platform that has made it very hard for me," Rodeheaver told Helen Sunday. In a 1927 letter, he outlined his concerns: Sunday's irritability was alienating local pastors, his essential support base. Sunday harangued the smaller crowds during the offering, unfairly expecting them to give as generously as the large crowds gave, back in the day. He was preaching for an hour and a half—twice as long as he used to—but his sermons were less focused. All of these paled in comparison to Rodeheaver's theological concern. Observing that Sunday's sermons now ended with a generic call to become a better person, Rodeheaver complained that he no longer heard a clear invitation to "accept Jesus Christ as personal Savior." Rodeheaver suggested that Sunday "make his invitation clear and plain," framed as "a definite, positive proposition to forsake their sins and confess Christ."[121]

Rodeheaver temporarily abandoned his usual diplomacy and drove to the heart of the matter. His words clearly stung—so much so that Helen Sunday refused to show the letter to Billy. But taken in context, Rodeheaver sounds like a protective son who wants to stave off more serious complaints coming from outside the family. A few months earlier, Upton Sinclair had released *Elmer Gantry*, a thinly disguised lampoon of Billy Sunday and Aimee Semple McPherson. The novel ignited a new wave of revival criticism from Lost Generation literary figures who sensed a weakness to exploit.

The 1927–28 season wobbled to a start with Sunday scheduled in small towns like Lawrenceburg, Indiana, and West Frankfort, Illinois. If all went well, Sunday would also visit Detroit and St. Louis, but he would do so with Homer Hammontree as songleader. Writing from his own meetings in Asheville, North Carolina, Rodeheaver adopted a conciliatory tone and called his years with Sunday "the very best years of my life."[122] He offered to resign so Sunday could make his relationship with Hammontree more permanent. He also restated his previous suggestions for improvement. "Whether you believe it or not, this letter has been written after careful consideration," Rodeheaver concluded, "and with a great deal of love in my heart for you and your work and the greatest possible sympathy for the troubles you have been having."[123]

Though Rodeheaver voiced his exasperation at several points, he never resigned from his position with Sunday—no formal breakup. Instead, their lives just drifted apart. Sunday's invitations came from smaller towns, often hosted by a local church rather than a citywide committee. As a result, Sunday cut his team to three assistants, all of whom did double duty to cover the needed tasks. Rodeheaver found himself in an opposite place, easily filling his schedule with personal appearances where he charged a standard fee of $250 per night (more than Sunday paid him for a full week). Like anyone else who ever traveled with Sunday, Rodeheaver continued to call him "boss," but now only worked with him a few weeks a year. The sawdust trail ended for Rodeheaver in 1930, after a final campaign with Sunday in Mt. Holly, New Jersey. The era of citywide tabernacle revivals was over, but Rodeheaver's gospel songs reached new heights by expanding into new formats: commercial recordings, radio, and film.[124]

4

COMMERCIAL GOSPEL MUSIC
"NO MATTER WHAT YOUR RELIGION, YOU WILL WANT THESE GRAND OLD HYMNS"

For anyone who yearns for the good old days when life was simple, the gospel music industry provides a wonderful lesson. In 1894, Elisha Hoffman wanted to license the hymn "Bring Them In," so he fired off a quick request to composer William Ogden: "Dear Ogden, may I use 'Bring Them In' in *Favorite Songs*? Cordially, Hoffman." The reply came back from Toledo, Ohio, three days later, even shorter: "Yes, my dear friend. Surely you can!"[1]

Ogden didn't even bother with a new piece of paper—he just scrawled his answer on the bottom of Hoffman's original letter and dropped it back in the mail. No money changed hands or was even discussed; the entire agreement was forged in twenty words. Ogden agreed to the request because he had his own hymnal projects, and soon would want to barter some of Hoffman's song copyrights, a straight-up trade. And Ogden knew what Hoffman's answer would be: "Surely you can!"

Just fifteen years later, when Homer Rodeheaver and B. D. Ackley compiled their company's first hymnal, they discovered how times had changed. Ackley wrote to Philip P. Bilhorn and asked for permission to use three of his songs. In return, Ackley offered the use of four of his own songs, a fairly standard trade. Bilhorn replied with an insincere counteroffer, suggesting that Rodeheaver could use the Bilhorn copyrights only if he also hired Bilhorn as the book's publisher and manufacturer.[2]

In other words—no deal. Rodeheaver had already contracted with E. O. Excell for the book's manufacture, which Bilhorn well knew. His only reason for

CHAPTER 4

FIGURE 4.1. Souvenir stand at Billy Sunday's tabernacle, featuring Rodeheaver's hymnals and sheet music. Courtesy of Rodeheaver Collection, Grace College, Winona Lake.

responding to Rodeheaver was to school the young publishers on the realities of the Chicago hymnal business. Copyrights were the new coin of the realm. Wealth and power would be measured in the number and quality of copyrights that a publisher owned. By controlling access to a large song catalog, the publishers could also control the manufacturing of hymnal plates, a profitable business in its own right.

In retrospect, Bilhorn's response was more tactful than the young upstarts probably deserved. Yes, Bilhorn knew exactly who Homer Rodeheaver was, because the young songleader had just replaced Fred G. Fischer—Bilhorn's nephew—on the Billy Sunday team. As a result, Bilhorn lost his lucrative contract to provide hymnals for the Sunday campaigns. And now Rodeheaver and Ackley came with their futile errand, asking for help on their competing project. Inadvertently or not, Rodeheaver was shaking up the Chicago hymnal trade.

In so doing, he moved gospel songs from the tabernacle into the public sphere, a transition that offered its own benefits and consequences. As gospel music developed into a commercial idiom, it became more than notes on paper—it became a remarkable array of related products, produced by a network of companies located in two Chicago business districts, Piano Row and Printer's Row. Such

FIGURE 4.2. Dearborn Ave. in Chicago, as seen from Rodeheaver's offices in the Monon Building, 1914–21. Courtesy of Rodeheaver Collection, Grace College, Winona Lake.

was the prediction of a trade magazine in 1918, having just sent a reporter to Billy Sunday's Chicago revival meetings: "Such ditties as 'Brighten the Corner Where You Are,' 'Throw Out the Lifeline,' and 'Rescue the Perishing' may not be great music or great lyrics, but it is good home stuff and it will be sung and listened to by many thousands," the magazine said. "Sellers of pianos and talking machines may find that the sawdust trail leads directly to good business for them."[3]

The sawdust trail built Rodeheaver's music company and in turn, a Chicago industry. Several factors contributed to its rapid rise, starting with a notable change to U.S. copyright law.

COPYRIGHT LAW

Though remembered as a horrible disaster, the 1871 Chicago Fire also ignited a unique civic reboot, a chance to rebuild the central business district from scratch. And it gave a new start to Chicago's hymnal printing industry. The fire put venerable firms like Root & Cady out of business, destroying their entire inventory of sheet music. The fire also threw copyright enforcement into a tizzy. Everything filed at the Chicago federal office, and any copyright document in possession of the owners—all destroyed. Perhaps it was just as well. The law itself needed a reboot.

On March 4, 1909, Homer Rodeheaver was just starting revival meetings in Pittsburg, Kansas. His brother Yumbert was still living in Jellico and operating a music store. If they had been following the news, they heard that Theodore Roosevelt finally signed a new copyright act, ending four years of congressional wrangling. But if Homer and Yumbert weren't paying attention, no one would blame them. Copyright law rarely made the news, though it would have an enormous impact on the gospel music industry.[4]

First, the 1909 law recognized the composer's rights in public performance. Songwriters were due a performance royalty even if they had sold their print rights to a music publisher. During the congressional debate, two competing interests had clashed: the individual composers (who wanted their performance rights to be recognized) and the restaurants and theaters (who did not want to pay for it). Once the new law clarified the performance rights, songwriters applied it to the rapidly growing segment of live radio. For musicians like Rodeheaver, who moved gospel songs out of the church and into the public sphere, the new law provided a new income stream. Of equal importance, the 1909 law granted an exemption for church and school performances. Without this clause, "public performance" could have forced churches to pay a royalty every time the congregation sang. The new law created a dichotomy, allowing gospel songwriters to have a "ministry" in church while still collecting royalties from the "secular" performances outside the church. Again—though not foreseen in 1909—this became enormously important when gospel songs were performed on the radio, a public performance.

Second, the new law created mechanical licenses for recordings, a two-cent-per-copy royalty to the copyright owner. In 1909 a "mechanical license" was primarily understood as a royalty on piano rolls, played mechanically on a player piano. Some industry prognosticators could also see how this applied to the early phonodiscs and cylinders, formats that soon eclipsed the piano roll craze. The new law provided another income stream for gospel songwriters, who in 1909 could barely conceive of any financial model other than their current system, where they churned out as many songs as possible and then sold them outright to a music publisher. Under the old copyright law, in the days before the songwriters gained performance rights and mechanical rights, a song's primary commercial value came from print rights. Songwriters worked in a system that strongly resembled the dominant business model of the era, factory piecework. Write as many songs as possible, sell as many songs as possible, build income through quantity, not quality.

The gospel hymnwriter Fanny Crosby provides an excellent example; her astounding output of 9,000 gospel song poems seem difficult to comprehend, unless one considers her financial model.[5] She never expected all 9,000 songs to become popular—she didn't even expect them to be published. She wrote song lyrics in bulk and her publisher paid her in bulk. Publishers paid low prices but had to buy a lot of song lyrics that they never used. The publisher made a relatively large investment while searching for a few songs of lasting character. In return, the songwriter received relatively small payments per song, but made up for it in quantity.

As gospel songwriters began to understand their new rights under the 1909 law, they were less interested in selling their songs in bulk. Instead, they wanted quality songs, "hits," that captured public attention on multiple platforms. The 1909 law completely upended the attitudes of songwriters, who learned it was unwise to sell their copyrights outright. Charles Gabriel's editorial contract with Rodeheaver paid $3,600 a year (when the average office worker made $750), but also gave Rodeheaver access to the valuable copyrights that Gabriel had retained in his own name. A typical Rodeheaver hymnal of the era contained about 40 Gabriel songs in a book of 256 selections. For top-tier gospel songwriters, the Gabriel contract was the wave of the future. For now, it was also unusual.

We mention this to explain how Rodeheaver benefited from a sweet spot just after the 1909 law was passed. In market terms, gospel song copyrights were temporarily undervalued. Most songwriters were still selling their songs outright at the old, relatively low, prices. But the new law added *future value* to the songs, making them more valuable than they had been in the print-only paradigm—if, that is, the new songs were well suited for recordings and media. Eventually the market corrected itself and publishers could not snap up song rights as cheaply as Rodeheaver did.

For gospel musicians whose songs were recorded in various formats, the mechanical license granted abundant blessings and one potential curse. Legally speaking, the mechanical licenses were *compulsory*. The song owner had to grant recording rights to anyone who asked, as long as they paid the royalty.[6] This part of the new law had been provoked by hardball tactics from a group of Tin Pan Alley publishers who tried to bundle and sell exclusive rights to their songs—locking out every other publisher in an unfair monopoly. Once the 1909 law took effect, it regulated commerce with a fair-trade clause. By establishing a standard two-cent royalty and by making the license compulsory, the law treated songs like they were manufacturing raw materials, fair game for anyone to record as long as performers paid the fee.

Barely understood at the time, the compulsory mechanical license took away one potential right of song ownership—the right to refuse a contractual relationship. For gospel song musicians who lived a "practice what you preach" moral code, questions cropped up rather quickly. What if a non-Christian artist wished to record a gospel song purely for its economic (not devotional) potential? The law stated that such recordings must be allowed, even if the artist was not devout. The gospel songwriter had no refusal rights—as long as the royalties were paid. Rodeheaver quickly understood the consequences of this point. In chapter 5, we see how he promoted his own Rainbow Records as a label where the musicians still believed what they sang, which Rodeheaver argued was no longer the case with the gospel music produced by the big corporations. The new copyright law seemed to create an ethical quandary for gospel musicians, and the situation became even more complicated.

Could anyone have prevented the Ku Klux Klan from recording "The Old Rugged Cross" multiple times in the early 1920s? Our account of Rodeheaver's life explores this question from several angles. According to the 1909 law, the song owner (Rodeheaver) had no legal recourse to refuse the Klan's license as long as they paid the two-cent royalty per copy. That was the unintended consequence of a *compulsory* mechanical license. And because the law remained untested on the matter of parody songs, the Klan could rewrite gospel song lyrics to suit their own hooded needs.[7] The question of Klan songs remains difficult to understand. In chapter 8, we frame this question as "What did Rodeheaver know and what did he do about it?" For now, we ask a different question. What *could* Rodeheaver have done to prevent the Klan's use of his songs (whether or not he knew ahead of time)? In short—nothing, except to wield the power of the pulpit. If he could not prevent the song's commercial misuse, he could at least condemn the practice as it happened. But he chose silence as the issue unfolded in a very public way. More will be said about this later—the incident remains a complicated one to sort out.

As a third consequence of the 1909 copyright law, gospel songwriters were motivated to produce more songs in a recognizable style. Now that copyright infringement was defined in precise terms, record companies grew more cautious about recording existing songs without permission. Instead, they sought out new songs that sounded like existing hits, a process that affirmed the emerging categories of jazz, blues, and country as having distinct and recognizable sounds that could be repeated.[8] As argued in the next chapter, another style should be added to this list—the emerging category of gospel music.

The broader problem of soundalike music brought embarrassment to Rodeheaver. In 1918, he had pulled out all of the stops to promote his wartime song, "We'll Be Waiting When You Come Back Home."[9] According to Rodeheaver, the idea for the song came to him while visiting an army camp, talking to a soldier boy who worried about losing his girlfriend back home. Rodeheaver took the idea back to Charles Gabriel, who wrote the words to Rodeheaver's tune. At least that's the story Rodeheaver told.[10] But the melody, the basic idea, and many of the lyrics sounded suspiciously close to "Keep the Home Fires Burning," a 1915 hit.[11] So close, in fact, that Rodeheaver found himself slapped with a copyright infringement suit. According to the *Music Trade Review*, Chappell & Co. had successfully sued four different companies in 1918, all with knockoffs of their hit song.[12] Rodeheaver withdrew the song and rewrote it, creating a great deal of embarrassment for a company that was supposed to be operating on a higher moral plane.

CHICAGO: GOSPEL HYMNAL CAPITAL OF THE WORLD

The 1909 copyright law helped the Chicago gospel hymnal publishers by solidifying a legal point. Two sections of the new law established the right of corporations to hold copyrights.[13] Authorship became a legal concept (rather than a person), and could be defined by contractual terms. This concept—a work created for hire—codified a business practice that was already established among the hymnal publishers. In the years after Ira Sankey, the publisher E. O. Excell built the first great catalog of gospel song copyrights by cultivating the best writers and purchasing the best songs.

Though the phrase *vertical integration* was not yet used, Excell developed his for-profit business model with similar ideas. Not only did he own the songs, he paid a Chicago typesetter to make beautiful printing plates, which he then marketed as part of a package. Excell was the first Chicago publisher to make song usage conditional on a manufacturing contract. Those who wanted to use Excell's copyrights had to rent his printing plates and use Excell as the print vendor. Excell offered his package deal to many groups that wanted to produce private-label hymnals, including Rodeheaver's first publishing efforts.

In 1910, Excell gave the Rodeheaver-Ackley Co. a desk and a place to store their inventory in Chicago's Lakeside Building. Almost never in the office, Rodeheaver and Ackley sent out their business correspondence from wherever the Sunday team happened to be in a given week. Excell also made introductions to Charles Gabriel, a freelance songwriter and editor who eventually worked for Rodeheaver fulltime. When people asked, Excell was quick to divulge the reason for his successful company. "It is to Gabriel's songs . . . I owe so much for any success I have gained."[14]

Excell's growth accelerated a transition that was already occurring. The first generation of gospel song publishers had worked directly with D. L. Moody, including Ira Sankey, Excell, Daniel Towner, and—toward the end—Charles Gabriel. Though Sankey had established Biglow & Main's office in New York,

Chicago became the production center. A later study concluded that the gospel hymnal publishers became the most prominent segment of Chicago's publishing industry between 1900 and 1920.[15] Near the end of his life, the Moody-era soloist George C. Stebbins suggested that "Chicago has been the home, at some period of their lives, of more celebrated writers, singers and leaders of evangelistic song than any other city in the world."[16]

Major companies of the era include E. O. Excell (Fine Arts Building, 410 Michigan Ave.), Biglow & Main (Lakeside Building), Meyer & Brother (108 Washington St.), Bible Institute Colportage Co. (250 LaSalle Ave.), S. Brainard's Sons (145 Wabash Ave.), Bilhorn Bros. (136 W. Lake St.), Hope Publishing (5707 Lake St.), Glad Tidings Publishing Co. (Lakeside Building), Evangelical Publishing Co. (Lakeside Building), Charles Reign Scoville (2203 Campbell Park), and Tabernacle Publishing (14 W. Washington St.). A dozen or so smaller companies also contributed to the local economy, usually by using services provided by Excell, Hope, or Bilhorn.[17]

PRINTER'S ROW AND PIANO ROW

The hymnal publishers flourished because Chicago had also become a center for printing services. Many typesetters and printers were located on South Dearborn between W. Congress and W. Polk, including the side streets of S. Federal and S. Plymouth. By the late 1880s, the area was known as Printer's Row or Printing House Row. A similar district was known as Piano Row, a stretch of South Wabash between Adams and Van Buren.[18] For fifty years the street reigned as a retail mecca for every kind of music. More pianos were sold on Chicago's Piano Row than anyplace on earth, according to *Music Trades* magazine.[19] On the northeast corner of Wabash and Jackson, Lyon & Healy billed itself as the largest music store in the world.[20] By 1923, the district sold more sheet music, musical instruments, and phonograph records than anyplace else in the world, according to researchers who studied Chicago's retail scene.[21] Such statements sound a bit fantastic, but they do help establish the business climate for the Rodeheaver Co., which maintained its headquarters in Chicago until its 1941 move to Winona Lake.

One more factor to note: Chicago never had a Church Row or a Religion Row, but it nevertheless became a center for denominational headquarters, church-related independent publishers, Christian magazines, seminaries, and various colleges. The hymnal publishers certainly benefited from proximity to their major customers. Many of the religious organizations eventually moved to the western suburbs or out of state, but for a time, Chicago also reigned as the "Capital of Evangelicalism."[22]

FIGURE 4.3. Joseph, Yumbert, and Homer Rodeheaver, about 1910. Courtesy of Rodeheaver Collection, Grace College, Winona Lake.

RODEHEAVER'S PUBLISHING MISSION

The Rodeheaver Co. described its publishing mission in relatively simple terms. They published new music for congregational singing. The songwriter Charles Gabriel served as the company's chief apologist for new music, believing that "young people of today do not enthuse over the music of fifty years ago."[23]

"Our mission is to get the people to sing!" Gabriel said. "They love music, and will sing if given songs that appeal to them. This we are trying to do. We are not concerned about the critic; as a rule, the song that is most severely criticized is the one the majority of the people like best."[24] Later, as Homer Rodeheaver expanded gospel music's audience through recordings, radio, and film, he offered the same essential "mission" justification.

THE RODEHEAVER MUSIC COMPANY

Though it seemed tragic at the time, the blaze that destroyed Yumbert Rodeheaver's Jellico music store proved to be fortuitous, the final impetus for Yumbert to move north and join Homer's new Chicago publishing venture.[25] The company began with Homer's money and natural gift for promotion, but its growth came through Yumbert's low-key management and business acumen. Yumbert claimed that he had "no training whatever" as a music publisher, and whatever success he enjoyed was because "I simply did the best I could, guided and helped by my friends."[26]

Yumbert's most obvious friend in the publishing business was Charles Gabriel, who had close relationships with both brothers. This became evident in August 1911, when the Rodeheaver Co. moved its offices from the Lakeside Building to the Methodist Book Concern building at 14 W. Washington St. The move made sense—Charles Gabriel had just signed a full-time contract with Rodeheaver, whose Lakeside office was really just Yumbert and a few clerical workers. It was easier for Gabriel to stay put and the Rodeheavers to come to him. His fourth-floor office suite had long served as a hangout for Chicago's gospel song community, where the aging group of Moody-era songwriters held court with the rising generation of younger publishers, Yumbert included.

The Rodeheaver Co. opened a Philadelphia office in 1913, which became the distribution node for his East Coast sales. Two other gospel song publishers were headquartered here. The composer William J. Kirkpatrick owned Praise Publishing Co., still one of the largest producers of Sunday School songbooks. The Hall-Mack company (J. Lincoln Hall and Irvin H. Mack) had grown quickly by purchasing smaller competitors. Most notably, it owned the valuable copyright to "In the Garden."[27] Like their Chicago counterparts, all three of the Philadelphia publishers traded back and forth on copyright usage.

In 1914, the Rodeheaver Co. moved its headquarters to the tenth floor of the Monon Building, 440 S. Dearborn St., which in 1890 had been Chicago's first thirteen-story structure. The Monon Railroad occupied the bottom floors, and the rest of the building was devoted to law offices and publishers.[28] Having signed long-term editing contracts with Rodeheaver, Charles Gabriel agreed to move his office studio to the new location. Now situated on the north end of Printer's Row, Rodeheaver's office was adjacent to the vendors he used for typography and printing. As the company expanded, so did his offices, and soon they moved to the thirteenth floor.

The move came at the same time Rodeheaver was making a significant industry investment. While planning for his next hymnal project, he purchased the music typographer who had been supplying plates to E. O. Excell.[29] Music plate production was enormously expensive, which was the reason why smaller publishers rented plates from E. O. Excell. But by owning his own plates, Rodeheaver could position himself in the same way Excell had—the go-to printer for anyone who wanted to produce a private-label hymnal. Rodeheaver quickly recouped his investment with the release of *Songs for Service* (1915). After using the new hymnal for Billy Sunday's revivals in Boston, Philadelphia, and New York, Rodeheaver had created his own bestseller. He never again paid anyone for plates, and he could advertise full services for anyone who wanted to publish a hymnal.

Songs for Service became notable for another reason: the debut of the company's new logo, which was embossed on the cover of his hymnals and printed on sheet music.[30] The artwork quoted a line from one of Rodeheaver's best-known songs, "If Your Heart Keeps Right," which became a hit after Rodeheaver featured it in his tabernacle meetings and recorded it for all of the major labels. Now the song—and the logo—seemed to sum up his new style of "cheer up" gospel song: "Every cloud will wear a rainbow if your heart keeps right."[31]

Rodeheaver's expansion also drew a target on his back. He released *Gospel Hymns and Songs* in 1917 and immediately caught flak from industry insiders who were ticked off about the new book's title. Not backing down, Rodeheaver took the dispute public, in the form of a full-page ad on the back cover of *Christian Worker's Magazine*: "Some of our competitors are making very strenuous objections to the title of our new song book, *Gospel Hymns and Songs*, claiming that it is an infringement on a book of somewhat similar title that they brought out about 42 years ago."[32] Without naming anyone Rodeheaver managed to tell the whole story, that his new hymnal title was too close to *Gospel Hymns and Sacred Songs* (1875), and that the heirs of Sankey who operated Biglow & Main ("some of our competitors") had complained vociferously.

Rodeheaver turned the flap to his benefit, using the ads to announce a name-the-new-hymnal contest, with the winner receiving 100 copies of the new book. Behind the scenes, Rodeheaver and his Chicago friends knew the truth of the matter. The old guard from New York, the heirs of Sankey who operated Biglow & Main, saw their business evaporating. Their real beef was not with the title; it was with the gospel songs that Rodeheaver used. Rodeheaver realized that the copyrights had expired on many of the original Sankey and P. P. Bliss hymns, so he made new plates and published them royalty-free. Rodeheaver's new book had the best of the older gospel songs, plus the best of his new songs—so why would anyone continue to purchase Sankey's older books?

The whole mess actually turned out well for Rodeheaver. Though Sankey's name garnered much respect, the incident made his family look petty. And when Rodeheaver announced the winning title, *Awakening Songs*, the publication delay allowed him time to incorporate his newly purchased hit, "The Old Rugged Cross," further boosting sales. His fraternal competitors may not have appreciated his rapid ascent, but Rodeheaver was now the go-to source for gospel hymnal publishing. It would be impossible to list all of the hymnals he produced during the era; perhaps one example will show how his system worked.

William M. Runyan worked with the aging Daniel Towner to edit *Songs of the Great Salvation* in 1918. The project turned out to be Towner's last before his death in 1919 and also one of the first for Runyan, who later composed "Great Is Thy Faithfulness." Following the business model of E. O. Excell, Rodeheaver allowed Runyan and Towner to use his existing plates for standard hymns like "All Hail the Power," along with older Sankey-era songs and some newer Gabriel songs. Rodeheaver also made plates for twenty-four of Runyan's new songs, plus printing, binding, and shipping services. As a final benefit, Runyan could use Rodeheaver's address at the Monon building (Runyan lived in Wichita, Kansas, and Towner no longer kept office hours). This project was only one of hundreds produced by Rodeheaver, who rapidly became the jobber of choice for private-label hymnals.

In 1921, Rodeheaver moved his offices to the McClurg Building, 218 S. Wabash Ave., a move that carried with it some symbolism. The Rodeheaver Co. moved from Printer's Row to Piano Row, part of an overall strategy to position the company as a "gospel music" company, not just a gospel hymnal publisher. He needed the extra space to build a recording studio for Rainbow Records, and he hoped for a greater retail presence (though his core business was mail order). His final move came in 1932, when Rodeheaver Co. moved to the Steger Building at the other end of Piano Row (28 E. Jackson Blvd.). His last decade in Chicago was marked by expansion into the church market with choir octavos, vocal ensembles, sheet music, and organ music. Though his product line diversified, his core business remained gospel hymnals, worth a closer look here.

THE TABERNACLE HYMNALS

The Rodeheaver-Ackley Co. started in 1910 with a simple plan to produce hymnals and songbooks for the W. E. Beiderwolf tabernacle meetings. The plans were interrupted when Billy Sunday offered Rodeheaver a position on his revival team. Rodeheaver's hymnal project instantly grew in scope—Sunday was drawing larger crowds and had promised Rodeheaver full ownership of the tabernacle hymnal sales. During the tabernacle years, Rodeheaver released a new hymnal every two or three years.

With every new hymnal release, Rodeheaver's introductory preface seemed to say the same thing: His customers loved the previous book so much that they claimed he could not possibly improve on it. But nevertheless "we have been constantly collecting and trying out new songs," and now the customers agreed that the next book was even better.[33] Marketing blurbs aside, Rodeheaver accurately reported his zeal for finding new and better congregational songs. During the tabernacle years, each successive hymnal featured about 40 percent new content—Rodeheaver had no qualms about cutting his own copyrighted songs if he could purchase ones that performed better. The resulting line of hymnals became an unstoppable juggernaut in evangelical churches. Any church that supported the Billy Sunday tabernacle meetings was also interested in

Rodeheaver's line of gospel hymnals. Many churches began a practice of purchasing two books for their auditoriums, their official denominational hymnal and a gospel hymnal, which sat side-by-side in the hymnal rack. Rodeheaver's song selection emphasized basic doctrinal ideas (the gospel), or as his critics charged, no doctrine at all. Either way, the song appealed to a broad range of Christian denominations. "No matter what your religion, you will want these two grand old hymns," one newspaper review gushed.[34] And it was true—Rodeheaver was creating a line of hymnals and recordings that appealed to Protestants of all stripes.

Rodeheaver supported the main hymnal line with a full line of ancillary products. In addition to three binding options (cloth, limp, and manila), he also produced a Special Tabernacle Edition with photos of the Billy Sunday team. For a time, the hymnals were also released in Canadian Editions, basically the same hymnal as the U.S. version, but replacing "America" with "God Save the King." For about 25 years, starting with *Great Revival Hymns No. 2* (1913) and ending with *Christian Service Songs* (1939), his tabernacle hymnals were published with orchestrations, usually with ten to fifteen instrument parts. Though valued by big-city churches and Sunday Schools, the orchestrated hymnals were expensive to produce. Rodeheaver eventually dropped the idea, though he loved the sound of a band accompanying the congregation.

Rodeheaver's experiments with shape note hymnals met the same fate. Starting with *Awakening Songs* (1917) and lasting until *Triumphant Service Songs* (1934), Rodeheaver went to the expense of producing shape note editions of each major hymnal, one of the few publishers to publish in dual formats.[35] Some of the impetus came when he purchased his own type and equipment, making the process cheaper. Another factor was his Billy Sunday schedule, which increasingly featured southern cities after 1917. Rodeheaver produced shape note editions for as long as they made money, but he was not a true believer. Unlike James D. Vaughan and the southern publishers, Rodeheaver was not on a Lost Cause mission to preserve the shape note system.

GOSPEL PEARLS

Despite a reputation for obstructing denominational requests, the Chicago publishers helped produce *Gospel Pearls* in 1921. The seminal hymnal of the National Baptist Convention U.S.A. included at least 40 songs from the Chicago publishers, songs that Black congregations were already singing.[36] *Gospel Pearls* is well remembered for including older Black composers like Charles A. Tindley, plus gospel songs from younger Black composers like Thomas A. Dorsey, Carrie Booker Person, Lucie E. Campbell, Charles Price Jones, and E. C. Deas. The book also includes several Sankey-era gospel songs and twenty-four copyrights that would be owned by the Rodeheaver Hall-Mack Co.[37] Other northern companies such as Hope, Charles Alexander, and Biglow-Main participated, as did southern companies such as John T. Benson and James D. Vaughan, and A. J. Showalter. The book also became known for its collection of spirituals, ones that were being sung by congregations of the era. When Homer Rodeheaver sang with the Wiseman Sextet for Rainbow Records, they sang some songs straight from *Gospel Pearls*, such as "I Know the Lord." More than any other book of the period, *Gospel Pearls* shows the breadth of what gospel had become: northern, southern, Black, white.

One wishes that more documentation existed for this important project. Some of what we know can be understood only with careful sleuthing. Given Rodeheaver's affinity for Black music, how much did he help with this project? We know that *Gospel Pearls* used many of Rodeheaver's plates, both of his gospel songs and of the standard hymns.[38] Rodeheaver may have printed the hymnals for the National Baptist Convention U.S.A. or at least provided plates for another printer to use. Either way, the book became enormously influential.

OLD RUGGED CROSS

Homer Rodeheaver bought the copyright to "The Old Rugged Cross" from songwriter George Bennard in 1918, but no one remembers exactly what he paid. When interviewed for this book, the former Rodeheaver Company vice president Bruce Howe could not say for sure. "I've heard stories about two dollars and five dollars. It might have been as much as $50," he said.[39] Even if it was, the prices seem low for a song that would sell millions of copies. Some of the details provide a clearer picture of the way the gospel hymn industry worked.

George Bennard had written the first stanza and chorus in 1912, finished it and copyrighted it in 1913, and licensed it to publishers for five years, including Homer Rodeheaver's first hymnal use in 1917.[40] When Bennard's wife was pregnant with their first child, Rodeheaver offered to buy the song, and the Bennards quickly agreed. If Howe is correct about the $50, it would have covered all of the family's medical expenses for the birth. The $50 ($900 in today's dollars) was not much money, but the Bennard family had no complaints about the deal, for two reasons.

First, the 1909 copyright law allowed for a copyright renewal period after the first 28 years. At that point, no matter who owned the song, the songwriter could renew. Though the law called for a relatively short copyright period of 28 years, the renewal clause tended to work as a safety valve if a song became popular. If a publisher under-paid the first time and had a hit, they ended up paying the songwriter considerably more at renewal time. Second, after the gospel hymnal publishers joined ASCAP (discussed below) many of the songwriters joined as well. At the time of George Bennard's death in 1958, he was receiving quarterly

ASCAP checks of $3,000 to $5,000, a comfortable sum (and this amount includes only his performance royalties, not his record royalties). The copyright law of 1909 gave songwriters more ways to sell their music. For the top gospel songs, the performance royalties could make composers comfortable, if not wealthy.

RODEHEAVER COMPANY ACQUISITIONS

The gospel song publishers continued to purchase song copyrights from songwriters, but this avenue eventually dried up when songwriters became skeptical about selling their songs outright. Publishers had a second method—purchasing entire song catalogs as competitors left the business.[41] Most of the time the purchases were motivated by some sort of assessment of the song catalog's value, based on its current annual royalties. But Rodeheaver's first acquisition was also his most unusual. He purchased Philadelphia's Praise Music in 1917, inheriting quite a bit of prestige from owner William J. Kirkpatrick, along with some copyrights. Kirkpatrick's influence began in 1859 with his *Devotional Melodies*, a hymnal that defined the gospel song genre even before Ira Sankey popularized the name.[42] Also a Methodist, Kirkpatrick visited with Rodeheaver every summer during their annual visits to Ocean Grove Camp Meeting in New Jersey. All of these were worthy reasons for Rodeheaver to purchase the company, but as it turns out, not his actual motivation. Rodeheaver still needed a manager for his Philadelphia office and had tried several times to recruit George Sanville from Praise Music. Now Rodeheaver tried a different tactic—he bought the company.[43] With Sanville's industry connections and proximity to the New York market, he proved his worth many times over in the coming years. Rodeheaver's largest acquisition came in 1936 when he purchased the Hall-Mack Co. of Philadelphia. After Hall died in 1930, Mack approached Sanville and Rodeheaver with an offer to sell. They respected Mack and asked him to remain with the merged company until his retirement.

Mack was a good enough friend to speak forthrightly when needed. Joseph Rodeheaver had written Mack soon after the merger, expressing concern that Homer, now nearly 60, needed to slow down. Mack agreed but also said, "I don't know just what you can do about it. He is as he is, and perhaps continued suggestions on your part will bring about the desired results . . . I have already spoken to him concerning the heavy load he is carrying."[44] Their concerns were warranted. Rodeheaver suffered various heart ailments for the rest of his life, never really slowing down, never making any lifestyle adjustments.

The merger created plenty of work. Immediately the Philadelphia office began reprinting some of the Hall-Mack hymnals with the new name, Rodeheaver Hall-Mack Co. And the new company was able to expand its church music offerings with additional solo music, choral music, and Sunday School songbooks from the Hall-Mack catalog. All of this gave Rodeheaver a strong justification for the acquisition, but the actual motivation was much simpler. Rodeheaver wanted the crown jewel of the Hall-Mack Co., the copyright to "In the Garden." One thing had not changed about the Chicago gospel music industry. Publishers would not survive for very long without a steady stream of new copyrights.[45]

FORMATION OF THE CHURCH MUSIC PUBLISHERS ASSOCIATION

In addition to their personal relationships and proximity in Chicago, the gospel hymnal publishers also forged informal agreements on hymnal pricing. While sharing the same typesetters and print vendors, the industry had settled on a standard format, the 6 × 9-inch cloth-bound hymnal of 256 pages. Individual copies sold at 25 cents each, or a bulk discount of $20.00 per 100. Keen competition among the publishers kept retail prices frozen, even though printing costs continued to rise. As early as January 1918 they met together to discuss a possible price increase, a coordinated shift to $25.00 per hundred, with every publisher announcing the increase at the same time.[46] Eighteen months later, as their production costs continued to rise, the same publishers met again, proposing to raise prices to $30.00 per 100.

Yumbert Rodeheaver attended the publisher's meeting in September 1919 and in practical terms held most of the cards. As the largest publisher, he could avoid a price increase the longest and—if he wished—could probably starve out his smallest competitors. Not wanting to make the final decision himself, Yumbert suggested that Francis G. Kingsbury write Homer (busy with a Billy Sunday revival in Davenport, Iowa). The letter, read today, provides a surprising amount of detail about the hymnal business. Kingsbury, the president of Hope Publishing, over-explains the financial situation because "some of us, perhaps, live a little closer than you to present-day problems."[47] The nicely worded barb reminded Rodeheaver that some of the companies were struggling and could not afford a price war. The proposed price increase went forward with Rodeheaver's approval.

Did these agreements constitute illegal price fixing? The publishers did not think so. Kingsbury noted how the hymnal publishers were already victims of this strategy. Paper, vellum, and other materials cost the same from vendor to vendor because "manufacturers have cooperated sufficiently to protect their business interests." Though declaring himself to be "unalterably opposed to monopolies and profiteering," Kingsbury suggested that the gospel publishers adopt "the same fraternal spirit that is now so pronounced in nearly all lines of industry."[48] Read today, his letter smacks of collusion, but his contemporaries in the business world did not see it that way. A few years later at the height of the Depression, fair-trade laws became popular legal strategies for fixing retail prices at a certain level. Such laws protected small independent business from the price-gouging tactics of large corporations. Applied here, Kingsbury was appealing to Rodeheaver's sense of fairness, understanding that he could play hardball if he wished.

The informal pricing agreements confirmed another transition, a power shift from E. O. Excell to Rodeheaver. The patriarch of the hymnal publishers, the man they all called "Uncle Ex" (at least behind his back), was in declining health, no longer enforcing his own price structures on the rest of his peers. When Excell died in 1921, the resulting vacuum created the perfect environment for more cooperation. In many ways, the Chicago hymnal publishers were already functioning as an informal trade organization, so it made sense to hold an organizing meeting in 1925. Ten publishers met at the Greenbrier Hotel in White Sulphur Springs, West Virginia, partly as a vacation and partly to craft bylaws for the Church and Sunday School Music Publishers' Association (CMPA).[49] Participants included the Rodeheaver Co., Hall-Mack Co., Adam Geibel Music Co., Tullar-Meredith Co., E. O. Excell Co., Hope Publishing Co., Tabernacle Publishing Co., Glad Tidings Publishing Co., Lorenz Publishing Co., and R. H. Coleman Co. The attendance list says quite a bit about the gospel publishing world in 1928. All of the companies were privately owned; no denominational publishers were allowed to join, a ban that included Christian colleges.[50] Six of the ten members were based in Chicago (and considering that Hall-Mack and Adam Geibel were soon purchased by Rodeheaver, the Chicago count became 8 of 10). Only one publisher represented the South, the Texas-based R. H. Coleman Co. All of the participants were men. And none of the companies were owned by Blacks or represented Black gospel music.

Early meetings emphasized what was clearly a genuine friendship among the participants. Wives attended and planned their own excursions while the men conducted business. Important business negotiations never got in the way of afternoon golf or the evening's restaurant choice. When it came time for substantive discussion, the early conversations centered around the hottest issue—a standard and equitable way to do business with each other. Members agreed that they would no longer withhold copyright permissions from each other and would develop a royalty structure that applied equally to all members. More to the point, the members agreed to limit the song licenses they granted to nonmembers. Once again, the denominational publishers came up short. In the previous system where the gospel publishers informally traded copyright permissions with each other, the denominations were locked out because they had few gospel song copyrights as trading capital. After the formation of the CMPA, the denominations were effectively blocked by formal group action. This point is worth remembering when reading gospel song denunciations of the era, usually voiced by critics representing the denominational publishers. Behind the scenes, the same denominations were asking the CMPA for permission to include the most popular gospel songs in their hymnals—and were routinely turned down.[51] From time to time, the CMPA approved an exception to the rule for the biggest projects (such as the gospel songs in the 1935 *Methodist Hymnal*).

Though his company was the biggest name in gospel music publishing, Homer Rodeheaver almost never attended the CMPA meetings, leaving such business to his brother Yumbert and George Sanville. Still, if an unresolved problem needed a bit more diplomacy, Homer entered the discussion, such as he did during a 1928 squabble. The Rodeheaver Co. had won a contract to print the 1928 *Cokesbury Hymnal*, which left Hope and Excell as the disappointed losing bidders. They both responded with an old-school threat, the possible withholding of their copyrights from the new book, even though they had promised to forgo such tactics when they formed the CMPA.

Homer Rodeheaver responded with a letter to both companies, reminding them that their action would "spoil the spirit and purposes of the gospel song publisher's organization." Taking a cue from Kingsbury's original letter, Rodeheaver appealed to their common business interests; together they could "counteract the influence of some of our big religious educationists who are trying to promote the hymns and kill our gospel song business."[52] The unstated subtext seems clear; Rodeheaver still held the upper hand. He had agreed to their earlier request about uniform pricing. Now the other gospel music publishers must toe the line on copyright permissions—they could not ask for a concession without expecting to give something in return.

Though it is not often viewed this way, the CMPA broke up the largest publishing monopoly in the religious world—the denominational publishers who controlled materials purchased by local churches. In 1925, the Sunday School Board of the Methodist Episcopal Church South surveyed 2,200 of its churches, asking which hymnal they were using. For a denomination seeking unity, the answer was shocking: 111 different books. Of these, only eleven of the titles had official Methodist sanction. The remaining 100 were from independent gospel hymn publishers, including four popular titles from Rodeheaver. Local churches actively ignored denominational attempts to "approve" certain books.[53]

The long-simmering tension with denominational publishing houses continued until the late 1930s. The previous lines of distinction started to erode when gospel publishers Haldor Lillenas and Tullar-Meredith sold their companies to a denomination, the Nazarene Publishing House. After Robert H. Coleman retired in 1939, he sold his copyrights to Broadman Publishing (owned by the Southern Baptists). And other denominational publishers such as Standard (representing Restoration Movement churches) had significant catalogs of gospel songs. Once the denominations controlled major blocks of gospel songs, they were invited to join the CMPA and share in the standard royalty system—finally achieving a truce.

FIGURE 4.4. Church Music Publishers Association in 1938: (Front) Yumbert Rodeheaver, Haldor Lillenas, Herbert Shorney, George Sanville; (Back) Isaac H. Meredith, Karl Lorenz, Irvin H. Mack, Robert H. Coleman, George Shorney. Courtesy of Hope Publishing Co. archives.

AMERICAN SOCIETY OF COMPOSERS, AUTHORS, AND PUBLISHERS

In 1932, the CMPA asked George Sanville to investigate "the broadcasting problem," a situation that illustrates complicated business angles in an era of rapid technological change. Now that the law recognized the songwriter's performance rights as a separate category from publishing rights, the music industry needed to administer the potential income stream from restaurants and theater royalties. As a result, New York's Tin Pan Alley publishers formed a trade organization in 1914, the American Society of Composers, Authors, and Publishers. By banding together they intended to protect and administer the performance rights of its members. Their timing was impeccable—the rise of music performances on radio gave their organization more clout.

At first, the old-school songwriters had a difficult time understanding how the plan worked. ASCAP collected fees for public musical performances by selling blanket licenses to restaurants and radio stations. Each venue paid ASCAP a quarterly fee for a license that covered all of its performances. Then ASCAP pooled the revenue and distributed it to members based on a points system. Popular songwriters and popular songs received a larger portion of the pie, but every ASCAP member received something.[54]

The venture grew quickly, and once most publishers and songwriters signed on, the ASCAP group controlled a functional monopoly. Songwriters couldn't join unless they were established and sponsored by an ASCAP publisher, giving ASCAP enormous control over who could be considered a songwriter. By the early 1920s it looked like ASCAP was deliberately excluding some elements of the songwriting market: no race music, no hillbilly music, and certainly no gospel.

But Rodeheaver's mission to inject gospel songs into public life had created an unexpected tension. No longer bound by the walls of a church or tabernacle auditorium, the gospel songs were increasingly encountered in public venues, where they mixed with the growing pool of American popular music. The gospel music publishers framed the licensing issues with a straightforward argument. Didn't the copyright law give the same protection to gospel music as it gave to every other style? If a theater orchestra or radio ensemble played "Brighten the Corner," shouldn't it earn royalties like any other song?

When the Church Music Publishers Association asked George Sanville to look into the matter, most of the gospel publishers felt locked out of ASCAP membership. At this point one could inject an editorial comment, that the gospel song publishers had been playing the same sort of exclusionary tactics with the church denominations who wanted to license their gospel songs. Now Rodeheaver and the CMPA were getting a taste of their own medicine. Nevertheless, Sanville's mission was to find a way into ASCAP, either through diplomacy or through brute force. He had previously helped C. Austin Miles gain ASCAP membership in 1925 (so far, the only gospel songwriter to be accepted, perhaps because of the secular songs he composed). In 1931, ASCAP allowed two gospel publishers to join, the Rodeheaver Co. and Lorenz, but no others.[55] Sanville encouraged Hall-Mack to send in an application, but ASCAP ignored it for a full year. After several meetings, the diplomacy route didn't seem to be working.

At the 1933 meeting of the CMPA, Sanville encouraged every member to apply to ASCAP in a coordinated attack, which in turn gave Sanville a stronger negotiating position.[56] If their applications were ignored en masse, he could legitimately threaten to cut off everyone's access to gospel song copyrights (a possibility that ASCAP's radio clients would not tolerate). The tactic worked, and by 1937 five gospel publishers were ASCAP members.[57] Because ASCAP paid royalties to both the publisher and the songwriter, everyone immediately reaped the benefit of Sanville's lobbying. In 1937, the Rodeheaver Co. received $7,339 in ASCAP payments (more than $130,000 in current dollars). And because the CMPA publishers disclosed their ASCAP royalties to each other, they finally had a measurable answer to a question of some interest. Which gospel music publisher was the largest? The answer surprised no one. Of the CMPA members, Lorenz commanded a 16 percent share of ASCAP's gospel song revenue, Hope Publishing a 23 percent share, and the Rodeheaver Co. a 58 percent share.[58] The new ASCAP numbers showed what had been long suspected—of the gospel song publishers, Rodeheaver had built the most valuable song catalog and had successfully brokered it to become a dominant force in the hymnal trade.[59]

Several of Rodeheaver's top songwriters also joined ASCAP, including the Ackley brothers and the surviving family of Charles Gabriel. The additional royalty income proved to be an unexpected windfall, despite the complicated system (which continued to puzzle members). At one point, B. D. Ackley tried to explain this to Ina Duley Ogdon, who wrote the lyrics to "Brighten the Corner" and ten other songs she had sold to Rodeheaver over the years. She could join ASCAP, Ackley suggested, and he even volunteered to sponsor her application. All she had to do was fill out the paperwork that Ackley mailed her, and the royalty checks would soon follow.[60] But like many other aging songwriters who barely understood their publication rights, the idea of performance rights completely befuddled her. In fact, she responded to Ackley with a curt letter of correction. She sold her lyrics outright to Rodeheaver years ago, she still had the bill of sale, and she was not expecting any further compensation. Furthermore, it was unseemly to suggest that anyone owed her more money.

"I'm absolutely certain that you are wrong as far as the use of your songs on the air is concerned," Ackley said in response.[61] Of course he was sure—he was already cashing his own checks from ASCAP. He tried one more time to explain the idea of performance rights, but Ina Duley Ogdon would have nothing of it. Sounded too much like a scam.[62]

Such accounts leave the reader wishing for a bit more. Chicago's gospel hymnal industry is worthy of more study—too much of what we know comes in the form of warm, devotional hymn stories. While this "Miracles Through Song" approach may tell us something about the way gospel songs contributed to American popular religion, it does little to illuminate the actual spirit of the times. As it turned out, gospel songs were big business. Rodeheaver avoided this topic, always describing his business dealings as a mission. As he added to his empire with recordings and radio and film, he always framed the new projects in the same terms: "Our mission is to get the people to sing!" But there is no way to get around the truth of the matter. Homer Rodeheaver, his brother Yumbert, and George Sanville were astute businessmen who engaged in sharp business practices to enlarge their own empire. Perhaps the aggressive tactics were consistent with Rodeheaver's personal mission, if understood in a certain context.

MONEY-MAKING ALTRUISM

Friends knew that certain subjects were off limits with Rodeheaver. Georgia Jay, for one. And later, the death of his half-brother Jack. And money. Homer

Rodeheaver wasn't shy about living the life of a well-to-do bachelor, but he didn't like to talk about his growing wealth or even his ideas about philanthropy. Interestingly, the town of Winona Lake had its own avowed approach to personal wealth, worth exploring here for its possible influence on Rodeheaver.

Soon after Rodeheaver began traveling with William E. Biederwolf in 1905, he met Biederwolf's friend Thomas Kane, the owner of a Chicago furniture manufacturing company. Kane's company specialized in industrial furnishings; his fortune came from building school desks. A Presbyterian, Kane served as president of the Winona Assembly and Summer School Association during its most prosperous years, the early 1900s. Kane and other Chicago business leaders purchased the Winona Lake land, built hotels and other amenities, and then bundled everything into a trust, preventing any one parcel or entity from falling into private hands. Unlike Rodeheaver, Kane talked about money all the time. And he encouraged his wealthy friends to adopt a thoughtful philosophy of wealth management that he called "Money-Making Altruism." He summarized this idea as six foundational financial principles that, in Kane's estimation, "should characterize every Christian layman: 1) make all the money he can; 2) take good care of his credit; 3) take good care of his property; 4) take good care of his family; 5) provide reasonably for rainy financial days; 6) do all the good possible with the remainder of the profits."[63]

During his years as Winona Lake's president, Kane tried to position the conference itself as "a lesson to the world of money-making altruism."[64] He frequently spoke on the topic and published several articles that distilled the basic concepts.[65] For a time, Winona Lake was known for its advocacy of money-making altruism. One shining example was E. O. Excell himself, whose aggressive business tactics certainly fulfilled the first of Kane's ideals. Less known was Excell's quiet philanthropy around Winona Lake, generous gifts that sustained the conference during lean years.

How much of this rubbed off on Rodeheaver? Hard to say, since he still wasn't talking about the money. But as late as 1944, a news reporter looked at Rodeheaver's life and concluded "it is all in accord with the longtime Winona tradition, for its motto is Money Making Altruism."[66] The article continued by quoting Kane's six principles and applying them to Rodeheaver. For now, while his Chicago publishing company was at its peak, Rodeheaver seemed to be doing well with the "make all the money you can" part. The rest would come in time.

5

NEW TECHNOLOGY TO PROMOTE AN OLD STORY
"AN OLD IDEA, ELECTRIFIED"

As the era of tabernacle revivalism drew to a close in the early 1920s, Billy Sunday and Homer Rodeheaver found themselves at an ideological juncture. Most Protestant theologians would acknowledge (some grudgingly) that Billy Sunday's populist approach still communicated the essential Christian doctrine of substitutionary atonement. But those old charges of a "vaudeville revivalist" were hard to shake. The Sunday and Rodeheaver supporters looked at the big picture of their successful ministry. But their detractors looked at the details, some of which were tawdry. Even their most ardent supporters understood how the essential character of their gospel message might be compromised by their method of delivery. Sunday responded by staying on the road and preaching to live audiences, perpetually skeptical about his future in recordings, radio, and film. Homer Rodeheaver took the modern path, quickly leaping past their audience limitation of 10,000 people a night.

By any measure Homer Rodeheaver would succeed as a recording artist, then a record label owner, then a radio star. And near the end, his early-adopter personality continued unabated as he experimented with film and television. As he leapfrogged from medium to medium, his overarching idea stayed the same. If the tabernacle era was over, at least the power of communal singing could be transferred through new technology.

CHAPTER 5

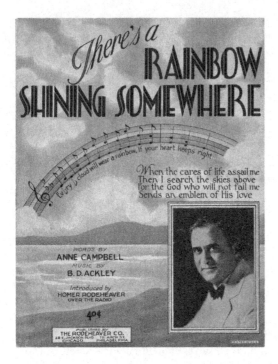

FIGURE 5.1. Theme song for Rodeheaver's radio programs in the 1930s.

CHICAGO'S PLAYER PIANO INDUSTRY

Some of these ideas can be illustrated through a quick look at Rodeheaver's brief foray into piano rolls. The Rodeheaver Co. offices were just around the corner from Chicago's Piano Row, known as the center for American piano production and also a center for piano roll production. Though Rodeheaver rarely stayed in Chicago for more than a few days at a time, the 1918 Billy Sunday meetings allowed Rodeheaver to work at length with the piano roll manufacturers.

As a populist commercial industry, the piano roll companies marketed popular song titles and later discovered they could also highlight popular personalities. Titles and names, that's what sold, as evidenced by their prominence in advertisements and product labels. Once the revivalists discovered the player piano market, their gospel songs were marketed the same way, prominently named as "Billy Sunday Songs" recorded by his star pianist, George Ashley Brewster, "with Mr. Rodeheaver giving his personal interpretation."[1] During their recording sessions, Brewster played a keyboard contraption that punched holes into a long roll of paper. Rodeheaver stood nearby, singing and conducting while Brewster recorded, producing interpretations that were recreated every time the piano roll was played.

For his March 1918 sessions, Rodeheaver contracted with the Imperial Player Roll Co., manufacturers of Songrecord piano rolls. Imperial leased space in the Lyon and Healy Building (57 E. Jackson Blvd.), just up the block from Rodeheaver's office. Since Piano Row was home to several competing piano roll makers, they each tried to market their product with a unique hook. In this case, Imperial billed its piano rolls as the perfect accompaniment for singing—the crucial point for Rodeheaver. Imperial printed the song lyrics down the side of the paper roll. As the piano player pumped the pedal mechanism, words scrolled past a window in the front of the unit, something like early karaoke. The piano roll industry thrived under one foundational precept—owning a piano should not require years of practice. "As simple as turning on a light," advertised the Cable Piano Co.[2] One could sit down and pump out any favorite tune, limited only by the owner's collection of piano rolls. Prognosticators were already suggesting that this new technology would change the essence of music. Rodeheaver saw potential benefits, which motivated his careful choice of a vendor. He wanted his piano rolls to sustain group singing.

Though Imperial's piano rolls proved to be the best option, they also came with a challenge. Imperial built its business on jazz and ragtime—mostly played by Charlie Straight, a young piano sensation with a gift for applying the jazz style to nearly any tune. The Rodeheaver and Brewster sessions were Imperial's first attempt at hymns and gospel songs, leading to humorous moments when Straight blundered into the studio to share some unwanted advice. According to the less-than-serious report in *Music Trade Review*, "Manager Thomas Kavanaugh spent a few busy hours sitting on the neck of Charlie Straight, the Imperial jazz king... Charlie had an idea that these hymns should have jazz accompaniments." The trade journal acknowledged that the religious piano rolls would likely be tremendous sellers but also asked each reader to "imagine for itself the demand these hymns would have created if Charlie had had his way."[3]

Humor aside, Rodeheaver was moving into uncharted territory. When he started his hymnal company in 1910, he had been mentored by a helpful network of old-guard hymn writers who taught him the business as if he would join them as Christian stewards, a formal apprentice in the gospel publishing fraternity. But Rodeheaver had no such network in the piano roll industry—he did business directly with people who generally did not understand his objectives and ideals. This critical nexus in the early 1900s, the cusp of commercial gospel music, has been studied for many years. Typical analysis centers on a growing tension between popular jazz-influenced idioms and traditional gospel songs—or looks at the financial angle, how the gospel songs made publishers wealthy. Our approach here is to explore a third path. Rodeheaver saw how modern technology could change the way we perceive and interact with music. As the era of tabernacle revivalism drew to a close, Rodeheaver sought out ways to preserve the communal experience. Rodeheaver advertised his new piano rolls as "beautifully phrased hand-played records of gospel songs, having the words plainly printed along the margin of the roll opposite the singing notes."[4] He still expected everyone to sing together.

EARLY RECORDS

For as popular as Rodeheaver's recordings became, they started slowly. The Victor Talking Machine Co. invited him to Camden, New Jersey for a test session in July 1913, where he recorded five selections. None were ultimately released, but the tests were promising enough that Victor invited him to return on September 10 for a formal recording session. Over the next three days Rodeheaver recorded at least twenty-five sides—twelve that Victor eventually released, and another thirteen that were rejected (usually for technical reasons, though Victor could also be finicky about repertoire). Such was the nature of early recording.

Sunday and Rodeheaver were in the middle of their Johnstown, Pennsylvania, campaign when Victor released the first six sides. Local dealers picked up the new records, as did every dealer in any city that had hosted the revivalists. Rodeheaver came with a built-in fan base, big enough to track in trade journals like *Talking Machine World*. Whenever Billy Sunday moved to a new city and started a campaign, the magazine reported a spike in local record sales. Convinced of his viability as an artist, Victor released the rest of his recordings from the 1913 sessions. The other labels noticed. While the industry continued to release various recording formats, popular recording artists could perform their hits with another company and another format, exactly what happened with Rodeheaver.

His next recordings came on March 9–10, 1914, when he and Sunday were conducting a campaign in Scranton, Pennsylvania. Rodeheaver took the train to New York City on his off days, recording six more songs on Edison Blue Amberol cylinders. Four of these were the same tabernacle favorites that Rodeheaver had just recorded with Victor: "The Old-Fashioned Faith," "If Your Heart Keeps Right," "I Walk with the King," and "Mother's Prayers Have Followed Me." Edison released them in time for their July catalog, which included a brief promo of their new artist. "He possibly sings to more people night after night than any other man in the whole world today," the magazine said, explaining Rodeheaver's market potential. "Mr. Sunday's Tabernacles seat from ten to fifteen thousand people, and they are filled nearly every night of the week."[5] In 1929, Edison abandoned the Blue Amberol cylinders; Rodeheaver was among the last to record in the format. He stayed with Edison long enough to release about 30 titles on their new Diamond Discs.

By the time he returned to the Victor studios in 1915, his main agenda was to record his latest hit, "Brighten the Corner," popular since its 1912 introduction in sheet music and revival hymnals. During the heyday of tabernacle revivalism, Rodeheaver released a new hymnal every two or three years and purchased gospel song copyrights by the hundreds. The Chicago hymnal industry could be called a midwestern Tin Pan Alley, following many of the precepts of its secular counterpart in New York. For both groups the perennial question of "hit-making" still depended on song pluggers who pitched their newest creations to popular live performers and their agents. In the world of revivalists, songs became popular through relentless plugging during the tabernacle meetings, Bible conferences, and (sometimes) the summer denominational meetings. As a prime example, Rodeheaver featured "Brighten" as a vocal solo, trombone solo, and mixed quartet. Or he invited various groups and delegations to visit the tabernacle and present their rendition of his new song. No matter who sang the verses, Rodeheaver invariably invited the entire audience to sing the chorus, all 10,000 or 15,000 in unison. The simple melody and repeating lyrics made it easy to learn, which was the secret to Rodeheaver's successful recording career. You could sing this at home, sing it with the record—anyone.

Having established a customer base with Victor and Edison, Rodeheaver now began recording with the last of the "big three" labels, Columbia. He repeated "Brighten," among others, a song he eventually sang at least a dozen times for nine different labels, including his own.[6] In the period between 1913 and 1920 Rodeheaver recorded with Victor, Edison Blue Amberol, Edison Diamond Disc, Columbia, Emerson, and Vocalion.

His experiences with the major labels can be characterized by what he did not record—a lot of his repertoire. The big three labels seemed uninterested in his rendition of the Sankey-era gospel songs (Rodeheaver frequently sang a poignant version of "The Ninety and Nine"). Victor and Edison both passed on his renditions of the spirituals (he used them in nearly every tabernacle meeting). And Rodeheaver's ideas about singing *with* Black ensembles? Forget it.

The big three did not want anything with a gospel piano sound, or his trombone, or for that matter, his half-sister. Also, nothing that made the southern singer sound too southern, and none of Rodeheaver's preservationist nostalgia—no duets with Charles H. Gabriel or E. O. Excell, the old guard of gospel publishing. Compared to Rodeheaver's tabernacle performances of the same era, the big three record labels kept Rodeheaver in a relatively narrow stylistic range, which eventually provoked him to start his own label.

In the most glaring omission of all, the record labels paid little attention to Rodeheaver's true passion, his desire to record mass tabernacle singing. In partial defense of the labels, what Rodeheaver wanted was nearly impossible. The horn-based equipment of the acoustical era was not very portable, nor was it suited for capturing thousands of voices at once. But on one occasion in 1917, Victor agreed to bring its recording equipment to Billy Sunday's New York tabernacle.

Chalk it up to the spirit of the times. Sunday and Rodeheaver Sunday's organizers had built his biggest tabernacle ever, with 16,000 seats and standing room for another 4,000. Critics saw the rising structure and dusted off their usual "he'll never fill it" stories. But two days before the campaign began, Congress declared war on Germany, the country was awash in patriotism, and suddenly New York needed God. Sunday squelched the usual questions about money, promising that his entire offering would go to the Red Cross. The *New York Times* responded with its own blessing, some of the best press Sunday ever received.

Rodeheaver asked his chorus to gather at the tabernacle on a Monday, the campaign's official day off, for a special recording session. Thousands more snuck in without invitation. Rodeheaver conducted them in eight songs of his own choosing, performed exactly as he did for a tabernacle meeting, with Bob Matthews and George Brewster at the two nine-foot Baldwin pianos. Six of the attempts were rejected for one reason or another, but Victor released "Sail On" and "America," one of the best examples of early mass choir recordings.[7] Victor later listed the chorus as 2,500 voices, a plausibly conservative number that does not include any of the spectators who sang along. The recording of "America" still sounds fresh and vigorous today, rolling forward with unstoppable enthusiasm until the final "let freedom ring," and then ending with a spontaneous cheer.

Rodeheaver's recording career entered a new phase when he started his own Rainbow Records label in 1920 (discussed in the next chapter). He also continued to record with major labels and smaller independents, including Gennett, Claxtonola, Silvertone, Herwin, Champion, Paramount, Brunswick, Okeh, Montgomery Ward, Conqueror, Decca, and International Sacred. All told, he released more than 500 songs on at least twenty-four different labels between 1913 and 1955. How many records did he sell, total?

As a test case, one could look at his duet recordings of "The Old Rugged Cross" with Virginia H. Asher, released on nine different labels between 1920 and 1925.[8] There is no way to overstate the song's enduring popularity, but also no authoritative way to measure its sales. In *Twenty Years with Billy Sunday*, Rodeheaver claimed to have sold more than a million recordings of the song.[9] Meanwhile, the discographer Allan Sutton has persuasively argued that such claims are impossible to verify during the acoustical era, even though "million-seller" attributions are made for any number of recordings.[10] Even if Rodeheaver exaggerated his "Old Rugged Cross" numbers (it wouldn't be the first time), his claim is at least interesting—impossible to verify, but also difficult to refute.

FIGURE 5.2. Wreckage of the Rainbow Records airplane after its 1921 crash in Winona Lake. Courtesy of Rodeheaver Collection, Grace College, Winona Lake.

TECHNOLOGY'S TRAGIC TURN

Any account of the Roaring Twenties could trace the remarkable progress of American ingenuity—and then discuss the challenges created by modernity. For Rodeheaver, this tension can be seen in his experiences with cars and airplanes. As was usually the case whenever a new gizmo came along, Homer Rodeheaver was the first member of Billy Sunday's staff to purchase an automobile—just another addition to the barnstorming hoopla of tabernacle revivalism. Having secured endorsement deals for his trombones (Conn, Wurlitzer) and his pianos (Baldwin), Rodeheaver added to the hype by endorsing Hudson automobiles and then orchestrating grand entrances by auto. Newspapers reported on Rodeheaver's "saucy little roadster," the women who rode with him, and the delegations who greeted him when he traveled from town to town.[11]

His auto accidents—at least four of them—also made it into the news, as did an incident with his half-sister, Ruth. At the start of the 1922 Winona Lake Bible Conference, she plowed a car into a willow tree as guests were arriving at the park entrance. She escaped with cuts and bruises but could not escape a greater awkwardness—the brand-new car, now demolished, was owned by Helen and Billy Sunday.[12] Darker incidents would follow. Billy Sunday Jr. died in a 1938 car wreck, then son Paul died in a 1944 airplane accident. Rodeheaver's brother Yumbert was seriously injured in a 1940 accident. But no incident was as tragic as Homer Rodeheaver's ill-fated scheme to buy an airplane.

Rodeheaver's disastrous plan started in 1918 during his WWI tour of France, where he met Lt. Lynn D. Merrill, a flight commander in the 166th Aero Squadron who flew out of the Maulan Aerodrome.[13] Perhaps Rodeheaver and Merrill flew together during this visit, perhaps not, but they stayed in touch after returning to the United States. Once home, Merrill bought his own plane and began a career as a commercial pilot. He made good money performing barnstorming stunts for airshows and civic celebrations, plus offering airplane rides at $20 each. All was fine until he attempted a risky air rescue of a drowning boy in Tampa, wrecking his plane in the process. Rodeheaver read accounts of the heroic deed and came up with a plan.

At the end of the war, the army unloaded its surplus of Curtis JN-4 biplanes, known as Jennys. A good plane could be had for $300, brand new and still in the shipping crate, at a fraction of its $5,000 production cost. And though veteran pilots like Merrill gravitated to the surplus Jennys, everyone else did, too. A new commercial industry was about to emerge as barnstorming pilots found all sorts of uses for the surplus planes. And at the end of the war, no license was required.

Rodeheaver purchased a Jenny for Merrill, who agreed to earn ownership by flying the plane for various Rodeheaver events. The idea, perhaps half-formed, came at the same time as Rodeheaver promoted his new record label, so it seemed natural to emblazon the wings with a giant Rainbow Records logo. Their first public appearance came when Rodeheaver and Merrill flew the plane into Winona Lake for the opening of the 1921 Bible Conference. They had left Cincinnati about two hours earlier, flying over several Indiana towns and dropping Rainbow Records leaflets as they buzzed overhead. Once they arrived at Winona Lake, Rodeheaver planned to use the airplane as another amenity for his hotel guests—those who stayed in a Rodeheaver hotel could also arrange for an airplane ride around the lake. It was the only airplane in the county—a surefire business opportunity. Rodeheaver also saw an opportunity for his half-brother Jack, who wanted to become a pilot. Now 18, Jack was just young enough to have missed the war; instead, he was returning home from a year at the McCallie Military Academy in Chattanooga, Tennessee. Jack immediately began flying lessons with Merrill.

All of Rodeheaver's reasons for owning an airplane, stacked end to end, still didn't amount to much. Nothing close to a well-planned business model. Rodeheaver loved new technology, pure and simple. But his risk-taking personality and his personal wealth made for a bad combination and sometimes resulted in impulsive decisions.

The resulting tragedy unfolded quickly as Jack and Lt. Merrill took off for his first training flight. The engine stopped in midair and the plane began to roll, then

Merrill reached over Jack's shoulder and promptly fell out of the open cockpit. An overly optimistic doctor later suggested that Merrill died of a heart attack before he hit the ground. Jack fared no better. Now upside down and unable to recover from the dive, the plane plunged into a cornfield adjacent to the golf course.

Newspaper accounts spared no detail, reporting that Jack's chest "was crushed almost to a jelly" and his head "was crushed so that his brains and blood oozed from his ears."[14] Some rumors suggested that Merrill's wife and Jack's mother actually witnessed the bodies fall, and were present when Jack's mangled remains were removed from the wreckage. Homer Rodeheaver raced to the accident site in his auto, having heard the news while sitting on the porch of his Rainbow Point home.

An indescribable gloom settled over the lakeside resort as vacationers quietly returned to their rooms, with nothing else to do. Conference organizers decided to move forward with the evening meeting, which G. Campbell Morgan turned into an impromptu prayer session and wake. He described the flyers "not as dead, but gone to meet their God face-to-face."[15] And Homer Rodeheaver, the man who lived his entire life on stage, was nowhere to be found. "The once jovial Homer Rodeheaver, a man who has witnessed all the horrors of war, yet made soldiers laugh in the face of these, is today broken in spirit and almost frantic with grief," the local paper suggested, but no one outside of his family really knew what Rodeheaver was feeling.[16] He never talked about it. In the aftermath of the accident, Homer Rodeheaver carefully avoided any mention of the tragedy in company publications or newspaper interviews. His stepmother dropped a few hints to a reporter, who wrote how the "dreadful airplane crash was a terrible blow to him, and one from which he has never completely recovered."[17] Nevertheless, Rodeheaver did not take any time off after the accident, and instead charged forward with a jam-packed schedule, which only seemed to aggravate his "nervous and run-down condition."[18] His doctor suggested a lengthy vacation away from Winona Lake, the impetus for Rodeheaver's 1923–24 world tour with W. E. Biederwolf. When Rodeheaver returned, he dove into radio ventures that took up the next decade of his life.

EARLY RADIO

The question of the "first" radio station in the United States is too complicated to unravel here—KDKA of Pittsburgh makes a claim for 1920, challenged by several contemporaries, with the final answer depending on the way the claim is worded.[19] Similar problems await anyone identifying the "first" religious radio broadcast. KDKA (again) makes a claim, a "radio chapel" broadcast in December 1921.[20] Conventional radio histories often cite these KDKA broadcasts as the start of religious programming, which can at least be called the best documented early

CHAPTER 5

services. Whoever might have been first, the idea of religious programming rose concurrently with the first viable radio stations of the 1920s.

Early radio seemed to attract niche interests. Chicago's first station, KYW, started by airing live performances of the Chicago Grand Opera, a quirky opera-only format. The station boasted of 200 radio receivers when they started and 25,000 after two months of broadcasting. Was this giant leap because of the station format, or the novelty? No one could say for sure—but religious broadcasters believed that if people would listen to opera, they would certainly listen to gospel songs and sermons.

Billy Sunday and Homer Rodeheaver began their foray into radio on April 26, 1922, during their Richmond, Indiana, campaign. The *Palladium* newspaper, owners of WOZ, persuaded the tabernacle musicians to broadcast a special Wednesday night concert. Performers included Rodeheaver, pianist Bob Matthews, Virginia Asher, Florence Kinney, and Albert Peterson. Listeners consisted of a vibrant group of amateur radio operators who organized listening parties around the city—two dozen radio receivers, at best. But in a fine stroke of publicity, the *Palladium* also installed a radio in Billy Sunday's hotel room, giving the newspaper an excuse to cover their own event with a front-page article. The reporter described the solos, duets, quartets, and trombone numbers, and detailed the quality of reception throughout the city. But the headline reported all that a person needed to know about Billy Sunday's future in radio: "Billy Enjoys First Program by Radio; Listens in His Room."[21] As the world changed around him and as technology changed revivalism, Billy Sunday would be a listener, not a performer.[22]

FIGURE 5.3. Rodeheaver and tabernacle musicians broadcast from WOZ Radio in Richmond, Indiana, in 1922. Reprinted from *Twenty Years with Billy Sunday*, 1936.

As Rodeheaver and Sunday continued to hold tabernacle revivals throughout the 1920s, they discovered that most of their host cities were adding radio to the promotional menu. As a result, Rodeheaver spent the next eight years honing his musical approach for the new radio audience. But Billy Sunday never succeeded in scaling his tabernacle delivery to fit inside the radio box. When WMC in Memphis wanted to broadcast Sunday sermons in 1925, reporters were not optimistic about the result: "Mr. Sunday is bound to get out of earshot of the microphone, rushing and running around as he does. Either he must change his ways or the WMC people must persuade him to put on a sunbonnet or some sort of headgear and attach the microphone to it."[23] The prediction proved to be accurate; though Sunday made radio appearances when his hosts requested it, he intuitively knew it was not his format. Near the end of his life, Sunday talked about radio in abstraction, as a problem he could solve in theory but not in real life. "Those who broadcast religious programs have not found the correct formula to win great numbers of religious listeners or to convert people into churchgoers," Sunday complained in the *New York Times*. "Personality is the ingredient that makes any show a winner. The evangelist is a gospel specialist who has learned the trick of appealing to the masses. Radio should be made his right-hand implement and aid."[24]

The next generation of evangelicals did indeed make radio the "right hand implement" of preachers, Paul Rader serving as an example. After a short stint at the Moody Church, Rader established his Chicago Gospel Tabernacle with the help of weekly broadcasts and political glad-handing. Rader was friendly with William Hale Thompson, the Chicago mayor who bought his own radio station and branded it as WHT. Thompson needed someone to manage his Sunday programming, so Rader volunteered and recruited Rodeheaver to help.[25] Between 1925 and 1929, Rodeheaver appeared on numerous WHT programs and also appeared on Chicago stations WGN, KYW, and WQJ. All of the broadcasts followed the same basic format, sticking close to the tabernacle repertoire and often assisted by various members of the Sunday party. Many of the printed broadcast schedules note the sponsorship of the Rodeheaver Co.[26] By 1925, Rodeheaver added a fifth Chicago station to his portfolio, a monthly program on WLS ("World's Largest Station"), owned by Sears, Roebuck & Co.[27] Here Rodeheaver tested his essential idea about radio, that it should be participatory rather than passive. In addition to his conventional mix of musical performances, he invited listeners to gather around their radio sets while he led singing. His programming ideas, his populist appeal, and especially his East Tennessee accent came at just the right time.

Deciding to focus on retail merchandising, Sears sold WLS to the publishers of *Prairie Farmer* magazine in 1928. The new owners understood how their magazine audience could become a listening audience; more importantly, they understood the social dynamics of rural-to-urban migration. More than half of their listeners now lived in cities, but they still wanted to hear live updates from Chicago's Union Stock Yards, commodities reports from the Mercantile Exchange, and above all, up-to-the-minute weather reports. WLS became "The Voice of the Prairie" for its increasingly urban audience.

Listeners also expected a certain style of music from WLS, including the standard repertoire of Protestant hymns and gospel songs. In the days before Christian broadcasting emerged as a distinct station format, stations such as WLS included a healthy mix of religious programing. Rev. John Holland worked at the station for several years as a part-time announcer who led morning and evening devotionals, plus the Sunday broadcasts of *Little Brown Church of the Air*. Rodeheaver helped with the show for several dates in 1929, apparently because he was already scheduled in the studio for his Saturday community sing program.

Rodeheaver persuaded WLS to run the format for a full week straight, December 19–24, 1929, billed as "The National Christmas Carol Sing." The program became the first nationwide test of Rodeheaver's essential idea about radio—that it would become a new platform for communal singing events. WLS promoted the broadcasts to "community groups, Boy Scout troops, Campfire girls, public and parochial schools, and churches of many denominations" and predicted the greatest radio audience ever.[28] In the weeks before the event, the radio station mailed Rodeheaver's Christmas carol booklet to any listener who requested one. WLS, trying to establish its own viability on a national network, billed the event as "the first time that a radio station has ever presented such a series of programs with the co-operation of listeners."[29]

After the success of the Christmas carol sing, Rodeheaver's monthly program picked up a sponsor, the Calumet Steel Fence Post Company. Now with a new name, the *Calumet Sociability Hour* also promoted a Rodeheaver community songbook, *Sociability Songs for Community, Home, School*.[30] Rodeheaver offered a bulk discount to the Calumet dealers, who then promised listeners a free songbook if they stopped by local stores. The program leaped in popularity when it ran as a network lead-in to the popular WLS National Barn Dance program on Saturday nights. Starting on February 1, 1930, and lasting until October 25, 1930, the *Calumet Sociability Hour* ended only because Rodeheaver received an even better offer.

In retrospect, Rodeheaver's growing radio career explains the real reason why he accepted fewer and fewer tabernacle campaigns with Billy Sunday. Rodeheaver had no trouble filling his schedule with radio broadcasts, recording dates, music conferences, one-night concert events, and frequent travel. Sunday, however, struggled to find cities that would commit to his preferred format of a multiweek tabernacle campaign. Most of Billy Sunday's biographers interpret Rodeheaver and Sunday's 1930 "break-up" as the result of Rodeheaver's growing dissatisfaction.

Rodeheaver had criticized Sunday's obsession with fund-raising and his approach to altar calls (see chapter 3). And Helen Sunday aggressively protected Billy from Rodeheaver's entrepreneurial schemes. But the real story was less dramatic—their careers just took different paths. Rodeheaver and Sunday continued as friends and neighbors; they never really broke up. Though they did not know it at the time, their final campaign together came in 1930 at Mt. Holly, New Jersey. Now approaching 70, Billy Sunday looked forward to quiet days at his hillside cottage in Winona Lake. Rodeheaver moved on to a nationwide radio career, but first took time for a five-week vacation to Germany, where he visited the famous passion play in Oberammergau. Traveling companions included brother Joseph and his new wife, Ruthella, and Homer's longtime friend, Grace Saxe.

For all that has been said about the women in Rodeheaver's life—his front-page romances with Georgia Jay and Aimee Semple McPherson, his awkward relationship with Helen Sunday (his real boss?)—his closest and longest female companion was rarely mentioned. Grace Saxe joined the Sunday team in 1911, a year after Rodeheaver, and continued through 1921, when her health waned. Billy Sunday called her the best Bible teacher in America. Her afternoon teaching sessions often filled Sunday's tabernacle on their own merits. No music, none of Rodeheaver's preliminaries, just a solid hour of instruction from an unmarried woman with a Bible. Rodeheaver gave her a regular column in his *Gospel Choir* magazine, the only part of the magazine that was not devoted to some aspect of church music. And Rodeheaver treated her as a close friend and confidante, though she was twelve years his senior. Of all the members of Sunday's team, Grace Saxe was the only one he vacationed with, including his 1923–24 world tour and this 1930 trip to Germany. Now they enjoyed one last trip together before her health gave out entirely.

NETWORK RADIO

While Rodeheaver traveled, NBC radio executives discussed the *Calumet Sociability Hour* and its possible suitability as nationwide community sing program. As soon as Rodeheaver returned, they pitched the idea for *Rodeheaver Sings*, a new show to originate from WEAF (later renamed WNBC) in New York. The program ran twice a week, Wednesday and Saturday nights, over the more prominent NBC Red Network. "Mr. Rodeheaver will urge the groups around the loud speakers to join in the choruses just as he attempted to get the congregations at the Billy Sunday services to unite in singing the hymns," a radio reporter said, describing the repertoire as mostly gospel songs and ballads.[31] The resulting format lived up to its billing in at least one place—Rodeheaver's hometown of Jellico, Tennessee, where crowds gathered at the local Methodist church for every broadcast.[32]

Rodeheaver introduced a new theme song for the show, "There's a Rainbow Shining Somewhere," which felt like a peppy, Depression-era sequel to "Brighten the Corner."

There's a rainbow shining somewhere,
There's a light across the skies;
There's a rainbow shining somewhere,
Like a gleam from Paradise;
Though today the clouds are drifting
Far across the stormy sea,
There's a rainbow shining somewhere,
That will some day shine for me.[33]

Like his other cheer-up songs, Rodeheaver viewed his radio theme as a gateway to religious music—not, strictly speaking, a gospel song with a clear declaration of Christian salvation. Rodeheaver's optimistic rainbow trope fit right in with other popular hits of the era, songs such as "I'm Always Chasing Rainbows" (1918) and Al Jolson's "There's a Rainbow Round My Shoulder" (1928).[34] And within the world of gospel music, The Stamps Quartet sang "Give the World a Smile" for Victor in 1927.[35]

Rodeheaver Sings ran from December 1930 to March 1931, a typical run for 1930s network shows, after which Rodeheaver tried to work up a replacement, *Worth While Poems*. His plan was to read poems "of the Edgar Guest type, poetry possessing an everyday and popular appeal," interspersed with stories and his commentary about the authors.[36] The idea sounded plausible—Rodeheaver was known for his poetry reading on the Chautauqua circuit and in tabernacle meetings. But the program never picked up an advertising sponsor, leading to its cancelation after a two-week tryout in April 1931.

His next radio venture came in the form of 1932's *Neighborly Songs and Poems*, his first attempt at a pre-recorded format.[37] Assisted by the Mendelssohn Male Quartet of Chicago and the ensemble of the Chicago Concert Company, Rodeheaver narrated a 15-minute programs of gospel songs and other familiar old songs. Produced in Chicago, the programs were distributed on 16-inch transcription disc, a new format that began to compete with live radio.[38] Judging from the relatively few broadcast schedules printed in local papers, the venture may not have been successful enough to justify its larger overhead. It ran on various stations from August 1932 to September 1934. By this point, the evangelical Protestants had established their own genre of radio broadcasts, the familiar music-and-preaching format that drew on a long tradition of tabernacle meetings and Bible conferences. Rodeheaver's radio programs took a somewhat different approach, aiming for a populist bridge from secular society and pointing to the church. Not preaching, per se, but brief sermons between songs to remind listeners of the power of music and the value of communal song.

PERSONAL TRANSITIONS

Rodeheaver's radio career stalled for a bit during the next few years, perhaps because he was temporarily distracted by business mergers (discussed in chapter 4), his trip to Africa (discussed in chapter 8), and increasingly, extended winter vacations in Florida. Also, the death of his stepmother, several associates, and Billy Sunday.

Rodeheaver stopped by Billy Sunday's Winona Lake cottage in October 1935, to ask a favor. Having been called away on business, Rodeheaver needed a fast substitute to cover a scheduled meeting in Mishawaka, Indiana. Sunday obliged, giving the congregation at First Methodist Church a happy surprise when he showed up as Rodeheaver's replacement. Sunday still preached with vigor despite his age, and when the service ended, 44 people hit the trail. The sermon turned out to be Sunday's last. A week later he died of a heart ailment while visiting his Chicago in-laws.

At the funeral service, Homer Rodeheaver offered a brief tribute that should have dispelled any notions of a breach between the long-time partners: "The members of Mr. Sunday's party want me to say to you that those of us who knew him best loved him most."[39] And behind the scenes he started working on a project to memorialize the tabernacle era. Over the years, Rodeheaver had tried to get Sunday to record sermons on his Rainbow Records label, tried to get Sunday to film a tabernacle service, and tried to stir up interest in various biographical projects. Nothing came of the proposals, mostly because they never made it past Helen Sunday. Now Rodeheaver began work on a book project without asking for Helen Sunday's approval. He finished the manuscript during his 1936 Africa tour, and then published it as *Twenty Years with Billy Sunday*.

Rodeheaver wanted to write his sincere impressions of Sunday "while they are still fresh in mind, as conscientiously as possible, with the hope that they will aid in preserving a clearer and more truthful portrait of one of the most colorful, picturesque, dynamic, and consecrated personalities of this or any other generation."[40] Read today, his tone comes off like someone who sat down to write a personal memoir after the funeral of a best friend. Which it was. Warm, effusive, and in places outright defensive, especially when discussing Sunday's finances and publicity. Rodeheaver's knack for storytelling detail became a bane and blessing for future researchers. He remembered and recounted particulars that no one else knew, but he also embellished stories in ways that make fact-checking difficult.[41]

During this time, Rodeheaver's stepmother, Bettie, was quite ill, spending most of her time at the home of daughter Ruth and James Thomas in Roanoke, Virginia. Rodeheaver left on his 1936 Africa trip with some trepidation, understanding that she was not well. A few months after his return, Bettie Rodeheaver passed away, on October 24, 1936. Then in December he received word that Grace Saxe was gravely ill with bone cancer in Waterloo, Iowa, where she had retired. Rodeheaver canceled all of the events on his schedule and made an emergency flight from New York to see her one last time, staying for two days while she was still alert. When she died on February 5, 1937, Rodeheaver returned again to lead the funeral at Walnut Street Baptist Church in Waterloo.

CRITIQUES OF TECHNOLOGY

This same period also afforded Rodeheaver some time to reflect on the changes of his own era, both in terms of gain and loss. "We appreciate the radio but must admit that it has taken from the young and old much of the initiative and desire for individual participation," Rodeheaver said in 1936. "The sale of musical instruments gradually declined with the advent of radio. The sale of sheet music has also materially decreased. Why learn the piano or violin when by simply turning a little knob you bring into the home the masterpieces of music?"[42]

His concerns echoed a familiar line of thought that can only be summarized here. In 1906, composer John Philip Sousa complained about the phonograph in "The Menace of Mechanical Music," calling it "a mechanical device to sing for us a song or play for us a piano, in substitute for human skill, intelligence, and soul."[43] As the discussion continued, T. S. Eliot predicted that technology would inevitably change musical perception, anticipating a day when "every theatre has been replaced by 100 cinemas, when every musical instrument has been replaced by 100 gramophones . . . when electrical ingenuity has made it possible for every child to hear its bed-time stories through a wireless receiver attached to both ears."[44] For Eliot, this zeal to "make life as interesting as possible" would only lead to "the fate of the Melanesians" (referring to an Australian tribal group decimated by the introduction of the gramophone).[45]

Such warnings—there were many—tended to argue that recordings and radio discouraged group participation, creating a generation of passive listeners. The church musicians of Rodeheaver's era were making the same point. In 1937, Charles Winfred Douglas attributed the poor condition of congregational hymn singing to "the almost universal misuse of the radio." He accused radio of luring the congregation into "a merely passive role" with "bad examples of the so-called hymn crudely and sentimentally sung."[46] His thinly disguised critique of gospel songs jabbed directly at Rodeheaver, and in retrospect, seems at least disingenuous. In 1933, Douglas had complained about congregations who "remain mute spectators at a Sung Mass."[47] Though he theoretically agreed with Rodeheaver on the importance of congregational singing, Douglas advocated a far different solution—the revival of ninth-century plainchants. As if this was not enough, Douglas insisted on publishing the ancient tunes in their original (and ultra-obscure) neume notation. Needless to say, his hymnals didn't sell quite as well as Rodeheaver's.

In addition to critiquing the "bad" music, traditional church musicians also argued that recordings and radio cultivated the expectation of a higher performance standard. According to Rodeheaver's friend Earl Harper, "the ideals of technical proficiency have risen high. The fumbling amateur is hardly safe from being 'razzed' by an audience made familiar with high qualities of technique and interpretation."[48] Near the end of Rodeheaver's life, his Youth for Christ friends offered the same opinion. "Radio has spoiled things for the careless gospel musician," wrote Torrey Johnson and Robert Cook, "for your young folk can hear, if they wish, worldly music, *perfectly produced*, any hour of the day or night."[49] But rather than lamenting the situation, the new generation of YFC leaders viewed this as a challenge to meet. Their recordings and live performances became increasingly sophisticated as they worked toward "perfectly produced" religious music.

FIGURE 5.4. Rodeheaver as radio host of "Come On, Let's Sing," 1936. Courtesy of Rodeheaver Collection, Grace College, Winona Lake.

After Rodeheaver, a new class of professional Christian musicians emphasized performance music, not just at Bible conferences and summer conventions, but also at the local church level.

Recordings and radio changed church music and gospel music, no doubt, but first Rodeheaver tried to use the new technology to re-create the old experience of mass singing. "Radio should make a more determined effort to re-create a desire for individual participation in music," he said.[50] And for a time it looked like he might be right.

"AN OLD IDEA, ELECTRIFIED"

Community singing on the radio airwaves enjoyed one last resurgence before disappearing from America's musical memory. Vic Knight of WABC-Columbia recruited Rodeheaver for another incarnation of the community sing format, now billed as *Come On, Let's Sing*. The program debuted on July 22, 1936, running on Wednesday nights at 9:30 p.m. It quickly attained the widest network distribution of Rodeheaver's radio efforts, and a respectable 6.5 audience share for its time slot.[51]

His song repertoire remained unchanged from earlier programs: "roundelays, barber-shop ballads, novelty songs, melodies of the Gay Nineties, and songs from 10 to 20 years ago."[52] He pointedly avoided the hottest Tin Pan Alley hits, arguing that "songs of today are much less in demand, both because they are replaced by others so quickly and because many of them are too intricate in rhythm and key changes for the ordinary person to sing."[53] Rodeheaver continued to preach a distinction between performance music and communal music, choosing songs only for their suitability to group singing.

The show quickly picked up a sponsor and a new name, *Palmolive Community Sing*, which ensured its big-budget status. Rodeheaver frequently invited guest conductors—radio celebrities—including Irving Kaufman, Elsie Janis, Frank Crumit, and Harry "Singin' Sam" Frankel. One additional feature of the new show contributed markedly to its popularity. Rodeheaver did the show live, using an audience of 1,000 enthusiastic singers accompanied by piano, accordion, and a core group of 40 rehearsed singers. "The world needs song today more than ever before," Rodeheaver told a reporter, reminding him of Shakespeare's famous epigram, "The times are out of joint." Rodeheaver explained his own antidote for troubled times: "If I can help them through group singing to forget their troubles, to put aside their burdens for a little while, then I have the satisfaction of knowing I'm doing my bit to help."[54] The *New York Times* proclaimed the radio community sings to be "An Old Idea, Electrified," and soon other competitors emerged to take the credit.[55]

NEW TECHNOLOGY TO PROMOTE AN OLD STORY

FIGURE 5.5. Newspaper advertisement for Rodeheaver's 1936 radio program. Reprinted from *Dayton Daily News*.

Another community sing made its CBS debut four months after Rodeheaver's show. Led by Wendell Hall, the show's format skewed toward comedy bits and novelty songs. The show also featured a very young Milton Berle, perhaps the reason why radio historians remember it more often than Rodeheaver's show. Another reason might be the title. After signing a sponsorship deal, the program crowned itself *The Gillette Original Community Sing*, a memorable but indefensible claim.[56] Back in Chicago, a WLS radio columnist complained that east-coast publicists were ignoring Rodeheaver's earlier contributions, which had existed on Midwest stations since at least 1930. "But perhaps this idea is new now that little old New York has at last approved it," the columnist griped.[57]

For a brief period in the mid-1930s, Rodeheaver appeared to have correctly assessed radio's potential. Families gathered around the parlor radio, singing together from their free copies of sponsor songbooks. Church groups, Boy Scout troops, society matrons—they all held singing parties while Rodeheaver's voice led them from the radio set. Then the trend faded just as quickly as it rose. Rodeheaver tried one more show on the NBC network in November 1939, but it failed to catch on. Even in the late 1940s, Rodeheaver continued to pitch radio ideas. He developed a pilot for *Rainbow Point with Homer Rodeheaver*, planned as a live half-hour broadcast from his Winona Lake home. A syndication company promised "magnificently interpreted sacred music, nerve-soothing philosophy, and hearty chuckles," but the program never got off the ground.[58] The community sing craze was over.

For those who are familiar with the historiography of gospel music, this account challenges conventional thought. During the 1930s and '40s, southern gospel quartets and Black gospel groups famously abandoned their earlier emphasis on songbook sales and communal singing, moving to new successes with recordings and radio. The next decades, often called a Golden Era, are remembered for their concert-style musical performances. The new-style quartets and soloists sang sophisticated arrangements with bravura flourishes, impossible for an audience to emulate. While historians are right to document this shift in emphasis, we should not define gospel music purely on the performances of quartets and soloists. Another stream of gospel music—congregational singing—remained enormously popular in evangelical churches, even as it was disappearing from the public sphere.

THE RADIO VOICE

In purely musical terms, Rodeheaver was a remarkably gifted vocal artist and a surprisingly average trombonist. On some nights, if he was tired, his playing was embarrassingly below average. This is the sort of observation that Rodeheaver never acknowledged in public, but certainly he knew it to be true. Otherwise, there is no reason to explain why he released over 500 recordings of his voice and only one trombone solo. Very early on, Rodeheaver's trombone had become part of his personal brand and an influential model for revival songleaders, but he had no illusions about his ability—it was a visual prop.

As Rodeheaver transitioned from the revival tabernacle to the radio, he quickly understood what worked in the new medium. After a few initial experiments, he abruptly stopped playing his trombone on radio broadcasts. When asked, Rodeheaver explained ("a bit wistfully," according to a reporter) that his trombone had no "radio personality." Compared to the tabernacle performances, "its chief fascination lies in being able to see its antics and gyrations, an appeal which is lost in radio."[59]

If Rodeheaver's trombone had no future in radio, his voice certainly did. His greater potential as a soloist had been identified early on, when he was leading the children's meetings at the 1906 Lemon Hill revival meetings. Ada Turner Kurtz, a Philadelphia voice teacher, happened to hear him sing and immediately suggested lessons. During the revival years, he also studied with Oscar Seagle, a Tennessee-born Columbia recording artist. Having started out as a revivalist singer, including appearances at Billy Sunday meetings, Seagle later recorded the gospel song repertoire with Columbia.[60]

Rodeheaver studied with Seagle to build his foundational skills, a coping strategy for the nightly rigors of unamplified tabernacle singing. His interest in vocal solos started as an afterthought, a third talent that could be added to his vaudeville-like repertoire of entertainments. First came his reputation as a communal song director (well deserved, without peer); then came critical notice as a trombone player (surprisingly positive reviews), and then much later, his vocal abilities.

In musical terms, Rodeheaver could be classified as a lyric bass-baritone, possessing a two octave range from F below the bass clef staff to F above. He became famous for singing his own brand of gospel songs, traditional hymns, African American spirituals, and patriotic songs. Though less remembered today, his performance repertoire also included sacred art songs, solos from Mendelssohn's *Elijah*, early-twentieth-century recital repertory, plus the basic parlor songs expected of any Chautauqua singer. He could also be classified by what he did *not* sing—he steered away from Tin Pan Alley, jazz, and the developing repertoire known as the Great American Songbook. Anyone who has heard the Rodeheaver recordings of "Molly and the Baby" or "De Brewers Big Hosses" understands how fragile and ironic this line of demarcation could be. He would not sing pop, but he was willing to sing Prohibition songs that sounded nearly the same.

Later, Rodeheaver studied with a third teacher, Oscar Saenger of New York, a Victor recording artist who developed a series of 20 experimental voice lessons on phonograph records. By this point, Rodeheaver was a mature artist and was enjoying a successful recording career that at least equaled Saenger's. After Rodeheaver returned home from his 1918–19 wartime tour, he seemed to understand that his career was taking a new turn. Perhaps this served as his motivation for remaining in New York to study voice for several months. The collaboration proved to be fruitful; Rodeheaver later encouraged other gospel song artists to study with Saenger. Most importantly, Rodeheaver began to navigate an adjustment to his own singing; his primary audience soon became the microphone.

EARLY FILM

By now our essential point should be clear, that Rodeheaver believed modern technology could advance his essential ideas about communal singing. One final example shows his experiments with sing-along moving pictures.

Just a few weeks before the 1928 election, the Democratic National Committee sponsored open-air rallies in support of presidential candidate Alfred E. Smith. The nightly theater crowds stopped at Forty-Sixth St. and Broadway for outdoor showings of a moving picture featuring orations from several notable Democrats. Probably boring, then as now, but then the film segued to Homer Rodeheaver waving his arms and directing the gathered crowd in "The Sidewalks of New York" as the words scrolled along the bottom of the screen.[61] The stunt worked brilliantly, even if Smith's candidacy did not. One trade magazine estimated that 50,000 people a night sang along to Rodeheaver's songleading.[62] The irony seemed especially delicious—Rodeheaver openly promoting a Roman Catholic who campaigned against Prohibition.

Meanwhile, Billy Sunday spent several weeks politicking in a more predictable way. The Anti-Saloon League paid Sunday an undisclosed amount for speeches in support of Herbert Hoover, the Republican prohibitionist who eventually won the election.[63] Sunday quickly tired of reporters who pestered him about his speaking fees—now they had an even better question to ask. After years of singing "Da Brewer's Big Hosses Can't Run Over Me," after years of Prohibition support, had Homer fallen off the wagon?

The incident had started back in July, when Rodeheaver filmed screen tests for Fox Movietone. The film industry had been experimenting with sound films for several years. While history remembers *The Jazz Singer* (1927) as the first feature-length "talkie," early one-reel short films often featured a surprising variety of musical and comedy acts. Movie houses had been offering an entire evening of entertainment: a feature film, a few live vaudeville acts, and a live orchestra or organist. Now the live bits were being replaced by short films of the same performances—vaudeville, legitimate theater, and recording artists. It made perfect sense to adopt the idea for community singing.

In December 1927, Vitaphone had released its first community singing film, led by Lynn Cowan, the Iowa-born vaudeville singer and Columbia recording artist.[64] Their original concept—a singer-songwriter leading his own new songs—proved to be ineffective. Audiences wanted to sing songs they knew. Perhaps this is why Movietone looked to Rodeheaver, whose repertoire always skewed toward the familiar. His screen tests resulted in one short film and at least one reel of outtakes. Movietone thought enough of the test to prepare a print with titles, "Homer Rodeheaver in Community Singing." Rodeheaver enters wearing a tuxedo and then immediately turns to the camera to address the audience. "You look like a crowd of mighty good-natured folk who would be willing to help a fellow try a little experiment," he says, inviting everyone to sing the words that appear on the bottom of the screen. "I will direct the singing just as if I were here in person. If you come along and help me we'll have a lot of fun, and maybe we'll start a revolutionary idea in community singing." After a single chord to establish pitch, he leads Stephen Foster's minstrel song, "Old Folks at Home" (1851), followed by a chorus of "Love's Old Sweet Song" (1884).[65]

While he was working with Movietone on the community singing films, they discussed another idea. A cameraman from Movietone News traveled to Winona Lake for a day at the Bible Conference, filming Billy Sunday, the tabernacle choir, and Rodeheaver leading the whole crowd in songs. The resulting footage became part of a Movietone News short film that was released the week of September 7, 1928.⁶⁶ By all accounts, the newsreel gave the Winona Lake revivalists a valuable burst of publicity. Then came Rodeheaver's film with Al Smith, released six weeks later.

Of course, Billy Sunday hit the roof. Or was Helen angrier? The incident seemed to rekindle the tension lingering from Rodeheaver's critical letters to Sunday. In the first place, Helen Sunday disliked any team member who challenged Billy in public. And she looked suspiciously whenever Rodeheaver floated a new idea about recordings, radio, and now film. To her eyes, Rodeheaver had already eclipsed her husband in popularity. The newsreel films would benefit Rodeheaver's career far more than Billy's. Everyone noticed Rodeheaver's absence from the 1928 fall revivals, and, not knowing that Rodeheaver had planned this leave of absence all along, naturally assumed that a breakup had occurred over the Al Smith film.

It took a full year to quash the rumors. Before his 1930 meetings in Elmira, New York, Rodeheaver wrote to a local pastor, attesting that he and Sunday were still on cordial terms. "I have never seen Mr. Smith and have never been at one of his meetings," Rodeheaver said, assuring him that he could pass any political litmus test. "I have been an enthusiastic supporter of Herbert Hoover's long before he was even nominated for president."⁶⁷ Then Rodeheaver explained what really happened: without his knowledge, Movietone sold the "Sidewalks" screen test to the Al Smith campaign. Rodeheaver had no real control over the way his film was used.

As for the other Movietone film, it was never shown in theaters (someone backed out of the deal, either Rodeheaver or Movietone). The embarrassing chapter drew to a close when Movietone mailed a 16mm print back to Rodeheaver in Winona Lake. He pulled it out and showed it to friends from time to time, then it sat in a box for decades until Bruce Howe rescued it at the 1980 Rainbow Point estate sale.⁶⁸

As for the lingering controversy, Rodeheaver seemed to approach political affiliation in the same way he looked at various competing fraternal organizations, or for that matter, doctrinal controversy—why can't we all just get along? In 1912, Rodeheaver wrote a campaign song for Teddy Roosevelt, the Progressive party ("Bull Moose") presidential candidate who lost to Woodrow Wilson.⁶⁹ This didn't stop Wilson from singing with Rodeheaver when they crossed paths during their wartime tours of France.⁷⁰ In 1931, Rodeheaver led a Christmas carol sing for a charitable event with President Herbert Hoover's wife, Lou.⁷¹ Then in 1935 Rodeheaver led community singing for a huge rally where Franklin D. Roosevelt announced his reelection campaign.⁷² In 1940, Rodeheaver led 250,000 people in a community sing during a Wendell Willkie political rally, where the

CHAPTER 5

FIGURE 5.6. Rodeheaver playing Santa for an Eleanor Roosevelt Christmas event, 1939. Courtesy of Gamma-Keystone.

Democrat-turned-Republican was in the middle of a futile campaign against Franklin D. Roosevelt.[73] But the event did nothing to mar his relationship with the Roosevelts; by December of the same year, Rodeheaver was playing Santa Claus at Christmas events hosted by Eleanor Roosevelt herself.[74] Anyone searching for a political pattern in all of this would be stumped, unless one understands that Rodeheaver went nearly anywhere to lead community singing.

ANOTHER FAILED EXPERIMENT

Rodeheaver turned his attention to more familiar territory when he embarked on one more project in 1931, a religious film. Making no small plans, Rodeheaver had contracted with RCA Photophone to produce a community sing film for churches—not just a few hymns, but the entire church service. His ideas had been brewing for some time, starting with an experiment during the heyday of his Rainbow record label. In 1923, Rodeheaver planned a series of "radio records" for syndicated broadcasts. He recorded all of the elements of a church service except the sermon and prayers—ten or twelve records packaged together and played on two specially constructed record players, "one machine overlapping the other by a newly patented synchronizing device, so that there is no break at the end of one record and the beginning of another."[75] His project had the backing of the National Broadcaster's League, a Midwest coalition of early radio stations, but came five years ahead of its time. Recordings of the acoustical era were too noisy for radio broadcast, and their three-minute length made for complicated disc-swapping problems that Rodeheaver never really solved. Five years later, using improved technology, Chicago's WMAQ distributed *Amos 'n' Andy* by transcription disc. Rodeheaver's initial efforts were largely forgotten.

Now he returned to his church service idea, this time on film. The *Los Angeles Times* called his idea "the first instance of a religious service recorded for the screen with sound."[76] As he had done with records and radio, Rodeheaver justified his movie experiments as a way to assist small rural churches. He recruited a stellar cast of big-city religious celebrities, including Rev. Charles R. Erdman reading scripture, the Westminster Choir with John Finley Williamson, and Rodeheaver himself conducting the congregational songs.

Everyone signed on to the project except for Rodeheaver's favorite preacher. Rodeheaver tried without success to enlist Billy Sunday, making him a grandiose promise to pay all of the production expenses and then give Sunday "regular and continuous income for every reel you make."[77] But Billy Sunday deferred. Actually, he had been turning down movie offers for more than ten years, starting with a 1917 offer of $200,000 from a major studio. "It is not that I am opposed to the movies," Billy had told the *New York Times* at the time, "but I won't commercialize my mug, and don't you forget it."[78]

Rodeheaver suspected, probably correctly, that Helen Sunday was behind the rejection. "She has never been willing to help me in any plans I have suggested," Rodeheaver complained in his letter to Billy Sunday. "She has never seemed to have much confidence in my suggestions."[79] In this case, however, Helen Sunday correctly guessed how the affair would end. Rodeheaver's letter explained his plan to "show it to the ministers and find out how many would be interested in a regular service of that kind. As soon as I get this reaction I will be able to go to some of the big companies and they will be willing to finance the making of the pictures."[80]

RCA organized a preview for New York clergy, hoping to interest them in the project, but the reaction was decidedly mixed. One pastor complained about the camera work—too many shots lingered on the soprano section, "in which there were several comely maidens with enough beauty to be conspicuous."[81] Another minister ranted about too much makeup: "The next time Mr. Rodeheaver gets a choir together, tell him not to let the girls use so much lipstick."[82] Such quotes were Christmas gifts to bored newspaper editors, who were happy to run the story. The kicker came when *Variety* and *Time* referred to the film as "Canned Church Services," a name that did not help Rodeheaver's promotional efforts.[83]

Nothing became of the venture, probably because of the cost. Rodeheaver planned to rent the films to churches for $15.00 a showing, but first the churches needed to upgrade their technology to a new projector that played the "talkie" format. With a cost of $500 (roughly the same as a new Ford Model A, about $6,000 in current dollars), the new projectors were still beyond the budget of the average church. And Rodeheaver's essential premise may have been faulty—small rural churches were not clamoring for a Sunday evening service with big-city production values. His idea of community sings on film—though temporarily popular in theaters—never really took hold in churches.[84]

FINAL FILMS

In the 1950s, Homer Rodeheaver tried one more time to resurrect the community sing idea on film. By this point, California had a vibrant independent film industry, 16-mm projectors were standard equipment in churches, and the growing Youth for Christ movement seemed especially friendly to Christian movies. Rodeheaver hired California producer Cordell Fray to assist with two 15-minute features, *Rainbow Shining Somewhere* and *Then Jesus Came*. The format stayed pretty close to the community singing genre, and for that matter, felt a lot like a tabernacle revival service. Backed by Audrey Meier on piano, Rodeheaver leads the Phil Kerr Harmony Chorus in several of his well-known songs while the lyrics appear at the bottom of the screen. He picks up his trombone and plays a stanza on "Brighten the Corner" and "In the Garden," the only known examples of his playing in the color film era.[85]

Again, Rodeheaver explained the project with his familiar reasoning: "It will be designed for churches in smaller communities which have no song leader."[86] But parts of it also sound like a promotional film for the Rodeheaver Boys Ranch, his new venture in Palatka, Florida. At the end of each film he encourages the audience to consider a gift to the ranch and to contact the Rodeheaver Hall-Mack Co. for any of their church music needs. For Rodeheaver, the project was the last of his community sing film experiments. The idea was well past trendy in the 1950s, though Mitch Miller tried to resurrect it one more time with his *Sing Along with Mitch* television show, running 1961–64.

Rodeheaver's next film venture came in 1954 with a set of three one-real films produced by Westminster Films in Pasadena, California. The company was owned by a Rodeheaver friend, William E. Brusseau, who began the company in 1952 to produce religious films for missionaries.

"We had been friends with Homer for some time when he contacted us about the possibility of putting together a film," Brusseau said in a 2006 interview with the authors. Perhaps a bit skeptical and well aware of Rodeheaver's precarious health, Brusseau suggested a screen test first. Rodeheaver traveled to Pasadena in July 1954, when Brusseau shot about fifteen minutes of exterior and interior tests. "We believe that people will be happier and better if we can get them to sing together," Rodeheaver said, launching into his regular pitch about communal singing. "It's mighty hard to be mad at your neighbors when you stand and sing with them. Have you ever tried that? Well, we know that you'll be happier and better if you try it."[87] Despite his comments in the screen test, the Westminster project did not feature any group singing.

"He had very specific ideas and we filmed it and edited it just like he wanted," Brusseau said of the films. "When it was done, he seemed happy with the result."[88] Rodeheaver's very specific ideas seemed skewed toward gospel music preservation, a film record of his essential gospel song ideas. Rather than using the community song format again, Rodeheaver created each film as "real, true stories of things that have happened because of the singing of the gospel songs." After an introductory vignette about the song, Rodeheaver performed a solo rendition of it. As if the old-school vibe was not clear enough, Rodeheaver recruited the help of Alfred H. Ackley (younger brother of B. D. Ackley), who accompanied on piano. Rodeheaver ended up completing three films, though he probably intended to do more: *Miracles through Song: "Heartaches"*; *Miracles through Song: "Somebody Cares"*; and *Miracles through Song: "When Malindy Sings"* (all 1955). The last of these, *Malindy*, featured Rodeheaver's blackface performance (discussed in chapter 7).

While Rodeheaver worked on the three *Miracles* films, he also finished the principal photography for a fourth and final Westminster film, based on his book *Twenty Years with Billy Sunday*. Nearly forty years after the height of tabernacle revivalism, Rodeheaver discovered that the subject keenly interested the next generation of revivalists, especially Billy Graham, Cliff Barrows, and Youth for Christ leaders. Since the mid-1940s Rodeheaver had been hosting their summer convention at his Winona Lake hotel. Now he found himself in the role of elder statesman, with memories worth preserving on film.

When Homer Rodeheaver passed away on December 18, 1955, Brusseau was still editing *Twenty Years with Billy Sunday* and was running into an unresolved problem.[89] Rodeheaver died before finalizing a distribution plan. After scheduling a premier at the Church of the Open Door in Los Angeles for a Youth for Christ meeting, Brusseau discovered that Rodeheaver had also promised the premier to another individual—who threatened legal action if the films were shown anywhere else. "What we didn't know at the time was that Homer had promised the first showing to more than one different group," Brusseau said. "He was a sweet man and near the end of his life—I'm sure it was a memory lapse. But it became a hot potato, a real mess."[90]

Brusseau pointed out the obvious, that the small, independent Westminster Films could not afford a protracted legal dispute. "So we did nothing. The master and print sat on a shelf for the next several years, until we dissolved the assets of Westminster Films in 1963." When interviewed in 2006, the ever-tactful Brusseau did not discuss the root of his problem—Helen Sunday found out about Rodeheaver's film plans and, right on cue, launched into evasive maneuvers. Except this time, Rodeheaver was dead, and her piercing "Rody!" commands were unheeded.

J. Palmer Muntz, president of the Winona Lake Christian Assembly, found out about the flap when Westminster Films approached him about showing the film during the 1956 summer meetings. "It is my impression that Mrs. Sunday is not overly happy about the way that the preparation or the planning of it was handled," Muntz said, discreetly noting that he heeded her wishes because Mrs. Sunday was a longtime supporter of their organization.[91] Brusseau responded with a truthful summary: "It was not until after we had actually completely produced this film and Homer Rodeheaver had passed away that we learned of the friction that existed between Mrs. Sunday and Homer Rodeheaver."[92]

As later researchers would discover, Helen Sunday was not given to introspection. She kept no journals. She did not save her correspondence unless it was business. She could have written a fascinating memoir but chose not to.[93] And she could have encouraged Billy Sunday to write his own account—but instead, she continued in her role of gatekeeper. She had her reasons, starting with the new biography that William G. McLoughlin Jr. had just released, *Billy Sunday Was His Real Name*.[94] The author had been nosing around Winona Lake for several years, working on his dissertation for Princeton and then working on the book. Gradually gaining their trust, McLoughlin interviewed nearly all of Sunday's former coworkers (still living), including Rodeheaver and Helen Sunday herself. But this did not prevent McLoughlin from addressing the difficult parts of Sunday's life, including his various critics, the tragic lives of his children, and above all, the money. McLoughlin wrote a lot about the money, and if it weren't for his book, Sunday's infamous "two dollars a soul" comment might have been forgotten.

McLoughlin's book was remembered as the first scholarly biography of Billy Sunday's life, and perhaps the greatest. A neutral reader would call the book warm, engaging, and thorough. Outside of Winona Lake, it was lauded. But around town, the locals nitpicked at the mistakes and carped about the tawdry details. Helen Sunday never trusted news reporters; now she extended her skeptical stare to researchers and authors. And film producers. Rodeheaver's final film remained on William Brusseau's shelf, seen by very few people until well after Helen Sunday's death. In 1963, Brusseau sold his *Twenty Years with Billy Sunday* negative to Irvin S. (Shorty) Yeaworth, who saw value in the existing footage. Rodeheaver's vignette about his early days with Sunday did, in fact, preserve the era in Rodeheaver's own voice. Yeaworth used as much of the Rodeheaver footage as he could, releasing it in a new film called *The Billy Sunday Story* (1965).[95]

HOW TECHNOLOGY CHANGED RODEHEAVER'S MUSIC

Homer Rodeheaver's career spanned a remarkable era of change. He began singing in tent meetings and wooden tabernacles without electronic amplification. He rode horseback to his first gigs, and by the end of his life he was flying from city to city. He successfully transitioned from piano rolls and silent film to Edison cylinders to 78 r.p.m. records to radio to "talkie" films to 45 r.p.m. records to stereo LPs and color film. Not many performers in any genre can boast such a diverse résumé. Given how his life's work was advanced by technological change, it seems fair to reflect on its negative impact as well.

The gramophone and the radio caused music to lose its original context. Music was now portable and could be radically divorced from its original context.[96] It could be bought and sold as an object and then carried into work or home. So jazz music did not stay in the saloons and dance halls—it even found its way into Billy Sunday's record cabinet. For that matter, church music did not stay in church. But this new portability challenged Rodeheaver's essential rationale in maintaining a clear distinction (at least in his own mind) between tabernacle music and church music.

Rodeheaver assumed that music would remain attached to a particular time and place—but his tabernacle music didn't stay in the tabernacle. He partly envisioned the consequence, how recordings might be bought and sold and exported around the world, and how recordings might be used in a Sunday evening service. But he failed to predict how easily his "cheer up" gospel songs could be transported straight into a worship service, replacing the standard hymnody he intended to preserve. And now that his gospel songs were fully portable, the artist had no control of his creation. Disconnected from their original context, his gospel songs could be dropped into the soundtrack for *Birth of a Nation* or repurposed as hymns to the Ku Klux Klan. When he started his own record label, Rodeheaver would soon understand the consequences of this idea.

6

THE MISSION OF RAINBOW RECORDS

"A LARGER AND MORE REPRESENTATIVE SELECTION OF GOSPEL SONGS"

In August 1920, Homer Rodeheaver set up a temporary studio in Winona Lake, his first attempt at recording his own material on his own record label.[1] Rodeheaver started with a favorite, "Safe in the Arms of Jesus," featuring a trombone solo, a vocal from his half-sister Ruth, and the famous piano chime effect that tabernacle audiences loved. Insiders understood that his song choice was not accidental; he had tried to record this song for Victor in 1913 and 1916, both times rejected, but now he was making the decisions himself. And he was charting new territory, creating the first record label devoted to gospel music.

The August recording sessions coincided with his Song Director's Conference, a two-week event that gathered many of the musicians Rodeheaver had met during his fifteen years on the revival circuit.[2] As always, Rodeheaver was thinking about the future, and dreaming about ways to harness the new technology to further the cause of gospel music. Over the next two weeks he recorded more than fifty sides, thirteen of which featured his own solo repertoire. The balance of the material demonstrated a wide variety of gospel music: solos, duets, male quartets, mixed quartets, spoken word recitations, piano solos, and a few sermons. He capped the August recording sessions by inviting everyone to participate in a mass choir recording session, a somewhat futile attempt at capturing 600 voices with his new acoustic recording system.

By September, Rodeheaver had nailed down the key decisions about Rainbow records, though the exact details are lost to time. Who pressed the early records? Unknown. Who printed his first labels? Unknown. Where did Rodeheaver

FIGURE 6.1. Rodeheaver recording at his Chicago studio with the Smith-Spring-Holmes Orchestra, c. 1922. Courtesy of Rodeheaver Collection, Grace College, Winona Lake.

purchase his equipment, and who engineered his early sessions? Also unknown, though we will offer a theory later in the chapter. Small scraps of the story can be gleaned from the scant documents that remain. By November, Rodeheaver had incorporated a new company known as the Rodeheaver Record Co., vested with $50,000 in capital. He had invited other investors to join in the partnership, as reported when the *Syracuse Herald* found out about possible local participants.[3] But the final list may have been closer to home—in his 1923 pocket planner, Rodeheaver penciled a note about two "Record Co. Investors," Grace Saxe ($5,500) and Florence Hay ($600). Saxe was Rodeheaver's longtime friend from the Billy Sunday team; Florence Hay was an illustrator who often drew while Saxe gave a Bible lesson.[4]

In November 1920, the first shipment of records (from the August sessions) arrived for distribution.[5] The new company prepared catalogs and ads for the Christmas season, and the Rodeheaver Record Co. listed a recording laboratory in Winona Lake, along with sales offices in Chicago and Philadelphia.[6] His ads may have been optimistic—the recording laboratory was at least planned, but no evidence exists to show it was operating yet. This much is certain: In 1920, Rodeheaver started a company, recorded at least 50 sides, arranged for vendors to produce the initial inventory, released a catalog and ads, and sold his first recordings. In a field glutted with "first" claims, no gospel label can claim to have started earlier.

RAINBOW AND VAUGHAN RECORDS

With the first recording sessions in August 1920 and the first releases in October 1920, the Rodeheaver Record Company began several months before Vaughan Records of Lawrenceville, Tennessee. Sometime in March or April of 1921, the Vaughan quartet traveled to Cincinnati and recorded jubilee-style arrangements of "Steal Away" and "Couldn't Hear Nobody Pray."[7] The Vaughan recordings became an important milestone in gospel music; in fact, Tony Russell uses their sessions to mark the start of his well-respected country music discography.[8] Still, very little is known about their early sessions, and until now, no one could say for sure where they were made. This much is known—the Vaughans did not record anything prior to spring 1921, at least seven months after Rodeheaver's initial efforts with Rainbow.[9] More to the point, the Vaughans actually made their first records with Rodeheaver's equipment, explored here in a moment. The two companies became enormously important to the development of American roots music, but neither one left documentation of its early years, leading to several decades of conflicting claims and misinformation about their history. Our account here seeks to resolve the confusion and to document the working relationship between Rodeheaver and Vaughan.

Their association began in 1920, when Rodeheaver invited a full complement of instructors and vocal groups to his summer Song Director's Conference. The guest list included the colorful Rev. Adlai Loudy, who had traveled for several southern publishers and later with the Chapman/Alexander evangelistic team.[10] Loudy possessed a robust, resonant tenor voice, honed in southern singing schools, but operatic in quality. Newspapers called him The Dixie Caruso. That was the normal part. Newspapers also called him The Samson of the Age, because at 27 he looked like a circus strongman, flaunting an almost comical, musclebound physique. As an ordained minister who favored tight-fitting t-shirts, Loudy often opened his sermons by bending an 80-penny nail or tearing a deck of cards in half with his bare hands.[11]

As a featured speaker at Rodeheaver's 1920 conference, Loudy was so well received that he ended up lecturing at the conference for several years running, teaching the musicians to improve their physical health and stamina.[12] Rodeheaver also recruited Loudy to sing in his ad-hoc Rainbow Quartet, which recorded "The Church in the Wildwood" and "Just Outside the Door" for the 1920 Rainbow releases. The all-star Rainbow Quartet included Dr. Frederick Martin, basso of the Metropolitan Opera Company; Homer Rodeheaver, baritone; Loudy as second tenor and soloist, and Dan Beddoe, noted Welsh recording artist, singing first tenor.[13] The early Rainbow Quartet borrowed from the southern tradition of publisher-sponsored male quartets, albeit with voices more suited to the opera stage. And the Rainbow Quartet had more than a conceptual similarity to the Vaughan group—the two groups were sharing the same tenor, Rev. Adlai Loudy, who sang with both quartets.

After his 1916 ordination in the Christian church, Loudy traveled to New York for further voice study, followed by a teaching appointment at James D. Vaughan's School of Music, Lawrenceburg, Tennessee. There he met Virgil O. Stamps and was asked to tour with Vaughan's National Quartet. After traveling by himself to Rodeheaver's 1920 conference and helping launch one gospel label, Loudy then returned home to help Vaughan launch another. They all meet Rodeheaver in Cincinnati the next spring, but in the meantime, Rodeheaver had many decisions to make.

TECHNOLOGY CONSIDERATIONS

Rodeheaver's decision to start a new record label turned out to be well timed. For two decades the American recording industry had been controlled by a coterie of companies in the New York–Philadelphia corridor. The period, known as the acoustical era, featured musicians who played directly in front of an acoustical horn while the record groove was cut into rotating wax blanks by a mechanical lathe. For a time, companies competed over various formats: cylinder vs. disc, vertical cut vs. lateral, recorded at several competing speeds with proprietary shellac formulas. Victor and Columbia settled a potential patent war with a new production agreement, charging everyone else royalty and solidifying the consensus for lateral-cut discs. Meanwhile, Thomas Edison continued with his vertical cut Diamond Disc, marketed as a better-sounding audiophile product.

By the time Rodeheaver began his label, the format wars were over, as was the East Coast monopoly. In 1917, the Starr Piano Company of Richmond, Indiana, retooled its factory equipment to manufacture phonograph cabinets, then started a new record label, Gennett. A few months later the Wisconsin Chair Factory in Port Washington, Wisconsin, began building record player cabinets, then started Paramount Records. Soon these new "indie" labels were joined by Rodeheaver, who did business with both companies.

CHAPTER 6

ECONOMIC CONSIDERATIONS

In addition to the technological considerations of recording formats, Rodeheaver also had to consider the national economic outlook, which was surprisingly bleak. A hundred years later, most readers have forgotten that the Roaring Twenties actually started with an economic recession, officially lasting from January 1920 to June 1921—the exact period when Rodeheaver was trying to start a new business venture. Economists still refer to the period as the Forgotten Depression and blame several forces: a spike in the labor force as soldiers returned home from the war, labor unrest, and inept monetary policy from the new Federal Reserve system. The recession was marked by rapid deflation and significant declines in industrial production. This national trend can also be seen in a drop in Rodeheaver's personal income. In his pocket planners, he listed an annual income of $32,733 for 1921 and $21,569 for 1922, a drop of about 35 percent.[14] The economic decline hit the recording industry a bit later than other industries, but when it came, it hit hard. Columbia was caught by overproduction and internal stock speculation, leading to a $2.3 million loss in 1921. Victor floundered more slowly and in 1925 failed to pay stock dividends for the first time since 1901. Edison, already the loser of the format war, would soon close his label.

What seemed like economic challenges also offered opportunity, especially to the upstart labels in the Midwest. As the East Coast companies laid off longtime workers, the new independent labels hired them and benefited from their industry experience (the reason why Rodeheaver successfully attracted so many industry veterans). As smaller East Coast companies were forced out of business, their equipment could be purchased cheaply (which is how Starr purchased its first recording machines, and perhaps how Rodeheaver did too). As long as the new independent labels had sufficient cash to weather a slow start (and Rodeheaver did), the future looked positive. Two years after Rainbow's start, a company catalog declared that "Homer Rodeheaver has made possible the success of the Gospel Song Record through the expenditure of vast sums of money and an untiring devotion to the cause."[15] Both were true—requiring a closer look at "the cause" that motivated Rodeheaver.

THE IDEA OF A CHRISTIAN RECORD LABEL

Technical and financial matters aside, Rodeheaver's record company venture was fueled by a basic idea. He viewed his record company as a mission, which he explained with evangelistic zeal whenever possible. By 1920 Rodeheaver understood that the heyday of tabernacle revivalism was over. He believed that the future of communal singing would be advanced by new technology, leading to experiments with piano rolls, recording, radio, and film. Rodeheaver also believed that the future of communal singing depended on a song style deliberately crafted for group singing. But after a plum career where he recorded with all of the big three record companies (Victor, Edison, Columbia) and a half-dozen smaller ones, he had not yet found a company that fully embraced his ethos. So once again he prepared to bypass the institutional gatekeepers. Rodeheaver had started his career with an end run around church leaders who opposed his gospel songs. Now his gospel hymnal sat side-by-side in the same pew rack as the official denominational hymnal. So he tried it again, aiming for a new record label that would exist side-by-side with the big three recording companies, all in the same record cabinet.

His campaign for a new record label started like many marketing projects—he created a need, a problem, and appealed directly to the evangelical network that became his customers. In 1920, he began using his personal column in *Rodeheaver's Musical News* as a pulpit for the project. He complained about the large companies who were "thousands and thousands of records behind with their orders" and awash in popular songs of the day, which he further demonized as "jazz music which can be furnished to the people who want to dance." He complained that "the big companies" weren't making any effort at all to supply the pent-up demand for gospel song recordings. And having worked with them for the past seven years, Rodeheaver had concluded the "large Eastern companies ... will not likely be willing or able to supply this demand." Rodeheaver now felt a burden to "counteract, in a way at least, the tremendous wave of popular songs." Sounding like a Lowell Mason disciple preaching the doctrine of musical uplift, Rodeheaver called for "a better grade of music," by which he meant his gospel songs.[16]

After stating the problem, Rodeheaver pitched a solution: "Would it not be possible to organize a company to record and manufacture sacred song records, exclusively?" After establishing the "large Eastern companies" as a bogeyman, Rodeheaver suggested a new midwestern record company, where "some of the splendid singers of the Middle West and the Southern states who would never have a chance to be heard otherwise could be given a chance to record some of their songs."[17]

Rodeheaver used his new enterprise to enforce boundaries between the evangelical musicians and the "professional singers who do not care anything about the songs they sing, except for the money they get for it." Instead, he promised songs "recorded only by people who really believe in what they sing."[18] He explained his efforts using the ministry language of Protestant evangelicals; but in secular terms, he was also defining the limits of a new genre. He avoided the generic *sacred* or *religious* designations used by record companies, terms so broad as to be meaningless. Rodeheaver intended to showcase the entire spectrum of *gospel music*, which he defined with an ideological boundary, as gospel texts sung by true believers. At the same time, he did not impose the boundaries of a particular musical style, a point that mystified the secular labels and continues to confound some researchers.

As if to anticipate any possible concerns about profiteering (a charge he frequently heard about his hymnals), Rodeheaver promised to "set aside a certain percentage of the proceeds to go for the training of young men and young women for religious work." His recording laboratory could become a tool for training the next generation of revival musicians, part of a summer institute that developed a self-perpetuating stream of young people who supplied "a constantly growing demand which would spread the Gospel message in song."[19] In subsequent advertising copy, the Rodeheaver Co. also continued to emphasize their core market of "little churches in out-of-the-way sections which do not have a preacher" who could purchase a record player for their church auditorium, and thus "conduct an entire service with the best music and best preaching possible to secure."[20]

Such was Rodeheaver's rationale for a new record company, as stated just before his 1920 summer recording sessions. Read today, his article also sounds like optimistic advertising copy; and to be sure, he pulled out all of the stops when marketing his new business. Established as a subsidiary of the Rodeheaver Co., the Rodeheaver Record Co. used a variation of the rainbow logo that Rodeheaver had been using on his hymnals since 1917. The original 1920 version of the label used the name Rainbow Sacred Records; later versions simplified this to Rainbow Records.[21] By late 1921, the label design was truly spectacular, a rainbow printed in four colors with a ring of gold metallic ink.

As a side benefit, rainbows were trendy, a 1920s trope. But choosing a popular name also caused problems for later researchers. Not only was *rainbow* used for

FIGURE 6.2. Rodeheaver's first issue on his Rainbow label, 1920.

FIGURE 6.3. Rainbow Sacred Records catalog, 1920.

various 1920s products and services, it also became the name of other record companies. In 1947, Eddie Heller started the Rainbow Recording Corporation in New York, featuring Latin and doo-wop groups. Heller apparently had no idea that an earlier label had used the same Rainbow name, or that Rodeheaver had restarted his version of the label in the mid-1940s. The two companies took a live-and-let-live approach to the brand confusion.[22]

RODEHEAVER COMPANY EXPANSION

Understanding that he would rarely be in Chicago long enough to run the company, Rodeheaver recruited Edwin H. Forkel to become general manager of Rainbow Records, starting on January 1, 1921. His hire was somewhat of a coup, Forkel having worked for the Methodist Book Concern for 25 years, where he became a fast friend of Rodeheaver's editor, Charles Gabriel. In addition to his business experience, Forkel was well connected to various causes and served as choir director at Washington Boulevard Methodist Church in Oak Park.[23] Though he had a stellar business reputation, he had no experience in managing a record company.

Rodeheaver also recruited L. E. Gillingham as recording engineer, whose résumé included 18 years at Victor Records, then Aeolian, and at some point, Columbia. Eventually he joined Rodeheaver full time, but for now Gillingham freelanced on Rodeheaver's projects. For instance, Rodeheaver reported that Gillingham had taken the recording machine to Nashville in May 1921, with the intention of making records of the "genuine old plantation songs" as sung by the student body of Fisk University. Rodeheaver's subsequent report offers several surprises.[24] First, though the Fisk Jubilee Singers have been thoroughly studied, no one has mentioned these sessions. Second, Rodeheaver's interest was not actually with the Jubilee Singers; rather, he wanted to capture a chapel service with "this wonderful body of negro singers in their own auditorium. This gives us a more nearly absolute correct idea of the genuine negro spiritual than can possibly be done by just a small group of singers." From his previous visits, Rodeheaver believed the congregational singing of spirituals sounded demonstrably different ("a more nearly absolute correct idea") than the well-known concert renditions performed by the Jubilee Singers.[25] Third, the audacity of Rodeheaver's idea, an engineer who traveled around with recording equipment for what amounted to field work by an amateur ethnomusicologist, was several years ahead of its time. But alas—as exciting as his Fisk University project might seem, the field recordings were apparently a failure. After Rodeheaver's enthusiastic announcement, none of the recordings were released.

Rodeheaver's reference to the 1921 Fisk sessions helps us better understand his activities in April and May, during the Cincinnati revival meetings with Billy Sunday. Rodeheaver had arranged for recording equipment to be shipped to Cincinnati, where his recording engineer set up a temporary recording laboratory. David Lewis later documented their output: perhaps as many as 100 sides recorded, including 23 that were added to the Rainbow catalog.[26] Some of the Cincinnati recordings are uniquely important documentation of tabernacle revivalism, especially Rodeheaver's continued attempts to record mass singing.

At this point we can solve the mystery about the earliest Vaughan recordings. Researchers knew that the Vaughans had traveled somewhere in 1921 for their first quartet recordings; for a time, this was thought to be Paramount Records in Port Washington, Wisconsin.[27] But then David Lewis matched the matrix numbers on the Vaughan records to the known series of Rainbow numbers used for the Cincinnati sessions, placing the Vaughans with Rodeheaver in April or May 1921.[28]

In Cincinnati, Rodeheaver also continued his usual practice of visiting local record dealers, holding recitals, and plugging his records. Though he now operated

FIGURE 6.4. Advertisement for an early recording demonstration in Cincinnati, 1921. Reprinted from the *Cincinnati Enquirer*.

his own independent label, Rodeheaver continued to promote his big-label recordings, to the appreciation of local dealers.[29] But bringing his own equipment to Cincinnati allowed him to go one step further, scheduling a recording demonstration at Shillito's department store. Along with Virginia Asher and pianist Robert Matthews, he made about a dozen test records while an audience listened to a lecture about recording science.[30]

The Cincinnati events also allow us to piece together more of the early Rainbow Records technical history. It seems likely that L. E. Gillingham served as recording engineer for the Cincinnati sessions and then immediately left for Nashville to record the Fisk group.[31] Perhaps Rodeheaver did not even own his own equipment. He had no known Rainbow sessions between the end of the 1920 Songleaders Conference and the start of the 1921 Cincinnati meetings. His Winona Lake studio existed only in advertising copy.[32] Gillingham (and the equipment) returned to Winona Lake in August 1921 for the next Song Director's Conference. In the June 1921 issue of the *Gospel Choir*, Rodeheaver promised, "We will establish our laboratory at Winona Lake during June, July and August," an interesting phrase that seems to indicate its temporary nature. He also promised to record "outside individuals who want individual, personal records." He further mentioned a new relationship for pressing the records, which seems to confirm that he used an outside vendor to produce his 1921 output.[33]

The quality of the 1920–21 Rainbows was decidedly mediocre for the era. Rodeheaver obliquely acknowledged the problem by saying, "Some of our first production were not as satisfactory as we had hoped, although we have ten or twelve numbers which we believe to be just as good as any others that can be secured. We are planning to remake the ones which are not entirely satisfactory."[34] Several reasons for this might be offered. Rodeheaver's equipment may have been inferior—perhaps even rented or secondhand. His pressings, whoever did them, were certainly low budget. And Rodeheaver kept a lot of takes that the big companies would have rejected. He took risks, such as the trips to Cincinnati and Nashville, driven by his passion to record the tabernacle experience. For Rodeheaver, capturing the moment on record was more important that its audiophile quality.

COMMUNAL SINGING RECORDS

Rodeheaver developed commercial recordings to teach congregational singing in churches, an idea strongly influenced by music educators with similar interests. Peter Dykema led a group of Progressive-era music educators who advocated community singing as a way to create social uplift and a shared musical culture. Using mass-produced booklets like *18 Songs for Community Singing*, their movement can be seen as a secular alternative to Rodeheaver's tabernacle sings.[35]

In 1916, the Victor Band recorded "Drink to Me Only with Thine Eyes" and "Flow Gently, Sweet Afton," with Victor ledgers noting that the music came straight from *18 Songs*.[36] Deliberately produced for Dykema's home and community sing-alongs, the recordings feature straightforward performances that sound oddly incomplete unless one considers that the singing voices are supplied by those listening around the Victrola horn. The sing-along trend continued for a dozen years, marketed in music education journals with ads that described the "stirring band accompaniment" as "strong, correct, inspiring."[37] By 1921, Columbia promoted a competing line of accompaniment records "that get everybody singing the minute they start to play. You no longer need a piano, an accompanist, or a leader."[38]

As the trend peaked in May 1921, Rodeheaver hired Thomas P. Ratcliff to help with a similar effort for Rainbow, recruiting an industry veteran who had produced Victor's community sing records. *Talking Machine World* played up Ratcliff's "thorough knowledge of the educational possibilities of the record field" and predicted he would do the same for Rodeheaver.[39] Radcliff immediately created ads and catalogs to market Rodeheaver's gospel song records with the same selling points as the community singing records. "How Rainbow Records Can Improve Your Congregational Singing," blared one headline, which then asked, "How would you like to have your congregations taught how to sing by Homer Rodeheaver?"[40] The advertisements promised the same "correct" renditions, framed as "real vocal demonstration of the correct rhythm, expression and interpretation to be employed to make your singing of gospel songs what it ought to be." As far as Rodeheaver was concerned, every church ought to buy a talking machine. And for churches without a choir or competent soloists, "Rainbow Records will provide the well-rendered solo, duet, male quartette, or other special selection which will save the service from that drab atmosphere which attends a service without special singing."[41]

Ratcliff's hire gave Rodeheaver the impetus for opening a New York office at 219 East 39th Street—Ratcliff worked from New York and sometimes traveled to Chicago for sessions. The New York office gave Rodeheaver a presence at the epicenter of the recording industry, important for now, but ultimately a short-term priority. While Ratcliff significantly shaped the label's promotion and industry presence, he did not stay with Rodeheaver much more than a year. In 1922, he moved back to London, where he continued his interest in community singing. Today he is most remembered for a community singing tradition he inaugurated at Wembley Stadium in 1927, the singing of "Abide with Me" before the Football Association Challenge Cup Final.[42]

1921 SONG DIRECTOR'S CONFERENCE

With the record company enjoying a successful launch, Rodeheaver spent the spring of 1921 promoting his summer Song Director's Conference. Rodeheaver viewed his conference as the natural successor to the singing schools he attended as a youth, using modern techniques to train evangelistic singers, songleaders, and church musicians. Among others, Rodeheaver invited the Vaughan quartet to appear, with Adlai Loudy singing in two quartets, Vaughan's and Rodeheaver's.

Vaughan and Rodeheaver agreed about the value of gospel songs for communal singing, though they approached it from somewhat different perspectives. Both men were interested in musical literacy, both believed that part singing produced the most robust communal singing, both produced songbooks that emphasized four-part vocal harmony. Rodeheaver aimed for the revival tabernacle audience, and frequently spoke of bridging the gap between secular life and personal religious transformation (his overall goal), which ultimately led to greater attendance at Sunday worship services. Vaughan started from a different place. Rather than the revival tabernacle, he aimed at the southern tradition of All-Day Singings, where families gathered in community public spaces to sing from shape note songbooks. As such, Vaughan was an evangelist for the shape note system of sight singing.

When the Vaughan quartet had recorded the first sides in Cincinnati, earlier that spring, they performed "Steal Away" and "Couldn't Hear Nobody Pray" straight from the just-released *Vaughan's Concert Quartet Book for Male Voices*.[43] Though he intended his quartets to teach the principles of sight singing and demonstrate his new songs, Vaughan understood that their performances were becoming popular in and of themselves, creating a new market for a different kind of quartet book. When the Vaughans recorded songs from his *Concert Quartet Book,* they were singing from a new type of product geared for the concert stage—the audience would not sing along with the quartet's increasingly complicated musical arrangements. Vaughan was by no means the only publisher to follow this path. Other southern hymnal publishers started their own quartets and quartet-oriented publications; soon the south was awash with professional singing groups who competed for market share. Historian Don Cusic used the 1941 death of James D. Vaughan to mark the end of southern gospel's first era, a convenient milestone for a transition already in progress. The All-Day Singings morphed into All-Night Sings, a new concert format organized by Wally Fowler in 1948. The original idea of a hymnal-based community songfest disappeared for the southern publishers. Rodeheaver, however, continued with his assumption that the new technology would encourage communal singing.

WINONA LAKE

One thing was clear—Rodeheaver pulled out all of the stops for the 1921 Song Director's Conference in Winona Lake. After the 1920 summer events, Rodeheaver made several bold moves. First, he formed a partnership with evangelist Mel Trotter to purchase the Winona Hotel, the famed gateway property to Winona Lake. Next, he remodeled the entire building, installed 50 private bathrooms, and generally prepared for an influx of guests the next summer. He also agreed to purchase the Westminster Hotel from a cash-strapped Presbyterian group, a building that became home to the Rodeheaver Co. And he bought the Mount Memorial building, where he talked about a recording laboratory for Rainbow Records. His Winona Lake buying spree had a certain logic to it. First, Rodeheaver's hymnal business made him wealthy. How wealthy? No one really knew, but everyone noticed that he paid for his real estate deals with cash. Second, Winona Lake's summer events created their own hospitality industry, which Rodeheaver now controlled by snapping up 75 percent of Winona Lake's hotel rooms. His stepmother, Bettie Rodeheaver, had done a fine job managing his smaller lodges around town; now her responsibilities would expand. And one more footnote made the transactions seem sensible: In 1920, the conference trustees had completed a giant tabernacle building and were scheduling a full slate of events for 1921, including a national Presbyterian conference.

For the final day of his 1921 conference, Rodeheaver planned to fill the new tabernacle for a gigantic concert. And the stellar musical guests also worked in the afternoons to make "a great list of new records," ensuring that Rainbow had "the greatest list of sacred songs that can possibly be secured anywhere in the world."[44] Rodeheaver also planned to use the Winona Lake recording laboratory for classroom instruction at the summer school. "There is a tremendous advantage to students in hearing their own work on the records," Rodeheaver said. "Certain errors and deficiencies can be corrected more easily if a student can hear the tone as the teacher teaches it."[45]

Ever the visionary, Rodeheaver's years of tabernacle revivals had also taught him the need for administrative talent, which he found in his brother, Joseph. After finishing his PhD at Boston University, Joe taught in South Dakota and then at the Iliff School of Theology in Denver. But his wife, Erma May Bashford, died in February 1920 after an extended illness. In 1921, Homer created a position for Joe as special consultant to the Rodeheaver Co. Joe began spending his summers in Winona Lake, where he served as dean of the Winona Lake summer school. Yumbert also drove down from Chicago for much of the summer, though he rarely appeared on the platform or taught classes. All three of the brothers remained close. Having grown up working together in their father's sawmills, they had no trouble working together in the family business.

Homer Rodeheaver capped off his preparations with a splashy entrance. On July 20, 1921, he arrived in Winona Lake in his new airplane, piloted by war hero Lt. Lynn D. Merrill. They had left Cincinnati about two hours earlier in true barnstorming style, flying over several Indiana towns and dropping Rainbow Records leaflets. Once they landed in Winona Lake, Rodeheaver planned to give the airplane a custom paint job, complete with Rainbow Records logo.

Guests began arriving at the Song Director's Conference, including the Vaughan quartet. Kieffer Vaughan also traveled with the group, having joined his father's company in 1918.[46] His ongoing music education included several months of lessons with Oscar Saenger of New York, the Victor recording artist who also taught Rodeheaver. Everyone understood that Kieffer was being groomed as Vaughan's next president, a position he assumed when his father died in 1941. A talented singer, teacher, and gospel songwriter, Kieffer later became mayor of Lawrenceburg, Tennessee, and president of the National Singing Convention—a worthy successor to his father's empire.

The question of successors had probably occurred to Homer Rodeheaver, now 40 years old, unmarried, and childless. He was paying for his half-sister, Ruth, to study music at Ohio Wesleyan University. And he paid for his half-brother, Jack, to attend a Chicago business prep school, living with Yumbert and working part-time at the Chicago office. While he was in high school, Jack also traveled to a few of the Sunday meetings, singing in a quartet with Homer and other staff members. The exact role Jack might have had in the Rodeheaver Co. or in Rainbow Records will never be known—this was the same summer as the tragic airplane accident that took his life at age 18. On the afternoon of August 25, members of the Vaughan

Quartet were playing a round of golf when they saw the plane overhead, flying close enough that they could witness Lynn D. Merrill's tragic fall and then Jack's upside-down plunge into the cornfield near the golf course (recounted more fully in chapter 5). Keiffer Vaughan started running and arrived at the crash scene first, a detail recalled by Stella Vaughan years later.[47] But there was nothing he could do—Jack was dead.

The conference did not end with its promised concert on August 27, which was supposed to feature the quartets and Rainbow Records artists. With a quick change in plans, the new tabernacle was instead used for Jack's funeral, attended by several thousand. And Rodeheaver was on the front page of the newspaper again—with a crash-site photo, three columns wide. In a perverse twist, the only thing recognizable in the wreckage was a crumpled wing and the words "Rainbow Records."

Gospel music would always have its tragic stories—the 1954 Blackwood Brothers plane crash comes to mind—and gospel performers have always managed to channel these moments into life-affirming music. Perhaps his friends waited for such a response from Homer Rodeheaver. Friends and supporters expected a new song, maybe a tribute recording, maybe a special page in the *Gospel Choir*, but nothing appeared.[48]

OFFICES IN NEW YORK AND CHICAGO

Six weeks after the airplane accident, the Rodeheaver Record Co. continued its business expansion by moving its New York office to 150 E. 41st Street. The New York recordings were to be supervised by C. R. "Johnnie" Johnston, a longtime Edison engineer who had recorded Florence Nightingale in 1888. The New York venture did not last long, open for about a year in 1921–22. Gillingham and Johnston are both known to have worked there, though one suspects their participation may have been part-time. According to *Talking Machine World*, the permanent laboratories of the company would still be maintained in Winona Lake, a claim that seems to be just the opposite of what happened. The popular summer resort was a hotbed of activity for precisely three months during the summer, a good place for a pop-up studio, but precious little happened the rest of the year. Rodeheaver's huge investment in recording equipment would be successful if he could keep the studio busy year-round, but this was impossible in Winona Lake.[49]

Instead, Rodeheaver made plans for a Chicago studio, which precipitated his move from his longtime offices in the Monon Building (440 S. Dearborn St.) to the McClurg Building (218 S. Wabash Ave.). He leased the entire sixth floor of the building and constructed publishing offices, stock rooms, and a recording studio, where Rodeheaver's recording equipment finally had a permanent home.[50]

In the first year of operation, starting in August 1921, Rodeheaver's equipment had moved at least three times for location recordings: the August 1920 Winona Lake sessions, the April 1921 Cincinnati sessions, the May 1921 Nashville sessions, and now the final move to Chicago in November 1921. For the first three location sessions, L. E. Gillingham traveled from New York to operate the equipment. When the Chicago studio opened in November 1921, Thomas P. Ratcliff visited from the New York office to engineer the first studio sessions.[51] Rodeheaver and several musical guests recorded fifty new sides for release on the Rainbow label, plus additional custom recordings with different branding.

THE SPECIAL LABEL

Discographers and collectors have long been interested in Rodeheaver's Special label, the custom division of Rainbow Records. The recordings released on the Special label are some of the most obscure records of the 1920s; no ledger or published catalog is known to exist for it, and no one is quite sure how many recordings were produced.

Rodeheaver's Special label possibly started in the summer of 1921 in Winona Lake, where Rodeheaver had promised to do "recording for outside individuals, who want individual, personal records."[52] More certainly, the label was up and running when Rodeheaver opened his Chicago studio in November 1921, when Thomas P. Ratcliff engineered the inaugural sessions. In addition to recording his own material for Rainbow, Rodeheaver also reported recording 56 numbers "for private individuals who wanted these records for Christmas gift purposes."[53]

The idea itself was not new. Columbia started a personal label in 1915, marketing its services to ordinary people who wanted to make recordings. But the Columbia process was not cheap. Columbia charged $1 each for the first 50 records, plus the cost of recording the master, at least another $50. So a modest run of 50 records might cost $2 each (about $25 each in today's dollars, pricey by any standard). "This was essentially a vanity business," says the researcher Tim Brooks, who noted that Columbia's chief customers were "churches and other religious groups, along with an occasional lodge or corporation that wanted a recording for promotional purposes."[54]

Rodeheaver described his Special customers in essentially the same terms, promising to record "songs, sermons, speeches, lectures, lessons, or any other subject." He suggested commercial applications such as "heart-to-heart talks to division executives and branch managers." And he encouraged local pastors to record their sermons, because church members would "treasure and repeat them for years to come."[55] His suggestion proved to be a radical development—until now, sermons could be preserved only by stenographers. Now every nuance of

> **HEAR YOURSELF**
> AS OTHERS HEAR YOU
>
> An opportunity long sought is now offered to all music lovers of Chicago and vicinity.
> We have just opened a modern
>
> **Recording Laboratory**
>
> where songs, readings and instrumental selections can be reproduced for phonograph records.
> An invitation is extended to all readers to call on us, where interviews will be cheerfully given on Private Recording.
>
> **The Rodeheaver Record Co.**
> 6th Floor, McClurg Bldg.
> 218 S. Wabash Avenue, Chicago

FIGURE 6.5. Advertisement for Rodeheaver's custom recording division, 1923. Reprinted from the *Music News*.

sermonic delivery could be preserved on record. Rodeheaver immediately suggested obvious applications for the idea, such as sermons for elderly shut-ins or sermons for churches without a minister. But another application, unmentioned for now, had a significant impact on twentieth-century preaching. The commodified sermons could now be packaged and sold, just like the gospel music.

Rodeheaver's production prices were somewhat lower than Columbia's, only 50 cents each for the first 50 records, plus $65 for the master recording. But even at these rates the process was expensive, $1.80 per record in an era when commercial recordings sold for 75 cents or $1.00. In other words, Rodeheaver's Special label was not yet a viable alternative for people who wanted to produce short runs and resell the recordings at a markup. The numbers just didn't add up. But for those who viewed the act of recording as preservation, or for those with altruistic notions of ministry, the idea could be attractive.[56]

The ads for Rodeheaver's Special label boasted that "music of every kind can be recorded."[57] Some recording artists fit neatly into Rodeheaver's conception of gospel music, such as Oscar W. Green, the Swedish baritone and professor of voice at North Park College who sang "O Kunde Jag Förtälja" (Special unnumbered) in Swedish. Henry Hugh Proctor, the African American pastor that Rodeheaver befriended during their 1917 Atlanta meetings, recorded his "Address to Negroes of America" (Special 2017); this was paired with the Nazarene Congregational Church Choir of Brooklyn singing "Lift Every Voice and Sing." At its best, the

Special label gave voice to individuals and groups who had no access to the big recording companies.

Some of the recording artists represented community music groups who had no personal relationship with Rodeheaver. The Ames Quartet, a college group from Iowa State University, sang "Sing Me a Song of Iowa State," "The Loyal Boosters," and "Fight, Ames, Fight" (Special 5089); the Chicago Newsboys Band recorded several marches (Special unnumbered); Eleanor H. Rosen played "School Days" as dance music for Chicago's R. G. Huntinghouse Dancing Academy (Special 2017-B). Again, for groups such as this, the Rodeheaver studio was one of the few places in the Midwest where they walk in off the street and cut a record.

Some of the Special recordings featured performers who seem fairly distant from Rodeheaver's own views, such as Bhagat Singh Thind, who recorded lectures on Sikh religious philosophy: "'Aum,' the Sacred Hum of the Universe" (Special 20115A) and "Purifying the Sub-Conscious Mind" (Special 20115B). One might ask why the Rodeheaver Co. allowed groups such as this to have access to their studios. No clear answer exists (other than the obvious default: there was money to be made). The question becomes more pointed with the discovery of several Ku Klux Klan–related projects on the Special label—a perplexing incident explored in chapter 8.

GENRE FORMATION IN THE RECORDING INDUSTRY

Rodeheaver's distribution network expanded in early 1922 as several large dealers signed on, such as Cabinet & Accessories Co. in New York, and A. J. Heath & Co. in Philadelphia and Baltimore.[58] Rodeheaver also recruited Sue Hewling from the Martin Band Instrument Co. for sales to the Chicago region, a territory she knew well.[59] His regular announcements in trade journals such as *Talking Machine World* also signaled another milestone—the industry was taking him seriously. Rodeheaver rightly took credit for a market reaction, where the big East Coast companies were now adding more sacred material to their catalogs: "Since Rainbow Records have been announced," Rodeheaver observed, "nearly all the other large companies have been supplying their dealers with gospel song records in greater number than they have ever been willing to supply before."[60] Something else was afoot.

Much later, researchers pointed to the early 1920s as a milestone, the moment when American vernacular music separated into distinct genres. Everyone understood how *jazz* became a catch-all term for popular music, especially dance music. Suddenly the midwestern companies like Gennett, Okeh, and Paramount, were recording and classifying music in categories such as *race* (jazz, blues, and other African American idioms), *hillbilly* (country, Appalachian folk, western swing, bluegrass), and *foreign* (nearly every immigrant group).[61] By any objective standard, Rodeheaver's genre could have been recognized as a fourth. The established labels on the East Coast suddenly found themselves outpaced by smaller competitors who used these labels to brand different categories of music for specific audiences—linking aesthetic styles with related social attitudes and beliefs connected to the music.[62] To catch up with the midwestern record labels, the East Coast companies began recording a wider variety of music, which was then advertised in different catalogs for each emerging genre.

This idea—still a matter of continuing research—is of interest here because of the way it illuminates Rodeheaver's mission. If read in the context of an era when race, hillbilly, and jazz genres were formed, Rodeheaver's statements help today's reader understand his intentions more clearly. Rodeheaver was deliberately and consciously creating a fourth distinct musical genre, the gospel music record.

"This is one of the reasons we have been so anxious to get more of our beautiful, practical gospel songs on phonograph records," Rodeheaver explained, positioning his gospel records in opposition to other emerging genres. "For so long the production has been centered in such a big percentage on the popular and jazz music that . . . it has been entirely impossible in some localities to secure sacred records and especially good gospel song records."[63] For Rodeheaver, establishing the viability of gospel music as a genre was more important than the success of his own label. Now that the industry leaders were marketing their own line of gospel song recordings, "we will all rejoice that they will be able to hear them in some way," even if it competed against Rainbow.[64]

Right on cue, *Talking Machine World* picked up on the religious music trend, though they didn't quite know how to approach it. "Despite the demand for records of popular and dance music of every type, many dealers report a very great demand from all classes of people, young and old, for sacred music," one article began.[65] The writer managed to sound surprised about the "millions of people in the United States who still go to church and who love the old hymns that they learned in the Sunday School in their youth." Offering a bit of helpful demographic analysis, the writer noted how "old hymns and the old songs make a very keen appeal to the millions of people who are middle-aged." Having spent the last twenty years of his life trying to reach out to young people, Rodeheaver could not have been impressed.

Then came the article's final flourish: "Some of these people looked upon the talking machine, because of its association with jazz, as something unholy, but when these old church-goers realized that the old standard hymns could be heard in their parlors on Sundays, as well as the old ballads, it delighted and consoled them."[66]

The record industry's condescending tone could not be more obvious—in one short passage the writer spoke of "these people" with their conservative social values, the "old" people who liked "old" music (used three times in one sentence), plus a thinly coded reference to their middle-class "parlors on Sundays." Such comments confirm that Rodeheaver's music was, indeed, emerging as a distinct genre, though barely understood (or respected?) by the companies who wished to capitalize on its potential.

THE MISSION OF RAINBOW RECORDS

Four years after establishing his new label, Rodeheaver stepped back to look at what he had created. He had a studio in Chicago, a sales office in Philadelphia, a summer headquarters in Winona Lake, and a dozen national dealers. In four years' time he had recorded 35 of his own solos and 12 duets with Virginia Asher, plus a breathtakingly diverse catalog that represented his conception of gospel music: solos, duets, a rootsy mandolin and guitar duo, several male quartets, an African American sextet and choir, opera singers, concert bands, and quirky acts that never gained notice past their own hometowns.

Feeling reflective, Rodeheaver wanted to summarize the first four years with a new statement of his essential purpose, which he did by recording a special spoken-word message intended for his Rainbow dealers.

"Rainbow Records are more of a mission than a business," he said, defining success differently than commercial record companies. "Ever since I made the first recordings of gospel songs several years ago, messages have been coming from all over the world, thanking me because of spiritual blessings and inspiration brought by the records."[67] Rodeheaver continued to believe his gospel song ministry would not have flourished through normal market channels, "because none of the big companies would record them." Rodeheaver also believed he could communicate the essential power of gospel music through recorded performances, which he explained in a series of testimonials: "A woman wrote me of her neighbor, an agnostic, who found it possible to have faith in God through hearing the records in her home. Another, of a grouchy husband who became kind and considerate through the record messages."

"So we want you to enjoy Rainbow Records because of their merit and the messages," he concluded, "but while you are buying them and boosting them, we want you to know that you are also helping in this great plan to spread the gospel around the world."[68] Yes, at the end of four years, Rodeheaver was still a true believer in the power of gospel music.

Rodeheaver continued to record for the major labels and stayed in touch with their executives, but didn't cut them any favors. After John S. MacDonald noted

Columbia's shaky financial picture in 1925, he tried to negotiate a few concessions from Rodeheaver, without success. Rodeheaver used the opportunity to remind MacDonald that his new Rainbow label sold about a million recordings in its first five years. "I would never have started to make them if the big companies like Victor and Columbia had agreed to make a big list of gospel song records and hymns," Rodeheaver said.[69] He had made his point—it wasn't about the money. He had broken free from the big labels, established his own Christian label, and recorded whatever he wanted. To an extent, after such an auspicious start, he had nowhere to go but down. He recorded very little after 1926, allowing the label to go dormant by 1929. Several factors played into this decision.

Recording technology changed again as Victor and Columbia released the first electric recordings (made with a microphone, not an acoustic horn) in mid-1925. Both companies used technology licensed from Bell Telephone Laboratories. Other companies followed: Brunswick with General Electric, Okeh with Columbia, Gennett with J. O. Prescott (Electrobeam). The choice was simple: anyone hoping to survive the transition had to license the new electric process from one of the big players.

Radio also made an impact. If live music (in any of the genres) could be heard on the radio, why purchase the recordings? For the same reason, movies (the new "talkies") grew in popularity. As seen in chapter 5, Rodeheaver's own interests shifted to radio and movies—again as a way to encourage communal singing. And like any other era, national economic trends could not be ignored. When the Roaring Twenties ended with the 1929 stock market crash, most of the independent labels did not survive.

In many ways, Rodeheaver's establishment of Rainbow Records can be judged a success. He established an early independent label that challenged the gatekeeping ethos of Victor, Edison, and Columbia. Somehow he managed to do so without alienating them; he continued to record the same gospel song material with the big labels. He also gave voice to people whose music had been pushed aside by the more popular jazz and dance trends. By giving each artist a great deal of artistic control, he successfully captured the broad range of styles that represented early gospel music.

He recruited well-respected industry professionals who shared his vision, established an independent network of dealers, and successfully promoted his label to the market segment he knew best, the Protestant coalition that supported tabernacle revivalism. His attempt to use recording technology in support of communal singing proved unsuccessful, but his failed attempt at least drew attention to his core beliefs about the purpose of gospel music. For the next fifteen years, Rodeheaver allowed the label to go dormant while he pursued other interests, but he returned to it one more time near the end of his life.

1940S REBIRTH

In 1944, Homer Rodeheaver restarted his Rainbow label, slightly ahead of the postwar rebirth of independent labels. He contracted with RCA Victor to press the recordings, then sent Bruce Howe to RCA's Chicago studios for training as a recording engineer. He also enlisted the help of Leigh B. Freed, a high school science teacher who lived in nearby North Manchester, Indiana. Many of the later Rainbows featured Rodeheaver re-recording his revival repertoire one last time, with piano or organ accompaniment. The recordings are not considered to be his best; his voice sounded tired, his pitch wavered, and the accompaniments sounded too much like 1920. More urgently, he was less successful at recruiting the next generation of evangelical recording stars. The Youth for Christ movement met in Winona Lake each summer and featured the best rising talent, but they all seemed to sign with other labels. Though he befriended George Beverly Shea and Cliff Barrows of the Billy Graham team, and though they hired Rodeheaver to print their crusade songbooks, he was unsuccessful in his attempts to sign any of them to a recording contract. Alfred B. Smith of Singspiration Records, the most aggressive and entrepreneurial of several new Christian labels, had locked Shea into an extended contract that eventually produced 27 sides.[70] After that, Shea signed with RCA Victor and never looked back.

After Rainbow Records limped along for several years, Rodeheaver made one final recording in the Winona Lake studios, a Christmas greeting that was sent to friends and family on December 16, 1955.[71] Homer Rodeheaver died two days later, just as his gift was arriving in the mail.

Three years after his death, the Rodeheaver Co. decided to close out its record label and concentrate on print music. Dealers advertised a four-for-a-dollar sale on Rodeheaver 78s until inventories were exhausted. Rainbow's closure might be explained by any number of reasons. First, the industry was in the middle of another technology change, briefly flirting with the 45 r.p.m. single format (used by Rainbow on several releases), then finding stability again when the market embraced mono LPs. Now record companies could potentially combine and repackage their 78 r.p.m. back catalog in the longer album format. But this required another capital investment and the assurance that their market segment would actually purchase the music again, a murky question for Rodeheaver's aging catalog of 1920s revival songs.

More importantly, the Rainbow label had always depended on Homer Rodeheaver's creative energy and salesmanship. After his death, the old guard staff could sustain his enterprise, but they never had another creative leader. Larger forces were also at play. The old-line gospel publishing families no longer held a monopoly on the Christian market, which now became glutted and strictly segregated by subgenre.

Rodeheaver's view of gospel music—which always transcended regional and racial distinctions—had nearly disappeared by the time of his 1955 death. Not only was his definition of gospel music disappearing, so was his essential idea. As seen here, Rodeheaver engaged every technological development with the assumption that it could be used for communal song. Just a few months before his death, he was still in front of the cameras, making one last sing-along film. Though he championed this communal singing objective in many interviews and articles, he never acknowledged what everyone else knew: he fought a losing battle. None of the new formats—not player pianos, not records, not radio, not film—would successfully encourage group singing. The new technology turned music producers into music consumers.

When the gospel song publishers started their own record labels, they intended the recordings to sustain sales of their hymnals—a gospel music market driven by communal singing. But now the performing groups took over, and turned this equation upside down. This can easily be illustrated by looking at the fate of the old-line southern gospel music publishers. Starting in the 1950s, the cash-rich performing groups started to buy out their parents, the publishing families. For instance, the Memphis-based Blackwood Brothers bought the Stamps Quartet Music Co., the Statesmen Quartet bought J. M. Henson Music Co., and then the two quartets formed a partnership to purchase the James D. Vaughan Publishing Co. By and large, once the quartets bought out their publishers, they stopped printing hymnals. The quartets knew that the valuable song catalog could be monetized through recordings, radio performances, and public concerts—communal singing was no longer necessary and was no longer a viable market. In the South, the fondly remembered All-Night Sing had become an All-Night Listen.

7

SPIRITUALS AND MINSTRELSY

"BORN AMIDST THE TRIALS AND TRIBULATIONS OF THIS RACE"

When telling the story of his own life, Homer Rodeheaver often mentioned his interest in African American music. His credentials were immediately obvious: He befriended Black pastors and visited their churches, he championed spirituals and performed them in revival meetings, and he underwrote expensive field work to transcribe spirituals as they were sung in African American congregations. He eventually published eight collections of spirituals and encouraged all churches—Black and white—to make them a part of their services. He recruited the Wiseman Sextet and Jackson College Jubilee Singers for his new Rainbow label and then sang *with* them for many of the sessions—early interracial recordings that showed evangelicals the promise of an integrated church.

When telling the story of his own life, Rodeheaver also skipped parts. He never explained how the Klan adapted "The Old Rugged Cross" as a racist anthem, nor did he speak of the Klan recordings that were made in his own studio in 1924. And he never understood how his own blackface performances (however well-intentioned) might be seen as racially insensitive.

As a public figure during turbulent times, Homer Rodeheaver reflected and shaped American ideas about race, provoking a host of questions that are challenging to untangle. To understand this chapter of Rodeheaver's life, we surveyed the diverse ways that American music scholars have interpreted racial issues and then asked how Rodeheaver fit into the ongoing discussion. Our approach here is not strictly historical—the questions we studied are still with us today, continuing as controversies in our own era. For instance, at the same time we were writing

CHAPTER 7

FIGURE 7.1. Rodeheaver with African American family on a return visit to Jellico, Tennessee. Courtesy of Rodeheaver Collection, Grace College, Winona Lake.

about Rodeheaver's historical blackface performances, a similar debate erupted over contemporary incidents. If a person judges such depictions as wrong *today*, were they also wrong in Rodeheaver's era? Of course, this is a question that historians prefer to avoid, ever wary about making judgments that smack of moral absolutes. But for anyone who wishes to understand Rodeheaver's community, American evangelicals, the question seems fair game. Their own identity is *built* on moral absolutes, based on their professed understanding of biblical teaching. So our approach, again, is to offer a straightforward analysis of Rodeheaver's own religious transformation. At the very least we can evaluate his religious life (and his views on race) by examining how he worked out his own stated ideals. The best introduction to this question comes by looking at the way Rodeheaver told his own story.

Homer Rodeheaver described his mother as beloved by both whites and Blacks, and he spoke of Black children who often came to serenade her when the family lived in Newcomb, Tennessee. She was "a ministering angel" to these youngsters, and Rodeheaver came to enjoy and love the spirituals they sang. According to his brother Joe, these relationships extended to church attendance, where the family "visited the negro churches and were warmly welcomed."[1] Years later, when Homer Rodeheaver spoke of his childhood, he invariably mentioned these early encounters with African Americans and their impact on his musical life. And while he was also steeped in southern mountain ballads, Rodeheaver said he "much preferred the negro spirituals to the hill-billy songs."[2]

In retrospect, Rodeheaver's comments about his early years are also significant for what they omit. By the time of his 1880 birth, the Compromise of 1877 had effectively killed the racial progress of the Reconstruction era, ushering in the regressive period that southern whites called *Redemption*. Rodeheaver never spoke of the rise of Jim Crow racism in his own hometown, nor did he mention the three lynchings in Jellico when he was twelve years old, or the Black family burned out of their cabin and forced to leave town. Such incidents must have left their own indelible impressions, even if he didn't talk about them.

Rodeheaver was learning of Black culture directly, through his own experiences and relationships. Later researchers characterized the songs Rodeheaver heard as *folk spirituals*, in contrast to the *concert spirituals* sung by choral groups and in contrast to the later *commercial spirituals*, created and sold to mimic the folk style.[3] By the time Rodeheaver encountered folk spirituals in rural Tennessee, the songs had already acquired their own conflicting origin stories, an ongoing search for "the first" and "the original." Scholars today have pretty much abandoned this search, and for good reasons. As an oral tradition, spirituals emerged from a primordial pool of diverse influences: African sources, slave shouts and ring dances, camp meeting songs, and evangelical hymnody. So the question of *when* (impossible to pinpoint) became much less important than *how*. Two aspects of this question drove later research: how African Americans developed a culture of their own, and how whites became aware of this developing culture.[4]

During Rodeheaver's early years, whites had a second introduction to Black culture that competed directly with the emerging spirituals—the development of blackface minstrelsy. In the 1830s, urban whites began imitating Black culture (or their conception of Black culture) for theatrical shows.[5] Often cited as the first form of American popular music, blackface minstrelsy provoked immediate questions: were these authentic depictions of Black life or deliberate racial ridicule? Our reasons for describing it as a *competing* introduction to Black culture will soon be clear. Rodeheaver's life illustrates how whites absorbed these conflicting streams of Blackness—and often had a difficult time separating real from faux.

Before the Civil War, blackface minstrel performances had become enormously popular among the northern working class. In most respects, these were horrible depictions, replete with racist stereotypes that revealed more about white attitudes than about African American life. Even so, the performances grew popular and could not be overlooked for their important impact on American popular music. By the end of the 1800s, blackface minstrelsy morphed into coon songs, a popular music genre built on racial stereotypes of Black people. But now the situation grew complicated as Black musicians also developed successful careers by writing and performing coon songs for Black traveling shows and early vaudeville.[6] African American popular music developed into cakewalks, ragtime, brass bands, jazz, and blues—all of them influenced, at least in part, by minstrelsy and coon songs, despite their vestiges of racism.

As explained by Rodeheaver, spirituals were a significant influence on his personal life and his brand of gospel songs. Interestingly, he never made similar statements about the influence of minstrelsy and its musical cousins—though he could have. Despite his lack of formal acknowledgment, our work here will show that Rodeheaver was clearly influenced by both genres, spirituals and minstrelsy.

RODEHEAVER'S SPIRITUALS

The spirituals took their name from two New Testament passages that speak of "psalms, hymns, and spiritual songs."[7] Evangelical Protestants of Rodeheaver's era considered this phrase to be a description of three distinct song genres in church music: *psalms* with texts taken straight from scripture, *hymns* as composed songs in the ongoing church tradition, and *spiritual songs* of recent origin.[8] Protestants agreed that these were distinct genres but had sharp disagreements over *when* the three should be sung. In particular, the idea of "spiritual songs" would be used to describe Black spirituals and gospel songs, but various denominational groups disagreed over when, exactly, they were appropriate. Should they be relegated to camp meetings and revival services, or could they be sung on Sunday morning? The question hovered over church music for the next century.

Though Rodeheaver learned folk spirituals in the oral tradition from Black neighbor children, his experience was becoming increasingly rare. Already some preservationists were worried that the antebellum spirituals were dying out. Early efforts to publish folk spirituals, such as the 1867 *Slave Songs of the United States*, tried to document what was already considered a disappearing culture.[9] At the same time Rodeheaver was learning folk spirituals, they were also morphing into a new form of concert spirituals. In the same year that *Slave Songs* was released, George L. White had organized a Fisk University choral group that toured extensively, sang mostly spirituals, and raised large amounts of money for the university. Renamed the Jubilee Singers in 1871, the widely imitated group developed a new style of formal arrangements in four-part harmony.[10] Rodeheaver believed folk spirituals and the concert spirituals were the first representations of authentic African American music, a position that is often discussed by current scholars.

"The spirituals became the first mass market music to have originated in the black experience," a recent study says, essentially agreeing with Rodeheaver.[11] Other studies have made competing claims about 1830s blackface minstrelsy, described as "the first formal public acknowledgment by whites of black culture."[12] Both statements, carefully worded, are interesting for what they affirm and what they reject (perhaps saying less than they seem at first glance). Yes, minstrelsy could be considered an earlier form of mass market music—but few people would argue that these performances originated in the Black experience and correctly represented Black cultural practices.

Aware of this, those who brought spirituals into public awareness immediately positioned them as being different than minstrelsy. The opening paragraph of *Slave Songs* critiqued songs like "Zip Coon," described as "spurious imitations manufactured to fit the somewhat sentimental tastes of our community."[13] In an 1868 magazine article about spirituals, John Mason Brown acknowledged that blackface portrayals resembled the genuine Black experience because of their "external resemblance, due to burnt cork." But Brown criticized minstrelsy as portraying "scarcely a feature of person, music, dialect or action that recalls, with any dramatic accuracy, the genuine negro slave of former years."[14] The spirituals were not only different, they were genuine.

When George L. White organized the first tours of a vocal group from Fisk University in Nashville, he deliberately avoided characterizing them as entertainers. To shift audience expectations, he stopped using phrases like "a band of negro minstrels" and branded the ensemble as the Fisk Jubilee Singers. As much as possible, early performances were booked in church auditoriums (not music halls) and billed as "services of song" (not concerts). Every service started with "Swing Low, Sweet Chariot," and immediately segued into a chanted version of "The Lord's Prayer," a liturgical touch that served as a coded affirmation to church people: this is not minstrelsy.

Dozens of Black vocal groups emulated the Fisk model as the concert spiritual developed its own distinctive traditions, always positioned as songs of religious devotion. Apologists such as Gustavus D. Pike commended the Fisk group as the appropriate alternative to "so much odium attached to negro concerts, as represented in burnt cork minstrels."[15]

In 1867, Thomas Wentworth Higginson used the term *Negro spirituals* to describe songs of a particular lyrical content: "more than a source of relaxation, they were a stimulus to courage and a tie to heaven" and "the vocal expression of the simplicity of their faith and the sublimity of their long resignation."[16] In a preface to the musical portion of *The Jubilee Singers*, Theodore Seward described spirituals as having an overtly spiritual purpose, received as gifts "bestowed upon them by an ever-watchful Father, to quicken the pulses of life, and to keep them from the state of hopeless apathy into which they were in danger of falling."[17] Later generations continued to interpret spirituals in the same way. James Weldon Johnson surveyed the tragic American slave experience and concluded that "the Negro took complete refuge in Christianity, and the Spirituals were literally forged of sorrow in the heat of religious fervor. They exhibited, moreover, a reversion to the simple principles of primitive, communal Christianity."[18]

CHAPTER 7

This essential idea—that spirituals were *spiritual*—became lost in ongoing research. Of course, spirituals also held additional meanings, such as their use as work songs or coded signals for secret meetings.[19] But these dual meanings led to approaches that framed spirituals in purely secular terms: as escapist/compensatory literature, as veiled protest songs, or as a deeper mental escape into one's soul.[20] These interpretations reflect "the ideological temper of the times," as E. Franklin Frazier noted in *The Negro Church in America*. Frazier complained about "the efforts of Negro intellectuals ... encouraged by white radicals, to invest spirituals with a revolutionary meaning or to claim that they represented disguised plans for escape from slavery." For Frazier, these approaches minimized the ways that spirituals "were essentially religious in sentiment and otherworldly in outlook."[21]

Though Rodeheaver drew much of his musical inspiration from folk and concert spirituals directly from Blacks, he was clearly influenced by another source that was far less pure. A new genre known as the *plantation spectacle* became one of the most popular entertainments of the 1890s. Black performers found steady work in traveling shows like *South before the War*, an early vaudeville musical with a "happy slave days" plot.[22] During its nine-year run, several different Black quartets were employed, singing songs like "De Gospel Pass" and "Hand Down De Robe." In 1894, while traveling with *South before the War*, the Standard Quartet released "Keep Movin'," often regarded as the earliest African American recording of religious song.[23]

These were not the folk spirituals Rodeheaver learned as a child—they were composed and marketed with a cursory nod to spiritual imagery but purely commercial in source and intent.[24] One is tempted to describe these commercial spirituals as the offspring of two unwed parents: folk spirituals and blackface minstrelsy. In the context of a plantation spectacle, the commercial spirituals were written into the obligatory camp meeting scene, which included parodies of the backwoods preacher, the slain-in-the-spirit women, and burlesques of Bible stories. At their worst, the commercial spirituals sounded more like the popular coon songs, a vaudeville parody of concert spirituals that, at the end of the nineteenth century, had nearly obliterated the Fisk conception of jubilee singing.[25]

All of this changed when a reorganized Fisk group recorded for Victor in 1909. John Wesley Work Jr. led sessions that resulted in ten sides, including eight spirituals and two recitations of poems by Paul Laurence Dunbar.[26] The new Fisk recordings became highly successful, reestablishing the concert spiritual as a viable alternative to minstrelsy. The singers released additional songs on Victor, Edison, Columbia, and much later, Rodeheaver's Rainbow Records.[27]

By the time of the Fisk recordings, Rodeheaver had just met Billy Sunday at summer Chautauqua meetings, beginning his own trajectory into public awareness. Rodeheaver had his own Victor contract by 1913, and he immediately tried to record at least one of the Fisk selections, a recitation of Dunbar's "When Malindy Sings."[28] The take was rejected for one reason or another, but the attempt shows Rodeheaver's early interest in the material.

Rodeheaver began visiting Black churches while he traveled with Sunday, part of a general strategy to visit local churches and promote the tabernacle meetings. During the 1915 Philadelphia revivals, Rodeheaver described one such visit, where he sang mostly old spirituals: "As I spent some of my early years down South, I knew a number of the old plantation melodies, and we all enjoyed ourselves hugely."[29] When he sang "I Walk with the King," Rodeheaver reported how they "broke out into a running fire, and for a few minutes we had a genuine, old fashioned sort of a time, just like the Plantation revivals, when everybody was 'happy.'"[30]

Buoyed by his success in Black churches, Rodeheaver began singing the same songs in the tabernacle meetings. His first recording of spirituals came in May 1919, a session for Columbia where he sang "Heab'n" and "Some of These Days" with Virginia Asher.[31] In 1916, he also published his first songbook to include spirituals, the *Rodeheaver Collection for Male Voices*.[32] The collection of 160 songs featured seventeen spirituals, "so arranged as to preserve their original characteristics," a phrase that needs some explanation. All of the spirituals had been arranged for male quartet, filtered through the strictures of conventional music notation and four-part harmony. The arranged songs could not be called folk spirituals, but they sounded exactly like the concert spirituals presented by the jubilee quartets.

Rodeheaver spent two years, 1915–1916, experimenting with ways to connect his long interest in spirituals to the tabernacle audiences. The breakout moment occurred at the 1917 Billy Sunday meetings in Atlanta, where Sunday and Rodeheaver enjoyed the endorsement of Black pastors and the support of Black colleges. Anticipating this positive response, Rodeheaver brought editors J. B. Herbert and Charles Gabriel to Atlanta to visit Black churches and transcribe spirituals as they were sung. "The men copied down as nearly as they could some old-time melodies and harmonies," Rodeheaver said, "and we have printed them in two separate volumes, and in some instances, in sheet music, in order that they may be preserved."[33]

The Atlanta collection was published in 1918 as *Plantation Melodies*, followed by a promotional onslaught.[34] Rodeheaver unleashed an aggressive campaign of catalogs, advertisements, and cross-marketing with recordings of the published songs—not to mention his nightly features in the tabernacle meetings.

To be clear, *Plantation Melodies* was not the first published collection of spirituals (despite the claims of his publicity department). It came nearly fifty years after *Slave Songs of the United States* and forty-five years after Pike and Seward's

CHAPTER 7

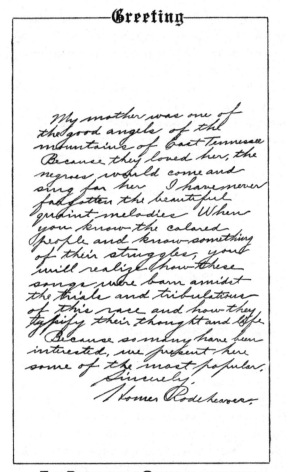

FIGURE 7.2. Rodeheaver's handwritten introduction to *Plantation Melodies*, 1918.

publication of spirituals in *The Jubilee Singers*. At least three earlier hymnals had included spirituals, all intended for Black churches.[35] And while Rodeheaver touted his personal knowledge and research, his book also borrowed from *Jubilee Songs* (1872) as a source. Of the forty-seven songs in Rodeheaver's collection, ten are identical or nearly identical to the earlier-published *Jubilee Songs* version.[36] Still, some of his field work for *Plantation Melodies* can be credited as a legitimate contribution. His book introduced an early published version of "Down by the Riverside," which was quickly adopted into the canon of standard American songs.

If Rodeheaver wished to claim a "first," *Plantation Melodies* represented the first time that spirituals were aggressively marketed to white churches in arrangements that could be sung by congregations and choirs. Unusual for his era, Rodeheaver believed that the spirituals were important for congregational singing and a valid liturgical resource. His book predated the inclusion of eighteen spirituals in *Gospel Pearls*, the seminal Black gospel collection released in 1921 and marketed to Black churches. His book also predated several important collections released during the Harlem Renaissance—books of spirituals compiled by William Arms Fisher, H. T. Burleigh, and the brothers James Weldon Johnson and John Rosamond Johnson. By 1925, Rodeheaver had produced two collections of spirituals, and (if he were modest) could at least claim to be ahead of the curve.

Rodeheaver used *Plantation Melodies* to outline his own theory about the origin of spirituals: "When you know the colored people and know something of their struggles, you will realize how these songs were born amidst the trials and tribulations of this race and how they typify their thought and life."[37] Rodeheaver believed that all people shared a "definite, natural and universal relation" that allowed them to respond to "the melodies and harmonies of these primitive songs."[38] Despite his optimism about the music's unifying power, the tabernacle audiences remained segregated.

In 1923, Rodeheaver began working on *Negro Spirituals*, a second compilation of spirituals collected during the Billy Sunday campaign in Columbia, South Carolina. As he had done for the Atlanta meetings, Rodeheaver sent Herbert to Columbia for formal field work where he was assisted by Turner H. Wiseman, the pastor of Columbia's Bethel African Methodist Episcopal Church, who also led a Black quartet and sextet.

In a letter to W. E. B. Du Bois dated August 26, 1923, Wiseman related how he came to meet Homer Rodeheaver. Robert Matthews of the Billy Sunday party contacted Wiseman to see if Black churches would be interested in attending three meetings in Columbia "for colored people" on consecutive Sunday mornings. The pastors demurred, not wanting to give up their own church services, but they agreed to one meeting. Rodeheaver and Sunday encouraged Wiseman to organize a choir.

"Here we had an aggregation of 800 Negro voices for the purpose of singing God's praises and to touch men and women's hearts for the higher life," Wiseman reported, emphasizing that he alone had trained the group. "Upon the day set apart, this great chorus sang as only Negros can sing the Songs of the Soul; Our Spirituals."[39] According to Wiseman, Rodeheaver was so impressed that "he invited us back to sing for the white services on [the] following Wednesday. We came—we sang—we made many friends. Mr. Rodeheaver and Mr. Sunday emphasized that God loves us all alike [and] that in Heaven we have to worship all together."[40] In his letter, Wiseman did not dig into the obvious implication of

FIGURE 7.3. A Rainbow Records catalog advertisement for the Wiseman Sextet recordings, 1922.

that phrase. If Blacks and whites expected to worship together eventually (when they were "in Heaven") what about here on earth?

Some of the answer can be gleaned by studying the five collections of spirituals that Rodeheaver published for congregational singing.[41] The preface of each book covered similar territory: Rodeheaver's belief that spirituals were an important contribution to American music, and his belief that they should be sung by all people. He continued his own campaign by including spirituals in his community songbooks[42] and in many of his gospel song hymnals after 1917.

In his ongoing effort to promote the spirituals, Rodeheaver continued to recruit Black artists and music editors. He renewed his acquaintance with Frederick Douglass Hall, who had sung in Rodeheaver's 1917 Atlanta chorus and now directed the Jackson College Jubilee Singers. When Sunday and Rodeheaver held meetings in Jackson, Mississippi, Hall's choir performed several times. Rodeheaver asked him to create a series of choir anthems based on spirituals, which was released by Rodeheaver Music Co. in 1925.

Frederick Hall continued to edit Rodeheaver's collections of spirituals for the next twenty-five years, including *A Group of Unusual Negro Spirituals for Choirs and Large Chorus Work* (1928), *Southland Spirituals* (1936), the male chorus collection *Negro Spirituals and Folk Songs* (1939), and *Sing Songs of the Southland*, vol. 1–3 (1955). Hall was also the motivating force behind *Sixty-Two Southland Spirituals* (1946), a collection that opens with "Lift Every Voice and Sing," identified as the "National Negro Hymn."[43] Along the way, Rodeheaver also befriended Worth Kramer, director of the Wings Over Jordan radio chorus. The relationship resulted in *Wings Over Jordan Favorite Spirituals of 1939* (released in 1940). The book contains ten songs billed as exact transcriptions as sung by the popular *Wings Over Jordan* radio choir.

Rodeheaver's marketing of spirituals followed the same rationale as his marketing of Rainbow Records, as "a mission, not a business." Given the cost of what he was doing, his original motives can be seen as an act of altruism. Rodeheaver paid for the field work and transcriptions up front. In practical terms, each spiritual cost him considerably more than the $10 flat fee he typically paid for a new gospel song. Such actions can be seen as Rodeheaver's consistent mission to "do all the good possible," one of the foundational tenets of Winona Lake's "Money-Making Altruism."[44] However positive his motivation, the coin had two sides. Winona Lake's altruism was also built on another foundational principle: that every Christian layman should "make all the money he can."[45] For Rodeheaver, this translated into a heavy dose of self-promotion.

Rodeheaver aggressively advertised his collections of spirituals and then claimed credit for making them popular. In 1928, *Time* magazine reported that Rodeheaver "likes to be thought of as the introducer and exploiter of Negro spirituals."[46] Other media outlets soon reported that "Homer Rodeheaver has contributed more to make the negro spirituals popular than any other concert artist." By demonstrating "how beautiful these negro spirituals really are," Rodeheaver helped church musicians understand how they "brought to their programs a new field of music that had never been used."[47]

The "never been used" claim was pure hyperbole, but it serves as an apt reminder of what often happened when whites of the era forged unequal partnerships with Blacks. Suddenly it was all about Rodeheaver, a revised history of spirituals that seemed to minimize the earlier work of the Fisk Jubilee Singers, other Black groups, and his own Black editors.[48] Perhaps this was not Rodeheaver's intention, but his publicity seemed to reinforce an old problem. "White Americans were morally obligated, in the most paternalistic way, to step in and solve the so-called Negro Problem *for* the Negro, not *with* him," Henry Louis Gates once said, a description that seems to apply here.[49]

CHAPTER 7

RECORDING THE SPIRITUALS

Homer Rodeheaver began recording spirituals more or less concurrently with his efforts to publish them. After his 1919 recordings with Columbia Records, he continued recording spirituals for Victor, his own Rainbow label, and others—more than forty times in all. Of these, the most notable are his 1923 recordings with the Wiseman Quartet and Sextet and a 1926 project with the Jackson College Jubilee Singers.

Rodeheaver started recording Black groups soon after he published the 1923 *Negro Songs*. "Realizing that so few white people could sing the Negro spirituals with the lilt and rhythm and the peculiar beauty of voice quality that the Negros have, I brought six Negros from the Southland into our laboratory in Chicago, and there we recorded some of the songs sung in the original beauty and simplicity of the old slavery days."[50]

A native of Missouri, Rev. Turner Henderson Wiseman (1896–1939) studied music in Los Angeles after serving in the racially segregated 25th Infantry Regiment during the Spanish-American War. At the time he met Rodeheaver at the 1923 Billy Sunday meetings in Columbia, South Carolina, Wiseman had been an ordained minister for fifteen years. Wiseman's Bethel Jubilee Quartet impressed Rodeheaver enough that he recommended the group to the Victor, who recorded twelve sides of spirituals with the group in July 1923.[51] Following the Victor sessions, the quartet traveled to Richmond, Indiana, where they recorded at least thirty-four sides for Rainbow and Gennett Records as the Wiseman Quartet and Sextet.[52] Rodeheaver himself sang on several of the Rainbow recordings. On "Hard Trials" several singers took a solo break to sing about various Christian denominations.[53] Predictably, Rodeheaver sang the verse, "Oh, Methodist, Methodist, is my name; Methodist till I die." Wiseman's arrangements were polished and well sung, and several of the Rainbow sides were also released on Paramount Records, a leading distributor of race records that were marketed to the African American community.[54]

In light of Rodeheaver's performances with a Black group, Wiseman wrote to Du Bois: "This is the first time in America that a noted white singer has recorded his voice with a Negro sextette. Mr. Rodeheaver sang the verse to a dozen songs with our sextette taking [the] chorus."[55]

In claiming that Rodeheaver was the first "noted white singer" to record with a Black singing group, Wiseman was probably unaware of earlier interracial recordings made between 1894 and 1917, featuring Jessie Oliver, Polk Miller, and Arthur Fields.[56] No matter. Rodeheaver's sessions with the Wiseman group remain important as very early interracial recordings. According to the Gennett ledgers, the Wiseman sessions in August 1923 came only a few weeks after Gennett's sessions with Jelly Roll Morton and the New Orleans Rhythm Kings, often cited as first interracial recording sessions in jazz history.[57]

Rodeheaver continued to sing spirituals with Black groups whenever he could. In 1926 he invited Fred Hall and the Jackson College Jubilee Singers to the Gennett studios. The sessions resulted in four sides, including "Little David, Play on Your Harp" with Rodeheaver as featured soloist (though he is not credited on the label).[58]

PRESERVING THE AUTHENTIC SPIRITUAL

Several of the Wiseman Sextet recordings on Rainbow began with an announcement by Rodeheaver, such as the one that precedes "Lord, I Can't Stay Away": "We present on this record one of the most typical of the real Negro spirituals and one of the most effective in revival meetings. You will hear it here with its strange minor and all the peculiar turns, just as you would hear it from one of the most talented congregations of the real South."[59] Rodeheaver intended to preserve what he called authentic versions of spirituals as they were sung by Black congregations. This also seemed to be his motivation for his 1946 collaboration with the Fisk Jubilee Singers, although the full nature of their relationship remains murky. At that time, Rainbow Records released six sides of spirituals that the Fisk group had recorded ten years earlier, possibly in Chicago's Studebaker Theater. Who actually made these recordings is not known—Gennett? Rainbow?—but these performances by an all-male octet led by Mrs. James Myers are artfully sung and well recorded.[60] The arrangements exhibit a sophistication and, at times—particularly shown with the chromaticism on "Dry Bones: The Old Ark's A' Movering"—a popular, commercial feel. When John Wesley Work Jr. wrote in 1915 that "forty-five years have naturally made some changes in the renderings of certain songs," he probably could not have imagined what another twenty years would do to them.[61] His Fisk Jubilee Singers had achieved a degree of refinement that compared favorably with any choral group in the land. Spirituals didn't sound anything like this on the plantation.

The question of authenticity—what constituted a "real" spiritual as they were originally conceived—was one that dogged the promoters and performers of this music from the outset. Early ethnographers of Seward's era were influenced by white European hymnody, white gospel music, minstrelsy, vaudeville, and art song, whether directly or subliminally. The same is true for later arrangers of spirituals (Coleridge-Taylor, Burleigh, and Johnson), and performers (Fisk Jubilee Singers and the Wiseman Sextet). Prior to audio recordings, musicians attempted to preserve the songs purely through music notation and approximations of slave dialect—what the authors of *Slave Songs* called "some very comical specimens of the way in which half-understood words and phrases are distorted."[62] On the other hand, it proved difficult to notate the nuances of music that fell outside traditional western, classical harmony, rhythm, and melody.

In 1897, Alice Mabel Bacon, who taught at Hampton Institute, believed strongly that an authentic performance of spirituals was not possible "when you take it out of its foreordained and appropriate setting in some part of the complicated negro religious ritual, and adapt it to be sung as regular four-part song by a choir or congregation, either white or black." This is exactly what the Fisk singers had done, and what Rodeheaver did, as well. According to Bacon, the process of codifying the spirituals in print made the songs "a totally different thing." Already aware of white critics who believed spirituals came from white sources, Bacon believed their misunderstanding was because spirituals had already "been subjected to this process of civilizing into regular written forms."[63]

Du Bois complained that the Fisk and Hampton groups provided good models for singing spirituals, but their imitators ("straggling quartettes") served spirituals poorly. Some arrangements caricatured the authentic sound of spirituals, "to spoil the quaint beauty of the music, and [have] filled the air with many debased melodies which vulgar ears scarce know from the real."[64] T. H. Wiseman, who was probably aware of Du Bois's published statements, used his 1923 letter to Du Bois to offer a defense of his new arrangements and recordings, which he felt went a long way in "preserving the racial songs." Wiseman's postscript to the letter was a plea: "Please let me know your opinion."[65] A reply from Du Bois has not been preserved.

Writing in 1958, Regina Dolan summed up the authenticity problem as a no-win scenario, where "some musical authorities complain that in most conventional versions of spirituals, there is too much melody and harmony. They assert that if you over-emphasize the melodic elements of spirituals, you produce a sentimental ballad of the Stephen Foster type. If you stress harmony, you get barber-shop choruses and if you concentrate on rhythmic idiom, you secularize the product, and the result is only a syncopated shout with the religious mood completely vanished. What then?"[66]

As a marketing strategy, Rodeheaver reassured his customers that his publications and recordings of spirituals were, indeed, authentic. He always enlisted the help of African Americans when producing his print editions of spirituals. He sponsored field work at African American churches. He garnered additional legitimacy by recording Black groups such as the Wiseman sextet, the Fisk Jubilee Singers, and the Zion Travelers. Authenticity, for Rodeheaver, meant the authentic replication of spirituals as they were sung in Black churches, with a special interest in the ways congregations sang them in corporate worship. If anything, Rodeheaver's work preserves the performance practices of Black churches in the early 1920s (not, strictly speaking, the original folk spirituals).

But the authenticity question can also deflect scholars from seeing the obvious. While busy charting ways that folk spirituals had changed—the European four-part harmony, the strictures of standard notation—it becomes easy to miss what had not changed. For Rodeheaver, the spirituals were authentically *spiritual*, and whatever changes he made to the form were designed to preserve this essential quality. While spirituals also had an enormous influence (in a secular sense) on American roots music, Rodeheaver was interested in their transformational effect on church congregations.

RODEHEAVER'S MINSTRELSY

Rodeheaver's approach to minstrelsy was completely different than his embrace of spirituals. For Rodeheaver, the influence of minstrelsy operated in the background, rarely discussed or acknowledged. Nevertheless, three vestiges of minstrelsy are clearly seen in Rodeheaver's public performances: his use of racial jokes, his adoption of African American dialect when reciting the works of Black poets, and his occasional blackface performances.

As discussed in chapter 2, Rodeheaver performed in blackface while a student at Ohio Wesleyan University in 1903 and 1904, as part of the school's annual "Dandy Darkies" minstrel show. The show was sponsored by the OWU Student Athletic Association, whose president was none other than Branch Rickey. Later in their lives, Rodeheaver became known for his interracial recordings of spirituals, and Rickey would be credited with hiring Jackie Robinson to break baseball's color line. But in their college years, both were involved in an entertainment that most white Americans considered to be completely acceptable, blackface minstrelsy.

A newspaper review of the OWU minstrel show remarked on the jokes and stories that "were told in true darky fashion."[67] Rodeheaver continued to use this material for many years during his personal appearances—more bits of schtick to warm up the audience between songs. His prodigious memory called up poems, epigrams, and anecdotes that suited every occasion. Crying babies? Latecomers? Groups of railroad engineers? Local heroes? Rodeheaver always seemed to have a story, followed by a seamless segue into the next musical selection. For someone famous for diplomacy, someone who rarely offended anyone, Rodeheaver's choices could be surprising.

At the 1917 Atlanta revivals, local church leaders had organized a meeting of African Americans during an unusually cold December. Rodeheaver led off with a racial joke, a Blacks-in-cold-weather story about a man who traveled to Chicago, was found frozen stiff on the street, and (the story goes) tossed in the crematory oven. Next came the punchline: "Hey there, white folks, shut dat door. Don't you know you're letting in a draft?"[68]

Rodeheaver caught a wave of laughter and transitioned into a homily about "warm weather Christians." Perhaps his story worked for the audience, at least according to news accounts (written by white journalists). Edgy, at least—a white man telling a racial joke to a Black audience. Where was the line—at what point does topical humor become racist? Rodeheaver didn't have a clear answer.

As he continued to use the racial stories, some of the jokes were reported in newspapers, accompanied by blackface cartoons.[69] These bits grew popular enough that he published them in two collections, *Worth While Poems* (1916) and *More Worth While Poems* (1929).[70] As late as 1949 he published *F'r Instance: A Collection of Jokes and Humorous Stories*. The book contains two dozen items that feature racial dialogue about Blacks (the book's index lists them as "Negro Stories") who are referred to as "darkeys" named Mose, Sambo, Rastus, Ephriam, or Sam.[71] These jokes and stories, told in African American dialect, make one wince today. Yet, such items were, at the time, standard fare on the white public speaking and entertainment circuit, to say nothing of the minstrel shows of Rodeheaver's early years.

A similar observation can be made about temperance and prohibition songs. By the time Rodeheaver joined Billy Sunday in 1909, alcohol had already become a major plank in the revival platform. Because of Sunday's famous "Booze Sermon," Rodeheaver found he could use temperance songs from the revival platform even if their secular slant didn't quite fit the genre of gospel music. Two of Rodeheaver's editors, J. B. Herbert and Charles Gabriel, had already published collections of temperance songs, so they were well familiar with the genre. Many of these were thinly disguised "coon songs" from the minstrelsy era, full of African American stereotypes and exaggerated dialect. In 1903, Gabriel had written music to "I Draws De Line Right Dar," with lyrics by T. C. Johnson:

> I's a 'Publican niggah, yes, I is, An' I votes dat ticket eb'ry time;
> But de Mastah, he say, I am his, An' my 'legiance in de heb'nly clime.
> So I votes fo'de man, ef he's all right, an' takes no liker at de bar;
> But ef fo' de whisky side he'll fight, Den I draws the line right dar. Hah! Hah!"[72]

Such songs were written by whites for a white audience, where, to say the least, the inherent racism was embraced, tolerated, or even unrecognized. Other Prohibition songs showed a milder form of minstrelsy, such as Herbert's "De Brewers Big Hosses," which Rodeheaver began incorporating in revival campaigns in 1911 and recorded for Victor in 1913.[73] With an easy-to-teach chorus and fun "train whistle" effects, the song bridged the gap between 1890s minstrelsy and novelty songs of the 1920s. And when the song became a hit, Rodeheaver bought it outright from Herbert and began publishing it himself.[74]

SPIRITUALS AND MINSTRELSY

FIGURE 7.4. "De Brewers Big Hosses," a Rodeheaver staple during tabernacle meetings. Reprinted from the *Live Wire*, 1914.

In 1912 Rodeheaver and Charles Gabriel collaborated to write *Old Black Sam: A Vision of Slavery Days*, a concert musical for narrator, chorus, and piano. The music came from Stephen Foster, white gospel songs, and Frédéric Chopin; no folk spirituals were employed. Told through the voice of a dying slave, Sam adopts a stereotypical house servant persona, speaks in broken dialect, and gives the audience an idealized description of his slave master. "He know dis nigga'd die for him mos' any day," Sam says, and claims his master was "de kindest one a darkey ever knew."[75] Taken as a whole, the production laments the tragedy of slavery but also romanticizes its history, resurrecting the old lie of Jefferson Davis, that slaves were "peaceful and contented laborers."[76]

Old Black Sam cannot be reconciled with Rodeheaver's avowed love of spirituals and his respect for African Americans. It can only be understood in the context of blackface minstrelsy, a continuing and unspoken influence on Rodeheaver's musical life. After the Jubilee Singers established a deliberate contrast between authentic spirituals and the faux Blackness of minstrelsy, Rodeheaver seemed to blur the distinction. As a rule, people who were comfortable with the minstrelsy genre were not above using the N-word when it seemed to suit the occasion.

When visiting Black regiments during the waning days of World War I, Rodeheaver praised them as "great soldiers and true patriots." But he also told jokes about "darkies in shell holes" and used the word *nigger* when he wasn't around them.[77] Rodeheaver's use of the word raises a larger issue worth discussing. As used by whites, *nigger* has always been a racist term. At no point in its long history was the word a neutral expression.[78] Many whites of the era tried to defend its "appropriate" use, like the 1930s writer who tried to differentiate between "the nigger, the 'colored person,' and the Negro—uppercase N." By establishing this distinction, whites could justify using *nigger* as a legitimate appellative for "bad" Blacks. Such pronouncements (always by whites) were accompanied by the author's imagined authority as one who was raised by Black nurses or because one played with Blacks as a child.[79]

Despite Rodeheaver's professed affinity for African Americans, there is no good way to justify his use of racist language. In Rodeheaver's era, the N-word was all too common, even among whites with progressive racial attitudes. On the subject of "enlightened whites" who thought they could use the N-word, many similar incidents could be cited.[80] Whether used as humor or irony, there was no way for whites to use the word without invoking the racism that was inherent from the beginning.

DIALECT, CODE-SWITCHING, AND VERBAL BLACKFACE

Rodeheaver began publishing and recording spirituals just before the rise of the Harlem Renaissance, where issues of Black life were reexamined by a rising generation of Black musicians and artists. In particular, the coon song fell out of favor. Having fueled the early careers of many Black musicians who used it to earn a stable living, the style was now viewed as an obsolete accommodation to white audiences. The spirituals, on the other hand, continued their emergence into popular awareness, albeit with a bit of baggage from the minstrelsy era. As Rodeheaver began printing the words of spirituals he wandered into yet another controversial subject, the matter of racial dialect.

The earliest collections of spirituals printed the lyrics in dialect.[81] Viewing their work as ethnographic preservation, the authors of *Slave Songs* even distinguished between the Gullah pronunciations of St. Helena Island, the inland pronunciations of North Carolina, and the "negro-French" of Louisiana. Standing at the intersection of the oral and written traditions, *Jubilee Songs* followed the same pattern, transcribing the words as they were pronounced and sung.

As academic inquiry continued, James A. Harrison published his *Negro English* dictionary (1884), followed soon after by the formation of the American Dialect Society.

In addition to the ongoing linguistic study, respected novelists and poets continued writing dialect to establish their fictional characters. Everyone remembers Mark Twain's Huck Finn, but the poet James Whitcomb Riley was also becoming known for his rural white "Hoosier" dialect, and for organizing annual meetings of the Western Association of Writers in Winona Lake. For a time, dialect was serious business, except when it wasn't.

For every instance where a serious ethnographer tried to accurately transcribe language—for every instance of dialect in serious literature—there was a competing attempt by a singer in blackface who abused dialect in pejorative ways. And in the middle stood a bunch of whites who couldn't tell the difference. Rodeheaver's use of dialect serves as another way to examine the ongoing tension.

Of the forty-seven songs in *Plantation Melodies*, forty-six of them could be traced to folk spirituals, either from *Slave Songs, Jubilee Songs*, or the much-touted field work that Rodeheaver sponsored during the 1917 Atlanta revival meetings. The one remaining song did not have folk music roots, a clear outlier that did not fit in with the others. In fact, "Where Am De Chil'ren?" was composed by Charles Gabriel, a white man writing in Black dialect such as this:

> Way ober Jordan dey shout an' sing,
> Loud do de heab'ns wid de music ring.
> Wearin' de robes ob a mighty King,
> Halle-hallelujah, my Lord![82]

His song serves as a classic example of a late 1800s commercial spiritual—composed in the tradition of folk spirituals, yes, but also heavily influenced by the popular minstrel songs. Rodeheaver's decision to include it in *Plantation Melodies* can only be seen as naive, given his stated goal of presenting "authentic" spirituals as they were sung in Atlanta's Black churches. Gabriel's song represents the faux Black culture of northern minstrelsy. Certainly not authentic, whatever *authentic* meant. If Rodeheaver could not yet tell the difference, apparently his Black editors could, dropping "Where Am De Chil'ren?" from all subsequent Rodeheaver collections. Starting with *Negro Songs* (1923), assisted by T. H. Wiseman, and continuing for the next twenty years with publications edited by Fred Hall, the song was never again used.

Black artists and musicians were beginning to draw a line between real and fake. For instance, Paul Laurence Dunbar had risen to fame in the 1890s by writing lyrics like "Who Dat Say Chicken in Dis Crowd," a demeaning coon song that made him decent money.[83] But he turned from his former career and found greater success in literature, writing novels, short stories, and poetry—especially dialect poems.[84] Though he did not live long enough to see the Harlem Renaissance, Dunbar's work was revered by the next generation of Black writers. James Weldon Johnson called him "the first poet from the Negro race in the United States to show a combined mastery over poetic material and poetic technique, to reveal innate literary distinction in what he wrote, and to maintain a high level of performance." Johnson noted that "Dunbar's fame rests chiefly on his poems in Negro dialect," which compared favorably to the Scottish dialect poems of Robert Burns. In Johnson's estimation, Dunbar was the first to use dialect "as a medium for the true interpretation of Negro character and psychology."[85] This affirmation was shared by W. E. B. Du Bois, H. T. Burleigh, and most Black literary figures of their era. They saw a clear difference between Dunbar's "Who Dat Say Chicken in Dis Crowd" (demeaning dialect, now passé), and "When Malindy Sings" (authentic dialect, a legitimate literary expression). The same distinction applied to spirituals, considered by Harlem Renaissance Blacks to be an important literary form, and also considered to be recognizably different than the dialect used in blackface minstrelsy.[86] But again—could whites could tell the difference?

Paul Laurence Dunbar's most famous and popular poem, "When Malindy Sings," serves as summary example. The 1896 poem extolls the virtues of Malindy, a character based on Dunbar's mother. Its nine verses offer a sentimental portrayal of Malindy's singing while drawing particular attention to her renditions of "Come to Jesus," "Rock of Ages," and in the poem's climactic lines, "Swing Low, Sweet Chariot." As printed, the poem serves as a classic example of *eye dialect* (a term that came into use during the 1920s).[87]

> *Ain't you nevah hyeahd Malindy?*
> *Blessed soul, tek up de cross!*
> *Look hyeah, ain't you jokin', honey?*
> *Well, you don't know whut you los'*
> *Y' ought to hyeah dat gal a-wa'blin',*
> *Robins, la'ks, an' all dem things,*
> *Heish dey moufs an' hides dey faces*
> *When Malindy sings.*[88]

After the 1909 "Malindy" recording by Rev. James A. Myers of the Fisk Jubilee Singers, the poem was recorded many times by Black performers, including the jazz singer Abbey Lincoln (1961), Oscar Brown Jr. (1962), and Maya Angelou (1994).[89] Ironically, Dunbar had constructed "Malindy" with its own social pretext, that the white Miss Lucy could never replicate the "raal right singin'" of the Black Malindy:

You ain't got de nachel o'gans
Fu' to make de soun' come right,
You ain't got de tu'ns an' twistin's
Fu' to make it sweet and light.[90]

Ignoring Dunbar's apparent warning, the Italian soprano Lina Cavalieri performed and recorded the song, despite her presumed lack of "natural organs" to make the sound come right.[91] And Rodeheaver had enough faith in his own "natural organs" to attempt the poem as a white male. Given its sentimental memories of motherhood, its veneration of spirituals, and its quotations of old gospel hymns, the poem seemed a natural fit for his repertoire. He frequently performed it from memory at his public appearances and recorded it six times.[92] It became one of Rodeheaver's signature works, praised as a recitation performed "with splendid effect."[93]

In contrast to those who used dialect to purposefully demean or humiliate Blacks through the use of racist humor, Rodeheaver intended his recitations of "When Malindy Sings" as respectful tributes. His performances hold up well when compared to the best Black performers of the same material (James A. Myers), avoiding excessive exaggeration. But unlike Myers, Brown, Lincoln, and Angelou, Homer Rodeheaver was white. However respectful, he mixed his performances of "Malindy" with "darky" jokes and Prohibition songs in minstrel dialect.

This sort of confusion illustrates why Dunbar's poetry fell in and out of favor, later criticized as an artifact of blackface comedy. "No white racist has ever caricatured the Negro folk more grossly than Dunbar," some claimed, comparing his work to long-held stereotypes of the "charming, happy-go-lucky darkey."[94]

To his credit, Rodeheaver hired Black editors who understood this distinction better than he did. In Fred Hall's introduction to *Negro Spirituals and Folk Songs*, he cautioned that spirituals were "deeply religious and should not be sung in such a way to suggest frivolity or ridicule." In particular, Hall addressed the white singers who attempted Black dialect. "In singing the songs, dialect must not be overdone," he said.[95] For instance, Hall advised singers to drop certain letters and elide certain syllables, such as the "d' and "r" from *children* (pronounced and spelled as *chillun*). He corrected singers who gave too much emphasis on *de* in "nobody knows de trouble I see," producing an exaggerated affectation. More subtly, he critiqued concert singers who weren't Black *enough*, who were rolling the final *r* in words like "river" and "over," a technique borrowed from art songs. But this guilty group included Black singers like Paul Robeson and Marian Anderson, whose recordings of spirituals frequently demonstrated the precisely rolled *r*.

In short, the matter of Black dialect was as perilous then as it is now. The term *code switching* was not yet used, but Black concert singers learned to shift dialects when moving between social settings, especially when navigating the world of (white) opera. And though the term *blaccent* was not yet used (or *verbal blackface*), Rodeheaver (and other whites) would put on Black dialect when it suited them. Looking at the situation from the vantage point of history, Rodeheaver's dialect could be grouped in the same category as several recent examples, where white speakers borrowed Black speech patterns and (however well intentioned) strayed into perilous territory.

THE "END" OF BLACKFACE

Though he was a child of the postbellum South, Rodeheaver lived long enough to see the sweeping cultural changes after World War II. His death on December 18, 1955, came just a few weeks after Rosa Parks refused to move to the back of the bus in Montgomery, Alabama. In the last decade of his life, he saw the beginnings of the civil rights movement—but was slow to understand the implications. Good-hearted but tone deaf, he put on the burnt cork one more time for a final film performance of "When Malindy Sings." The result proved to be embarrassing, and the film itself disappeared quickly.[96]

Rodeheaver planned his 1955 *Miracles through Song* film series to preserve his ideas about gospel music.[97] Of the three films he finished before his death (he may have planned more), he intended the *Malindy* film as a tribute to spirituals, and by extension, an illustration of the African American influence on gospel songs. His basic plan seemed solid enough—the film features the Zion Travelers singing two jubilee-styled spirituals: "Heav'n" and "You Must Come in at the Door." And Rodeheaver's choice of artists was spot-on; their film performances were excellent examples of the jubilee tradition. The Los Angeles–based quintet had been singing together for ten years and had toured extensively. But Rodeheaver seemed to sabotage his casting choice by asking the quintet to dress in bib overalls and straw hats, singing from a plantation porch. If his romanticized view of southern life was not clear enough, Rodeheaver's voice-over reinforces his version of the past: "Down in the days when the cotton fields looked like snowdrifts and the scent of the magnolia mingled with the sound of the mocking birds." Then in the next scene, Rodeheaver enters the house in full blackface and a wooly white wig, dressed as an elderly house servant and carrying a tray. He begins reciting "Malindy" in much the same way as his first performances of the poem, forty years earlier.

Two conclusions are inescapable. First, his good intentions are obvious—he intends his film as a respectful tribute. But secondly, he cannot disguise his own insensitivity to changing attitudes and the emerging civil rights movement.

From Rodeheaver's perspective, his blackface film followed the same tropes he had seen since his teen years. For instance, the 1892 plantation spectacle *South*

FIGURE 7.5. Rodeheaver in blackface for the filming of "When Malindy Sings," 1955. Courtesy of Rodeheaver Collection, Grace College, Winona Lake.

before the War had featured a white singer in blackface, Charley Howard, who appeared in a plantation scene with African American quartets.[98] The elderly house servant, the overalls and straw hats, the plantation porch setting—all of these were stock in trade for the 1890s minstrel show. Rodeheaver borrowed these for his 1903 and 1904 *Dandy Darkies* show, 1912 *Old Black Sam*, and his 1955 film.

During Rodeheaver's lifetime, blackface escaped public criticism and academic scrutiny for a surprisingly long time. In the early 1930s, the first serious studies of minstrelsy cast it as a legitimate expression of Black folk culture, even seeing it as a way to champion Blackness.[99] Such arguments perpetuated the categories of "good" blackface and "bad" blackface, a long-standing argument that positioned some forms of minstrelsy as tolerably inoffensive, unspoiled by racism. After all (the theory went), many Black composers and performers enjoyed successful careers in minstrelsy. Many Black Americans loved Eddie Cantor and Al Jolson—including their blackface performances (often labeled as respectful and authentic).[100] Of course these attitudes would eventually fade, but we mention them here because of their influence on Rodeheaver and his generation of evangelical Protestants. The concept of "good" and "bad" minstrelsy also helps explain the long, odd afterlife of minstrelsy in American culture. After World War I, minstrelsy seemed to be dead, if measured by theater performances or sheet music sales. Then came an unexpected resurgence through the Hollywood blackface musicals of the 1930s, followed by more sustained censure.

In Chicago, the blackface radio show *Amos 'n' Andy* came under a torrent of criticism from Bishop William J. Walls of the AME Zion Church. Blacks in Chicago remained split on the issue (the *Chicago Defender* gave a measured defense of the show), but the critical tide had turned.[101] When *Amos 'n' Andy* moved to television in 1951, the NAACP immediately filed a court injunction and kept up public pressure until the show was canceled in January 1955 (just a few months before Rodeheaver made his blackface film).

What changed? Why did blackface lose its general acceptance? One might be tempted to cite a change in societal values, with a new generation of scholars applying their moral beliefs to past eras of history (in other words, the sin of presentism). But another answer is available, one which fuels our analysis here. As we revisited neglected sources, we uncovered a long-simmering criticism that had *always* existed but was rarely studied. For instance, the abolitionist Frederick Douglass had preached against minstrelsy as early as 1848.[102] William Lloyd Garrison offered similar criticisms in his abolitionist newspaper *The Liberator*.[103] And when the Fisk Jubilee Singers began touring, the northern abolitionists deliberately positioned their concert spirituals as an alternative to racist minstrelsy. As a new generation of African American scholars looked at the historical record, they continued to acknowledge the influence of minstrelsy on American popular music, but they were no longer willing to overlook the full story.[104] Whatever positive impact that blackface minstrelsy may have had, it was also rooted in white racism—from the very beginning.

By pointing out Rodeheaver's insensitive attitude toward blackface, we should note another sad irony. If the subject is "white performers who didn't get it," Rodeheaver had plenty of company on film. Bing Crosby's *Holiday Inn* became famous for his hit song "White Christmas," but it also included Crosby's now-forgotten blackface tribute to Abraham Lincoln.[105] The scene was excised from subsequent releases, but the list of blackface performances continued: Milton Berle (1949), Joan Crawford (1953), Sophia Loren (1953), Bugs Bunny (1953), Frank Sinatra (1960) . . . and the reader understands how this embarrassing timeline has not yet ended.[106]

Rodeheaver's insensitivities—his minstrel shtick, his "darky" jokes, his blackface performances—did not seem to harm his friendship with African Americans (such as T. H. Wiseman, Thomas A. Dorsey, and Frederick Douglass Hall). If they challenged him in private, they continued their public support of his recordings, publications, and meetings. Joseph Rodeheaver later noted that Homer "prizes highly the confidence of his Black friends who have recognized in him a sympathetic, sincere friend."[107]

For Homer Rodeheaver, the motivation to use African American music and dialect was multipronged. First, he intended them as respectful tributes to a people who had given the world a great gift of song. Second, Rodeheaver wanted to introduce spirituals to white audiences as the true roots of American music. Certainly, he financially benefited from the sales of his songbooks and recordings of spirituals, music that was increasingly in demand by whites due to concerts and performances by Black Jubilee groups. But we have no reason to claim this as his primary motivation in promoting the genre. Rodeheaver genuinely loved spirituals. Finally, and most importantly, Rodeheaver was convinced that the Christian message of spirituals was "of value to everyone."[108] He wanted all congregations—Black and white—to share music from the African American musical tradition.

8

JIM CROW REVIVALISM MEETS THE KLAN
"THIS BIG DEVIL OF RACIAL PREJUDICE"

All things equal, Sunday and Rodeheaver preferred an integrated tabernacle audience, singing from the same hymnal. At the peak of their revival meetings, 1915–17, they conducted integrated meetings in major northern cities like Philadelphia, Detroit, Boston, and New York. Despite such moments, pressure for segregated meetings had been mounting for several years. During the 1915 Philadelphia campaign, delegations from Washington, DC, and Richmond, Virginia, came for official site visits. Sunday was booking dates for 1918 (three years out) and considering offers from southern cities. Both of the all-white organizing committees came to Philadelphia with one condition—segregated meetings. After a period of reflection and prayer, the Sunday team accepted the terms.[1]

"We always fell in with the local custom," Helen Sunday explained later, defending the segregated meetings as a decision forced by local committees in the south.[2] Despite Billy Sunday's powerful influence, he could not overcome the social reality of Jim Crow. But this also meant he couldn't dodge the inevitable criticism from the Black community. During the 1917 Atlanta revivals, the Black-owned *Atlanta Independent* ran critical editorials and called for a boycott of the Sunday meetings, but Sunday managed to keep the support of most Black ministers by holding several special meetings for Blacks and featuring their music. A year later, Sunday endured more criticism during the Washington, DC, meetings, followed by a significant disruption in Richmond.

On the opening night of the campaign, Blacks arrived at City Auditorium expecting the usual Jim Crow seating. The auditorium, like other public venues in Richmond, allowed Blacks in the gallery while the whites took the main floor.

FIGURE 8.1. Chicago klansmen gather for a cross-burning ceremony, 1921. Courtesy of *Chicago Tribune*.

Tonight, however, armed police officers stood at each door of the tabernacle, barring Blacks from even entering.[3] When respected Black ministers were turned away (and reported to their congregations the next day), there was no way for Billy Sunday to dodge the withering criticism. "His managers have deemed it advisable to show only white people the way to heaven," said the editor of the *Richmond Planet*, a local Black newspaper. "Somebody blundered in excluding one of the most loyal races of people on the face of the globe."[4]

Excuses were made. Fingers were pointed. The all-white local committee blamed the police, and the all-white police force claimed they were following the committee's directive. For a time, no one blamed Sunday directly, perhaps because everyone knew he was displeased with the venue from the start. His advance team wanted to build another temporary tabernacle to seat 10,000 people, the usual requirement for any city that invited Sunday. But wartime lumber restrictions discouraged new building construction so, at the last minute, Sunday settled for a quick remodel of the City Auditorium. Organizers promised to extend the gallery to both sides of the auditorium, creating 6,000 seats and a choir loft for 750. Gargantuan for anyone else, but way too small for Billy Sunday. To make matters worse, the Sunday team arrived on site and discovered the expanded gallery had not been completed. The auditorium seated precisely 4,358, the smallest venue Sunday had used since Rodeheaver joined him in 1909. The seating situation forced Sunday to preach multiple times each day—which quickly exhausted him. In the meantime, someone had approved a crass solution to the tight seating arrangements: ban the Blacks entirely. On the opening day of the Richmond revivals, Billy Sunday preached to 15,000 whites in three back-to-back meetings. According to the *Times-Dispatch*, 5,000 more were turned away (though the white-owned paper did not report their race).[5]

Billy Sunday tried to make amends by scheduling a special Blacks-only meeting, a too-late idea that earned him more criticism from the *Richmond Planet*. Rather than attending Sunday's meeting, the Black ministerial association hired Rev. William H. Skipwith to hold alternate meetings at a Black church. The ministers tactfully avoided calling this a boycott, saying "the Conference has never had any quarrel with the Rev. Billy Sunday, nor his campaign committee."[6] The Black ministers had a reputation for theological conservatism and an affinity for Sunday's evangelistic zeal. To their way of thinking, they had been locked out of the meetings and cornered into yet another separate but equal religious service. "While Mr. Billy Sunday is pointing the white folks the way to heaven from the City Auditorium, these leading evangelists are pointing the colored folks to the same place," the *Richmond Planet* said.[7]

The situation had blown up without Rodeheaver's usual diplomacy. His standard solution, as demonstrated in Atlanta, was to organize a massed choir from the Black churches, ensuring their participation. But no one reached out to the Black churches in Richmond. In fact, Rodeheaver missed the first week of the Richmond meetings, still finishing up his WWI tour of Europe. After the first few meetings sputtered along, Billy Sunday read a telegram from his absent partner, announcing that Rodeheaver would arrive the next day. The tabernacle erupted in cheers, a reminder of how much Sunday depended on Rodeheaver's preparatory work.[8] Ever the trooper, the exhausted Rodeheaver disembarked in New York and immediately boarded a train for Richmond. The next night he was on the platform of the cramped City Tabernacle, back to his old routine as Sunday's warm-up act.

On his first night in Richmond, always mindful of crowd favorites, Rodeheaver sang "Carry Me Back to Old Virginny" with Bob Matthews and George Brewster.[9] The old minstrel song inadvertently summarized the tensions and insensitivities of the Richmond meetings:[10]

> *Carry me back to old Virginny.*
> *There's where the cotton and corn and taters grow.*
> *There's where the birds warble sweet in the spring-time.*
> *There's where this old darkey's heart am long'd to go.*
> *There's where I labored so hard for old Massa,*
> *Day after day in the field of yellow corn.*

Full of nostalgia for southern plantation life, the song perpetuated the "happy darkey" fable about enslaved people, a Lost Cause idea cherished by white southerners and increasingly repudiated by Blacks.[11] And, oh, it was complicated—the song was written by the African American composer James A. Bland, who made a lot of money writing minstrel songs.[12] But the minstrelsy era was over, and for that matter, so was the war, a point driven home in stinging editorials from the *Richmond Planet*. "White folks and colored folks were being killed and wounded," and now the same soldiers who fought side by side were returning home, the paper said.[13] Now just a few months after Armistice, the inevitable social change was already occurring.

Pressing the point even further, the *Richmond Planet* cited Billy Sunday himself, who had preached a sermon on racial reconciliation just a few months earlier in Providence, Rhode Island. "If the Negro is good enough to fight in the trenches and buy Liberty Bonds, his girl is good enough to work alongside any white girl in the munition factories," Sunday had said. Quoting the Providence sermon at some length, the *Richmond Planet* asked a logical follow-up question: "It would be interesting to know whether or not Mr. Billy Sunday's opinions in Rhode Island are the same as Billy Sunday's opinion in Virginia." Of course, this was the exact question that Sunday was trying to skirt. Or as Helen Sunday answered thirty years later, "We always fell in with the local custom."

The postwar racial tension simmered for a few years, followed by Chicago's infamous race riots of 1919, where 38 were killed and more than 500 injured. The incident provided fertile ground for the Ku Klux Klan, now busy organizing local chapters. By 1920, the Klan had imbedded itself into Chicago's political, social, and religious leadership, operating openly among white Protestants. For the next five years, Sunday and Rodeheaver were pushed and pulled by forces on both sides of the issue. Meanwhile, the Klan touted its populism and projected an aura of invincibility. The truth was more complicated.

The Klan's Achilles' heel—secrecy—became a vulnerability for its opponents to exploit. In 1922, the Catholic-backed *Tolerance* newspaper began publishing weekly lists of Klan members, exposing Chicago business and government leaders under lurid headlines like "Is Your Neighbor a Kluxer?" A few months later, the Chicago aldermen voted to ban all city employees from Klan membership, and the *Chicago Tribune* printed names of state workers who joined. As political pressure increased, the Illinois legislature passed a law banning robes and masks from public meetings.[14]

Though the Klan hyped its relationship to local pastors, it quickly lost the battle among religious leaders. The Federal Council of Churches expressed opposition in 1922, targeting the Klan's "secret, private, and unauthorized" agenda.[15] Many Protestant denominations added their own anti-Klan resolutions and anti-Klan editorials in their denominational magazines.[16] Locally, the Chicago-area Baptist ministers passed an anti-Klan resolution in 1921, followed by a similar one from the Methodist ministers.[17] And for the most conservative Protestants, Charles Blanchard of Wheaton College spoke through the *Christian Cynosure* magazine to oppose *all* oath-bound secret orders—not just the Klan, but also freemasonry, Odd Fellows, Elks, Jesuits, even college fraternities.[18] For Blanchard, the secrecy not only bred racism, but also drunkenness, womanizing, and a host of other sins.[19]

The Klan, ever the populist movement, responded with an end run around the denominational leaders. Starting in 1922, groups of hooded Klansmen visited Chicago-area churches, timing their entrance after the opening hymns, just before the offering.[20] One well-publicized stunt featured a demonstration of 500 Klansmen who entered a church, dropped money in the offering basket, and quickly disappeared. Of course, they called the newspaper first. Klan donations were never made privately. The timing and amounts of the donations were always accompanied by public proclamation, despite the familiar teaching of Jesus in the Sermon on the Mount, which prohibited public displays of alms giving.[21]

The Klan called these church stunts *visitations* (or privately, *invasions*), part of a national strategy to shore up its tenuous support in Protestant churches. And if the tactic worked on the local level, why not target the most visible icons of Protestantism, the revivalists? An early instance came in Spartanburg, South Carolina, when a hooded Klansman approached Billy Sunday's platform carrying a letter and a cash donation of $650. Rodeheaver accepted the envelope with an attempt at humor, feigning a trembling of the knees. Then Maj. John D. Frost rose from the audience with an impromptu endorsement, reassuring the audience that the Klan stood "for law and order, joining with the churches of the land in upholding Protestantism and Americanism, fighting for the separation of state and church, daring to protect the purity of womanhood, advocating free speech and free press and believing in but one flag and one country and that [is] America."

Sunday's response to Frost sparked hearty applause: "I could say amen to everything Major Frost said, for I didn't hear anything objectionable in that. And if you are on the right side, the Ku Klux won't get you anyway.["][22]

The anonymous Klansman finished by presenting the Sunday party with neckties and flowers, then silently left the auditorium. Before introducing the next song, Rodeheaver offered an awkwardly neutral conclusion: "This is the first time we have ever been visited by the Ku Klux Klan and we shan't forget them."[23] And like always, Sunday kept the offering.

Previous Sunday biographers have treated these Klan incidents with some charity, describing Sunday's response in neutral terms and positioning his racial attitudes as moderately progressive for his era.[24] Perhaps Helen Sunday is responsible for some of this misdirection. When William McLoughlin Jr. asked her about the Klan visits, she claimed that Billy Sunday "never expressed himself much about it—they attended a meeting in a tabernacle in a body once, I remember, but do not know where."[25] Our analysis of the tabernacle Klan visits, based on newly available sources, offers contradictory evidence. From January 1922 to January 1925, Klan groups visited Billy Sunday meetings on at least nine

JIM CROW REVIVALISM MEETS THE KLAN

occasions, with each incident covered by reporters.[26] Put it this way: Sunday never turned anyone away.

Rodeheaver and Sunday's highly effective method for filling the tabernacle meetings—the delegation system—worked as a mutually beneficial publicity stunt. Organize a group, march in with banners, be ready to sing your favorite song when Rodeheaver called for it, and maybe even present gifts. A fine night out for any group, and a guaranteed mention in the next day's newspaper. The official policy of "any group" meant just that—local churches, temperance societies, the Y.M.C.A., Boy Scouts, and local factories and businesses. From time to time, a few rabble rousers would test Sunday's mettle by showing up with a delegation of saloon owners or chorus girls. But sure enough, everyone was welcome. As odd as this sounds, the strategy was wholly consistent with Sunday's evangelical ideals. "Go ye into all the world," Jesus said, and Billy Sunday was all too glad to welcome groups of sinners to hear and sing the gospel. So why not welcome the Klan?

In Charleston, West Virginia, four masked and hooded Klansmen shook hands with Sunday and presented him with a check for $200. Sunday was quoted with an ambiguous endorsement, mixed with white supremacy: "You needn't be afraid. The Ku Klux Klan is like the sheriff: it don't bother you if you obey the laws. The Ku Klux Klan stands for Americanism, Christianity and [after a pause], supremacy of the race."[27]

FIGURE 8.2. Cover of the Indiana Klan's sheet music version of "The Old Rugged Cross," about 1923.

195

CHAPTER 8

At other times, Sunday seemed fearful of the Klan's intimidation, as when twelve Klan members showed up in Richmond, Indiana, with a letter and check for $50. Sunday accepted the gift and then addressed the audience: "I'm glad they came in to bring me something instead of to get me, I'll tell you that."[28] On another occasion in Nashville, Tennessee, a Klan newspaper quoted Sunday as saying, "I don't know anything about this organization except what I read in the newspapers, but from the lies people tell about me, I believe that all they tell you is not true. I never heard of the Ku Klux Klan having trouble with anybody who was behaving himself."[29]

After the first few incidents, Sunday's responses seemed a bit too careful, a calculated fence-sitting strategy that tried to keep all of the emerging factions in the same revival tabernacle, as if that were still possible. As a result, Sunday came in for sustained criticism—this time, not about the money or flamboyant preaching. The *Coshocton (Ohio) Tribune* published an editorial denouncing his friendship with the Klan, sarcastically calling him into account for "the 'free speech' that is dispersed by hooded bandits masked as the custodians of 'liberty.' We congratulate Mr. Sunday upon this acquisition of new admirers. As water seeks its level, he has found his."[30]

Then came the rumors. Sunday could hardly complain about groups who manipulated news coverage (he was a master of the art), but now the coverage turned against him. The *Chicago Defender*, trusted by Chicago's African American community as the "World's Greatest Weekly," provoked controversy with a jarring headline: "BILLY SUNDAY KLANSMAN?" The 1922 news item reported a claim from Dr. C. Lewis Fowler, founder of Lanier University, Atlanta, that "Billy Sunday is the leading Klansman in America."[31] Though Lanier is largely forgotten today, the *Defender* readers would have recognized his name. A Baptist minister and avowed white supremacist, Lanier had invited the Klan to take over his self-named university a year earlier. He installed Imperial Wizard William Simmons as president and then introduced a new curriculum that taught "pure, 100 percent Americanism."[32] The *Defender* was reporting nothing more than Lanier's rumor, exactly the coverage the Klan wanted. Of course the Klan would claim Sunday, if they could get away with it.

A Knoxville newspaper picked up the controversy and ran another headline, "Noted Evangelist Is Member of Ku Klux Klan."[33] In this incident, Sunday had followed the wishes of the local organizing committee by planning a segregated Blacks-only service. When an organization of Black ministers came out against the segregated meetings, Klan-friendly reporters twisted the story into another assertion that Sunday had joined the Klan, which Sunday again denied.

For the record, we found no evidence that Sunday or Rodeheaver were Klan members. Their names were not among the 10,000 Chicagoans exposed by the *Tolerance* newspaper (one can presume that if *Tolerance* had something credible on the revivalists, it would have been used). We also checked extant Klan records for Kosciusco County, Indiana (which are embarrassingly detailed), but found no names connected with Sunday or Rodeheaver's ministry.[34] The claims of Klan membership can be chalked up to the Klan's ongoing campaign of dirty tricks, but the rumors did not have to be truthful to be effective. Besides, Sunday was too busy shooting himself in the foot.

In their efforts to fill the tabernacle each night, Rodeheaver and Sunday could be chameleons who reflected local culture, whatever it was. Though his father died fighting for the Union in the Civil War, Billy Sunday would tap into the South's Lost Cause rhetoric when he was in the right neighborhood. For the 1923 meetings in Columbia, South Carolina, Sunday offered a tribute to Robert E. Lee, Stonewall Jackson, Jeb Stuart, and "other warriors of the South." At the same meeting, Homer Rodeheaver—whose father had also been a Union soldier—greeted a delegation of thirty-five Confederate veterans by playing "Dixie" on his trombone, and the crowd roared with approval.[35]

As the Klan visitations continued, Rodeheaver would sometimes receive advance notice of their tabernacle visits. During the 1925 Memphis campaign, he warned the crowd that the Klan would be in attendance the next night and made a lame joke about their bedsheets.[36] This opened the door for a Klan newspaper, the *Fraternalist* of St. Joseph, Missouri, to report on "a fiery cross of red incandescent lights" in front of Sunday's pulpit. After Rodeheaver's opening songs, "the vast audience sat down and thousands of handkerchiefs went to tear-filled eyes" as the choir sang "The Old Rugged Cross" and twelve robed Klansmen entered. According to the Klan report, Billy Sunday was overcome with emotion and described the ceremony as "wonderful."[37]

Of course, this account was heavily embellished by the Klan's reporter—who knows what Sunday really said—but the event itself, stripped of the overwrought prose, could only be damaging. Having cultivated a reputation for fearless preaching against all forms of sin, Billy Sunday had fallen strangely silent about racial bias, an omission that now seems deliberate.

For example, Billy Sunday's advance team found itself in a bind when preparing for his 1919 Tampa revivals. The Boston Red Sox had already rented out the largest park for spring training. Having no better place to pitch their giant tent, Sunday's organizers accepted the invitation of the Tampa Bay Casino, raising eyebrows and creating predictable jokes. But Sunday showed no fear of his hosts. Once the meetings started, he peppered his sermons with the usual denunciations against card-playing and dancing.[38] He did the same when delegations of naughty chorus girls, liberal preachers, and saloon owners came to his services. Anyone was welcome to attend, as long as they understood that Billy Sunday would not temper his message for anyone. Yet a few years later, when surrounded by Klan members, Sunday offered no condemnation of their racism and corruption. On the contrary, he praised the Klan for helping to keep order in communities and "ridding the places of undesirable characters"—without addressing the Klan's definition of *undesirable*. After Sunday was presented with a letter from the Shreveport, Louisiana, Klan, the *Shreveport Journal* reported that "[Mr. Sunday] knew some outrages had been committed by wearers of robes, he said, 'but there are some bad folk in the church, and some are even found in the cabinet at Washington. But that's no reason to condemn the whole organization.' He said he would wager that the Klan would endorse prosecution of any violators."[39]

Sunday could shake off the fringe rumors of Klan membership, but he could not dodge those who drew attention to his silence on racial bias. Francis J. Grimké, the influential African American pastor of Fifteenth Street Presbyterian Church in Washington, DC, noted that racism "is the one subject that [Sunday] always studiously avoids . . . as if the religion of Jesus Christ had nothing to do with it, was in no way concerned with it." "Is it not strange," Grimké thundered, "that all other sins should be related to Christianity, should be brought under its condemnation, and that this darling sin, which so many are rolling under their tongues as a sweet morsel, should alone be allowed to escape?" Grimké spared nothing in his denunciation: "This man, Rev. Billy Sunday, at times, seems to be a little courageous, judged by his vigorous denunciation of many sins; but when it comes to this big devil of race prejudice, the craven in him comes out; he cowers before it; he is afraid to speak out; at heart, he is seen to be a moral coward in spite of his bluster and pretense of being brave."[40]

Understanding Sunday's enormous influence, the *Chicago Defender* grieved over a missed opportunity, complaining that "the sensational preacher Billy Sunday has never been loud in his denunciation of lynchings, and yet he is supposed to be one of the chief exponents of genuine Christianity." The *Defender* accused Sunday of "religious hypocrisy" and noted his influence on thousands of converts and followers. If Sunday's apathy continued unchecked, "further regression would follow," the *Defender* predicted.[41]

CO-OPTING "THE OLD RUGGED CROSS"

The Klan's popularity coincided with another 1920s trend, communal singing, which could be experienced two ways: tabernacle revivalism or the community song movement. Both forms radiated winsome ideals. Both forms of communal singing represented religiosity, patriotism, and wholesome fun—exactly the ethos the Klan wished to appropriate for their weekly meetings. Klan leaders made communal singing a part of each rally, one more attempt to make their bigotry and intimidation compatible with respectable citizenship.

Cloaked in anonymous white robes and hoods, crowds of native-born white Americans would surround a burning cross and sing together, led by a "Kladd" who conducted their efforts. The Klan repurposed nearly every song genre by writing new lyrics to extoll the organization and its goals. The most popular community songs became immediate fodder for new Klan lyrics. Some attempts were awkward ("My Old Kentucky Home" as "The Old Klansman's Home"); some were laughably clumsy ("Yes, We Have No Bananas" as "Yes, the Klan Has No Catholics").[42]

In particular, Christian hymns proved to be attractive targets. The official "Order of Business" for the biweekly Klan meetings specified five Klan songs set to familiar tunes: "From Greenland's Icy Mountains," "Home, Sweet Home," "Blest Be the Tie That Binds," "America," and "Just as I Am."[43] At mass rallies "Onward Christian Soldiers" became the favorite, repurposed as "Onward Christian Klansmen," "Onward Ku Klux Klansmen," and "Onward, Valiant Klansmen."[44]

Homer Rodeheaver would not be immune to these stunts. Having plugged "The Old Rugged Cross" until it reached national fame, his best-seller proved to be irresistible for Klansmen in search of another song. Between 1923 and 1924, at least six versions of his song appeared with Klan lyrics, the most popular of which were "The Bright Fiery Cross" by Alvia Otis DeRee of the Indiana Klan, and "The Old Fiery Cross" by Paul Stone Wight of the New York Klan.[45] Both songs demonstrate subtle differences that say something about the Klan's reach into American culture.

Alvia DeRee's version functions as an over-the-top secular parody that strips out much of the religious imagery:

"THE OLD RUGGED CROSS" WORDS BY GEORGE BENNARD	"THE BRIGHT FIERY CROSS" WORDS BY ALVIA OTIS DEREE
On a hill far away stood an old rugged cross, *The emblem of suff'ring and shame,* *And I love that old cross, where the dearest and best* *For a world of lost sinners was slain.*	*Over the U.S.A., the fiery cross we display,* *The emblem of Klansman's domain;* *We'll be forever true, to the Red, White and Blue,* *And Americans always remain.*
Refrain: *So I'll cherish the old rugged cross,* *Till my trophies at last I lay down;* *I will cling to the old rugged cross,* *And exchange it some day for a crown.*	Refrain: *So, I'll cherish the Bright Fiery Cross,* *Till from my duties at last I lay down;* *Then burn for me a Bright Fiery Cross,* *The day I am laid in the ground.*

As somewhat of a contrast, Paul Stone Wight's version of the song uses most of Bennard's religious imagery for the first two stanzas, then offers a subtle misdirection in the third stanza:

"THE OLD RUGGED CROSS" WORDS BY GEORGE BENNARD	"THE OLD FIERY CROSS" WORDS BY PAUL STONE WIGHT
To the old rugged cross I will ever be true,	*To that old rugged cross I will ever be true,*
Its shame and reproach gladly bear;	*Its duties I gladly will bear;*
Then He'll call me some day to my home far away,	*He'll recall me some day to my home far away,*
Where His Glory forever I'll share.	*Where its glory forever I'll share.*

The comparison reveals a bit of theological mischief. Bennard's original stanza refers to the Christian afterlife, when Jesus Christ calls the believer to heaven, and the believer shares in Christ's ("His") glory forever. Wight corrupts the standard theology with an ambiguous pronoun. "He'll recall me some day" no longer has a clear antecedent, creating a question as to who, exactly, will recall the Klansman to heaven. But when they arrive in the afterlife, the Klansmen will eternally share in "its" glory—the Old Fiery Cross, not Jesus Christ.

No documentation has been found that shows that Rodeheaver approved these rewrites or benefited from any licensing arrangement. Given his business acumen and reputation for protecting his copyrights, Rodeheaver may have viewed these as infringements. The first page of the DeRees "Bright Fiery Cross" carried a disingenuous copyright notice: "Music Copyright 1913 by Geo. Bennard. Homer A. Rodeheaver, owner."[46] As the original song's composer, Bennard had registered a copyright for "The Old Rugged Cross" in 1913, licensed it to Rodeheaver for his 1917 hymnal *Awakening Songs*, and then sold the copyright outright to Rodeheaver in 1919.[47] For the average customer who looked at the cover art with its large cross and eight hooded Klansmen, and then saw the official-looking copyright notice, it seemed like Rodeheaver approved of the new project.

Like many other Klan activities, the truth hides behind a veneer of respectability. DeRee used "Music Copyright 1913" as a clever dodge. Rodeheaver owned both the words and music to "The Old Rugged Cross," but now DeRee had printed the music with competing Klan lyrics, for which he claimed a different copyright (but did not disclose it on the sheet music).[48] DeRee publicized his song in the *Fiery Cross* newspaper, then he convinced the Criterion Quartet to record it for the biggest Klan label, a sure way to generate sheet music sales.[49] And make no mistake—it was all about the money.

The Klan membership system existed to line the pockets of its leaders. Local recruiters took a cut of the annual dues ($10 per person) and then passed the rest to state leaders and the national leaders, the Imperial Wizard William J. Simmons and Imperial Kleagle Edward Clarke. Klan members were required to purchase their robe and hood from Clarke, who was also the exclusive vendor of bottled water used at Klan initiations ($10 a quart, supposedly from the Atlanta's Chattahoochee River, no substitutions allowed). "The 1920s Klan is best described as an enormously successful marketing ploy," a recent study concluded. "A classic pyramid scheme, officials at the top getting rich off of the individuals at the bottom, energized by sales agents with enormous financial incentives to sell hatred."[50]

Of course, the rank-and-file members wanted in on the action. The tightly controlled Klavern meetings funneled wads of cash to the leadership. But this left room at the bottom for closet industries run by local operators: Klan newspapers, dry cleaning, restaurants, photography studios, funeral services, tchotchkes of every sort. And music—piano rolls, recordings, sheet music. One researcher counted more than 100 Klan songbooks in the early 1920s, some with professional production values, others looking homemade.[51]

Chicago's music publishers took the Klan money when it came, creating all sorts of interesting ironies. A leading music engraver of sheet music, Rayner, Dalheim & Co., produced Klan songs such as "The Mystic City" (1922) and "Don't Forget America Needs You" (1925). The venture proved short-lived, and fifteen years later, the same Chicago company became the go-to vendor for Black gospel publishers such as Martin and Morris Music, who may not have known about Rayner's previous Klan business. The Klan's closet industry required mainstream vendors who were willing to accept Klan projects, especially the specialized trades like sheet music and record production.

KLAN RECORDINGS

The Klan's rapid growth in Indiana made Indianapolis a natural center for Klan-related business enterprise. With the Gennett Record Co. located only 70 miles east, Klan musicians used their studios several times in 1923 and 1924. None of the Gennett family were members of the Klan, but their custom division welcomed any customer who paid cash up front for a private-label recording.[52] And like the production vendors, many gigging musicians would take whatever studio dates came their way. The Criterion Quartet took the Klan projects and the Klan money, but cloaked their participation under a pseudonym (100% Americans). Other musicians openly supported the Klan, such as the Vaughan Quartet, who recorded "Wake Up, America, and Kluck, Kluck, Kluck" for Gennett in April 1924.[53] The recording was released on the Vaughan label with the Vaughan quartet listed as performers. And the sheet music, with its now-infamous hooded Klan artwork on the cover, was also published by James D. Vaughan.[54] The incident became an embarrassment to the company after the Klan craze collapsed.

The Rodeheaver Co. steered clear of the Klan sheet music business, but the Rodeheaver Recording Laboratories made several Klan recordings in 1924—a story that continues to perplex researchers. Homer Rodeheaver had positioned himself (and his company) as a supporter of African American music, including his use of spirituals in the tabernacle meetings, his published collections, his support of Black musicians, his recordings of spirituals. Yet someone at his company approved the Klan project. What did Homer Rodeheaver know of these deals?

Unfortunately, the trail grows cold in key places. Some of the midwestern record companies like Gennett and Paramount have studio ledgers or file cards to document recording sessions and personnel. But no such documentation exists for the Rodeheaver Co. Instead, researchers rely on the remaining evidence of newspaper accounts, trade journals, extant recordings, company catalogs, biographical information about the participants, and reconstructed timelines. Here is what we know so far.

In the summer of 1924, Paul S. Wight recorded six songs at the Chicago Rodeheaver studios, which were released with the red and gold Special label and "Rodeheaver Recording Laboratories" imprinted around the label rim. All six sides were unabashedly pro-Klan songs, with the label featuring the singer's name, Paul S. Wight, and his city, "Scottdale, Penn."

FIGURE 8.3. Paul Stone Wight's version of "The Old Fiery Cross," produced by Rodeheaver Records in 1924.

JIM CROW REVIVALISM MEETS THE KLAN

KLAN SONGS RECORDED BY PAUL S. WIGHT ON RODEHEAVER'S SPECIAL LABEL[55]

[K-1]: "Casey Jones" (9055), "God Knows We're Here to Stay" (9031)
[K-2]: "Then I'll Take Off My Mask" (9030), "The Old Fiery Cross" (9032),
[K-3]: "The Klansman and the Rain" (9056), "The Stuttering Klansman" (9054)

Born in Ohio to a minister of the Christian Church (Disciples of Christ), Wight dropped out of Moody Bible Institute in Chicago after two semesters[56] and traveled as a musician with several revivalists.[57] He married, had three children, and settled into ministry at the Christian Church in Scottdale, Pennsylvania, where he was active in the local Klan chapter. On July 4, 1924, he spoke at a Klan rally attended by 12,000, followed by his prominent role in a similar event on Labor Day weekend. The local paper reported that "Rev. Wight aroused much enthusiasm among the Klansmen by singing a number of Klan songs."[58] Sometime before the Labor Day event, Wight recorded his six songs, and was now positioning himself as a Klan musician. Confident that he was on the right side of a populist wave, Wight participated openly, ditching his hood and printing his full name and city on the Klan records.

His confidence proved to be misplaced. As an ordained minister with the Christian Church, he was openly bucking his church's anti-Klan stance. For two years, their denominational magazine had been running anti-Klan articles, followed by their formal adoption of a resolution condemning the Klan.[59] The situation blew up just three weeks after the Labor Day Klan rally, when Wight's church hosted a meeting of the Western Pennsylvania Christian Missionary Society. His invited guest speaker blasted the Klan's racial bias, right from Wight's own pulpit. The Scottdale church took its cue and pressured him to resign.

A few weeks later Wight showed up in Buffalo, New York, as the new pastor of the Glenwood Ave. Christian Church, which also became the headquarters of his new Klan front, the International Music Co.[60] Having learned a lesson (sort of), he lowered his Klan profile and ordered a new supply of his Special records, this time without his name on the label. The new version also replaced "Scottdale, Penn." with "International Music Co., 894 Glenwood Avenue, Buffalo, New York," which proved to be the same address as his new church. At roughly the same time, early 1925, he published *American Hymns*, a 36-page Klan songbook with "special prices to Klaverns and Dealers" advertised on the cover.[61] Cheaply produced, the book feels like a marketing strategy, with the last four pages advertising Klan recordings and sheet music. The book is full of suggestive sales strategies, such as this notice under "The Old Rugged Cross": "Above song recorded with sacred words on Record No. 1015. With Klan words No. K-2 and No. 75001." In a classic Klan bid for mainstream respectability, Wight had cited the famous Rodeheaver

```
┌─────────────────────────────────────────────┐
│        KLAN RECORDS FOR HOLIDAYS            │
│          Latest Double Disc Records         │
│ K-1  "Kasey Jones" (Humorous)               │
│      "God Knows We're Here to Stay."        │
│ K-2  "Then I'll Take Off My Mask" (Humorous)│
│      "The Bright Fiery Cross."              │
│ K-3  "The Stuttering Klansman" (Humorous)   │
│      "The Klansmen and the Rain" (Humorous) │
│ 75003 "The Cross in the Wildwood" (Quartette)│
│      "Why I Am a Klansman" (Quartette)      │
│ 75006 "Daddy Swiped the Last Clean Sheet" (Humorous)│
│      "The Gathering Klan."                  │
│           Player Word Rolls                 │
│ R-1  "The Bright Fiery Cross"               │
│ R-2  "The Mystic City"                      │
│              Sheet Music                    │
│ The Bright Fiery Cross..............35c     │
│ Then I'll Take Off My Mask..........25c     │
│              Klan Books                     │
│ "Why the Ku Klux Klan"..............25c     │
│ "Babylon the Harlot"................25c     │
│ All records and rolls $1.00 each. By mail $1.10│
│          Address THE RECORD CO.             │
│ ℅ W. C. Steen, Mgr.  4th Floor, 459 Washington Ave. Buffalo.│
└─────────────────────────────────────────────┘
```

FIGURE 8.4. Klan advertisement in the *Buffalo Truth*, a New York Klan newspaper, 1924.

and Asher recording of the original (No. 1015) and then juxtaposed his own Klan version (No. K-2) and the Deree Klan Version sung by the Criterion Quartet (No. 75001).

In addition to the six Klan songs he recorded himself, Wight released two additional Klan records on the Special label,[62] sung by the Chicago Male Quartet, plus a puzzling sixth recording of two patriotic songs sung by Rodeheaver, "Hats Off for Old Glory (The Flower of the U.S.A.)"[63] and "Battle Hymn of the Republic," both of which featured their original (not Klan) lyrics.[64]

All of these details are offered as a way to state the obvious: Wight had the assistance of someone at the Rodeheaver Recording Laboratory—someone who sold him a custom recording package that included six of his own Klan songs with custom labels and then helped Wight with a second release several months later, this time with a revised (and anonymous) label. And someone at the Rodeheaver Co. helped Wight issue two additional Klan quartet records, plus two patriotic songs that Homer Rodeheaver had previously recorded and not released.

In fairness, some of this cooperation between Wight and Rainbow Records may have been the direct result of the 1909 copyright law, which mandated a *compulsory* mechanical license (discussed in chapter 4). Copyright owners could not deny unsavory vendors from licensing their songs; any use was legal as long as the royalty was paid. We should also note the limits of Rodeheaver Co.'s cooperation. The Wight recordings on the Special label are never mentioned in Rodeheaver Co. ads, nor were they sold through Rodeheaver catalogs. Rodeheaver did not publish any of Wight's Klan music, or in any way promote the alternate Klan versions of "The Old Rugged Cross" (and as stated earlier, probably viewed these as infringements). Also, Rodeheaver did not sell Klan recordings or Klan songbooks at Billy Sunday's tabernacle book stall, or promote the Klan products from the tabernacle platform. Nothing can be found to indicate that Homer Rodeheaver promoted the Klan music.

But the Rodeheaver Co. did take the Klan's money, just as surely as Billy Sunday kept the Klan offerings when they were given. The essential incongruities cannot be missed: Gennett established itself as a pioneer label for African American music at the same time it recorded Klan groups; Rayner, Dalheim & Co. printed Klan sheet music and then became the primary print vendor for Black gospel publishers; and the Rodeheaver Co. produced seminal recordings of African American spirituals at the same time as it made six Klan recordings.

Meanwhile, Chicago's *Tolerance* newspaper saw no reason to regard the situation as a murky ethical quagmire, reminding its readers of a simple option: "Turn Down Klan Cash." The paper reported how the St. Louis Boy Scouts turned down a $15,000 donation from the Klan, which the Boy Scouts called "insidious propaganda to worm its way into this organization."[65] According to *Tolerance*, the Boy Scout's refusal preserved the purity of their mission—and was rewarded by other supporters who made up for the lost donation.

In its short fifteen-year history, the Rodeheaver Co. had grown from nothing to become one of the most influential gospel music publishers in the country. Known for aggressive business tactics and a huge marketing budget, the company had become a major player in the Chicago publishing scene, supporting a network of Chicago vendors that produced its products for national distribution. But despite all of this business growth, Rodeheaver consistently positioned his namesake company as a *mission*. Given his repeated claim, it seems fair to ask if he had achieved this objective, as suggested by the available evidence. It appears as though the Rodeheaver Co. followed the same model as any other midwest music vendor—good ole-fashioned business pragmatism. Any private customer was welcome as long as they paid cash on the barrelhead.

If the Rodeheaver Co. was losing track of its mission, the point can be further demonstrated by looking closely at the way its business model shifted from 1923 to 1925. When Rodeheaver started Rainbow Records in 1920, his intention was to record all kinds of gospel music. The Rainbow label released music from the top soloists and groups on the revival circuit. Lesser-known groups were released on the Special label, sometimes with pressings of a dozen copies or fewer—a classic vanity publishing model. Famous or not, all of the groups fell into Rodeheaver's idea of "sacred" music.

During his first three years in the recording business, some of Rodeheaver's assumptions proved unsustainable. His New York office didn't generate enough business to stay open. His Winona Lake office was successful for exactly two months during the summer, followed by ten months where his equipment was little used. His only real chance for sustainable success came from the Chicago office, but his prime location on Wabash Avenue's Piano Row brought the company a different sort of business.

Starting in September 1923 and extending through the early 1925, the Chicago Rodeheaver studio recorded surprisingly few sides for its own Rainbow label. Instead, a majority of the projects were for outside clients, many for release on Paramount Records and other labels. The list of groups who recorded at the Rodeheaver studio reads like the crossroads of American roots music: Wallin's Svenska Records, Jelly Roll Morton's Steamboat Four, Sodarisa Miller, Monette Moore, Ukelele Bob Williams, Thelma La Vizzo and the New Orleans Creoles, Papa Charlie Jackson, O'Bryant's Washboard Band, and more. From a purely musical standpoint, the output was remarkable, except for the nagging question of "what's missing." The Rodeheaver Co. had strayed from its mission.[66]

Another clue can be seen by examining Rodeheaver's schedule for the same time period, a classic "when the cat's away" scenario. Rodeheaver left on his world tour in September 1923 and did not return until June 1924. Once home, he immediately began a travelogue tour on the summer circuit, singing the songs he learned and telling exotic stories of the countries he visited. Then came his summer music conference in Winona Lake, followed by the start of the 1924 revival tour with Billy Sunday, including multiweek campaigns in Elmira, New York; Nashville, Tennessee; Jackson, Mississippi; and Newport News, Virginia. His nonstop schedule took its toll, and Rodeheaver was hospitalized with exhaustion in March 1925, missing two weeks of the Newport News meetings. In short, Rodeheaver spent almost no time in Chicago. He left the Rodeheaver Co. in the care of his brother, Yumbert, who held the title of treasurer and functioned as de facto CEO. Though the record division shared the same floor of the McClurg Building as the rest of the Rodeheaver Co., it was separately incorporated, led by its own business manager and recording engineers.[67]

One is tempted to paraphrase the Watergate question—what did Homer Rodeheaver know about the Klan business, and what did he do about it? We may never know, other than to surmise that Rodeheaver must have learned the details by the fall of 1924. His next steps seem like a classic "circle the wagons" response. Rodeheaver hired a person he could trust—his brother Joseph—to join the firm as business manager of the Rodeheaver Record Co. With a PhD in philosophy and a long career as a seminary professor, Joe seemed like an unlikely choice to lead a record company. He had no training in the technical aspects of record production and little stomach for the sharp tactics of the Chicago music business.

But Joe was family, and he was suffering through a difficult personal transition. After several years living in Denver and teaching at Iliff School of Theology, Joe's wife had taken ill and died, one of the reasons that Homer invited him on the world tour. After their return home in June 1924, Joe continued his usual summer role as dean of the summer sessions in Winona Lake. Then came an offer from Northern Baptist Seminary in Chicago, a part-time teaching position for the fall semester, which meant Joe was available to help with the company business for at least two days a week.

Right away he redirected the company's prevailing business strategy. If the Rodeheaver Record Co. could not subsist on gospel music alone, perhaps music educators could provide the sustaining income, rather than the jazz bands and blues singers. Soon Joe had blanketed the trade magazines with an announcement "of particular interest to singers and teachers." Make a test record at the Rodeheaver Record Co., hear your own voice, and then make additional recordings every few months to track your improvement. Joe also sent personal invitations to fifty of Chicago's best-known voice teachers, offering the first record "for about the price of one lesson."[68] By the end of 1925, Rodeheaver had stopped recording jazz and blues groups for Paramount, though it is hard to say if this was the result of the new business strategy, or (also likely) a sign that Rodeheaver's acoustic recording equipment was growing obsolete in the new electrical era. More to the point, the company's brief flirtation with Klan business was also over.

The Klan fell apart during a series of scandals in 1925, the biggest of which was the rape and murder trial of the Indiana Klan leader D. C. Stephenson. Any veneer of respectability vanished amid widespread reports of booze parties, sexual harassment, and financial corruption. The support of local clergy evaporated just as quickly, and with it went the target demographic of white Protestants, who stashed their robes in the attic and tried to paper over their racist past. The Klan music industry evaporated—though Alvia DeRee and others tried to repurpose its agenda as American nationalism. In 1928, he published yet another version of "The Bright Fiery Cross," morphing his racist song into an anthem about the American flag ("to this wondrous flag I will ever be true").[69] Meanwhile, after four years in Buffalo, Paul Wight bounced to yet another church in Wilkes Barre, Pennsylvania, where his first sermon was "How Long Can We Keep America American?"[70]

Homer Rodeheaver, meanwhile, continued his personal quest to understand African American music, a curiosity that would take him to Africa ten years later.

SINGING BLACK

In the Preface to *Singing Black*, Rodeheaver's account of his 1936 trip to Africa, he gave readers his answer to a nagging question: What is the origin of African American spirituals?

"Now here is an interesting thing about the spirituals," he wrote. "The rhythm came from Africa with the slaves. Mixed with the culture, refinement and religious

FIGURE 8.5. Rodeheaver filming during Africa trip, 1936. Courtesy of Rodeheaver Collection, Grace College, Winona Lake.

background of the southern white people, the spiritual was born." Rodeheaver said this on numerous occasions, both before and after his Africa trip, though he did so without any scholarly or ethnographic support. Yet the Preface to *Singing Black* continued with a tantalizing statement: "I made this trip to Africa to find out the source of the negro spirituals."[71] Having long advanced his own theory, Rodeheaver made it sound like the trip would provide the long-awaited, definitive key to understanding this important subject. Unfortunately, the Preface to the book was the last readers were to hear about this reason for the trip.

Rodeheaver traveled with Methodist Bishop Arthur J. Moore (1888–1974) and others, and *Singing Black* reads like a travelogue transcribed from Rodeheaver's personal diary, where he tells of visiting villages, observing work of missionaries, and encouraging workers in African hospitals and schools. Sometimes Rodeheaver took out his trombone to attract a crowd and then sang several spirituals. *Time* magazine reported that he "often [started] alone in a clearing and eventually attracting 1,000 or so black heathens." His trombone, it seems, was his means of security. "Rodeheaver said he needed no guards or protection from the savages. When he was in danger, he just tooted his horn, and it pacified the wild men."[72] He left behind a few copies of his *Southland Spirituals* and hoped they would be translated and sung for him on a return trip that never occurred.

But the origin of spirituals? The trip to Africa and *Singing Black* revealed no new information, and Rodeheaver avoided the subject for the rest of the book. His journey to Africa and his book about his travels provided him with entertaining stories and home movies for audiences when he returned home. Newspapers were full of accounts of the trip that seemed to grow taller and taller with each telling. Articles repeated Rodeheaver's claim that "Africans like spirituals" and "all Africa is singing spirituals now," including his belief that "the natives" loved his rendition of "De Brewer's Big Hosses." One reporter called this "doubly remarkable, because Congo villages have no horses, never saw a big 'brewery wagon.'"[73]

Bishop Moore would later preside over Homer Rodeheaver's funeral on December 20, 1955, held at First Methodist Church of Warsaw, Indiana. Moore eulogized his friend and cited examples of how Rodeheaver touched lives, starting with a story from their Africa trip. But Moore did not wax eloquently about Rodeheaver playing his trombone in the jungle, or his singing of spirituals to groups of people in remote villages. Nor did he talk about Rodeheaver's recordings and publications of spirituals, something Rodeheaver himself felt were among his most important achievements in advancing the musical and spiritual legacy of African Americans that he had first encountered in his childhood. Instead, Moore said, "Come with me. We're on the banks of a river way back in the jungles of Africa, a thousand miles from an electric light and they bring up a little hunchback, black boy with eyes I can never forget. He's a preacher today because Rody loved him and helped him through school."[74] It was Rodeheaver's love and respect for the individual and his desire to help those who were disadvantaged—regardless of race—that Moore remembered in the hours after the death of his friend.

In evaluating Rodeheaver's views on race, we discovered a complex jumble of attitudes, actions, and inactions. There is no denying that he missed opportunities to condemn racism, and that he failed, in critical times and ways, to live up to his own stated ideals. Yet Rodeheaver's view of racial issues should not obscure what we know was his genuine affection for Blacks, his care for and employment of many African Americans, and especially his promotion of spirituals. For a white man who grew up in the Jim Crow–era South and lived through a time of immense social and cultural change, Rodeheaver's advocacy of spirituals pointed forward to a better understanding of Black music, what he called "the beauty and artistry and religious power of these songs of an heroic race."[75]

9

PRESERVING AND EXPORTING THE GOSPEL SONGS
"BRIGHTENING THE CORNER AROUND THE WORLD"

In 1923, Homer Rodeheaver embarked on a world tour with his old friend, W. E. Biederwolf, part of an entourage that included his brother Joseph, Bible teacher Grace Saxe, illustrator Florence Hay, and news reporter Theodore T. Frankenberg. Their travel schedule was a bit open-ended, but they planned to be gone for at least nine months, visiting Hawaii, Japan, China, Korea, the Philippines, Thailand, Ceylon, India, Australia, Egypt, the Middle East, and then home.[1] More to the point, Rodeheaver missed Billy Sunday's entire 1923–24 revival season, their second extended separation.

By this point, Biederwolf had retired from the revival circuit and was serving as director of the Winona Lake Christian Assembly, allowing him more time to travel. Now 42, Rodeheaver had reached the pinnacle of success, whether measured by the spiritual goals of a revivalist or by the secular metrics of annual income, brand awareness, and celebrity appeal. Perhaps he was a little bored of the revival format, but he never tired of travel. After the revival years, he rarely lived in one place more than two weeks at a time. His stepmother, Bettie, continued to live at his Rainbow Point home in Winona Lake, keeping the upstairs bedroom ready. But he rarely stayed long.

Like many other successful middle-aged men, Rodeheaver began to think about his legacy, which for him, meant the legacy of gospel songs. A few days into the world tour he explained his reasons for the trip to a Hawaiian magazine writer, who reported, "Mr. Rodeheaver will sing and play and endeavor to introduce American singing methods in the mission field.... He believes that phonograph records of Gospel forms can be a big help in spreading the Gospel message."[2]

FIGURE 9.1. World tour, 1923–24. Courtesy of University of Arkansas Library Special Collections, Theodore Thomas Frankenberg Collection, Fayetteville, Arkansas.

Though he was using new technology, Rodeheaver was by no means the first American to export gospel songs to foreign countries. Notable earlier trips included the Moody and Sankey tour of Great Britain in 1873–75, the Fisk Jubilee Singers tours of Great Britain and Europe in 1875–78, and the world tour of gospel singer Philip Phillips during the same period. Later tours included the 1913 Sunday School Tour Around the World, featuring gospel pianist Alvin Roper (who soon published an instructional book with Rodeheaver). And the grandest tours of all were mounted by R. A. Torrey and Charles Alexander, who circled the globe nonstop between 1902 and 1907. Though these earlier trips did not take advantage of recordings, they sold millions of gospel hymnals. (Sankey and Alexander's international sales were particularly robust.)

As researchers continue to study these early gospel music tours, they have reevaluated conventional interpretations, where American musical culture is said to have emerged on the world scene during World War I, primarily through the influence of ragtime and jazz. Yes, but one should not overlook the influence of American evangelists and missionaries who spread American gospel songs to Europe, Africa, and Asia as early as the 1870s. If an international audience heard "American" music before 1900, it was probably a gospel song. Embarking on their world tour, Rodeheaver and Biederwolf were preparing to export the Gospel Song Evangelistic Movement, that uniquely American formula of winning souls "by means of gospel singing and evangelistic address."[3]

EXPORTING GOSPEL SONGS

Spurred on by Frankenberg's publicity and headlines such as "Around the World with the Gospel Horn," Rodeheaver propagated his essential idea, that "gospel music is the universal language."[4] He reported that international interest in gospel songs transcended language and culture: "Even where they could not understand the words at all, they would sit and listen as long as we would sing or play the gospel songs and hymns."[5] As Rodeheaver became convinced of their international value, he began to consider ways to equip missionaries to use gospel songs more effectively. "I am especially anxious to develop our school and conference ideas," he wrote to Billy Sunday while steaming from Hawaii to Japan, continuing their ongoing conversation about training the next generation of evangelists and songleaders.[6]

Rodeheaver believed his idea was straightforward and simple: teach American gospel songs to indigenous cultures, translating the lyrics to local languages as much as possible. Then, use technology (printing, sound recordings, radio) to propagate the message. But only a few weeks into his trip, Rodeheaver ran into complications that challenged his assumptions. Rodeheaver wrote Billy Sunday with his surprised observation, that "the songs we hear and know as Hawaiian have been written by music teachers who have come in there from England or America or some other country." But Rodeheaver wanted to hear "the real Hawaiian music," which he described as having a chantlike similarity to Native American music. Rodeheaver noted how the westernized "Hawaiian" music was becoming more popular than the indigenous expressions. He also observed that the Hawaiians "seem to have a little of the same attitude about their music as some of the finicky Negro churches have about their spirituals."[7] As seen in his correspondence with Billy Sunday (and in his earlier experiences in Atlanta), Rodeheaver could recognize one part of the problem: the local cultures who were giving up their indigenous music in favor of the "better music" advocated by missionaries and educators.

Rodeheaver had stumbled into long-standing issues that proved troublesome for musicologists and anthropologists who studied the spread and acculturation of American musical idioms. More to the point, Rodeheaver was about to be confronted with the natural consequence of his own ideas—he became guilty of the same problem he noted in Hawaii. As gospel music spread around the world, it influenced indigenous approaches to religious music making—and in many cases, stifled local creativity in favor of the styles preferred by American missionaries.

The problem had been brewing since the early 18th century, when various Protestant groups began spreading their ideas beyond their own borders. For instance, Moravian missionaries left Bohemia to establish colonies in North and South America, Asia, and Africa. In addition to preaching the Christian gospel, they exported their traditions of congregational part singing, choral music in the German style, and brass choirs. No doubt their musical displays created quite a local stir—imagine the astonishment of Native Americans hearing a group of Moravian trombone choir players for the first time![8] But too often the missionaries viewed this indigenous curiosity (or flat-out bewilderment) as confirmation that their brand of church music had some sort of universal power, some sort of mysterious unction that could be transmitted between cultures.

Several problems were surfacing. Many of the missionaries failed to appreciate or respect indigenous culture, assuming that "primitive" cultures were inferior to the western tradition. This neglect was accompanied by strong suspicions about musical idioms used in the ritual of non-Christian religions. Back home, their supporting churches were actively rejecting emerging American idioms tainted by what they considered to be immoral associations (seen in their condemnation of ragtime and jazz). So certainly the same standard of purity must be enforced on other cultures, they reasoned. While the phrase is over-worn and not at all accurate, the missionaries saw music as a "universal language," but this idea often functioned as a thinly-disguised code for "western music," now imposed on other cultures. In time, evangelicals would implement more nuanced approaches, but for now, Rodeheaver was observing a brewing problem. His own approach to Protestant Christianity was not exclusively Western—he recognized the problem of acculturation in African American churches and later in Hawaiian churches. But in retrospect, he did not see his own missionary strategy as part of the growing problem. His experiences in Japan provide a classic example, offering insight into the ongoing beliefs and expectations of American gospel song performers.

Before he arrived, Rodeheaver had met many Japanese onboard his ship, returning to Tokyo to find their families after the recent earthquake. The revivalists arrived in Japan on September 30, 1923, less than a month after the *Kanto Daishinsai* (great Kanto earthquake) caused more than 100,000 deaths and left two million people homeless. Rodeheaver planned to meet Japanese friends who had already understood his revival music. Juji Nakada studied at Moody Bible Institute (1896–98), where he became active in the International Holiness Union

FIGURE 9.2. Ugo Nakada, Rodeheaver's Japanese protégé. Courtesy of Rodeheaver Collection, Grace College, Winona Lake.

and Prayer League. Having the Moody and Sankey model of preaching and singing the gospel, Nakada began to apply the same idea when he returned to Japan. He cofounded the Oriental Mission Society, the Tokyo Bible Institute, at least nine churches, and *Tongues of Fire*, a Holiness journal. Many called him "the D. L. Moody of Japan."[9]

If so, Juji Nakada was missing one important part of the revivalist model, a Sankey-like singing evangelist. Hoping that his own son Ugo might develop into such a role, Nakada had enrolled him in a Tokyo mission school in 1915. When a missionary played Rodeheaver's recording of "Since Jesus Came into My Heart" on a Victrola, the song captured Ugo Nakada's interest even though he could not understand the English words.[10] After gaining permission to take the disc home, Nakada played the record repeatedly and memorized the lyrics, syllable by syllable. According to Rodeheaver's later account, Nakada "did not understand their meaning, but he did understand the spiritual appeal of the music."[11] Rodeheaver believed the gospel songs possessed an essential spiritual quality that could be understood by any culture, even cultures that had a limited understanding of English or Western music.

The Nakadas eventually wrote to Rodeheaver in America, asking for more records, which he was happy to send. This may have been the impetus for Rodeheaver recording four gospel songs in Japanese for his Rainbow label.[12] Then Ugo Nakada traveled to the United States in 1920, visiting the Billy Sunday Cincinnati meetings but narrowly missing a chance to meet Rodeheaver, a major disappointment. So when Rodeheaver planned his 1923 Japan tour, the elder Nakada assigned Ugo to be Rodeheaver's pianist and translator, hoping the relationship would develop into a mentorship opportunity.

The situation worked out famously; Rodeheaver told and retold Ugo Nakada's story for years, offering it as another illustration of the power of gospel music.[13] In a spoken word recording for his Rainbow Records dealers, Rodeheaver reported that Nakada "had no one to teach or help him, so he got all my records he could secure. Through studying and imitating them, he became the best gospel singer in Japan."[14] On the surface this seems like another of Rodeheaver's hyperbolic marketing claims, but in this case, the breathless praise of Nakada was true.[15] Quite taken with his young friend, Rodeheaver paid for his return to the United States for additional study.

Strongly influenced by Rodeheaver's music and methods, Ugo Nakada made a career of adapting American gospel music for his Japanese audience. With the help of Satoshi Moriyama, Ugo Nakada founded *Ogikubo Eikou Kyoukai* (Ogikubo Glory Church in Suginami, Tokyo), part of a growing network of Japanese Holiness churches. He served as the church's music director, started a publishing company known as *Seika no Tomo* (Friends of Seika), published a Japanese translation of Handel's *Messiah*, and wrote Japanese gospel songs for children, youth, and adults. Working directly with Rodeheaver, he produced a Japanese-language hymnal used by immigrants to the United States, *A Special Selection of Revival Hymns in Japanese*.[16] Today, Nakada is regarded as a seminal leader of evangelical church music in Japan. Rodeheaver's method of spreading gospel songs—through missionary endeavor and new technology—would be repeated in many international locations, though space does not permit a full exploration here.

At the end of the nine-month tour, Rodeheaver returned home and released a Rainbow Record to preserve some of his thoughts about the trip. "On our trip around the world we sang 'Brighten the Corner' in the language of practically every country we visited," Rodeheaver said and then demonstrated by singing verses in Hawaiian, Japanese, Korean, Amoynese (Xiamenese), and Mandarin Chinese.[17] The trip kindled an amateur fascination with world languages. On each leg of the trip he asked his hosts to translate "Brighten" and teach him the lyrics phonetically. His 1923 pocket planner includes hand-written phonetic pronunciations of "Brighten the Corner" in the five languages he recorded, plus eight additional languages: Tagalog, Chinese-Swatow (Shantou), Chinese-Canton, Cantonese-Bangkok, Siamese, Burmese, North New Ireland, and Egyptian (Arabic).[18] After

CHAPTER 9

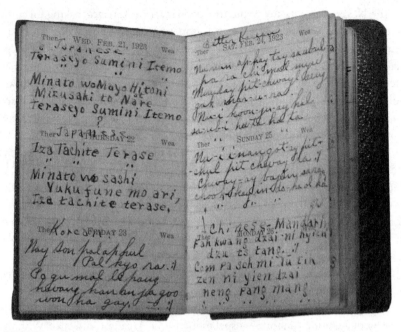

FIGURE 9.3. Rodeheaver's world tour diary with his phonetic translations of "Brighten the Corner," 1924. Courtesy of Rodeheaver Collection, Grace College, Winona Lake.

returning from his trip, he continued to use these translations as he gave travelogue concerts in the United States.

Rodeheaver's plan to export gospel songs proved successful enough (he accomplished his objective of spreading the Christian gospel through song) but also full of unintended consequences and resulting controversies. The account cited at the beginning of this chapter framed his activities as a form of Americanization: "Mr. Rodeheaver will sing and play and endeavor to introduce American singing methods in the mission field."[19] Another news report promised that "American methods of mass singing will be taught."[20] Like other musicians of his era—secular and sacred—Rodeheaver had been zealous in developing a "true" American music. Having accomplished this objective, the Americans now measured their success by the speed at which they achieved international cross-cultural recognition. As argued earlier, the missionaries and traveling evangelists who spread their American gospel songs may have been "first," influencing cultures before the global spread of American ragtime, jazz, and blues. Nevertheless, all of these sprang from the same well—the American vernacular tradition.

When discussed in relation to England and Europe, America's first cultural exports (vernacular music) were regarded in a positive light. Today, cultural theorists continue to defend these as "good" exports—especially jazz, now described as "Americanization at Its Best."[21] But when viewed in relation to its impact on developing countries, this Americanization came to be seen as an imposition, not a benefit. Beginning in the 1970s, terms such as *cultural imperialism* and *cultural hegemony* entered the scholastic vocabulary as negative assessments of America's cultural exports.[22] Influenced by this ongoing conversation in the academy, evangelicals after Rodeheaver began to question their wholesale transplanting of American church music to other cultures.[23]

Much could be learned from an in-depth study of Rodeheaver's international outreach; perhaps others will make this a subject of further inquiry. For now, it helps us understand the global impact of American music in a more nuanced way. And it helps us understand more about Rodeheaver himself—the insatiable curiosity that allowed him to approach the uncertainty of modern life with his trademark optimism. But like his experience with African American music, Rodeheaver stumbled into complicated ideas. He embraced notions about the power of music but struggled to define what, exactly, that power *was*. He believed in musical universals with a naive assumption that gospel songs communicated universal spiritual ideals. Whatever one makes of this, one of his essential ideas has ongoing merit. In his newspaper interviews from 1924, Rodeheaver emphasized communal singing as the essence of American music ("American methods of mass singing"). As such, his idea provides an interesting alternative to current studies, which frame Americanization as the global spread of jazz and other roots music (essentially performance, not communal, idioms). Rodeheaver was probably disappointed when he discovered that gospel songs did not actually have universal appeal, especially in developing cultures. But his attendant ideas about communal singing resonated with nearly every world culture he encountered. In his own way, he stumbled onto a possible universal: the worldwide appeal of communal song.[24]

SISTER AIMEE

In addition to leaving plenty of time for philosophical ruminations, steamship travel allowed Rodeheaver time to correspond with old friends, including the celebrity evangelist Aimee Semple McPherson. Their friendship had been the subject of much speculation—a romance? a business relationship? No one knew for sure. Rodeheaver and Sister Aimee wrote back and forth for the duration of his world tour, mostly about business and their mutual embrace of gospel songs.[25]

Just before leaving from Los Angeles on their world tour, Biederwolf and Rodeheaver agreed to lead a service at the Angelus Temple, recently constructed by McPherson.[26] Rodeheaver had known her since 1919, when she arrived in Tampa at the tail end of a Billy Sunday campaign. She rolled into town in her custom-painted "gospel car," set up another revival tent, and held competing meetings—a blatant breach of the unwritten revivalist code. McPherson also contracted with the *Tampa Times* to serialize her Easter sermons, inadvertently bumping Sunday's coverage. Sister Aimee was 29 years old and attractive. Billy Sunday looked all of his 56 years, sometimes tired and grumpy, and surrounded by a team of middle-aged assistants. Two women on his team, Grace Saxe and Virginia Asher, had forged their own national reputations as highly respected Bible teachers. But both were now in their 50s and dressed as respectable business leaders or society matrons—nothing like Sister Aimee's carefully cultivated flapper persona.

When interviewed many years later, Helen Sunday recalled Billy's ire during the 1919 Tampa meetings. McPherson attempted to pay her respects by visiting a Sunday meeting, but he banned her from sitting on the platform with the other ministers. No surprise. McPherson's second husband had filed for a separation in 1918, claiming she had abandoned him for the revival circuit. And McPherson never joined the International Evangelistic Association, the Winona Lake watchdog group that looked suspiciously at her flamboyant breach of doctrinal and social conventions.[27] When newspapers started calling her "the female Billy Sunday," the real Billy Sunday seemed to draw a line.

According to Helen Sunday, Billy Sunday's irritation in 1919 did not rub off on Rodeheaver, who was busy escorting McPherson to Tampa's bathing beaches in the afternoons.[28] What was their relationship, exactly? Rodeheaver still enjoyed his status as a perpetual bachelor; Sister Aimee flouted her legal separation from Harold McPherson. They should not have been surprised at the gossip and speculation. At the very least, they forged a business agreement for the Rodeheaver Co. to print the first Foursquare denominational hymnal, *The Pentecostal Revivalist*, as well as several later editions. And Rodeheaver visited Angelus Temple multiple times between 1923 and 1931, giving concerts and leading songs at special events. They were at least friends. No one could be blamed for asking questions and floating rumors.

Though ten years her senior, Rodeheaver understood her better than most, especially their mutual need for perpetual motion. They both knew the loneliness of the road, the peril of celebrity, and the unexpected problems of sudden wealth. And while Rodeheaver differed with McPherson's ideas about Pentecostal healing, he and McPherson agreed on one important idea: the appeal and importance of gospel songs.[29] A month before Rodeheaver's 1923 visit, one observer described an Angelus Temple church service like a tabernacle meeting, with a grand piano, pipe organ, 20-piece-orchestra, and 80-voice choir joining the congregation of 5,000 in singing old gospel songs.[30]

McPherson took Rodeheaver's ideas considerably further than he intended. Rodeheaver maintained a distinction between standard hymns and gospel songs ("never intended for a Sunday morning service").[31] McPherson spliced the liturgy of tabernacle revivalism directly into her Sunday worship services. While Rodeheaver had not yet abandoned the revival circuit, he could see the future by observing McPherson, a next-generation revivalist who left the sawdust trail to build a local church through an aggressive media presence. Paul Rader did the same at his Chicago Gospel Tabernacle.

After returning home from the world tour in June 1924, Rodeheaver continued his periodic visits to Angelus Temple, provoking more questions about a possible romance. When he was away, McPherson had flirted through the newspapers, telling reporters her dreamy hopes for a perfect husband: "He must be good looking, six feet tall, a preacher, a trombone player, sing well, and be 'a good and holy man.'" Though the wire report ended with, "She has not met one like that yet," her description sounded suspiciously like Rodeheaver.[32]

Then in February 1930, *Time* magazine passed along a rumor about Rodeheaver's engagement to Sister Aimee, a gossipy story that also printed her denial. McPherson confirmed that Rodeheaver had given her a ring—but apparently not that sort of ring. Despite the frothy headlines and the tantalizing possibility of a Christian celebrity wedding, nothing came of the news.[33] Several McPherson biographers later probed for any evidence to confirm a possible engagement, always coming up short. Seventy years after the supposed event, daughter Roberta Semple Salter could offer only a fleeting memory of Rodeheaver. "He wanted to marry my mother, but Mother said no. She liked him fine but didn't want to marry him."[34]

In 1931, Sister Aimee found a third husband in David Hutton. The marriage lasted until Hutton sued for divorce in 1934, complaining that his weekly allowance was too small and the gossip was too invasive. Thoroughly disenchanted with the shenanigans, evangelical magazines continued to print her name as "Aimee Semple McPherson Hutton." As the debacle settled, Rodeheaver stopped participating in Angelus Temple events. He never returned after 1931 and apparently breaking off personal contact. Another wishful engagement rumor surfaced in 1935, immediately denied by Sister Aimee, who claimed to be greatly surprised. "So surprised, in fact, I can only think of one who might be more surprised," she said. "That one would be Mr. Rodeheaver."[35] Which was true. Another reporter quoted his denial: "You may tell the world that we are not going to get married."[36] After considerable gossip-mongering, all that the reporters could find was a business relationship: "He said his only relations with Aimee centered about the sale of his songbooks in her meetings," one report concluded, ending the matter for good.[37]

CHAPTER 9

RAGTIME AND JAZZ

As Rodeheaver stumbled into complicated questions about exporting American culture, he also became embroiled in a moral panic about musical style—ragtime and jazz. When the Atlanta newspaper reporters described Rodeheaver's gospel songs as ragtime in 1918, their description sounded like a compliment rather than an indictment. "Brewster literally fights the keys, bringing out the harmony in great thunderous chords, while Matthews' hands run up and down the keyboard of the other piano in ragtime accompaniment," Ned McIntosh had said, calling it "thrilling, contagious, infectious."[38]

The newspaper accounts of Rodeheaver's "ragtime" demonstrate how flexible the term had become. Born in African American communities and popularized by piano-playing composers such as Ernest Hogan, Scott Joplin, and Thomas Turpin, true ragtime featured distinctive syncopated rhythms played in a relaxed, unhurried way—not just a rhythmic pattern, but also a characteristic feel. Ragtime drew from several traditions, a happy merger of the vernacular and cultivated, the urban and rural, the European and the Afro-Cuban. The 1893 Chicago World's Columbian Exposition is often cited for bringing the ragtime piano style into public awareness, as was true with Sankey's gospel songs. After the fair, ragtime found a home in the music hall and early vaudeville, where it was embraced by instrumental combos, bands, and theater orchestras. The word *ragtime* became a generic label for any popular music with syncopated rhythm, a catch-all for popular music that included cakewalks, coon songs, and even two-step marches.

At the peak of tabernacle revivalism's popularity, jazz seemed to eclipse ragtime. The all-white Original Dixieland Jazz Band migrated from New Orleans to Chicago in 1916, when Joseph Swerling visited the Shiller Cafe and called it "The First Jass Band."[39] Researchers debated his claim for the next hundred years. Swerling's review for the *Chicago Tribune* described a new musical style where "wind instruments predominate and the music is very raggy."[40] Though Chicago became the northern gateway for jazz groups, Rodeheaver was not likely to have heard jazz in its natural environment. A lifelong teetotaler, Rodeheaver did not frequent saloons and clubs.

A year later, by a fluke of history, the Original Dixieland Jazz Band had moved to Manhattan for an extended stay at Reisenweber's Cafe—just before Billy Sunday and Rodeheaver arrived for their ten-week revival meetings. And the jazz group recorded its seminal sides with Victor just a few months before Rodeheaver's tabernacle recordings with the same label. So it seems appropriate to note the proximity and coincidence. The rise of jazz occurred at the high point of tabernacle revivalism but did not yet achieve popular attention. Sunday made no mention of the new jazz craze during his New York sermons, though he had plenty to say about drinking and dancing.[41]

Like ragtime, *jazz* quickly became a misused term. When the Paul Whiteman Orchestra played a repertoire of dance music, vaudeville, and Tin Pan Alley, the critic Wilder Hobson refused to call it jazz. "Whiteman's publicity was a particularly striking example of why the word 'jazz' quickly lost any semblance of a generally accepted meaning," Hobson wrote. "Before Whiteman's debut it had at least had definite connotations of noise and confusion; afterwards it was applied to virtually any music in fox-trot or one-step tempo."[42] Hobson's complaint reveals a changing context where jazz became identified as a lifestyle, not just a musical style.

The revivalists had been complaining about the jazz lifestyle all along. More than just music styles or emerging genres, words like *ragtime* and *jazz* were metaphors for the progress and problems of modernity. Jazz became shorthand for the corruption of morals, especially the corruption of modern women who were enticed into jazz culture (meaning unfettered hedonism).[43] This had been Joseph Swerling's point from the very beginning, when he described a Chicago jazz club where "everybody was drinking, smoking, laughing, dancing. The dancing was as raggy as the music. Delightful Bohemianism prevailed.... As one lady passed she blew a puff of cigaret smoke at a boy next to me."[44]

Such accounts help us understand how Billy Sunday used *ragtime* as shorthand for all that was wrong in the world: "Girls, don't be one of the fudge eating, rag time, painted faced, frizzle headed sassity sissies that can can't turn a flapjack without flopping it on the floor," he told a group of high school students.[45] Ever the faithful sidekick, Rodeheaver made it clear that he did not play ragtime or jazz. At the height of the jazz craze in 1922, an overly creative writer claimed to have interviewed Rodeheaver's trombone, quoting it as saying, "Rody plays lots of things on me, but it is mostly gospel music, never jazz." His trombone further claimed that "I go best when it comes to gospel songs, with a full chorus in swing behind me, and a huge audience going good out front. I tell you, boy, that is the life." The anthropomorphic interview ran with a giant photo of the trombone and a blaring headline: "This Is Rodeheaver's Trombone Which Has Never Played Jazz Music."[46]

A few months later, Rodeheaver again denied that his gospel songs sounded like ragtime and jazz. He said his goal was just the opposite—he intended songs like "Brighten the Corner" to replace the popular styles. In 1922, Rodeheaver told a news reporter that men in the offices and shops were "singing and whistling them in preference to the old-time jazz hits."[47]

Rodeheaver and Gabriel considered their music to be rhythmic, but not actually jazz or ragtime. According to Gabriel, "The use of good music in the home and church cannot be too strongly emphasized in these days of 'rag-time' and 'jazz.' We must come back to sane music, and the music-loving people must lead the way."[48] Gabriel freely conceded that songs like "Brighten" used "that radical form of syncopation popularly known as *ragtime.*" Gabriel suggested the technique could be used judiciously for "language requiring syncopated interpretation," valuable for communicating that "the most pathetic passions of the heart, the direst grief, the keenest anticipation and humblest devotion may be most beautifully expressed."[49] But using a few ragtime rhythms did not make a song ragtime, at least in Gabriel's mind. Rodeheaver acknowledged that his songs used "a certain bit of melody and rhythm" but cautioned against those who "go to the extreme and have too much rhythm of a certain kind, because then we have the jazz music of the day."[50] After Rodeheaver's songs were distributed on records and on the radio, Rodeheaver also argued that he had an audience who viewed the two genres as distinct—and preferred the gospel songs. He cited "managers and officials of the big stations" as saying the gospel songs were "the ones most often requested as encores or repeats," as reported by "the home loving population of America."[51]

Rodeheaver and Gabriel articulated a view held by all of the gospel song publishers, who saw their music as essentially different from popular idioms. In Cincinnati, the Fillmore Brothers kept their gospel hymnal business separate from their line of band music—until, that is, the second generation over blurred the distinctions. Henry Fillmore, the same Henry who conducted summer revivals with Rodeheaver, became famous for composing rags like "Lassus Trombone." In one memorable instance he quoted the first few measures of Handel's "Hallelujah" chorus, repurposed with ragtime trombone smears and impudently titled as "Hallelujah Trombone." J. H. Fillmore, Henry's hymn-writing father, hit the roof, furious at the appropriation of sacred music as a ragtime tune. Believing that a line had to be drawn somewhere, J. H. Fillmore allowed the song to be published but demanded that Henry change the name, resulting in the secular-sounding "Shoutin' Liza Trombone."

Charles Gabriel saw the same second-generation transition when his son returned home from the war with a new interest in popular music. Like all parents, Gabriel tried his best to understand the changes—at one point defending the new ragtime fans as "our sons and brothers who have given up the pleasures we are enjoying today, and have gone to face the hardships and dangers of army life."[52] The same question perplexed Billy Sunday, whose own children apparently had a taste for jazz. Many decades after the Sunday home was turned into a museum, the researcher Bill Firstenberger thought to check the inside of Billy Sunday's Victrola cabinet—and found a significant stash of dance music, where a well-worn disc of "Loose Feet" by the Tampa Blue Jazz Band sat right next to Rodeheaver's recording of "Jesus Is All the World to Me."[53] Whatever distance Rodeheaver and Sunday were trying to maintain between gospel songs and jazz, the difference was less clear to the next generation—and unclear to their critics.

In 1928, the *New York Times* reported a recent meeting of the United Lutheran Church in America, where delegates voted not to include "Brighten the Corner" in the next edition of their denominational hymnal. Delegates complained it was too jazzy, the *Times* said.[54] The incident produced a few exuberant headlines, implying that the Lutherans had seriously considered the song, but the scenario seems unlikely. The United Lutherans had kept their distance during the tabernacle revivals, never fans of Sunday's preaching or Rodeheaver's music. And at the time, the Rodeheaver Co. was continuing the quiet policy of refusing to license their songs to denominational hymnals. The Lutheran "vote" smacks of grandstanding—never a real controversy. But the event does serve as a cultural marker. The question of jazzy gospel songs, originally framed as an issue related to tabernacle revivalism, had now spilled over into the Protestant church.

Though Rodeheaver viewed his new gospel music as merely a bridge to traditional church hymnody, his influence had ignited a broader discussion about the influence of popular music on congregational song. In 1924, Earl Harper complained about "gospel rag-time" and "jazz gospel music," calling it "in many respects an evil thing" that "puts the church in league with cheap and inartistic expression."[55] Even after discounting Harper's imprecise use of the ragtime and jazz labels, his words still read like a thinly veiled shot at Rodeheaver and Gabriel.

Harper also acknowledged a weakness in his own position, admitting that congregational singing had been in a steep decline before Rodeheaver, an understandable motivation for embracing fresh music. According to Harper, "the hymns have been dragged down, drawled along, crushed out of all semblance to rhythmical compositions. And then the ministers and leaders of the church have wondered why the young people don't love the great hymns of the church!"[56]

THE ORIGINAL TEMPO OF GOSPEL SONGS

Much later, the music historian Talmadge Dean suggested the "jazz" accusations were perpetuated by a later generation of church musicians, "people of the 'microphone' generations who sing their hymns in acoustically deadened auditoriums."[57] Dean, who drew on his own childhood recollections of a Sunday meeting, felt the jazz elements disappeared "when the song is sung (or heard) in a 'live' wooden tabernacle by a congregation of five to twenty thousand people."[58] Dean claimed that the song, when compared to its later performances in the 1950s, was sung much slower in the revival era. "My own childhood recollection (and it is vivid) is that the tempo was at least andante by modern standards."[59]

Dean's point about slower tempos can be heard in extant recordings of the era. Rodeheaver's earliest performances of 'Brighten the Corner" feature tempos that vary between 85 to 90 beats per minute.[60] While the syncopated rhythms remain, the supposed jazz feel is nonexistent. Rodeheaver and Gabriel felt strongly about modeling correct tempos for their gospel songs—so much so that they left an unusual artifact. Their 1917 release of *Gospel Hymns and Songs* includes metronome tempo markings for nearly every song. They were virtually alone in this publishing practice; congregational hymnals almost never use metronome markings. In this case, they printed the "Brighten the Corner" as 96 b.p.m., which seems to be the upward limit of their revival-era performances.[61] Late in life, when Rodeheaver led "A Billy Sunday Tribute" in Winona Lake, he resurrected his old "Brighten" stunts, assigning each line of the chorus to different sections of the Billy Sunday Tabernacle. With B. D. Ackley at the piano, Rodeheaver immediately locks in on his tabernacle tempo of 96 b.p.m., but with a bounce—a surprising lilt that confuses anyone who does not understand the difference between tempo and mood.[62]

With the passing of time, no one remembered the true vibe and feel of tabernacle revival singing. When 1960s-era church musicians and critics resurrected the "jazz" accusations about "Brighten," their memories were influenced by the tempo and instrumentation of 1960s recording artists, not the original tabernacle performances. For instance, the jazz inflections are obvious in Ella Fitzgerald's 1967 version, where she sings the chorus at 108 b.p.m. and is backed by a jazz combo, orchestra, and chorus.[63] Mainstream pop artists had been covering "Brighten" since 1950, when the Andrews Sisters recorded it for the Decca Faith Series.[64] In the next twenty years, it was recorded more than 50 times, by a wide range of artists including the Mills Brothers, Red Foley, Burl Ives, Tennessee Ernie Ford, and Anita Bryant, plus dozens of southern gospel quartets (apparently locked in a competition to see who could sing it the fastest).[65] By this point. pop artists had identified an acceptable canon of gospel songs that could be successfully divorced from their revivalist roots and recorded commercially. "Brighten" completely lost Rodeheaver's original conception as a warm-up song for group singing—now it was only sung in performance, almost never as communal song, and considerably faster than Rodeheaver's tempo.

RODEHEAVER'S PARLOR SONGS

If Rodeheaver's gospel music style can't be described as ragtime or jazz, what was it, exactly? Perhaps the best answer is *parlor songs*, a broad category of nascent popular music that predates ragtime and jazz. In the era immediately before World War I, popular music styles could be described as several overlapping categories of vernacular music: parlor songs, minstrelsy, band marches, vaudeville, and eventually ragtime. And though another category is sometimes forgotten, one could add gospel songs, which drew on the others and markedly influenced them.[66]

A reviewer of Ira D. Sankey's gospel songs had recognized these intertwined vernacular sources as early as 1876: "Determine the pleasure that you get from a circus quick-step, a negro-minstrel sentimental ballad, a college chorus, and a hymn all in one, and you have some gauge of the variety and contrast that may be perceived in one of these songs."[67] When Sankey's successors perpetuated these categories in urban revivalism, they followed the same path of influences.

Which category came first? The question has no good answer, and it probably doesn't matter. The American vernacular tradition developed from a common primordial pool of musical ideas. The early categories should not be seen as separate idioms nearly so much as they are separate places where one could encounter music. The designation as "parlor" songs describes their location, and also their role as communal music shared in family venues. The industrial revolution created a market for inexpensive parlor instruments, especially the reed organ and piano, and thus created a market for inexpensive sheet music written simply enough for the average amateur. Eventually, the parlor songs could be heard in music halls, Chautauqua events, and vaudeville, but they never functioned as pure audience-centered performance music. In the same way, gospel songs (as conceived in the era from Sankey to Rodeheaver) were less about individual performances and more about communal expressions of group prayer, group singing, and group testimony.[68] Parlor songs and gospel songs were to be played and sung and enjoyed as communal music, with the audience as performer.

In essence, many of the gospel songs *sound* like parlor songs. Our assertion could be sustained by lengthy analysis but can be more easily demonstrated by singing both kinds of songs and listening to period recordings, where the similarity becomes immediately obvious. More important for our discussion of Rodeheaver, gospel songs and parlor songs also shared similar lyrical themes, especially infused with tropes from the genteel tradition. Both formats feature the same stock characters as seen in nineteenth-century sentimental literature: the dear departed mother, the dying child, the wayward (prodigal) son. Both formats encouraged moral reform, honorable struggles against difficult causes, and the promise of an eternal reward.

For Rodeheaver, whose own mother died when he was only eight, the sentimental "mother" songs and poems were a significant part of his repertoire. He began with "Tell Mother I'll Be There," written by Charles M. Fillmore (brother of J. H., uncle of Henry), and popularized by Charles Alexander, who explained its appeal in straightforward terms: "It reaches all classes, because everybody has a mother."[69] When Rodeheaver began singing "Tell Mother" in tabernacle meetings, the feature became so popular that he developed a full repertoire of similar songs and poems. Nearly every meeting had some sort of "mother" moment, with Rodeheaver eventually recording most of the repertoire.[70] He reached the saturation point with "Mother's Prayers Have Followed Me," which he published in a dozen versions and recorded more frequently than any other song except "Brighten the Corner."[71] He also published his "mother" recitations in two poetry anthologies, *Worth While Poems* and *More Worthwhile Poems*.[72] Most tellingly, his book *F'r Instance: A Collection of Jokes and Humorous Stories* features many jokes about fathers and sons—but no funny stories about mother.[73] Mother was serious business.

All of this met the approval of Billy Sunday, who shared Rodeheaver's soft spot. Sunday's father died in the Civil War, and his destitute mother sent the children to the Iowa Soldier's Orphans Home. Decades later, Sunday's spiritual journey began as a baseball player who heard Chicago street musicians singing "Where Is My Wandering Boy Tonight." For the rest of his life he listed the song as his favorite. The "wayward son" songs functioned as close cousins to the "mother" songs.

Parlor songs and gospel songs were birthed at the same time, emerging from the same nineteenth-century social forces and musical influences, and sharing many of the same themes. Rodeheaver and Gabriel freely acknowledged the connections. After critics painted the revivalists as ragtime proponents, Charles Gabriel corrected the impression by disclosing his musical sources. "Ragtime appeals to the feet and amuses the sensual nature, and has its place," Gabriel said. "Folk and home songs with their beautiful harmonies appeal to the spiritual side of life, and, touching the heart, satisfies."[74] In Gabriel's mind, gospel songs drew from the same well as "folk and home songs." Never quite ragtime, never quite jazz, and strongly influenced by the spirituals, gospel songs joined other American forms at the fountainhead of the American popular tradition.

FINDING THE GOSPEL IN GOSPEL SONGS

Here we offer a modest critique of current scholarship. Researchers who apply techniques from musicology and social history will glean key insights from their academic disciplines—and yet miss the essential point of the gospel song. Musical and social forces are not the *primary* reason gospel songs became popular. Rather, the gospel songs fostered personal spiritual transformation for the people who sang them.

Rodeheaver frequently spoke of his role in acquiring, testing, and winnowing the best songs. Advertisements described how Rodeheaver "selected each song for some particular point of merit and special purpose," resulting in song collections that were "thoroughly tried and approved." But these were not musical or literary standards. Rodeheaver wanted songs that "aroused a wonderful spiritual uplift whenever used."[75]

FIGURE 9.4. Rodeheaver conducts a community sing in Chicago's Orchestra Hall, 1940s. Courtesy of Rodeheaver Collection, Grace College, Winona Lake.

Of course, such statements prove troublesome for researchers who wish to quantify a factual basis for social and cultural history. Anyone who attempts to measure spiritual transformation quickly discovers how elusive the task can be. One analysis of Rodeheaver's lyrical themes showed that he most frequently used "songs of rejoicing," 25 percent; "songs of exhortation and spiritual invitation," 20 percent; and "songs of doctrine and faith," 15 percent. The study also estimated that Rodeheaver's tabernacle music touched on political themes 5 percent of the time (mostly Prohibition songs), and "songs of sentiment" 10 percent of the time. For critics who tagged the revivalists as being overtly political and sentimental, these numbers are surprisingly low.[76] Though such studies can reveal interesting insights, they touch only around the edges of Rodeheaver's essential assertion, that his songs aroused a wonderful spiritual uplift "whenever used."

RODEHEAVER'S POWER OF MUSIC

Rodeheaver struggled to explain how, exactly, the gospel songs brought about this spiritual change. From within his own evangelical theology, he could have attributed this spiritual uplift solely to the unseen working of the Holy Spirit (the Christian belief about supernatural conviction of sin leading to repentance and conversion). Frankly, had Rodeheaver stayed within this theological boundary, he would have been on safer ground among his evangelical peers. Instead, Rodeheaver seemed to treat the power of music as a secular force, one that could be summoned in either a tabernacle meeting or a community sing. Just before Rodeheaver left on his world tour, Peter Dykema released another of his studies on community singing, addressing "the power of music to elevate the taste of its listeners without external aid or guidance."[77] Overcome by his faith in musical Progressivism, Dykema seemed to believe this power was automatic—listen to this music and you will become a better person. Dykema also spoke of a musical progress from "poor" music to "very good" music, using well-written popular songs, then light classics, then grand opera. His theories sound remarkably close to the way Rodeheaver and Gabriel had described "Brighten" as a stepping stone to better church music.

As such, Rodeheaver's conception of the power of music had an overlapping role with the power of the Holy Spirit. At times Rodeheaver seemed to mix the two powers, leaving the observer with a confusing dilemma. Were sinners converted by the power of the Holy Spirit or by the power of music? Rodeheaver, the World's Greatest Songleader and acknowledged master of crowd dynamics, often emphasized the power of music, leaving himself open to charges of emotional manipulation.

One example can be seen by looking at "That Little Chap 'O Mine," a favorite Rodeheaver poem that he often recited at Billy Sunday's men-only meetings. "I do not know who wrote this," Rodeheaver said of the poem, "But it has helped so many folks I like to pass it on. . . . Men have told me they have been saved through this poem." Comments like this always raised the eyebrows of Billy Sunday's doctrinaire supporters. The "Little Chap" poem told a sentimental, heart-rending story without a shred of biblical content. The concluding lines—the ones that supposedly led men to spiritual conversion—didn't sound very spiritual:

And I am trying hard to be the man he fancies me to be,
Because I have this chap at home who thinks the world 'o me.[78]

For revival preachers like Billy Sunday, "I am trying hard" wasn't going to cut it. Their salvation sermons hinged on a clear proclamation of the gospel (the death, burial, and resurrection of Jesus Christ) as essential to personal spiritual transformation. According to Rodeheaver's theory of tabernacle music, the sentimental repertoire with light or nonexistent theology served as a gateway to the all-important preaching about the Christian gospel. But sometimes Rodeheaver became so captivated by what he saw as the power of music that he believed his song repertoire would produce genuine spiritual reform, all on its own.

His sentimental take on the doctrine of salvation extended to his view of the Christian Bible. Later in life Rodeheaver wrote to the retired evangelist M. B. Williams, tossing a few bouquets to an old friend. "It is always a joy to be able to tell the people about you and our friendship throughout the years, whenever I sing 'My Mother's Bible,'" Rodeheaver said. "That's one of the greatest songs on the Bible ever written."[79] Not many evangelicals agreed with his fawning assessment. The best the song could offer were a few mawkish lines of parlor theology:

There's a dear and precious book,
Though it's worn and faded now,
Which recalls the happy days of long ago;
When I stood at mother's knee,
With her hand upon my brow,
And I heard her voice in gentle tones and low.

Such examples, overtly sentimental and sappy as they are, help explain why the next generation of church musicians often criticized Rodeheaver's approach. Some of his favorite songs lacked theological integrity; their popularity came from the commercial appeal of the parlor song idiom, not because of their lyrics. Once the parlor songs faded from popular culture, so did his sentimental gospel songs. But in the meantime, Rodeheaver could stave off the decline by updating his technology and marketing the songs in new ways. The "power of music" could be harnessed to communicate the Christian gospel, using proven Progressive-era methods that could be taught, reproduced, and exported. If Rodeheaver and Dykema were correct, the gospel songs should have achieved lasting results in any culture and in any era. But an obvious question surfaced, provoked by dwindling tabernacle crowds and declining music sales. Rodeheaver believed his ideas about the power of music were correct, but it seemed like he could no longer invoke it whenever he wished. The genie could not always be called to come out when Rodeheaver rubbed his lamp. Was the power fading, or did it ever exist at all?

10

FALLING OUT OF STEP AT THE CLOSE OF AN ERA
"WE HAVE IN RECENT YEARS LOWERED OUR STANDARDS"

The slow decline began with a car accident. Yumbert Rodeheaver traveled from Chicago to Winona Lake on August 3, 1940, riding with family friends.[1] The party planned on staying at Homer's home for a few days while visiting the summer Bible conference. But something went horribly wrong when they were only a half-hour from their destination. One vehicle veered into the path of another on a tight two-lane highway, resulting in a gruesome wreck and two fatalities. Yumbert suffered a fractured pelvis and other injuries. After several weeks of hospitalization, the family understood that Yumbert, now 72, would never be the same. He spent most of his time in a wheelchair and needed a nurse attendant for the rest of his life. The quiet man who transformed Chicago's hymnal industry would never return to the office.

The accident became the catalyst for family and business consolidation. A few months later Homer Rodeheaver remodeled his Rainbow Point home, which now became his year-round residence. On April 30, 1941, the Rodeheaver Co. announced the closure of their Chicago and Philadelphia offices, moving the entire operation to the Westminster Hotel at Winona Lake. Homer Rodeheaver hired a 20-year-old Winona Lake resident, Bruce Howe, to assist with the move. Howe remained with the company for fifty years, and after Rodeheaver's death, took responsibility for protecting his legacy.

The decision to leave Chicago was inevitable, even without Yumbert's accident. From a business standpoint, there was no clear reason to keep the offices, order fulfillment, and printing plant in Chicago's South Loop district. "The publishing

FIGURE 10.1. Rodeheaver's Rainbow Point home in the early 1950s, site of countless summer gatherings. Courtesy of Rodeheaver Collection, Grace College, Winona Lake.

company decided it was foolish to be paying city prices for a mail order business, so decided to move to Winona Lake," Ruthella Rodeheaver wrote in her memoir.[2] During the next decade, most of the old-line printing companies left Printer's Row for the suburbs, citing the same reason.

Rodeheaver asked the manager of the Philadelphia office, George Sanville, to move to Winona Lake and manage the consolidated operations.[3] B. D. Ackley had moved from Philadelphia the year before and was already settled into his new Westminster Hotel studio. Joseph Rodeheaver resigned his position from Chicago's Northern Baptist Seminary and took a greater role in the day-to-day office operations, with Homer giving him a partnership share in the company. Then in 1942, his half-sister Ruth and her husband moved from Roanoke, Virginia, with James Thomas becoming administrative assistant at Rodeheaver Music. It seemed natural for the Thomases to move into Rainbow Point as well, with Ruth becoming unofficial hostess for Homer's impromptu parties. Pie and coffee seemed to magically appear after every Winona Lake event, whether Homer returned home with five or fifty friends.

With all the company changes and the consolidation to Winona Lake, Homer should have taken a cue and slowed down himself. Despite the advice of his

CHAPTER 10

FIGURE 10.2. Rodeheaver "rested violently" in Winona Lake, never slowing down for retirement. Courtesy of Rodeheaver Collection, Grace College, Winona Lake.

brothers and friends, Homer continued his whirlwind travel schedule and neverending ideas for new projects. And when everyone else came to Winona Lake to rest, Homer managed to find more things to keep him busy. He "rested violently" in the summer months, a reporter said, "riding surfboard, playing tennis, swimming, diving, playing, driving his speedboat recklessly, entertaining as many friends and passersby as can crowd under his roof."[4] Homer's rhythm of life had but one speed—*on*.

DOCTRINAL CONTROVERSY

The matter of Rodeheaver's friends became a hot question. In 1946, Rodeheaver became embroiled in a theological flap when he invited a Seventh Day Adventist group to sing at the famed Bible conference run by the Winona Lake Christian Assembly.[5] The quartet was attending his School of Sacred Music during the day; Rodeheaver saw no problem with them singing for the evening session of Bible conference. (The two events ran concurrently, meeting together for the evening sessions.) Rodeheaver ran his School of Sacred Music with the same attendance policy as the old tabernacle meetings. As a result, he attracted a wide consortium of Protestants who were interested in gospel music training.

Back in the days of citywide revivals, Rodeheaver loved to tell a convoluted anecdote about inter-faith cooperation: A Jewish man whose leg was amputated by an Episcopalian doctor in a Catholic hospital, further assisted by a Methodist woman who donated the wooden leg of her deceased Baptist husband, delivered to the hospital by a Lutheran messenger—and on the story went, always good for a laugh, always affirming the cooperative ethos that made citywide revivals possible.[6] But the theological landscape had changed after the fundamentalist-modernist split of the 1920s, with fundamentalists and evangelicals further fragmenting into distinctions that befuddled Rodeheaver. If an SDA quartet attended his music conference, why couldn't they also sing at the evening Bible conference?

"To Rodie, doctrine was not as important as friendship," explained Bob Jones Jr., a longtime friend.[7] But after the quartet sang in 1946, Rodeheaver was blasted by Robert G. LeTourneau, the conference president. "I am surprised; I am stunned; I am sorry you are ruining yourself hobnobbing with, and trying to defend, Seventh Day Adventism," began one of his letters to Rodeheaver.[8] Because Rodeheaver was still a conference trustee, LeTourneau also sent carbon copies to every board member. LeTourneau pointedly asked Rodeheaver to "get down on your knees and ask God to forgive you and bring you back to the gospel Billy Sunday preached."[9] Rodeheaver, deeply offended, resigned from the board.

"I have been rather loyal to that Bible Conference for twenty-five long years," Rodeheaver later complained to Helen Sunday.[10] He didn't need to state the obvious, that "rather loyal" meant donating thousands of dollars. Rodeheaver also complained that leaders had been "laying plans and making efforts for the last four or five years to get me out of the way."[11]

Helen Sunday's reply is not known, but the flap helps us better understand Rodeheaver's theological attitudes. He was most comfortable with the Protestant coalition of the early 1900s, where Presbyterians like Chapman, Biederwolf, and Sunday could work closely with Methodists like Rodeheaver and Charles Gabriel. Though their theological systems were different, they agreed on the orthodox doctrine of soteriology (the doctrine of personal salvation). All of the revivalists—Methodists, Presbyterians, and Baptists alike—agreed on the deity of Jesus Christ and the important doctrine of substitutionary atonement, the original theme of gospel song lyrics. During the era of tabernacle revivalism, the doctrinal disputes were left to denominational leaders to iron out. But during the 1930s and '40s, the fights over Protestant orthodoxy seemed to be pointing toward an uncomfortable conclusion, that Protestants would never again cooperate for citywide evangelism.

FLAT NOTES

As if to add insult to injury, other Winona Lake observers dared to state the obvious. Rodeheaver's trombone playing—never strong—was declining to the point of embarrassment. Chicago's WMBI Radio had committed to live broadcasts of the conference but started to cut away during Rodeheaver's segments. "Our reasons for this were simple," said station manager Walter Carlson in a memo. "His singing and playing were below our standards, the musical talent he put on the air usually failed to meet our standards, [and] his talk was objectionable, due to blarney and extreme promotion of his School of Music."[12] Perhaps Carlson had also seen a recent record review in *Billboard* magazine, which commended Rodeheaver's song material as "full of meaning," but noted that he "puts it over crudely." While older listeners might remember his glory days as Billy Sunday's soloist, "the new generation may object to the wobbly pitch."[13]

Given Rodeheaver's continued reputation as the World's Greatest Songleader, the WMBI snub was noticeable ("Rody has many friends," the memo acknowledged). Then Carlson relented somewhat, explaining that "as a friendly gesture, however, we have in recent years lowered our standards for a part of the Conference and put him on the air." At least somewhat aware of the political ramifications, Carlson reminded the radio announcers that "the situation calls for tact and wisdom from above" (though a person could argue that his memo wasn't all that tactful).[14]

THE NEXT BILLY

However badly his performance skills may have declined, Rodeheaver influenced the next generation of revivalists, especially Billy Graham. They met when Graham was attending the Florida Bible Institute in Temple Terrace, a suburb of Tampa. The Bible training school got its start when a local country club went bankrupt; it rapidly became a popular winter retreat for northern preachers. The list of guest faculty read like a Who's Who of evangelicalism, including Rodeheaver. Graham was only 19 and had not yet preached his first sermon, but his path would cross with Rodeheaver many times in the next few years.[15]

Graham quickly connected to a network of loosely affiliated evangelicals who held Youth for Christ events around the country. Though their local efforts began without formal organization, the various meetings shared common traits: a fast-moving succession of musical acts, celebrity testimonies, and vaudeville-like bursts of comic relief. And the programs invariably began with a period of communal singing, often led by trombone-playing songleaders such as Lloyd Fessmire, Ted Ness, and especially Bob Cook, who later became YFC president. "You need a competent song leader who knows God," Bob Cook explained. "Bad song leading, or even good song leading with the flesh in it, can kill your meeting."[16]

For anyone who has forgotten the connection to Rodeheaver's trombone, Cliff Barrows serves as the best example. Billy Graham and Barrows met at a 1945 revival meeting in Asheville, North Carolina. As the story goes, Graham discovered he did not have a songleader to begin the meeting, only to be rescued by Barrows, who was traveling through town on his honeymoon. Barrows had his trombone in the trunk of the car, and his wife, Billie, happened to play piano. None of the participants realized that the inauspicious event would lead to a 65-year partnership. Instead, the evening ended with a few cursory thank-yous before everyone departed in different directions.[17]

However random the moment might have seemed, Barrows had been studying Rodeheaver from a distance. In an interview for this book, Barrows said the impetus for adopting Rodeheaver's songleading style came from Helen Griggs, his aunt. She played piano at First Baptist Church in Ceres, California, and was familiar with Rodeheaver from her days at Moody Bible Institute. Barrows was playing trombone in the Modesto High School band when Rev. Paul Jackson asked him to lead the Sunday evening song service, so her suggestion seemed to be a natural fit. "I would bring the trombone down on the downbeat and then hold it up when we were holding a note out. I enjoyed it so much!" Barrows said, recalling his early imitation of Rodeheaver.[18]

Barrows soon experienced Rodeheaver's songleading in person, during chapel services at Bob Jones College. Even before meeting Rodeheaver, Barrows had thoroughly absorbed his songleading ethos, to the point where it was obvious to any observer. Thirteen days after his wedding, Barrows received a glowing review from a North Carolina reporter who was already saying, "Mr. Barrows is the equal of Homer Rodeheaver, songleader for the late [Billy Sunday], so skillfully does he lead the large crowds in congregational singing."[19]

A month later the two trombone-playing songleaders finally met, at the first Youth for Christ convention in Winona Lake.[20] By this point, Rodeheaver and Helen Sunday had pledged support of the new organization, the primary reason why the summer meetings were held in Winona Lake. Rodeheaver gave them use of his Westminster Hotel and made generous gifts to support the movement. The 1945 Youth for Christ meetings were important for another reason—Billy Graham and Cliff Barrows spent significant time together, joined by a young soloist with a growing radio career, George Beverly Shea. Graham preached, Barrows led songs, Shea sang—and Rodeheaver took notice. Soon they were all sitting on Homer Rodeheaver's porch and watching the sunset, finally getting to know each other. Rodeheaver enjoyed their attention and their questions, and with a little persuasion would pull out the scrapbooks and movie projector.

In addition to his personal influence on the Graham team, Rodeheaver strongly influenced the philosophical direction of the new organization, which he saw as the logical next step after tabernacle revivalism. When YFC leaders drafted their organizational documents over the next few days, their purpose statement sounded remarkably familiar. "YFC is a youth rally, rather than a church service," they explained, using an argument that came straight from Rodeheaver.[21] By drawing a distinction between the function of an evangelistic youth meeting and the function of a church service, the YFC leaders justified a growing body of

CHAPTER 10

FIGURE 10.3. Billy Graham with Rodeheaver, early 1950s. Courtesy of Billy Graham Evangelistic Association, Cliff Barrows Papers, Charlotte, North Carolina.

commercial-sounding Christian pop music. YFC's point of view, which became controversial, was certainly not new—in fact, it sounded exactly like Rodeheaver's frequently quoted defense of tabernacle revival music: "It was never intended for a Sunday morning service . . . its purpose was to bridge the gap between the popular song of the day and the great hymns and gospel songs."[22]

The young YFC leaders presented a vibrant program that seemed to widen the gap between past and present. Sensing a shift, the conference director J. Palmer Muntz privately told Shea that the YFC week "will be one of much greater blessing and spiritual power" compared to Rodeheaver's usual program. And then Muntz quickly added, "though I do not care to be quoted."[23] Of course not. The YFC generation took over, yes, but they avoided the divisiveness that LeTourneau had stoked. Rather than burning bridges, Billy Graham and Cliff Barrows venerated Rodeheaver even as they shifted to new music styles.

THE NEXT GENERATION OF GOSPEL MUSIC

Rodeheaver's friendship with Graham, Barrows, and Shea progressed in predictable ways. The Youth for Christ leaders wanted an official songbook, and the

Rodeheaver Co. wanted to recapture the evangelical youth market. Now Rodeheaver could exert a bit of friendly pressure. For the 1945 Winona Lake meetings, the young songleaders had used cheap-looking mimeographed song sheets, lyrics only, without copyright attribution.[24] (Imagine their awkward moment when Rodeheaver sat down in the Billy Sunday Tabernacle and was handed a pirated sheet of his own songs!) Rodeheaver could also point out the consequences of their delay in creating a songbook: other enterprising publishers had already stepped into the vacuum. Al Smith's successful *Singspiration* series had been in print since 1941 and had released one or two new editions per year, full of the most popular YFC choruses, but without YFC endorsement.[25]

The YFC leaders agreed to work with Rodeheaver on a songbook project, but by the time it was released in 1948, *Singing Youth for Christ* seemed late to the game.[26] In addition to its delayed release, *Singing Youth for Christ* also seemed remarkably safe: 21 of 115 songs were 1920s-era gospel songs owned by Rodeheaver, along with many Moody-Sankey favorites and traditional hymns. By contrast, Al Smith's *Singspiration* books featured the new-style songs featured on WMBI radio and Christian recordings. The Rodeheaver song catalog, once criticized for its trendy ragtime and jazz influences, now seemed tired. The rising postwar youth generation opened *Singing Youth for Christ* and saw their parent's music. So they had two choices: write new songs, or create fresh instrumentation for the older repertoire. Soon the YFC groups did both, but Rodeheaver couldn't seem to keep up with either trend.

The limitations of Rodeheaver's song catalog stemmed from his aging business model. As the owner of a cash-rich private company, Rodeheaver bought gospel songs in bulk and waited for them to become hits. Or sometimes he bought entire song catalogs from competitors who were leaving the business. But these old ways of doing business weren't attractive to a new generation of singer-songwriters like George Beverly Shea, who understood the financial benefits of keeping his own copyrights. Of course, this change was already afoot in the broader realm of American popular music, but for the Christian market, the song that broke the old model was Shea's "I'd Rather Have Jesus." In 1931, Shea had discovered a song written by Rhea F. Miller and had written a new tune, which he now sang everywhere and sold in sheet music.[27] As the featured singer on ABC's *Club Time*, Shea had a national audience.

A few months before the 1945 Winona Lake meetings, Rodeheaver had written to Shea with a conventional offer to purchase the song outright. "I would pay you a good price," Rodeheaver promised, explaining his old-school way of doing business: "I like to own the good songs I find, and am willing to pay a good price for them whenever I find people who would rather have the money than keep the songs."[28] Shea, however, declined the offer. He wasn't selling the song to anyone, not even Rodeheaver.

CHAPTER 10

But then Shea bumped into an old problem when he tried to publish his own collection of gospel songs—and needed Rodeheaver's permission to use four copyrights. The reply came from George Sanville, Rodeheaver's business manager, who schooled Shea on the realities of gospel music publishing. Yes, the gospel publishers were trying to adapt to the new system ("I have tried my best to forget some of our hard and fast rules"), but Sanville had been making deals like this since well before Shea was born. If the young singer-songwriter wanted to publish Rodeheaver songs in another hymnal, he would need to come to the table with something to trade. The Rodeheaver Co. would grant permission, "provided you will let us have the privilege of using one of your copyrights, 'I'd Rather Have Jesus.'"[29]

Now Shea found himself in a complicated bind. He couldn't agree to Sanville's trade because he only owned the tune for his song—Rhea F. Miller had copyrighted the words. They had both agreed to publish a solo version in sheet music and split the profits, but Miller had been declining all overtures to market the song in other ways. The idea of composers and lyricists sharing ownership became a major disruption to Rodeheaver's publishing model. Shea told Miller that industry insiders "were somewhat amazed" when Shea split ownership with her, because the gospel song industry "has not gone past the giving of $5.00 per poem," at least not until now.[30]

Undeterred by the status quo, Shea made one more attempt to persuade Sanville of the deal, pointing out how the radio market gave publishers new ways to barter. Shea had been featuring Rodeheaver songs on his nationwide radio broadcast, amounting to lots of free publicity (and ASCAP royalties for Rodeheaver). Shea carefully implied that this situation could continue only if Rodeheaver shared his publication rights—that was the trade. A few days later Sanville relented, telling Shea that his request was "contrary to our usual method," but agreeing to the terms.[31] And Shea kept his part of the bargain, continuing to feature Rodeheaver's songs on his *Club Time* broadcasts. The Hammond organ would swell, the announcer would intone "George Beverly Shea and the Club Time Aluminum Choral Singers present America's favorite hymn . . . 'The Old Rugged Cross,'" and everyone was happy.[32]

George Beverly Shea had broken free of the old model, where gospel publishers owned the songs, took all of the financial risks, and kept most of the profits. Now he had one more lesson to absorb. After recording "I'd Rather Have Jesus" for RCA Victor in 1951, he expected to receive RCA's standard royalty of two cents per record (which he planned to split with Rhea F. Miller). But when his first checks came in, he asked why his song ownership only netted .01 per record. The explanation seemed unfair: "When an individual holds the copyright it is RCA Victor's policy to pay a royalty of $.01," a representative explained, "because we are not receiving the backing and promotion of a publishing house."[33]

The solution seemed pretty obvious. A few years later, Shea wanted to record another of his songs, "The Wonder of It All." Before his recording session, he filed papers to start Chancel Music and then transferred the ownership of all his songs to his newly formed publishing house and captured the full royalty from RCA.[34] Shea's insistence on controlling "I'd Rather Have Jesus" became a watershed moment, signaling how the rising generation of singer-songwriters formed their own companies instead of selling their gospel songs outright. Rodeheaver's model, a Christian music industry built on congregational singing and hymnals sales, rapidly changed.

THE NEXT GENERATION OF CITYWIDE REVIVALS

George Beverly Shea continued to travel with Billy Graham and Cliff Barrows for the next 65 years, a remarkable relationship that began with the influence of Homer Rodeheaver. When the Graham team left Youth for Christ work to concentrate on citywide "crusades," they unabashedly borrowed nearly every aspect of the Sunday-Rodeheaver's tabernacle meetings.

Soon after joining forces, Graham and Barrows were described as being "as famous as the Billy Sunday–Homer Rodeheaver or the Moody–Sankey evangelistic duos."[35] Given the dozens of early articles that make this same comparison, one can suspect that the idea likely originated with the Graham organization's press kit. And now the Barrows backstory was subtly reframed to sound a lot like Rodeheaver's own story. A magazine writer could have described the ruggedly handsome Barrows as a high school baseball player, or a tennis star (both true). Instead, a 1946 profile described Barrows as "a former cheer leader in high school" and quoted Barrows as saying "I got my idea from cheer leaders."[36] The Graham team began releasing publicity photos with Barrows affecting Rodeheaver-like songleading gestures, leaving no doubt where Barrows got his songleading ideas.

Graham and Barrows returned to Winona Lake for the 1949 Youth for Christ meetings, where both were reappointed as vice presidents. This time, their long talks with Rodeheaver took on a new urgency. In six weeks, they would open their 1949 Los Angeles crusade, the event that propelled both of them to national attention. Bruce Howe later recalled how their 1949 Winona Lake conversations took on a more serious tone, with Rodeheaver passing along his regrets and misgivings about the old system of tabernacle revivalism and stressing the importance of personal integrity.[37] Helen Sunday had similar advice, believing that her wayward children might have turned out differently if she had spent more time at home.[38] And Winona Lake locals spoke of The Lost Prayer Meeting, held in the Rainbow Room of the Westminster Hotel, where YFC leaders prayed through the night and dedicated Graham for his future meetings.[39]

CHAPTER 10

The Los Angeles meetings cemented the Graham-Barrows transition from youth meetings to citywide evangelism. Now they needed a new songbook. In 1950, Barrows partnered with Rodeheaver to publish *Singing Evangelism: Billy Graham Campaign Songs*, a collection that looked like an expanded version of *Singing Youth for Christ*.[40] Barrows dropped 16 songs and added 42 different ones in the new book, but none of the added songs were newly written. For the next 25 years, the Rodeheaver Co. published updated editions of the Billy Graham songbooks, never straying very far from the core canon of hymns and gospel songs established during Rodeheaver's era.

Graham and Barrows were not shy about playing up their relationship to Rodeheaver, whom they treated as a respected mentor and a model for ministry. "We had him come to every crusade when he was alive until he died in 1955," Barrows said, a point supported by early Graham scrapbooks and newspaper accounts.[41] During the same period, Rodeheaver suffered two heart attacks and often looked unwell, but he accepted nearly every invitation that came his way. Rodeheaver's appearances for Graham included bits of congregational singing, a few vocal solos, and a ringing endorsement of the Graham team.

As Graham, Barrows, and George Beverly Shea sat behind him, Rodeheaver asked the crowd, "Have you ever known anywhere a whole combination of an evangelistic party just as near 100% perfect as this one here? Of course, we know the preacher is; but your choir leader—you've got the greatest in the nation. And these two boys here at these instruments [piano and organ], they just can't be surpassed." And though Barrows timed his service order down to the minute, he let Rodeheaver ramble as long as he wished. "I shouldn't be taking this much time to talk," Rodeheaver would say and then add a plug for his new Rainbow records, and then another plug for his Boys Ranch, and then a story about J. Edgar Hoover, and another testimony about his old friend Mel Trotter, and then, finally, a closing stanza of "Then Jesus Came."[42]

The Graham team did not expect stellar musical performances. "He had a difficult time with his pitch. He would play flat quite often," Barrows told us, years later.[43] In essence, Walter Carlson's memo was right. Rodeheaver's singing and playing were below standards—the new radio and television standards. Instead, the Rodeheaver appearances felt like an aging rock star jamming on stage with the up-and-coming young bucks, a Greatest Hits tour where nostalgia reigned (but no one expected perfection).

Having borrowed many of Rodeheaver's ideas, Barrows also discarded them when necessary. From 1947 to 1954, Barrows led and accompanied revival singing with his trombone—then suddenly stopped. When Graham and Barrows launched their 1954 meetings at London's Harringay Arena, they were surprised by bad press. A headline in the *Daily Express* called Barrows "The Genie of the

Golden Trombone," which didn't turn out to be a compliment. "You couldn't imagine anything more comic than the choir leader when he produces a gold-plated trombone and plays it to increase the enthusiasm while the choir is singing. I think he realized it himself," the paper said. "But it didn't destroy the atmosphere that was building up. He and his wretched trombone didn't matter a tinker's cuss. What did matter was that thousands of British people were there who were feeling the need for God."[44]

Graham's preaching style didn't fare much better, forcing the young evangelists to consider how their approach was viewed by their expanded audience. They could not build their international ministry with nostalgia for the American sawdust trail. Barrows stopped waving his trombone, Graham toned down his rapid-fire sermon delivery, and both of them gave up their garish hand-painted ties.[45]

Until now, Homer Rodeheaver's influence on Billy Graham and Cliff Barrows has received little scholarly attention. In his autobiography, Graham moves through the early 1950s fairly quickly—and from a curious emotional distance—telling the reader very little about the formation of his ideas. None of Graham's biographers explore the Rodeheaver relationship, but this oversight also reflects their limited access to Graham's personal correspondence. Billy Graham's 2018 death triggered the release of his Montreat, North Carolina, office files, including the letters and program transcripts we have cited in this section. As a result, Rodeheaver emerges as more of an influence than previously noted.[46]

For Rodeheaver, the Billy Graham Crusades provided yet another platform for his ongoing campaign to preserve gospel songs. For the Graham team, the Rodeheaver appearances gave them evangelical credibility with their expanded demographic (the parents of the Youth for Christ generation). And for anyone who still didn't get it, Rodeheaver concluded his performances with a final reminder: "You know the best part of it—not the singing nor the song—the best part of it is that it's true and could happen to anybody in this tabernacle tonight if you'll just open your heart and let him come in."[47] For Rodeheaver and the Graham team, the value of the gospel songs came from their musical affirmation of the gospel that Graham preached.

PROFITS AND PHILANTHROPY

After the Rodeheaver Co. consolidated its business interests in Winona Lake, Rodeheaver began to think more seriously about his own accumulating wealth. Throughout his career he had donated to various causes, keeping careful records in his pocket planners. But a closer examination does not reveal any particular pattern to his gifts. He did not seem to follow the Methodist doctrine of tithing

10 percent of personal income to his church, though he sometimes gave generous one-time gifts. His philanthropic efforts were geared toward projects and ministries sponsored by his friends, who showed no compunction in courting his support. In the early years, Rodeheaver's primary beneficiary was the Winona Lake Christian Assembly. Later, he supported Youth for Christ initiatives and the Graham crusades. He gave $25,000 to Bob Jones University, which was used for the construction of Rodeheaver Auditorium.[48] Most importantly, he began to work on the major philanthropic project of his life, the Rodeheaver Boy's Ranch in Palatka, Florida.

In 1944, Rodeheaver purchased a swath of lakefront property at Melbourne Beach, Florida, planning to develop a "Christian Colony in Sunny Florida" for retired evangelists. He even built a retirement cottage for his brother Joseph, but the larger plan fell apart when Joseph suffered a heart attack and died on January 28, 1946. The planned community never came to fruition.[49] In the 1940s, Rodeheaver also began purchasing parcels of land near Palatka, Florida, about an hour south of Jacksonville. He had become a savvy real estate investor during the Winona Lake years, skilled at finding distressed properties at a bargain price. Now he tested these skills on a gargantuan scale, having learned of a failed Florida land scheme. Unscrupulous developers had subdivided a section into 10-acre tracts, offering it to overzealous northern investors who thought they could flip the property for a quick profit. After the real estate bubble burst and prices collapsed, Rodeheaver swooped in and started buying up the parcels, eventually amassing 30,000 acres on St. John's River. He enlisted a local extension agent, Harry Westbury, as a minority investor and property manager. Now came the more obvious question—what did Rodeheaver have planned for all that land?

From all indications, Rodeheaver didn't have a plan. Parts of the land had been a timber business with a sawmill and planer, familiar territory for Rodeheaver. Part of the land had been a cattle ranch, which Rodeheaver and Westbury continued for several years.[50] The property also included a huge five-bedroom house with wraparound porch, large social rooms, and a large kitchen. Though it was in the middle of nowhere, the house felt a lot like his Rainbow Point house in Winona Lake, so Rodeheaver named it Rainbow Ranch and used it as a vacation home. Bruce Howe recalled wintertime trips in the early 1940s, when Rodeheaver invited B. D. Ackley, George Sanville, and others to join him at the ranch.[51] But everyone who visited wondered the same thing: 30,000 acres?

Sometimes Rodeheaver spoke of a Christian conference center and vacation site or a training school for Christian young people. At other points he dreamed of a work camp for unemployed men.[52] As Westbury later explained, their eventual plan developed by chance. Needing some informal foster care (and a quick solution), a Putnam County deputy brought a boy to the ranch and asked the Westburys to care for him temporarily. Not an unusual problem. In the late 1940s, communities lacked a fully developed social services network and sought informal solutions such as this. What started as a spur-of-the-moment idea quickly expanded as more boys needed care.[53] The *Orlando Evening Star* puffed the growing venture, calling for an executive director who "must be something like Father Flannigan was," a tough-minded inspiration, because the potential residents "will not be Sunday School boys."[54] Suddenly, Rodeheaver and Westbury found themselves in over their heads but still quite passionate about the idea. As one who lost his own mother when he was only eight, and as one who never had children of his own, Rodeheaver finally arrived at a fitting idea for his property.

The ranch was chartered on June 27, 1950, with a newly formed board and plans to build a properly designed orphan home. The first unit was finished in the fall of 1951 with room for nine boys ages 12 through 16.[55] As the ranch quickly grew, so did the continued comparisons to Father Edward J. Flanagan at his Boys Town compound in Omaha, Nebraska. Though Rodeheaver had plenty of ideas about what should be done, he also understood his own limitations; he knew very little about running a child-care facility. He wisely hired a competent staff, organized an independent board, and turned the management over to them. Rodeheaver's ongoing role was the one job he did better than anyone else: promotion and fund-raising.[56] He expanded the Boys Ranch board and persuaded friends to join, including Norman Vincent Peale, Bishop Arthur J. Moore, and Asa G. Candler, the founder of Coca-Cola. Most notably, Billy Graham joined the board and immediately began promoting the Boys Ranch on his *Hour of Decision* broadcasts. Graham's interest in the project stemmed from his continued ties to Palatka. During his student days at Florida Bible Institute, Graham preached at area churches and at the nearby Lake Swan Bible Conference. A Southern Baptist preacher baptized Billy Graham in Swan Lake, and the Peniel Baptist Church ordained him to the gospel ministry in 1939.[57]

Understanding all of Graham's ties to the region, Rodeheaver also offered to sell him a portion of the 30,000-acre ranch, a vacation place where he could unwind with his family in privacy. Graham (and especially his wife) had grown tired of summer tourists driving by his current home in Montreat, North Carolina. So in 1951, Billy Graham purchased 600 acres of Rodeheaver's Florida property. The son of a dairy farmer, Graham took the next logical step and purchased a herd of cattle to go with it, paying Harry Westbury to manage the herd. Rodeheaver and Westbury liked the young preacher and wanted him to be successful; there was no real way the transaction could go wrong. At this point in his life, Graham needed a bit of paternalism; the youthful Graham could be manipulated and sometimes used, like the time Alabama Congressman Frank Boykin offered to give Graham a new bull for his Florida herd. Boykin, a troublemaker for most of his political career, naturally expected political favors in return.[58]

Graham's side career as a Florida rancher proved to be short lived. He became too busy to visit his property, and if solitude was the goal, his wife had a better idea. She had located an equally remote 150-acre farm on Black Mountain, not far from the family's current Montreat home. She persuaded Billy to sell their Florida property back to Rodeheaver (along with the herd)—a friendly transaction where Rodeheaver returned the same sum Graham had originally paid. The Grahams used the money to develop their Black Mountain compound, which Ruth Bell Graham named Little Piney Cove. And as an added benefit, Graham was free from Boykin's political bull.[59]

Rodeheaver continued his Florida real estate ventures while making a few end-of-life plans. In 1944, he incorporated the Rodeheaver Foundation and endowed it with his hymnal profits. He originally intended the foundation to fund his education efforts, especially to encourage and promote gospel music. The Rodeheaver School of Sacred Music rarely broke even, and any new training ventures probably wouldn't, either. The foundation also supported various Winona Lake causes, such as the music department at Grace College. With all of his real estate investments and philanthropic efforts, Rodeheaver's wealth became a matter of open speculation. The idea of the millionaire hymnal publisher was too good to pass up—was it true?

Maybe. Much of Rodeheaver's personal wealth was tied up in real estate, making it difficult to assess cash value. He also held 50 percent ownership in the Rodeheaver Co. (the remaining shares were controlled by his brother, nephew, half-sister, and brother-in-law). But again, no one could accurately assess the market value of a privately held publishing company, at least not at the time. Much later, we would discover a profit-and-loss statement, misfiled in Winona Lake and ignored for years. For the fiscal year 1954–55, just prior to Rodeheaver's death, the company had total sales of $528,955, with overhead of $221,587—an annual profit of $307,408 ($2.8 million today).[60] By any standard, Rodeheaver was wealthy. At any rate, with the Boys Ranch off to a solid start, Rodeheaver and Westbury sold off the rest of the Rainbow Ranch property, netting $1 million for their 24,604 acres. At the time, the transaction was the largest-ever land deal in Putnam County.[61] Rodeheaver dumped a good deal of his profits into the Rodeheaver Foundation.[62]

Though it started out as an informal idea, Rodeheaver Boys Ranch became Rodeheaver's last big project in a lifetime of big projects. The ranch remains in operation today, still enjoying community respect and support, still committed to providing a Christian environment for at-risk children. Its motto remains unchanged from the Rodeheaver era, "It is better to build boys than mend men."

END OF THE RAINBOW

After living at a furious pace for most of his life, the end came quickly for Homer Rodeheaver. He suffered a cerebral hemorrhage on December 18, 1955, four days after another heart attack had confined him to bed. "I was delivering Sunday papers to him," Bruce Howe recalled. "Mrs. Thomas came to the door and said 'I think Rody's gone.' And I ran upstairs and he had passed away."[63] Howe, who also served as the Winona Lake fire chief, tried without success to resuscitate him. By the next morning, Rodeheaver's obituary ran in all the major papers, sparking a hasty funeral reunion for the aging crew of tabernacle revivalists, plus a few of the next generation, including Cliff Barrows. As guests arrived the night before the funeral, they naturally gravitated to Rainbow Point, where the pie and coffee were waiting, one more time.

"They asked me to stand by his casket at the piano at Rainbow Point and lead some of his favorite songs," Cliff Barrows told us. "And I did—I led 'Beyond the Sunset, O Blissful Morning.'"[64] His song choice seemed to be a fitting benediction. According to Winona Lake legend, Virgil and Blanche Brock wrote the song right there, two decades earlier, while watching the sunset from Rodeheaver's porch.[65]

Beyond the sunset, O blissful morning,
When with our Savior heav'n is begun.
Earth's toiling ended, O glorious dawning;
Beyond the sunset, when day is done.

A week before Rodeheaver died, Billy Graham met with the Protestant Council of New York City and accepted their invitation to hold a campaign in New York City the next year.[66] After quietly courting the Council for months, Graham had hoped his New York effort could attract theological liberals while also retaining the support of his conservative base. But this time, there would be no cooperation—the fundamentalists loudly withdrew their support of Graham. Having limped along for years, Billy Sunday's Protestant coalition had now shattered.

One could ask if the same fate awaited Rodeheaver's gospel songs. Forty years had passed since the high point of the tabernacle era, when everyone sang his new songs with abandon. The next generation of gospel songwriters had more diverse platforms for their new music: Youth for Christ rallies, radio choirs, Black gospel and southern gospel performers, and secular musicians who incorporated at least some gospel into their concerts. The newer songs were popular, yes, and clearly influenced by trends in pop music. But many of the new gospel songs of the 1940s and '50s became popular as performance music, not through communal singing.

By 1955, the shift was clear to B. D. Ackley, who pointed out the difference in a letter to songwriter George S. Schuler. "There is sometimes a noticeable drift that we term 'modernism type'—which to our old-fashioned mind takes away

CHAPTER 10

FIGURE 10.4. Cliff Barrows leading songs with trombone in hand (Billy Graham and Bev Shea, center), c. 1948. Courtesy of Billy Graham Center Archives, Wheaton, Illinois.

from the smoothness and general usefulness of gospel songs," Ackley said. Then he explained what he meant by *modernism type*. "You fellows can take a choir or chorus and train them carefully with your type of material—if it's the modern type—and put it over the air so that it sounds like a million dollars. Yet none of our people believe that these same songs could be put over in a general book with the average congregation." Now 83, Ackley felt the campaign to perpetuate gospel songs hadn't perpetuated Rodeheaver's essential ideal of communal singing. "It's about time that I gave up entirely," Ackley concluded, sounding worn out.[67]

DEATH OF THE RODEHEAVER COMPANY

When Rodeheaver passed away, his company claimed to be the largest independent church music company in the country—unverifiable, of course, but none of his competitors challenged the assertion. Now the Rodeheaver Co. faced the same challenge as any other family-owned company, the question of the next generation's role. Except in this case, Homer, Yumbert, and Ruth had no children, and Joseph's son, Joseph Jr. (with his doctorate from Harvard) was well into his career as a high school administrator.

After several years of informal conversations, James and Ruth Thomas agreed to sell the Rodeheaver Hall-Mack Co. to Word Music of Waco, Texas, owned by Jarrell McCracken and minority partner Marvin Norcross. When the sale became final on July 1, 1969, Word billed itself as "the world's largest producer of religious recordings," now with a robust print division and a Midwest distribution center.[68] More importantly, Word acquired 6,000 Rodeheaver songs, which *Billboard* described as "an overwhelming majority of the most used, most loved songs in America."[69] As for James and Ruth Thomas, the actual sale amount was never announced, though insiders later disclosed the amount as $1 million ($6.5 million in today's dollars). In addition to receiving a windfall, the Thomases received a guarantee that the Winona Lake office and warehouse workers could keep their jobs. Most importantly, the Rodeheaver brand would continue as a subsidiary of Word.

"The Rodeheaver name is forever in sacred music circles," Bruce Howe later explained to *Billboard*. "When we sold to Jarrell McCracken in 1969, he agreed that there would always be music carrying the Rodeheaver logo."[70] Howe's comment accurately represented the hopes of the Rodeheaver management, who viewed the sale as the next step forward for the company. But not everyone saw the sale in such positive terms. Roland Felts, the longtime music editor who had worked closely with Rodeheaver and the Ackley brothers, started cleaning out his office. "I am not interested in the kind of 'entertainment' they are producing," Felts complained to the songwriter Oswald J. Smith right after the Word sale. "And since they feel that I am not a fit writer for them, I shall be leaving the company." Felts echoed the same concerns Ackley had raised before his death, that the new style of "modern" gospel song was written for musical performances and recordings, rather than congregational singing. For Felts, the Rodeheaver sale was a final confirmation that his era was ending. "I hate to see the Lord's work change so completely that entertainment is more important than the gospel," Felts wrote.[71]

For about a hundred years, the gospel song hymnal industry was controlled by a small coterie of family-owned companies. The wider entertainment industry might not have taken note if it weren't for the popular performers who turned gospel songs into a mass market commodity. But now the entertainment industry had, in fact, taken note. In 1974, the American Broadcasting Co. approached McCracken and Norcross with a plan that sent reverberations throughout the industry—an offer to purchase Word Music for 300,000 shares of ABC stock. When insiders read the *Billboard* article, they could do the math. ABC stock was selling for about $23 a share, about $7 million for the transaction. Jarrell McKracken was wealthy. His private company, including the old Rodeheaver catalog, was now a publicly traded corporation.[72]

Years later, we stumbled on a document that explained the value of Rodeheaver's song catalog. An unpublished financial report listed Rodeheaver's top 50 songs for Fiscal Year 1973–74, starting with "The Old Rugged Cross" ($31,974), "In the Garden" ($31,968), and "Beyond the Sunset" ($14,429). The company disclosed annual royalties of $152,844 ($600,000 today), plenty enough to attract investor attention.[73]

After the sale, ABC kept the Rodeheaver offices open in Winona Lake, even expanding the warehouse at 100 Publishers Drive.[74] Bruce Howe became a vice president of ABC, in charge of the print music division that remained in Winona Lake. Lu Ann Inman, who started working in the Rodeheaver offices in 1978, recalls the final years: "The Rodeheaver Ladies—that's what I called them—were all in their sixties and seventies," a group that included Gertrude Ackley Dye, B. D. Ackley's daughter. "When Rodeheaver sold to Word in 1969, the Rodeheaver ladies had all of the history and the knowledge and knew how all of the copyright licensing worked."[75]

But times were changing. Ruth Rodeheaver Thomas died on February 11, 1979, followed by James Thomas in 1980, followed by a memorable estate sale at Rodeheaver's Rainbow Point home.[76] Hordes of souvenir hunters carried away a lifetime of knickknacks and home furnishings. Bruce Howe, ever loyal to the boss he called Mr. Homer, plunked down money for Rodeheaver's Victrola, stacks of records, boxes of old recordings and film, framed photos—and one gold-plated trombone.[77] In a fitting irony, George Beverly Shea sold Chancel Music Co. to Word a year later, including his best-selling favorite, "I'd Rather Have Jesus."[78] Forty years had passed since Rodeheaver first tried to purchase Shea's song; now it was listed as "assigned to the Rodeheaver Co. (a division of Word, Inc.)." The fine print at the bottom of the music confirmed a new reality: the Rodeheaver name existed primarily as a song catalog owned by ABC through its subsidiary, Word Music.

Then came the long-feared corporate downsizing. In 1987, ABC announced the closure of the Winona Lake offices, moving everything of value to the Word Music headquarters in Waco, Texas.[79] Everything of present value, that is. Workers loaded trucks with the remaining inventory—hymnals, choral music, and other religious print music. Then they wheeled out a bank of filing cabinets with copyright information about the song catalog. The rest of the stuff—75 years of gospel music history—went into a dumpster parked in the side alley. Bruce Howe retired to his Dream Lake estate outside of town, and for old time's sake he continued to list the Rodeheaver Co. in Winona Lake's phone book. But now the phone rang in his garage office.

At this point the ownership of Rodeheaver's song catalog becomes difficult to track, a twisted tale that exemplifies corporate music dealings at the end of the twentieth century. In 1986, Capital City Communications purchased ABC for $3.5 billion and forced Jarrell McCracken's resignation from Word; then in 1992,

Capital Cities/ABC sold Word Music for $72 million to Thomas Nelson (world's largest Bible producer); then five years later Nelson split off the music division for $120 million to Gaylord Entertainment (parent company of the Grand Old Opry), conservatively reporting its investment gain as $16 million. Ecstatic investors looked at the flurry of transactions as final proof that the Christian music industry could generate an ever-increasing revenue stream.[80]

Until the bubble burst. Few insiders could see it, but the market was significantly overvalued—starting with the value of older song catalogs. Word Music owners boasted of owning 40,000 songs, but the inflated figure did little to describe their value to shareholders.[81] The copyright to "The Old Rugged Cross" had expired in 1988, as had most of the revenue-producing songs from the era of tabernacle revivalism. Though it seems obvious now, the people who remembered and sang these songs were expiring, too. And the very idea of a hymnal, Rodeheaver's core business, was rapidly disappearing from churches in a new era of performance music. When Word Music released *The Celebration Hymnal* in 1997, it contained 12 songs from the old Rodeheaver catalog—the last hymnal to list Rodeheaver as a copyright owner. Then the Rodeheaver song catalog ceased to exist as an entity, swallowed up in industry consolidation.[82] As it turned out, Bruce Howe was wrong about the company's longevity. The Rodeheaver name was not "forever in sacred music circles."

The 1997 sale to Gaylord marked the pinnacle of Christian music capitalization, followed by ten years of free fall. Measured in dollars, the Christian market dropped by half between 1999 and 2005.[83] Cutting their losses, Gaylord Entertainment offered Word Music to AOL Time Warner for $84.1 million in 2001, writing off $29 million on the sale.[84] Time Warner continued on a random buying spree that baffled many observers. Having reached its goal of becoming the largest media company in the world, it was also awash in $30 billion debt—unsustainable in any economy. In 2003, it sold the entire Warner Music Group (including Word/Rodeheaver) to Edgar Bronfman's investment group for $2.6 billion. Lovers of irony could now point out that the Rodeheaver catalog, built on Christian hymns and Prohibition songs, was now owned by a Seagram's whiskey heir. But not for long. In 2016, the Warner Music Group sold Word Entertainment Group to Curb Records, meaning that the Word/Rodeheaver catalog was now privately owned again. For now.

In retrospect, the inflated value of Christian song catalogs can be traced to a fundamental discontinuity. In 1995, the music industry began using its Soundscan technology to track Christian music sales, with hopes that they would better account for a genre that was notoriously difficult to define.[85] The next few years of data showed "remarkable growth" in Christian music, with skyrocketing sales figures reported in *Billboard* and other trade journals.[86] The industry trusted the numbers enough to embark on a buying spree, where a majority of Christian music publishers were bought by publicly traded companies. In many cases, like Word/Rodeheaver, the companies were bought and sold several times. But the inflated sales reports cloaked a basic weakness in the Christian market. The rest of the music industry fell apart because consumers stopped purchasing CDs and instead found their music online, the well-documented shift from an acquisition model to an access model.[87] Meanwhile, the Gospel Music Association and Soundscan goosed its numbers by counting any music that could be plausibly sold in a Christian bookstore, even the soundtrack to *Oh Brother, Where Art Thou*, and "Butterfly Kisses" by Bob Carlisle. While the rest of the music market collapsed, the Christian sales figures appeared to increase, but only because everything counted as Christian music.

The aging generation of gospel songwriters like B. D. Ackley and Roland Felts had suspected this development and didn't like it. Had they lived to see the rise of Contemporary Christian Music in the 1980s, they might have been forced into some honest reflection: Rodeheaver's ideas had unintended consequences. When Rodeheaver introduced the first Christian record label as "more of a mission than a business," he successfully convinced his generation of gospel songwriters to enforce a clear distinction between the two. But now, looking back, many observers study the rise and fall of the Christian music industry and reach a different conclusion. The money won out.

Rodeheaver's followers also defended his essential reasoning, that some song styles were "never intended for a Sunday morning service" and could "bridge the gap between the popular song of the day and the great hymns and gospel songs."[88] But Rodeheaver did not anticipate how his brand of "bridge the gap" gospel music would actually become standard fare in evangelical worship services. For a time. Then the Youth for Christ musicians saw a new gap and created new music, justifying their choices as an application of Rodeheaver's "bridge-the-gap" philosophy. And though we do not have space to develop this idea further, one could easily observe how the next generation of Contemporary Christian Musicians borrowed Rodeheaver's reasoning yet again when justifying their stylistic changes.

As a result, whether or not one agrees with the musical transition that occurred in evangelical churches, modern worship music became a commodity, the exact problem Rodeheaver wished to avoid. And on Sunday morning, when the evangelical church gathers together to watch the performers, very few would argue that the congregation sings together like Rodeheaver intended.

11

EPILOGUE

"IT'S UP TO YOU, RODY, TO FREE THEM"

When the credits rolled for Rodeheaver's last movie, his name flew across the screen with a splashy title: "Homer Rodeheaver, the Dean of Gospel Singers." He probably thought of it himself. Thomas A. Dorsey had already claimed *father* of gospel music. Mahalia Jackson would always reign as *queen*. And southern gospel quartets continue to argue like Christ's disciples, asking who is the greatest in the kingdom.

FIGURE 11.1. Homer Rodeheaver, 1950s. Courtesy of Rodeheaver Collection, Grace College, Winona Lake.

CHAPTER 11

The idea of greatness often perplexes the biographer. After living close to a person through many years of research and writing—and after the patient reader wades through the interesting and mundane details of a person's life—is it still appropriate to ask about greatness? The question feels unseemly, perhaps a violation of scholarly detachment, the impudence of making a moral judgment, or even worse, *liking* the person.

Perhaps we should answer as he would answer. If we were to meet Homer Rodeheaver today, he would not waste any time trying to prove his greatness, but he would certainly make sure that we liked him. A warm handshake, introductions all around, a quick compliment, a funny story. And when the discussion turned serious, he would expect a spirit of fairness and a winsome response. So as we've introduced Rodeheaver to new audiences through this book, we wanted these qualities to be evident, even after balancing his version of the story with our concern for accuracy and context.

Rodeheaver could project his essential likability to the back row of the tabernacle. He brokered this basic quality into a long career as the nation's songleader, the world's largest gospel music publisher, successful record company owner, prolific recording artist, radio star, self-proclaimed ethnomusicologist, and generous philanthropist. By any measure, he was a success. His influence remains evident in the evangelical world and in the broader sphere of American music.[1]

At the time of his death, Homer Rodeheaver had become something like a jazz elder: the patroller of boundaries, keeper of traditions, expounder of official stories, teacher of the next generation.

That's not true jazz, the elder says, and in many ways Rodeheaver took on this same role for gospel music. He devoted a good deal of his life to marking boundaries for gospel music, which quickly became misunderstood. His hymnals and his Rainbow Records surprised everyone: the Blacks spirituals in a "white" songbook, the classical music in a revival tabernacle, the pop tunes that he insisted could be a gateway to a more serious worship service. He marked these boundaries at the exact same time the record companies were carving music into genres like hillbilly music, race music, and classical; yet Rodeheaver was recording all of these and calling it gospel. In his era, the northern whites were surprised by his inclusion of Black and southern music. Today the opposite is true—Blacks and southerners ask if Rodeheaver's gospel music belongs in the same category as their performance music. For some, his brand of congregational singing will never be *true* gospel.

But as all elders do, Rodeheaver did draw boundaries. Because he was a religious leader, part of this biography has strayed into the difficult intersection of religion and social history. His theological beliefs and devotional practices are a key part of the story, but to be honest, if we were young academics finishing a dissertation or seeking tenure, we would avoid such a touchy subject. Many who study gospel music find it easier to discuss the music or the history or the social forces that influence American culture. Discussing the spiritual and transformative aspects proves much more troublesome. So our approach here has been to at least suggest that Rodeheaver's religious views were transformative *for him*.

It was Homer Rodeheaver who interrupted choir rehearsals with an altar call, reminding his singers to consider the gospel message of the lyrics. It was Homer Rodeheaver who castigated record executives when they allowed virtually anyone to sing the gospel. No surprises here—the boundary that Rodeheaver drew around gospel music is the same boundary Billy Sunday drew in his tabernacle meetings, a clear line between unbeliever and believer. Not *true gospel*, but *true believer*.

The gospel elder keeps traditions and expounds official stories. Rodeheaver did his share of this, carefully documenting tabernacle revivalism with books, recordings, and several film projects. Even as early as 1920, when he saw the dwindling crowds and the fading methodology, Rodeheaver tried to record tabernacle music as it had been, a deliberate act of preservation. As researchers, we later stumbled onto a great irony of his life, that corporate caretakers had thrown away a good deal of the artifacts he tried to preserve. But this part of the story ended better than we expected. By focusing new attention on his life, we met many others who also had an interest in Rodeheaver's work and who helped us recover important sources. We have tried to name many of these new friends in our Acknowledgments section.

The gospel elder is teacher of the next generation, a job that Rodeheaver took seriously. His summer schools come to mind, but also his books, pamphlets, and the countless hours he spent talking to everyone on the porch of his Rainbow Point home. But when he told the old stories and showed the films—especially his blackface film—the enlightened younger generation performed its usual role, telling the elder that we don't talk that way anymore.

Homer Rodeheaver seems like such a likable chap. We want to like him, really. But how should we think about his failures, especially the times he failed to meet his own stated ideals, the gospel that he claimed to preach? Or to use a word that he would have used, how do we deal with his *sins*? In surveying his life we've seen principles of altruism that sometimes looked more like greed. We've seen musical ideals that sometimes looked like a marketing ploy. We've seen a love and respect for African American music that did not always extend to African Americans as a people. Or in his words, *God's children*.

Most troubling of all, why do honorable people see wrongdoing in their world and sometimes respond with silence?

As biographers who aspire to at least some form of scholarly detachment, it seems wrong for us to cast the first stone. So we look at the difficult questions we want to ask of Rodeheaver, and instead ask them of our own age, and of ourselves. How do we wish others to view our own failures? With forgiveness, certainly. This attitude frees us to pursue another virtue: the wisdom to look critically upon the spirit of our own age, and the courage to report its flaws. This is the lesson of a true biography.

* * *

Near the end of his life, Homer Rodeheaver took a halfhearted stab at writing an autobiography. Only a typewritten chapter survives, where he looks at his own life and remembers a fragment of wisdom from long ago, that "most lives are second bests." True success, Rodeheaver explains, would have been his original career goal—a lawyer. Then, after he types the paragraph, he scrawls an interrupting note in the margin: "But destiny or God ruled otherwise."

He never finishes the book, but the project helps him recognize his own transformation: "Life and your own capabilities have a way of finding you out and leading you away from whatever it is that you may have set up as a goal, toward the work that is really yours to do. I believe that as firmly as I believe anything."[2]

If we were to meet Homer Rodeheaver today, he wouldn't waste all of this time on talk. By now, with the introductions finished, he would have us all singing. He would conjure up something about *brightening corners* and *hearts wearing rainbows* and then the cynics among us would roll our eyes because people don't talk that way anymore. And we certainly don't sing together. We can't even make it through "The Star-Spangled Banner" without turning it into a political statement. So go ahead, Rody, just try to make us sing.

And he would. He would wave his arms and blow his trombone and we would sing whether we wanted to or not, because he is the World's Greatest Songleader and can get anyone to sing—*anyone*. Somehow Homer Rodeheaver knew that the "second best" of his life was actually his destiny, the thing he must do because no one else could. He would give himself the pep talk one more time, just like the old days, and he would face all of the problems of the world, utterly convinced that they could be made better through song—people singing together.

> *These thousands of men and women have come here because they are seeking something. Each of them—that capable looking business woman, that drunk with a week's beard on his chin, those girls giggling and nudging the sailors beside them, that bank president with the poker face—has his or her own world. They are caught in them. They are the prisoners of their own fears and anxieties, their own memories and hopes.*
>
> *It's up to you, Rody, to free them. You've got to weld all those diverse worlds into one.*[3]

EPILOGUE

Did he free them? Rodeheaver thought he had. He believed gospel music embodied the doctrine of personal salvation, true spiritual transformation. And for the religious skeptics among us, Rodeheaver's gospel music at least offers a positive antidote to our increasingly disjointed and disrupted world. He leveraged his vague "power of music" ideology to build character, strengthen families, and improve the moral fabric of society. Perhaps Homer was on to something, that communal music could be—somehow and in some way—a unifying, healing balm to bring people together.

In the years since Rodeheaver's death, pop musicians have continued to write communal anthems that speak to their generation. And every decade or so, music educators revive the community sing idea, their recurring act of defiance against the entropy of individualism. In the midst of divisions, we try to come together by singing together. We don't always succeed, but that's no reason to stop trying.

Or as Rodeheaver would say, *Come on, let's sing!*

ACKNOWLEDGMENTS

"No man is an island," John Donne wrote in 1624, a fitting warning for researchers who view their work as an isolated enterprise. Having begun with the intention of marshaling several different disciplines in a study of Homer Rodeheaver's life, we finished with a remarkable appreciation for the wide spectrum of people who helped us with the project. We could not have done this ourselves, so we will do our best to give credit where credit is due. If we have neglected someone who assisted us, please accept our apology and our sincere appreciation.

The project was supported by the research of a dedicated team in Winona Lake, Indiana, where Grace College continues to support the Winona History Center, the Billy Sunday Home Museum, and the Morgan Library Archives & Special Collections. Long before we began pawing around and asking questions about Homer Rodeheaver, they were guardians of many bits and pieces of his musical and spiritual empire. Jared Burkhalter, Rhoda Palmer, Nina Ferry, Tonya Fawcett, Bill Firstenberger, Mark Norris, Steve Grill, Terry White, and the late Carol Forbes were of immeasurable help as we asked them to dig deeper into what they knew they had, even as our insistent desire for more led them and us to new discoveries in closets they had not opened for many years. Our project became the impetus for gathering and consolidating many undiscovered resources. Through their tireless research efforts, the Rodeheaver Collection will become an ongoing resource for future study, a fitting companion to the library's well-known William "Billy" & Helen "Ma" Sunday Collection.

ACKNOWLEDGMENTS

The Billy Graham Center Archives at Wheaton College continues to be the most significant archive of Christian evangelism in the nineteenth and twentieth centuries. Bob Shuster and Katherine Graber gave us unfettered access to this unparalleled collection, along with additional material located by David Osielski, Keith Call, and David Malone of the Buswell Library Special Collections at Wheaton College. At the time of our research, the Papers of William Franklin "Billy" Graham Jr. (and other documents from the Billy Graham Evangelistic Association) were kept at the BGCA in Wheaton. In June 2019, the Graham papers were moved to the Billy Graham Archives in Charlotte, North Carolina.

Dell Moore of the Billy Graham Evangelistic Association (BGEA) arranged an interview with Cliff Barrows before his 2016 death. By this point, Barrows was declining all interview requests (mostly from aggressive obituary writers!), but he still wanted to talk about Rodeheaver and the trombone. Other key interviews included Bruce Howe, retired vice president of Rodeheaver Music; Donald Hustad, retired music professor and former Billy Graham organist; Kurt Kaiser, former vice president of Word Music; and William E. Brusseau, owner of Westminster Films—all of whom passed away while we were writing. "Any man's death diminishes me," John Donne also wrote, and we found ourselves immeasurably blessed by these timely interactions.

Additional insights were gleaned from interviews and emails with Barry Ogdon, great-nephew of Ina Duley Ogdon; Kris Yeaworth, son of the filmmaker Shorty Yeaworth; Terry York, author of a fine PhD dissertation on Charles Gabriel; Stan Moser and Roland Lundy, former Word Music executives; and Lu Ann Inman, director of copyright and licensing for Warner Chappell Music.

A long list of archivists, museum curators, librarians, college professors, musicians, gospel music aficionados, and research assistants answered our queries, helped us look for answers, and patiently endured our persistence when we just *knew* there was something more to be found. Among these are (alphabetically), Stephanie Bandel-Koroll and Olivia Beaudry (Center for Popular Music, Middle Tennessee State University); Margaret Downie Banks (National Music Museum); Wesley Barber (Hocking County Drafting Department); Beth Beach, Carol Holliger, Melissa Previtera, and Eugene Rutigliano (Ohio Wesleyan University); Ryan Bean (University of Minnesota Libraries); Christine Bolyard (Preston County Assessor's Office); Paul Boucier (Wisconsin Historical Society); Joanna Bouldin (McClung Historical Collection); Rev. Deb Bowsher (First Presbyterian Church, Mt. Gilead, Ohio); Andrea Cartell (University of Arkansas Libraries); Christy Cherney and Corie Zylstra (Moody Bible Institute Archives); Eddie Clem (Indiana University Kokomo); Stacey A. Cordery (Monmouth College Archives); Danielle Cordovez (Rodgers and Hammerstein Archives of Recorded Sound, New York Public Library); Steve Dillon (Dillon Music); Elizabeth B. Dunn

ACKNOWLEDGMENTS

(Duke University); David Earll (Ithaca College); Laura Eliason (Indiana State Library); Ruth Frasur (Hagerstown-Jefferson Township Library); Emily Gattozzi (Ohio Wesleyan University Historical Collection); Trent Hanner (Tennessee State Library & Archives); Kyle Hovious (Special Collections, Hodges Library, University of Tennessee); Stan Ingersol (Nazarene Archives, Lenexa, Kansas); Paul Jantz and Patrick Robbins (Bob Jones University); Debra Madera (Emery University); Robert Luckett (Jackson State University); Judy Stolz Maniskas (Hocking County Historical Society); Kurt Nauck (Nauck's Vintage Records); Jeffrey Norman (Arizona State University Music Library); the staff of Palatine (Illinois) and Toledo (Ohio) Public Libraries; Mark Rhodes (Bethel College); Jason Runnels (Southwestern Baptist Theological Seminary); Scott Schwartz, (Sousa Archives and Center for American Music, University of Illinois at Urbana-Champaign); John Shorney, Scott Shorney, and Steve Shorney (Hope Publishing); Jillian Sparks (University of Iowa); Geoffrey Stark (University of Arkansas Libraries Special Collections); Michael Stauffer (Indiana Historical Society); Mark J. Tidwell (Jellico Public Library); Robert Vejnar (Emory & Henry College); Greg Wilsbacher (Moving Image Research Collections, University of South Carolina); Steve Wunderley and Steve Zeleny (Foursquare Archives).

Several discographers and researchers were helpful in unraveling the story of Rainbow Records, starting with the tireless work of David N. Lewis but also including the efforts of Michael Khanchalian, Charlie Dahan, Richard Raichelson, and Robert Marovich; and Richard Martin and Meagan Hennessey of Archeophone Records.

Over the years, other writers have introduced Homer Rodeheaver's life and work in articles and books, especially David N. Lewis, Terry White, and Bert H. Wilhoit. A doctoral dissertation by Thomas Henry Porter was especially valuable, capturing important documentation before the destruction of Rodeheaver Company records. Porter offered support and encouragement for our project prior to his 2017 death.

Craig Bentley of the Columbus Revival Heritage Museum, whose interest in Rodeheaver intersected with his decades-long research on Ohio Methodism, provided invaluable assistance and undertook a pilgrimage to find the Rodeheaver homestead near Union Furnace, Ohio. Yoshioko Nakamura (Raleigh Christian Academy) provided translations from Japanese and information about Rodeheaver's influence in Japan subsequent to his 1923 visit; Craig Kridel (University of South Carolina, emeritus) offered extremely helpful insight on our chapters on Rodeheaver and race. The editors of the *Historic Brass Society Journal*, Stewart Carter and Howard Weiner, saw Douglas's article about Rodeheaver to print, helping to fine-tune its arguments and expression. Melissa Meyer edited our proposal and early chapters.

ACKNOWLEDGMENTS

Homer had no children; neither did his brother Yumbert or their half-sister, Ruth. After much searching we found grandchildren of Joseph Rodeheaver, Thomas Rodeheaver, and Barbara Rodeheaver Fong, who were exceptionally generous in sharing family documents, clippings, letters, photos, and insights, as well as rare recordings that featured Homer, Joseph, and Ruth.

We reserve special thanks for Laurie Matheson and Jennifer Argo at University of Illinois Press for their confidence in our book proposal and their encouragement as we worked.

To our wives, Carla (Kevin) and Patricia (Douglas), there are no words to adequately express our thanks. Long-suffering and patient, yes, but also encouraging and supportive. We chased after small details for weeks and shouted *Eureka!* when we found bits of the Rodeheaver puzzle that ended up as a single sentence in the book. Still, they listened and read patiently, even when bemused by the whole enterprise. And sometimes they hauled us back to earth—back into this century—with a raised eyebrow and a well-timed "Seriously?" Emerging from the deep cave of Rodeheaver research, we count ourselves blessed to have wives that are the embodiment of the well-worn but never more true words from Paul's letter to the Corinthian church, "Love bears all things, believes all things, hopes all things, endures all things. Love never ends."

Joint authorship does not always work out neatly, but in our case, our relationship has deepened over these years of researching and writing. We emerged with our friendship not only intact, but more vibrant. In these years of working together, our lives have changed quite a bit—the death of parents and grandparents, the marriages of children, the birth of grandchildren. Now that Douglas has moved from Arizona to Illinois (thank his grandkids), we find ourselves happily living near each other and ready to start the next shared project. Cue the raised eyebrows from Carla and Patricia.

NOTES

INTRODUCTION

1. Bill Darr (retired library director, Morgan Library, Grace College, Winona Lake), interview with Kevin Mungons, January 9, 2015. Homer Rodeheaver pronounced his last name as *ROW-duh-hay-ver* and spelled his nickname as *Rody*.

2. "Sunday's 19 Aids Draw Trail-Hitters," *New York Times*, January 28, 1917, 6.

3. Though *gospel song* became his term of choice, Rodeheaver occasionally used *gospel hymn*, *gospel music*, and just plain *gospel*. Even today, these names have roughly equivalent meanings that shift from user to user.

4. Homer Rodeheaver, "Leading Revival Singing," *Etude* (November 1942), 744, 772, 778; see also his similar explanation in "Suggestions for the Songleader," *Hymnal Handbook for Standard Hymns and Gospel Songs* (Chicago: Rodeheaver Co., 1930), v–x.

5. Homer Rodeheaver, *The Practical Song Director* (Chicago: Rodeheaver Co., 1925), 4.

6. "Gospel Hymns," *Grove's Dictionary of Music and Musicians*, vol. 6: American Supplement (Philadelphia: Theodore Presser, 1920), 224. The Rodeheaver omission can be read only as a deliberate snub by Waldo Selden Pratt, the volume editor and Presbyterian church musician who often criticized Rodeheaver's brand of gospel songs.

7. "Gospel music," Stephen Shearon, Harry Eskew, James C. Downey, and Robert Darden, *Grove Music Online*, 2012.

8. Standard works on southern gospel music include Don Cusic, *Saved by Song: A History of Gospel and Christian Music* (Jackson: University Press of Mississippi, 2012); James R. Goff Jr., *Close Harmony: A History of Southern Gospel* (Chapel Hill: University of North Carolina Press, 2002); and Douglas Harrison, *Then Sings My Soul: The Culture of Southern Gospel Music* (Urbana: University of Illinois Press, 2012). Two books on country music also address southern gospel; see Bill C. Malone and Tracey Laird, *Country Music USA: 50th*

Anniversary Edition (Austin: University of Texas Press, 2018); Tony Russell and Bob Pinson, *Country Music Records: A Discography, 1921–1942* (New York: Oxford University Press, 2008).

9. Standard works on African American gospel music include Eileen Southern, *The Music of Black Americans*, 3rd ed. (New York: W. W. Norton and Company, 1997); Horace Clarence Boyer and Lloyd Yearwood, *The Golden Age of Gospel* (Urbana: University of Illinois Press, 2000); Robert Darden, *People Get Ready* (New York: Continuum International Publishing, 2004); *Nothing but Love in God's Water Volume I: Black Sacred Music from the Civil War to the Civil Rights Movement* (University Park: Penn State University Press, 2014); and Robert Marovich, *A City Called Heaven: Chicago and the Birth of Gospel Music* (Urbana: University of Illinois Press, 2014).

10. This is essentially the approach taken in the 2012 *Grove Music Online* article, with more consideration for earlier sources. See also Charles E. Morrison, "Aldine Kieffer and Ephraim Ruebush: Ideals Reflected in Post–Civil War Ruebush-Kieffer Company Music Publications," (DEd diss., Arizona State University, 1992).

11. See the account in Rodeheaver's obituary, "Homer A. Rodeheaver Dies; Funeral to Be Tuesday," *Warsaw (IN) Times*, December 19, 1955, 1. The incident probably did not occur, at least not in Toledo; the authors read two full months (April–May 1911) of the *Toledo Blade* but found no mention of a tabernacle fire.

12. The authors collected hundreds of newspaper and magazine profiles, as well as consulted Rodeheaver's *Song Stories of the Sawdust Trail*, *Twenty Years with Billy Sunday*, and the unfinished draft of an autobiography project.

13. Mark Katz, *Capturing Sound: How Technology Has Changed Music* (Berkeley: University of California Press, 2010). See also Greg Milner, *Perfecting Sound Forever: An Aural History of Recorded Music* (New York: Faber and Faber, 2009); Robert Philip, *Performing Music in the Age of Recording* (New Haven, CT: Yale University Press, 2004).

14. David Suisman, *Selling Sounds: The Commercial Revolution in American Music* (Cambridge, MA: Harvard University Press, 2009), 15. Suisman writes of a new commercial class of music makers clustered in New York City; his analysis sounds strikingly similar to a parallel development with Chicago's gospel hymnal publishers.

15. For a summary, see Theodore Winston Thurston, "A History of Music Publishing in Chicago: 1850–1960" (PhD diss., Northwestern University, 1961), 202.

16. Hugh Barker and Yuval Taylor, *Faking It: The Quest for Authenticity in Popular Music* (New York: W. W. Norton, 2007), 12. "Certain whites of the period seem to have been more interested in celebrating what they considered the most primitive, elemental, and backward-looking African American musicians they could find."

17. See the description of Charles Wolfe, *In Close Harmony: The Story of the Louvin Brothers* (Jackson: University of Mississippi Press, 1996), 14. His Texas attribution for Kim and Nyland cannot be correct but is interesting for its misconception.

18. George Pullen Jackson, "The Genesis of the Negro Spiritual," *American Mercury* (June 1932), 243–48. See also George Pullen Jackson, *White and Negro Spirituals: Their Life Span and Kinship* (Locust Valley, NY: J. J. Agustin, 1943). For a critique of Jackson (there are many), see Dena Epstein, *Sinful Tunes and Spirituals: Black Folk Music to the Civil War* (Urbana: University of Illinois Press, 2003), xiii. "Today it is hard to believe that serious writers could

have questioned the African element in African American music and dance ... only half a century ago," Epstein pointedly observes.

19. Karl Hagstrom Miller, *Segregating Sound: Inventing Folk and Pop Music in the Age of Jim Crow* (Durham, NC: Duke University Press, 2010), 7. For a similar viewpoint, see Richard A. Peterson, *Creating Country Music: Fabricating Authenticity* (Chicago: University of Chicago Press, 1997). These approaches can be applied directly to the problem of "authentic" gospel.

20. Scholars continue to debate whether evangelicalism should be defined as primarily a theological movement or as an imagined community of sociocultural identity. Our research of Rodeheaver should prove interesting to both viewpoints.

21. Rodeheaver used this topical approach in *Twenty Years with Billy Sunday*, and William G. McLoughlin chose this same device when writing his topical biography, *Billy Sunday Was His Real Name* (Chicago: University of Chicago Press, 1955).

22. Eileen Southern, *The Music of Black Americans*, xx.

23. Homer Rodeheaver, *Singing Down the Sawdust Trail: The Life Story of Homer A. Rodeheaver*. Undated, unpublished manuscript with handwritten corrections by Rodeheaver, Rodeheaver Collection at Morgan Library Archives and Special Collections, Grace College, Winona Lake, Indiana.

24. Homer Rodeheaver, "Song Director's Conference," *The Gospel Choir*, August 1919, 26.

CHAPTER 1. PROLOGUE

1. Narrative details of the 1917 Atlanta revival are from contemporary news accounts published in the *Atlanta Constitution*, *Atlanta Independent*, and *Atlanta Georgian*. Billy Sunday held meetings for Blacks on November 19 and December 1, 8, 15, and 22, and he invited Black choirs to a whites-only meeting on December 6. See also the Atlanta accounts written by various Sunday biographers: William G. McLoughlin Jr., *Billy Sunday Was His Real Name* (Chicago: University of Chicago Press, 1955), 272–73; Lyle W. Dorsett, *Billy Sunday and the Redemption of Urban America* (Grand Rapids: William B. Eerdmans, 1991), 97–98, 153–54; Roger A. Bruns, *Preacher: Billy Sunday and Big-Time American Evangelism* (New York: W. W. Norton, 1992), 225–47. Additional background details can be found in *African-American Religion: A Documentary History Project*, www3.amherst.edu/~aardoc.

2. Ned McIntosh, "Berlin, Damrosch and Toscanini Are All Forgotten When Brewster and Matthews Begin Fighting Ivories at the Sunday Meetings," *Atlanta Constitution*, November 5, 1917, 1, 7.

3. Ibid., Ned McIntosh, "Sunday Meetings," 7.

4. *Atlanta Constitution*, December 7, 1917, 4.

5. See McLoughlin, *Billy Sunday*, 88, and Bruns, *Preacher*, 101. For the perspective of Jolson's boastful publicity agent, see A. Toxen Worm, "The Business of Being a Press Agent," *The Theatre*, June 1917, 372.

6. Vincent Bryan (words) and Harry von Tilzer (music), "When Billy Sunday Comes to Town," (New York: Harry Von Tilzer Music Publishing, 1915).

7. "Rody Learns about Singing and Sunday about Emotion When Negroes Hit the Trail," *Atlanta Constitution*, November 20, 1917, 1.

8. John Dittmer, *Black Georgia in the Progressive Era, 1900–1920* (Urbana: University of Illinois Press, 1977), 196.

9. Homer Rodeheaver, *Singing Black: Letters from a Music Missionary in Africa* (Chicago: Rodeheaver Co., 1936), 9.

10. "Atlanta Colored Music Festival" and "Henry Hugh Proctor" in the *New Georgia Encyclopedia*, www.georgiaencyclopedia.org; additional background from Altona Trent Johns, "Henry Hugh Proctor," *The Black Perspective in Music* 3 (Spring 1975), 25–27, 30–32.

11. Henry Hugh Proctor, "The Theology of the Songs of the Southern Slave" (Yale Divinity School BD dissertation, 1894). See also the edited version published in the Hampton Institute's journal as H. H. Proctor, "The Theology of the Songs of the Southern Slave," *Southern Workman* 36 (November–December 1907), 584–92, 652–57; later reprinted in *Journal of Black Sacred Music* 2 (1988).

12. Proctor was also well known to the northern revivalists; he had preached at the first Winona Temperance Conference on the topic "The Attitude of the Colored People towards Temperance in the South." See *Winona Year Book and Programs* (Winona Lake, IN, 1908), 23.

13. See the historical summary in "Ebenezer Baptist Church: Historic Structure Report" (Atlanta, GA: Southeast Region National Park Service, 2001), 9–13.

14. "Ebenezer Church Will Celebrate Anniversary," *Atlanta Constitution*, November 19, 1917, 6.

15. H. H. Proctor, "Billy Sunday in a New Role: A Peacemaker Between the Races in the South," *Congregationalist and Advance* 111 (December 27, 1917), 933–34.

16. Borglum quit soon after the project started, which was eventually completed in 1972 as a memorial to Confederate soldiers. The Klan's contractual right to hold meetings at the site was not revoked until the land became state property in 1972.

17. For a summary of Imperial Wizard David C. Stephenson and Klan corruption, see Wyn Craig Wade, *The Fiery Cross: The Ku Klux Klan in America* (New York: Simon and Schuster, 1987), 239–47.

18. Ned McIntosh, "Birth of a Nation Thrills Tremendous Atlanta Audience," *Atlanta Constitution*, December 7, 1915, 7.

19. W. E. B. Du Bois, "Of the Faith of the Fathers" in *The Souls of Black Folk* (Chicago: A. C. McClurg and Company, 1903), 191.

20. O. B. Keeler, "Evangelist Himself Is Right," *Atlanta Georgian* home edition, November 20, 1917, 9.

21. For Dorsey's participation in the Sunday revivals, see Horace C. Boyer, "Thomas A. Dorsey: 'Father of Gospel Music,'" *Black World Magazine* (July 1974), 21. Using Dorsey as a source, Boyer attributes the incident to a 1911 Billy Sunday revival meeting in Atlanta and gives Dorsey's age as 12. But Sunday and Rodeheaver did not visit Atlanta until 1917 and did not visit any southern cities prior to this date. Our summary adjusts Dorsey's recollection of the date (and his age) to fit the timetable of Billy Sunday's Atlanta meeting and contemporary news accounts. See also Eileen Southern's account added to the third edition of *The Music of Black Americans*, drawing on Boyer.

22. See Michael W. Harris, *The Rise of Gospel Blues: The Music of Thomas Andrew Dorsey in the Urban Church* (New York: Oxford University Press, 1992), 47–62. Also see the Harris account of Dorsey's religious conversion, 67–68.

NOTES TO CHAPTER 1

23. Details of the Dorsey and Rodeheaver friendship are from Dorsey's interview with Anthony Heilbut, *The Gospel Sound* (New York: Simon and Shuster, 1971), 57–58.

24. See the analysis in Harris, *The Rise of the Gospel Blues*, 68–69. Also see Horace Clarence Boyer and Lloyd Yearwood, *The Golden Age of Gospel* (Urbana: University of Illinois Press, 2000), 41–44. The hymnal's lengthy influence was remarkable; it has remained in print, unchanged from the 1921 edition.

25. John Godrich and Robert M. W. Dixon, *Blues and Gospel Records, 1902–1942*, 3rd ed. (London: Storyville Publications, 1969), 235. For an analysis of this omission, see Tim Brooks, "'Might Take One Disc of This Trash as a Novelty': Early Recordings by the Fisk Jubilee Singers and the Popularization of 'Negro Folk Music,'" *American Music* 18 (Autumn 2000), 308. Goodrich and Dixon corrected this omission in their 4th edition (1997).

26. W. E. B. Du Bois, "Of the Faith of the Fathers" in *The Souls of Black Folk* (Chicago: A. C. McClurg and Company, 1904), 192–93.

27. See his own summary in W. E. B. Du Bois, *The Autobiography of W. E. B. Du Bois: A Soliloquy on Viewing My Life from the Last Decade of Its First Century* (New York: International Publishers, 1968), 181. For an in-depth exploration of Du Bois's religious views, see Jonathon S. Kahn, *Divine Discontent: The Religious Imagination of W. E. B. Du Bois* (New York: Oxford University Press, 2009).

28. Hugh Barker and Yuval Taylor, *Faking It: The Quest for Authenticity in Popular Music* (New York: W. W. Norton and Company, 2007), 8–19. See also Benjamin Filene, *Romancing the Folk: Public Memory and American Roots Music* (Chapel Hill: University of North Carolina Press, 2000).

29. This is the number given in "Ira D. Sankey Dies, a Song on His Lips," *New York Times*, August 15, 1908, and can be viewed as a conservative estimate. Many other sources place the number at 80 million. See William Revell Moody, *The Life of Dwight L. Moody* (Chicago: Fleming H. Revell, 1900), 170–81.

30. "Sacred Concert Given Friday by Versatile Sunday Workers," *Atlanta Constitution*, December 15, 1917, 11.

31. Ibid.

32. Homer Rodeheaver and Charles B. Ford Jr., *Song Leadership* (Winona Lake, IN: Rodeheaver Hall-Mack Co., 1941), 23.

33. "Rody Learns about Singing," 1.

34. Known by various titles. Published as "Going to Shout All Over God's Heav'n" in *Gospel Pearls* (1921); also known as "I Got Shoes" and "All God's Children Got Wings."

35. "Rody Learns about Singing," 1, 5.

36. Ibid.

37. Homer Rodeheaver, *The Christian Worker's Magazine*, May 1916, 684. From an address Rodeheaver gave to the student body at Moody Bible Institute during the 1915 Billy Sunday revival meetings in Chicago.

38. "Negro Leaders Laud Billy Sunday's Work," *Atlanta Constitution*, December 22, 1918, 9.

39. Ibid.

40. Ibid.

41. Francis Grimké, "Billy Sunday's Campaign in Washington, DC," *Addresses Mainly Personal and Racial*, vol. 1 in *The Works of Francis J. Grimké*, ed. Carter G. Woodson (Wash-

ington, DC: Associated Publishers, 1942), 554–59. Billy Sunday's failure to condemn Jim Crow was later denounced by Grimké and others (further explored in chapter 8).

42. Steve Goodson, *Highbrows, Hillbillies, and Hellfire: Public Entertainment in Atlanta, 1880–1930*, revised ed. (Athens, GA: University of Georgia Press, 2007).

43. Martin Luther King Sr., "What Part Should Singing Play in Our Church Worship?," *Georgia Baptist*, March 1, 1936, 4.

44. Ibid.

45. Martin Luther King Jr., "Questions and Answers," transcript of informal discussion, December 18, 1963, MLK at Western Collection, University Libraries, Western Michigan University. The hymn allusion is from "In Christ There Is No East or West" by John Oxenham, a pseudonym of William Arthur Dunkerley (1852–1941).

46. "In Memory of Mama King," *Ebony*, September 1974, 144.

CHAPTER 2. SOUTHERN ROOTS AND EARLY YEARS

1. This account is based on a photograph of the July 4, 1890, Jellico town celebration, McClung Historical Collection, Knoxville, Tennessee.

2. Homer Rodeheaver, *Singing Down the Sawdust Trail: The Life Story of Homer A. Rodeheaver*, 12. Undated, unpublished manuscript with handwritten corrections by Rodeheaver, Rodeheaver Collection at Morgan Library Archives and Special Collections, Grace College, Winona Lake, Indiana. For other first-person accounts of Homer Rodeheaver's early life, see Charles H. Gabriel, ed., *Gospel Choir*, September 1921, 3–7; "A Brief Biography of Rodeheaver—Famous Gospel Singer," undated clip sheet (c. 1940s), Moody Bible Institute Archives.

3. Rodeheaver's family tree was researched through ship passenger lists, United States Census records, and census slave schedules; birth, marriage, death, and burial records; and Civil War records accessed through genealogy websites. Thomas Rodeheaver and Barbara Rodeheaver Fong also provided access to family records and photographs, and Mark J. Tidwell, librarian of the Jellico Public Library, was of immeasurable assistance.

4. The Rodeheaver surname has been spelled in various ways including Rothenhauffer, Rothenhoeffer, Rothenhofer, Rothenheffer, Rhodehaver, Rodaheaver, Rodahaver and Rodehaver.

5. Boyd B. Stutler, *West Virginia in the Civil War*, 2nd ed. (Charleston, WV: Education Foundation Inc., 1966), 6.

6. Otis K. Rice and Stephen W. Brown, *West Virginia: A History* (Lexington: University Press of Kentucky, 1993), 99–153.

7. Thurman Rodeheaver mustered with Company H, 3rd Virginia (later West Virginia) Volunteer Infantry on June 28, 1861. The regiment's designation was changed to 6th West Virginia Volunteer Cavalry on January 26, 1864; he was discharged August 14, 1864.

8. Thurman H. Rodeheaver, *T. H. Rodeheaver. Co. H, 3rd Virginia Volunteers: This memorandum book purchased at Clarksburg, Harrison County, VA, Monday, the 7th Day of May, 1861*, unpublished handwritten diary, Rodeheaver family collection. Quoted with permission of Barbara Rodeheaver Fong and Thomas Rodeheaver.

9. Established first as New Cadiz, the town became Five Mile Furnace in 1854, named for the iron ore company that was established in the area, before becoming Union Furnace.

10. *History of Hocking Valley* (Chicago: Inter-State Publishing Co., 1883), 1044. See also Rodeheaver, *Sawdust Trail*, 7.

11. *History of Hocking Valley*, 1044.

12. Rodeheaver, *Sawdust Trail*, 7. For the *Mayflower* passenger list, see www.mayflowerhistory.com/mayflower-passenger-list/.

13. D. J. Lake, "Map of Starr Township," *Atlas of Hocking County, Ohio* (Philadelphia: Titus, Simmons & Titus, 1876), 41. See also *Deed from Isaac A. Guthrie & Wife to John J. Rodeheaver* [sic] *and Thurman H. Rodaheaver* [sic], Hocking County, Ohio, Registry of Deeds, Volume V, page 511, March 21, 1867. See also Charles H. Gabriel, ed., *Gospel Choir*, September 1921, 4.

14. *History of Hocking Valley*, 993–94.

15. Though difficult to access, Homer Rodeheaver's abandoned birth home still stands today. Edward Sudlow described the site in 1976: "Now for many years disassociated from human habitation and much the victim of the elements and of vandalism, it still feebly, perhaps a bit ghost-like, manages to stand on its original foundation of hewn stone masonry." Edward L. Sudlow to Hocking County Historical Society, April 7, 1976, Hocking County Historical Society, Logan, Ohio. The home looked much the same in 2016; see Craig Bentley, "Homer Rodeheaver Birthplace," YouTube video, 9:51, August 20, 2016, youtu.be/VU6Q8ilxSCM.

16. "A Brief Biography," clip sheet.

17. Last Will and Testament of Homer A. Rodeheaver, March 11, 1953, Kosciusko County Clerk of Court, Warsaw, Indiana.

18. Rodeheaver, *Sawdust Trail*, 11–12.

19. "Beulah Land," written by Edgar Page Stites (words) and John R. Sweney (music), was released in a few Sunday School hymnals, and then came to widespread use when it was included in *Gospel Hymns No. 3*, Ira D. Sankey et al., eds. (New York: Biglow & Main, 1878).

20. Donald P. Hustad, "D. L. Moody and Church Music," *Mr. Moody and the Evangelical Tradition*, ed. Timothy George (London: T & T Clark International, 2004), 107–16.

21. While Homer Rodeheaver always gave his birthdate as October 4, 1880, the *Starr County (Ohio) Probate Court Record of Births* (1880, p. 330), gives his birthdate as September 4 and his name as "Alvie H. Rhodehaver."

22. Rodeheaver, *Sawdust Trail*, 8.

23. *Gospel Choir*, September 1921, 7.

24. Property deed, *Andrew and Elizabeth Lawson to T.H. Rodeheaver*, December 23, 1882. Campbell County, Tennessee, Registry of Deeds, 1882 book, 595–96. See also Miller McDonald, *Campbell County Tennessee USA: A History of Places, Faces, Happenings, Traditions, and Things*, Volume III (LaFolette, Tennessee: County Services Syndicate, 1994), 4, 13.

25. *Gospel Choir*, September 1921, 6.

26. "Nationally Known Speakers Feature of Air Tour Sunday," *Logan (OH) Daily News*, October 2, 1953, 1.

27. "Lancaster Camp Ground Activities," *Lancaster (OH) Eagle-Gazette*, August 3, 1928, 21. See also John Franklin Grimes, *The Romance of The American Camp Meeting* (Cincinnati: Caxton Press, 1922), 196.

28. *Gospel Choir*, September 1921, 7.

29. Rodeheaver, *Sawdust Trail*, 10.

30. Ibid., 11.

31. *Gospel Choir*, September 1921, 5.

32. Photos and commentary about the Rodeheaver Company Band, showing Homer Rodeheaver with bass drum and cornet (1890–92) are found in *Gospel Choir*, September 1915, 5, and October 1915, 5.

33. *Gospel Choir*, September 1921, 5.

34. *Fifth-Eighth Catalogue of Ohio Wesleyan University* (Delaware, OH, 1902), 60–61.

35. Rodeheaver, *Sawdust Trail*, 29–30.

36. Transcript of Homer A. Rodeheaver. Ohio Wesleyan University, 1900–1901. Courtesy of the Registrar of Ohio Wesleyan University.

37. "College News," *The College Transcript* (Delaware, OH), October 31, 1896, 3.

38. "Wesleyan Man Won," *Ohio Wesleyan Transcript* (Delaware, OH), May 6, 1903, 47.

39. Homer Rodeheaver [sic], *Certificate in Lieu of Lost or Destroyed Discharge Certificate*, April 4, 1940. Winona History Center Archives. However, Rodeheaver's enlistment date is given as November 12, 1898, in *Spanish-American War Records: Service Record of Those Serving with the First, Second, Third and Fourth Tennessee Regiments of Infantry, United States Volunteers*. Tennessee State Library and Archives.

40. *Gospel Choir*, September 1921, 5.

41. "Niggah Smears! Henry Fillmore's version of a 'cullu'd fambly' of enthusiastic 'slip horn' players." Advertisement for Fillmore Music House, Cincinnati, Ohio, *Musical Messenger*, February, 1919. Fillmore's advertising art featured perpetuated the racial stereotypes of minstrel performers.

42. Paul E. Bierley, *Hallelujah Trombone! The Story of Henry Fillmore* (Columbus, OH: Integrity Press, 1982), 24–26. The source for this account is Ruthella Feaster Rodeheaver (1891–1989), second wife of Joseph N. Rodeheaver, who offered Bierley a bit of family lore. Newspaper accounts have not corroborated Ruthella's memory and Homer Rodeheaver never spoke about it publicly, but the basic story seems plausible. Fillmore and Rodeheaver remained friends and often promoted each other's products.

43. Roger Butterfield, "Homer Rodeheaver: A Happy Christian with an Old Trombone Is Successfully Preaching Salvation through Song," *Life*, September 3, 1945, 66.

44. Rodeheaver purchased the trombone from David Herbert Jemison (1871–1964), who in 1911 went on to found Kappa Sigma Pi, or the Modern Knights of St. Paul, an international and interdenominational boys' brotherhood for churches and other religious organizations. In 1917, Rodeheaver became National Organizer of Jemison's group and subsequently became its Grand Chancellor. See David H. Jemison, *The Boy Problem Solved* (Cincinnati: David Jemison, 1911); Grimes, *The Romance of the American Camp Meeting*, 149–50.

45. Rodeheaver, *Sawdust Trail*, 31.

46. Ibid.

NOTES TO CHAPTER 2

47. "Musical Missionary," *Time*, June 29, 1936, 27.

48. Roger A. Bruns, *Preacher: Billy Sunday and Big-Time American Evangelism* (Urbana: University of Illinois Press, 2002), 103–4.

49. *The New Wonder Slide Trombones* (Elkhart, IN: C. G. Conn, 1924), 43.

50. "Homer Rodeheaver and Entertainers Score a Hit," *Lancaster (PA) Daily Eagle*, August 31, 1927.

51. *The Rodeheaver Party*, Chautauqua Season c. 1917, 4.

52. Ring W. Lardner, "Our Helping Hand," *Chicago Tribune*, March 14, 1918.

53. Eugene Bartlett Jr., quoted in Thomas Henry Porter, "Homer Alvan Rodeheaver: Evangelistic Musician and Publisher" (EdD diss., New Orleans Baptist Theological Seminary, 1981), 191.

54. "Musical Missionary," 26.

55. Carl. F. Henry, "Gabriel, Blow Your Horn," *Sunday School Promoter*, December 1943, 27–28.

56. Curtis Brown, "Man with the Trombone and His Great Army: Newest and Strangest Ally of the Dignified Old Church of England," *Courier-Journal*, Louisville, KY, February 25, 1900.

57. Douglas Yeo, "Homer Rodeheaver: Reverend Trombone," *Historic Brass Society Journal* 27 (1995), 57–88.

58. Will Rogers, "You Can Hear Holy Trombone at Winona," *El Paso Evening Post*, August 11, 1928.

59. Basil Miller, *Ten Singers Who Became Famous* (Grand Rapids, MI: Zondervan Publishing House, 1954), 72.

60. Rodeheaver, *Sawdust Trail*, 11–12.

61. See *Thirty Years of Lynching in the United States: 1889–1918* (New York: National Association for the Advancement of Colored People, 1919); Elliot Jaspin, *Buried in the Bitter Waters: The Hidden History of Racial Cleansing in America* (New York: Basic Books, 2007); Carrie A. Russell, "Reckoning with a Violent and Lawless Past: A Study of Race, Violence and Reconciliation in Tennessee" (PhD diss., Vanderbilt University, 2010).

62. "Threaten Negro Miners: Whites of Tennessee Surround Barricaded Blacks—Sheriff Summons Posse," *New York Times*, August 18, 1908, 5.

63. "Report Negroes Burned: Tennessee Mobs Said to Have Destroyed Family in Cabin," *New York Times*, August 19, 1908, 2.

64. See Daniel W. Crofts, *Reluctant Confederates: Upper South Unionist in the Secession Crisis* (Chapel Hill: University of North Carolina Press, 1989), 43; also see historic population data for Campbell County and Jellico, University of Tennessee Hodges Library Special Collections. By 2010, the Federal census reported only 125 Blacks in Campbell County, out of a total population of 40,716.

65. Homer Rodeheaver, *Plantation Melodies* (Chicago: Rodeheaver Co., 1918), n.p., inside front cover.

66. Property deed, *Ella Smith to T.H. Rodeheaver*, February 17, 1901. Campbell County, Tennessee, Registry of Deeds, 1901 book, 397–99. The home stood until 2019 when it was torn down. The site is now a vacant lot.

67. *Gospel Choir*, September 1921, 4.

68. "Charters Granted," *The Tennessean*, April 2, 1904, 6.

69. Grace Moore, *You're Only Human Once* (Garden City: Doubleday, Doran & Co., 1944). Homer Rodeheaver also took credit for Grace Moore's first music lessons. See Homer Rodeheaver, "There's a Song in Your Heart," *Radio Guide*, week ending October 24, 1936. See also Homer Rodeheaver, *Twenty Years with Billy Sunday* (Winona Lake: Rodeheaver Hall-Mack Co., 1936), 81.

70. "Students Will Participate," *Ohio Wesleyan Transcript*, May 18, 1904, 483.

71. "All Is Ready for Friday Evening's Fray," *Ohio Wesleyan Transcript*, May 18, 1904, 481.

72. "Athletic X," *Ohio Wesleyan Transcript* (May 18, 1904), 482; "Delaware's Dandy Darkies," May 12, 1904, concert program.

73. Rodeheaver repeated the Walton story in countless interviews. See a typical example in "A Brief Biography," clip sheet.

74. "Personalities of Men Conducting Revivals," *Daily Times* (Davenport, IA), April 7, 1906, 30.

75. James Paul Cogdill Jr., "A Major Stream of American Mass Evangelism: The Ministries of R. A. Torrey, J. W. Chapman and W. E. Biederwolf" (PhD diss., Southern Baptist Seminary, 1990). Other Biederwolf resources include Mark Sidwell, *William E. Biederwolf and Urban Evangelism: A Fundamentalism File Research Report* (Greenville, SC: Bob Jones University, 2004); William G. McLoughlin Jr., *Modern Revivalism: Charles Grandison Finney to Billy Graham* (New York: Ronald Press, 1959), 393–396; and one sympathetic biography, Ray E. Garrett, *William Edward Biederwolf: A Biography* (Grand Rapids, MI: Zondervan, 1948).

76. IAE Membership peaked during World War I, followed by a steep decline that would mirror the decline of citywide revival meetings. In 1920 the IAE changed its name to Interdenominational Evangelistic Association. Some organizational documents can be found in a collection at Morgan Library and Special Collections, Grace College, Winona Lake, Indiana. Also see various collections at the Billy Graham Center Archives, such as the papers of Milan Bertrand Williams, BGEA Collection 601. The organization continued through the 1940s, bolstered by generous gifts from Helen Sunday, who often hosted meetings at the Sunday home.

77. "Personalities of Men Conducting Revivals," 30. Several Sunday biographers suggest, in passing, that Rodeheaver toured with Biederwolf in 1904, but no evidence supports their meeting prior to 1905.

78. The two songs that Rodeheaver cowrote for *Hymns for His Praise No. 2* seem derivative and entirely forgettable. Though he owned the copyrights, Rodeheaver cut both songs from his subsequent hymnals.

79. Transcript of Myrtle Henderson. Ohio Wesleyan University, 1904–9. Courtesy of the Registrar of Ohio Wesleyan University. Henderson returned for an additional year of study, 1911–12, but did not graduate.

80. "Matrimonial," *Reading Times*, March 18, 1908, 8.

81. W. E. Biederwolf and Homer Rodeheaver, eds. *Hymns for His Praise No. 2* (Chicago: Glad Tidings Publishing, 1906).

82. *Philadelphia North American*, February 11, 1906, 1.

83. In addition to local news reports, see the description in Ford C. Ottman, *J. Wilbur Chapman: A Biography* (New York: Doubleday, Paige, and Co., 1920), 120–35.

84. "Lemon Hill Services Begin Sixth Season," *Philadelphia Inquirer*, July 1, 1907, 13.

85. "J. N. Rodeheaver," *Rodeheaver's Musical News* (n.d., 1921), 7.

CHAPTER 3. GOSPEL SONGS AND URBAN REVIVALISM

1. Narrative details of the Gospel Song Evangelistic Movement are from contemporary news accounts in the *Chicago Tribune*, *The (Chicago) Inter Ocean*, Moody Bible Institute's *Institute Tie*, and Henry B. Roller, *Twentieth Century Revival* (Cincinnati: Jennings and Graham, 1911), 88–90. See also the Daniel Towner Papers in Moody Bible Institute archives.

2. "12,000 Pray at Year's Dawn," *Chicago Tribune*, January 1, 1909, 5.

3. "Eulogizes Moody's Evangelistic Work," *The (Chicago) Inter Ocean*, December 31, 1908, 7.

4. "Notes and Suggestions," *Institute Tie* (December 1908), 334.

5. "Hymns of Sankey Sung in Memory," *Chicago Tribune*, August 26, 1908, 3.

6. Our summary here will look at two campaigns that exemplify Rodeheaver's approach to revival music and congregational song, as seen in Toledo, Ohio (1911), and Philadelphia (1915). Our chapter cannot replace the many Billy Sunday biographies, which contain more detail about individual Sunday/Rodeheaver revival campaigns.

7. For details about the Winfield Chautauqua, see W. Stitt Robinson, "Chautauqua: Then and Now," 1998 Presidential Address, *Kansas State Historical Society* 22 (Summer 1999): 132–41; Roland Mueller, "The Chautauqua in Winfield, Kansas," *Kansas Quarterly* 15 (Summer 1983): 15–19.

8. "Winfield, Kan.: Leavening a Community," *Lyceumite and Talent* (December 1911), 23.

9. According to local newspaper accounts, the Joplin meetings ran from November 21, 1909, to January 3, 1910, though several Sunday biographers omit them from lists of Billy Sunday campaigns.

10. "Concert Proves a Big Success," *Joplin (MO) News Herald*, January 4, 1910, 3.

11. "All Ready for Revival Wave," *Daily Times* (Davenport, IA), March 31, 1906, 20.

12. "Fred Fischer—A Local Estimate," *Daily Review* (Decatur, IL), February 16, 1908, 13.

13. The songleader Fischer used his middle initial to distinguish himself from Chicago's other Fred Fischer, the popular songwriter who wrote "If the Man in the Moon Were a Coon" (1905). After selling three million copies of his hit song, the other Fred Fischer changed his name to Fred *Fisher* and wrote "Chicago (That Toddlin' Town)," with its famously dismissive line, "The town that Billy Sunday could not shut down." But alas, the two Fred Fischers were not related.

14. Peter Philip Bilhorn, Fred G. Fischer, John R. Clements, and W. Stillman Martin, *Hymns of His Grace No. 1* (Chicago: Bilhorn Brothers, 1907).

15. Billy Sunday to Homer Rodeheaver, March 1, 1910. Location unknown; photocopy in author's collection.

16. Sunday to Rodeheaver, March 1, 1910.

17. Sunday to Rodeheaver, March 8, 1910.

18. Sunday biographers offer conflicting information. See the discussion in W. A. Firstenberger, *In Rare Form: A Pictorial History of Baseball Evangelist Billy Sunday* (Iowa City: University of Iowa Press, 2005), 45.

19. Homer Rodeheaver to M. B. Williams, February 10, 1940, BGEA Collection 330.

20. Theodore T. Frankenberg attributes the Bellingham story to the *Steubenville Gazette*; see *The Spectacular Career of Rev. Billy Sunday: Famous Baseball Evangelist* (Columbus, OH: McClelland & Co., 1913), 92–93. Helen Sunday offers essentially the same account in *'Ma' Sunday Still Speaks* (Winona Lake, IN: Winona Lake Christian Assembly, 1957), 25–27.

21. Edwin M. Long, *The Union Tabernacle; Or, Movable Tent Church* (Philadelphia: Parry and McMillan, 1859), 229. The practice was well-established by the time D. L. Moody constructed his network of tents for the 1893 World's Columbian Exposition.

22. Lyle W. Dorsett, *Billy Sunday and the Redemption of Urban America* (Grand Rapids, MI: Wm. B. Eerdmans, 1991), 53–54.

23. *Toledo Blade*, March 8, 1983.

24. "Sunday Preached at Addie Joss' Funeral," *Portsmouth (OH) Times*, April 17, 1911, 1.

25. *Toledo Blade*, May 22, 1911, 1.

26. Statistics reviewed in *Toledo Blade*, April 17, 1966.

27. Homer Rodeheaver, B. D. Ackley, and W. E. Biederwolf, eds. *Great Revival Hymns* (Chicago: Rodeheaver-Ackley Co., 1911), n.p. Sunday rarely endorsed products of any sort and did not endorse any other Rodeheaver hymnal after the first.

28. "Sunday Finds Music Great Aid in Gospel Campaigns," *Toledo Blade*, April 29, 1911, 1.

29. Torrey directed Alexander to give up bookstands at their revival meetings—as a condition of their staying together for fall meetings in Toronto. R. A. Torrey to A. P. Fitt, December 19, 1905. A. P. Fitt Collection, Moody Bible Institute Archives.

30. *Record of Christian Work* (December 1911), back cover.

31. Popular (and romanticized) accounts of Ina Duley Ogdon's life should be approached with caution. For the best attempt, see Joseph H. Gardiner, "Hymn Story, Hymn Myth: The Case of Ina Ogdon," *The Hymn* (July 1986), 30–34. Gardiner was married to Judith Kimball Ogdon, a granddaughter. See also "Ina Duley Ogdon" clipping file in the Local History Collection of Toledo Public Library. Note: By some irony, Toledo was home to two famous gospel songwriters, William Ogden and Ina Duley Ogdon, with nearly identical last names (which are sometimes confused).

32. Terry York, *Charles Hutchinson Gabriel: Composer, Author, and Editor in the Gospel Tradition*. Unpublished DMA dissertation. (New Orleans Baptist Theological Seminary, 1985), 63–64. York discovered several contracts between Rodeheaver and Gabriel on file at the Rodeheaver offices in Winona Lake, Indiana. The contracts are no longer extant, apparently destroyed when Word Music moved the offices to Texas.

33. Located at 701 Terrace Drive, Winona Lake, Indiana.

34. Located at 905 Sunday Lane, Winona Lake, Indiana (with adjacent Annex at 907 Sunday Lane). Rodeheaver's properties and Billy Sunday's home are now on the National Register of Historic Places as part of the Winona Lake Historic District.

35. "Just Getting Tip, Says Rodeheaver," *Chicago Tribune*, June 4, 1914, 13.

36. Rodeheaver discussed the song many times, including: Homer Rodeheaver, "Brighten the Corner Where You Are," *Song Stories of the Sawdust Trail* (New York: The Christian Her-

ald, 1917), 1–24; *The Practical Song Director: A Resume of Successful Methods in Twenty Years of Song Leadership* (Chicago: Rodeheaver Co., 1925); and *Twenty Years with Billy Sunday* (Nashville, TN: Cokesbury Press, 1936), 78–79.

37. Various sources give conflicting accounts. It seems most likely that the song was distributed as a leaflet in Columbus, Ohio, and then released as part of *Great Revival Hymns No. 2* for the Wilkes-Barre, Pennsylvania, meetings. See the scrapbook of undated newspaper clippings compiled by Ina Duley Odgon, now in the possession of Barry Ogdon, a grandnephew.

38. E. O. Excell (words and music), "O That Will Be Glory," *Make His Praise Glorious* (Chicago: E. O. Excell, 1900), hymn #54. This hymnal also debuted Excell's version of "Amazing Grace," with his now-standard harmonization of the NEW BRITAIN tune.

39. Helen Cadbury Alexander with J. Kennedy MacLean, *Charles M. Alexander: A Romance of Song and Soul-Winning* (London: Marshall Brothers, Ltd., 1920), 65.

40. Mary Kanazawa, "B. D. Ackley 'In the Service of the King,'" *Baptist Herald* (June 15, 1943), 8.

41. Homer Rodeheaver, B. D. Ackley, and Charles Gabriel, eds. *Great Revival Hymns No. 2* (Chicago: Rodeheaver-Ackley Co., 1913), n.p.

42. Charles H. Gabriel, *Personal Memoirs* (Chicago: Rodeheaver Co., 1918), 48.

43. Homer Rodeheaver, *The Practical Song Director* (Chicago: Rodeheaver Co., 1925), 7. His "most popular" claim smacks of typical hubris, but his larger point is worth evaluating. The song is usually left off compilations of the 1920s "greatest hits," a clear omission.

44. Dorothy C. Haskins, "Homer Rodeheaver, America's Foremost Musical Evangelist," *The Lighted Pathway*, January 1955, 9.

45. Rodeheaver, *Practical Song Director*, 7.

46. Rodeheaver, *Twenty Years*, 78.

47. Ibid.

48. Rodeheaver discussed his use of warmup songs in a lecture to Moody Bible Institute students; see Homer Rodeheaver, "The Music at the Billy Sunday Meetings," *Christian Workers Magazine* (May 1916), 684.

49. Lizzie DeArmond (words) and B. D. Ackley (music), "If Your Heart Keeps Right," *Great Revival Hymns No. 2* (Chicago: Rodeheaver Co., 1913), hymn #16.

50. A. H. Ackley (words) and B. D. Ackley (music), "In the Service of the King," *Great Revival Hymns No. 2*, hymn #101.

51. See the reprint of "Brighten the Corner" in *(Philadelphia) Evening Public Ledger*, January 5, 1915, 2.

52. Carrie Ellis Breck (words) and Charles H. Gabriel (music), "Help Somebody Today," *Great Revival Hymns No. 2*, hymn #13.

53. Edgar T. Corfield (words and music), "Is the World Any Better?," *Great Revival Hymns No. 2*, hymn #48.

54. W. C. Poole (words) and Charles H. Gabriel (music), "A Glad Way Home," *Great Revival Hymns No. 2*, hymn #123.

55. Edith Sanford (words) and B. D. Ackley (music), "Song of the Sunbeams," *Great Revival Hymns No. 2*, hymn #168.

56. Rodeheaver, "The Music at the Billy Sunday Meetings," 683.

57. J. Gresham Machen to Mary Jones Gresham, quoted in Ned B. Stonehouse, *J. Gresham Machen: A Biographical Memoir* (Grand Rapids, MI: Eerdmans, 1954), 232–33.

58. "Billy Sunday's 'Trailhitters' Soothed by 'Rodey's' Music," *Musical America* (May 19, 1917), 38.

59. Rodeheaver, "The Music at the Billy Sunday Meetings," 684; 682–85.

60. Charles H. Gabriel, *Church Music of Yesterday, To-day, and To-morrow* (Chicago: Rodeheaver Co., 1921), 14. For instance, Gabriel cited the connection to Matthew 5:16, "Let your light so shine before men, that they may see your good works."

61. "Miss Jay Tells Why She Sued," *Chicago Tribune*, June 7, 1914, 12.

62. His letters were read in court and later quoted in news reports; see "Trifling? Oh, No! Says Homer," *Cincinnati Enquirer*, May 30, 1914, 9.

63. Roberta W. Nicholson, the only female member of the Indiana legislature, introduced the first "anti-heart-balm" statute, see "Recent Cases: Domestic Relations. Constitutionality of 'Anti-Heart-Balm' Statute,'" *University of Chicago Law Review* (1945), 375–80. For a recent analysis, see Laura Belleau, "Farewell to Heart Balm Doctrines and the Tender Years of Presumption, Hello to the Genderless Family," *Journal of the American Academy of Matrimonial Lawyers* (2012), 375–76.

64. "Sues Revivalist for Heart Balm," *Chicago Tribune*, May 14, 1912, 1.

65. Dialog in this exchange is reported in "Singer Tells of His Courtship," *Chicago Tribune*, June 4, 1914, 8. More of the testimony is recorded in "Just Getting Tip, Says Rodeheaver," *Chicago Tribune*, June 4, 1914, 13; "Billy Sunday Aide Admits Love Facts," *Racine (WI) Journal-News*, June 5, 1914, 16.

66. *The Eagle* (Bryan, TX), June 8, 1914, 2.

67. The IAE released a statement exonerating Rodeheaver, who spoke at their annual meeting in August; see *Chicago Tribune*, July 12, 1914, 4. Also see Biederwolf's official declaration of support in "Dollar Heart Balm," *Xenia (OH) Daily Gazette*, August 3, 1914, 4.

68. "Miss Jay Tells Why She Sued," *Chicago Tribune*, June 7, 1914, 12.

69. Homer Rodeheaver to Mrs. A. W. Jones, quoted in *Wichita Daily Eagle*, June 5, 1914, 5.

70. Rodeheaver, *Twenty Years*, 141.

71. "Sunday's Choirmaster Reported Engaged to Metropolitan Opera Singer," *Wichita Beacon*, February 14, 1918, 1.

72. Carol Leon, "The Life of American Workers in 1915," *Monthly Labor Review*, U.S. Bureau of Labor Statistics (February 2016).

73. In 1926, Georgia Jay married Stanley Clarkson, a coal company salesman from Minnesota, where she lived until her death in 1940.

74. "Through with Women, Says Rodeheaver," *Pittsburgh Press*, March 24, 1915, 4.

75. The term *mainline* was popularized by the sociologist E. Digby Baltzell in *Philadelphia Gentlemen: The Making of a National Upper Class* (Glencoe, IL: Free Press, 1958). The term *mainline Protestant* suffers from the same imprecision as *evangelical* and *fundamentalist*, but it is useful here to describe the growing rift among American Protestants. See Elesha J. Coffman, *The Christian Century and the Rise of the Protestant Mainline* (New York: Oxford University Press, 2013), where the author traces the term's use but also suggests that mainline Protestants were never *mainstream*.

76. "Leaders in State and City Herald 'Billy' Sunday," *(Philadelphia) Evening Public Ledger*, January 1, 1915, 7.

77. Rodeheaver, *Twenty Years*, 127. In addition to Rodeheaver's chapter on the delegations system, see Jennifer Wiard, "The Gospel of Efficiency: Billy Sunday's Revival Bureaucracy and Evangelicalism in the Progressive Era," *Church History* (September 2016), 587–616.

78. Rodeheaver, *Twenty Years*, 129.

79. Though this point is often forgotten, many of these groups formed as a mutual aid network, a form of social insurance for immigrants and working-class laborers before the rise of labor unions. See Felix John Vondracek, "The Rise of Fraternal Organizations in the United States, 1868–1900," *Social Science* (Winter 1972), 26–33.

80. Rodeheaver was initiated as a Mason on December 22, 1914. at the Lake City-Warsaw Lodge No. 73, earning the three requisite degrees on December 22, 25, and 30; he later enrolled in the Grand Army of Princes of the Royal Secret, 32nd Degree, Ancient and Accepted Scottish Rite of Freemasonry, June 1, 1917, Buffalo Consistory, Buffalo, New York; he then initiated in the Ancient Arabic Order of the Nobles of the Mystic Shrine, July 1, 1919, Ismailia Temple, Buffalo, New York. All dates are from Rodeheaver's freemason certificates, courtesy the Rodeheaver Collection at Morgan Library Archives and Special Collections, Grace College, Winona Lake, Indiana. See also Norman G. Lincoln, "A Masonic Gospel Team," *Knights Templar Magazine* (March 1998), 25–26.

81. "I am proud that I am the daughter of a Mason and the mother of a Mason," Helen Sunday once said, referring to her son George. *The State* (Columbia, SC), March 17, 1923, 2.

82. Rodeheaver, *Twenty Years*, 129.

83. For the earliest known printed edition of the sermon, see William A. Sunday, *Get on the Water Wagon* (Fort Wayne, IN: E. A. K Hackett, 1908). For an earlier transcription of a Kankakee, Illinois, sermon under a different title, see Billy Sunday, "Cut Out the Booze," *Fort Payne (AL) Journal*, Wednesday, March 6, 1907, 5.

84. For the most complete list of Sunday team members, see W. A. Firstenberger, *In Rare Form: A Pictorial History of Baseball Evangelist Billy Sunday* (Iowa City: University of Iowa Press, 2005), 124–25.

85. "Billy Sunday Workers Spend Very Busy Day," *Pittsburgh Press*, January 13, 1915, 1–2. For a recent study of Billy Sunday's assistants, see Wiard, "The Gospel of Efficiency," 587–616.

86. Dorothy Giles, "Homer Rodeheaver: Cosmopolite of the Month," *Hearst's International Cosmopolitan* (May 1938), 111.

87. "Ackley, Sunday's Pianist, Resigns; Pay Too Small," *Philadelphia Inquirer*, June 15, 1915, 1, 4.

88. "Billy's Sermons Not All Original Says B. D. Ackley," *Scranton (PA) Republican*, June 18, 1915, 2.

89. "No Compromise in Sunday Fight, Declares Ackley," *Philadelphia Inquirer*, June 16, 1915, 1.

90. "Rodeheaver Denies Ackley's Charges," *Philadelphia Inquirer*, June 18, 1915, 3.

91. "Rodeheaver Denies 'Cheating' Ackley," *Pittsburgh Press*, June 18, 1915, 19; "Billy Sunday Is Silent on Ackley Charges but Ma Sunday Isn't," *Coffeyville (KS) Daily Journal*, June 23, 1915, 2.

92. "Ackley Backs Down, Asks Forgiveness, Blames 'Weakness,'" *Wilkes-Barre (PA) Times Leader*, June 22, 1915, 7.

NOTES TO CHAPTER 3

93. McLoughlin Jr., *Billy Sunday Was His Real Name* (Chicago: University of Chicago Press, 1955), 269. McLoughlin interviewed Helen Sunday, Homer Rodeheaver, and B. D. Ackley himself, but it seems doubtful that any of the three would have framed the issue as McLoughlin did.

94. Bob Jones Jr., *Cornbread and Caviar* (Greenville, SC: Bob Jones University Press, 1985), 97–98. Jones described Ackley's wife as "a real battle ax of a woman, without sympathy or understanding either of his faith or of his work in the ministry," but then qualified his words somewhat: "I may have been entirely wrong in the impression I gathered, but nothing Ackley ever said or did tended to change the impression."

95. "Brags of 'Using' Sunday's Pianist," *Des Moines Register*, June 21, 1915, 5.

96. Ibid.

97. Bruce Howe (vice-president of Word Music, retired), interview by Kevin Mungons, Winona Lake, Indiana, June 26, 2006.

98. Joe Leahan (words) and Charles Bender (music), "When Billy Sunday Comes to Town" (New York: Popular Music Co., 1914).

99. Joseph H. Odell, "A Revival Judged by Results," *Outlook* (April 11, 1914), 804–5.

100. Joseph H. Odell, "The Mechanics of Revivalism," *Atlantic Monthly* (May 1915), 585–92.

101. Odell, "A Revival Judged by Results," 805.

102. Throughout the book we have used the Consumer Price Index Inflation Calculator from the Bureau of Labor Statistics, expressing "current dollars" in 2020 dollars and rounding where appropriate. These estimations give a rough approximation of current value.

103. Sunday pared down his travel for the 1914–15 season, agreeing to only four campaigns (Des Moines, Omaha, Philadelphia, and Paterson, New Jersey), but planned each to run eight or ten weeks.

104. John Reed, "Back of Billy Sunday," *Metropolitan* (May 1915), 9–12, 68.

105. Carl Sandburg, "Billy Sunday," published simultaneously in *The Masses* (September 1915), 11, and *International Socialist Review* (September 1915), 152–53. This unexpurgated version was later published as "Billy Sunday" in *Billy Sunday and Other Poems*, George Hendrick and Willene Hendrick, eds. (New York: Harcourt Brace and Co., 1993), 3–6. Another previously unpublished poem in this collection, "God's Children," also references Sunday, 7.

106. Reed, "Billy Sunday," 9.

107. Ibid., 68.

108. Ibid.

109. "Unitarians to War on Billy Sunday," *Brooklyn Daily Eagle*, April 3, 1915, 7.

110. Brett Page, *Writing for Vaudeville: with Nine Complete Examples of Various Vaudeville Forms* (Springfield, MA: Home Correspondence School, 1915), 6–12. Quoted in Robert M. Lewis, ed., *From Traveling Show to Vaudeville* (Baltimore, MD: The Johns Hopkins University Press, 2003), 336.

111. "Revival Hits Box Office: Business So Poor That Company Could Not Pay Board Bill," *New York Tribune*, November 28, 1905, 12.

112. Lewis, *From Traveling Show to Vaudeville*, 336.

113. Edwin Milton Royle, "The Vaudeville Theatre," *Scribner's Magazine* (October 1899), 485–95. Quoted in Lewis, *From Traveling Show to Vaudeville*, 324.

114. Bernard A. Weisberger, *They Gathered at the River* (Boston: Little, Brown, and Co., 1958), 219.

115. Heywood Braun, "Sunday Holds His Title in Slang," *New York Tribune*, September 16, 1915, 7. Cohan's Broadway play later became a 1918 silent film.

116. "40,000 Cheer for War and Religion Mixed by Sunday," *New York Times*, April 9, 1917, 4.

117. Ibid.

118. Homer Rodeheaver to Billy and Helen Sunday, September 29, 1923, Papers of William A. and Helen Sunday, Morgan Library of Grace College and Theological Seminary, Winona Lake, Indiana. According to the ship manifest, Rodeheaver left Hawaii for Japan on September 24, 1923.

119. "Sunday's Campaign Hits Snag at Niagara Falls," *News Herald* (Franklin, PA), September 22, 1923, 10.

120. Other authors have written about this incident in the context of Billy Sunday's life; see Dorsett, *Billy Sunday*, 134–40; Bruns, *Preacher: Billy Sunday*, 286–87.

121. Homer Rodeheaver to Helen Sunday, July 3, 1927, Sunday Papers, Winona Lake.

122. Homer Rodeheaver to Billy Sunday, October 24, 1927, Sunday Papers, Winona Lake.

123. Homer Rodeheaver to Billy Sunday, October 20, 1929, Sunday Papers, Winona Lake.

124. After Rodeheaver left in 1930, Sunday continued with song leader Harry D. Clarke for two more full seasons, as well as intermittent dates through 1934.

CHAPTER 4. COMMERCIAL GOSPEL MUSIC

1. Elisha A. Hoffman to William A. Ogden, January 13, 1894; reply from Ogden on January 16, 1894, Collection 138, Billy Graham Center Archives, Wheaton, Illinois.

2. Bentley D. Ackley to Peter P. Bilhorn, January 23, 1911; reply from Bilhorn to Ackley, February 4, 1911, Rodeheaver Collection at Morgan Library Archives and Special Collections, Grace College, Winona Lake, Indiana.

3. "The Sawdust Trail and Music," *Music Trade Review*, March 23, 1918, 30.

4. See Russell Sanjek, *American Popular Music and Its Business*, vol. 2: *From 1790 to 1909* (New York: Oxford University Press, 1988), 25–33, 395–401. Sanjek primarily addresses popular music. Our work here applies the same ideas to gospel music.

5. The 9,000 figure, though unattributed, comes from Sanjek, *American Popular Music*, vol. 2, 188.

6. The compulsory mechanical license clause was revised again in 1976, stipulating that the copyright holder reserves the right to make the first recording of a song. See Copyright Act of 1976, Section 115.

7. Subsequent changes to the copyright law and subsequent legal precedent would clarify the legal difference between *parody* and *satire*. Groups like 2 Live Crew could release "Pretty Woman" (1989) as a legal parody of Roy Orbison's "Oh, Pretty Woman" (1964). But this legal distinction was entirely absent in the 1920s, resulting in a loose approach to song borrowing.

8. William Howland Kenney makes this point of country and blues (though he did not include gospel music as an emerging genre). See *Recorded Music in American Life: The Pho-*

nograph and Popular Memory, 1890–1945 (New York: Oxford University Press, 1999), 132–33, 140.

9. Charles H. Gabriel (words) and Homer A. Rodeheaver (music), "We'll Be Waiting When You Come Back Home" (Chicago: Rodeheaver Co., 1918). See also "We'll Be Waiting When You Come Back Home" revised edition, published by the same composers later in 1918.

10. Homer Rodeheaver, "We'll Be Waiting When You Come Back Home" (article), *Rodeheaver's Musical News*, Spring 1918, 9. Rodeheaver debuted the song during the 1918 Washington, DC meetings, and advertised it heavily during his 1918 Chautauqua meetings.

11. Lena Guilbert Ford (words) and Ivor Novello (music), "Keep the Home Fires Burning" (New York: Chappell & Co., 1915).

12. "Infringing Song Withdrawn," *Music Trade Review*, April 13, 1918, 54.

13. Copyright Act of 1909, Sec. 3: "The copyright upon composite works or periodicals shall give to the proprietor thereof all the rights" and Sec. 23 "or of any work copyrighted by a corporate body, or by an employer for whom such a work is made for hire."

14. George C. Stebbins, *Reminiscences of Celebrated Writers and Singers of Gospel Songs* (New York: George H. Doran Co., 1924), 325.

15. Theodore Winston Thorson, "A History of Music Publishing in Chicago: 1850–1960" (PhD diss., Northwestern University, 1961), 202. Prior to 1900, three additional cities served as regional hubs for gospel hymnal production: New York, Philadelphia, and Cincinnati. Measured by any standard, Chicago dominated the gospel hymnal market between 1900 and 1920. When printing technology shifted from metal plates to offset presses, the industry decentralized to several regional centers.

16. Stebbins, *Reminiscences and Gospel Hymn Stories*, 260.

17. For brief profiles on gospel publishers of the era, see Thorson, "Music Publishing in Chicago," also see Chicago city directories. Most of these firms moved more than once. The addresses given here are for 1910, the year Rodeheaver began his company.

18. Less commonly, the district was called Music Row, a more inclusive name that never really caught on.

19. "Something about Piano Row," *Music Trades*, August 6, 1921, 11.

20. Today a faded sign can be seen on the brick exterior, "everything known in music."

21. Carol Baldridge and Alan Willis, "Business of Culture," *Chicago History* 19 (Spring–Summer 1990), 49.

22. Russell T. Hitt, "Capital of Evangelicalism," *Christian Life* (April 1952), 15–18, 46–52; Martin E. Marty, "Chicago's Influence on Religion," *ATLA Summary of Proceedings* 60 (2006): 79–87.

23. Charles H. Gabriel, "Editorial," *Gospel Choir* (February 1918), 4. His choice of "fifty years ago" was a reference to the first generation of gospel songs from Sankey and others.

24. Ibid.

25. *Gospel Choir*, September 1921, 5.

26. Ibid., 7.

27. Hall-Mack purchased the Adam Geibel Co. in 1909, gaining the song catalog of Adam Geibel and C. Austin Miles.

28. Rodeheaver leased the office space when it was vacated by *The Show Window*, the trade journal of the National Association of Window Trimmers of America. By this point, Printer's Row was awash in magazines and publications of every sort.

29. The purchase of the T. C. Meredith Co. was completed in late 1913, and by 1914 Rodeheaver was advertising his own plate-making capability. The company began in 1879 as Robert R. Meredith & Sons, billed as the only music printer in Chicago. In the ensuing years, the Anderson Brothers emerged as a competitor, leaving Chicago publishers with only two options for hymnal typesetting.

30. The Rodeheaver Co. filed a trademark for its rainbow label on March 26, 1917, a full two years after it was in use.

31. Lizzie DeArmond (words) and B. D. Ackley (music), "If Your Heart Keeps Right," *Great Revival Hymns No. 2* (Chicago: Rodeheaver Co., 1913), hymn #16.

32. "100 Cloth Bound Song Books Free for a Name" (advertisement), *Christian Workers Magazine*, November 1917, back cover.

33. Ackley, *Great Revival Hymns No. 2*, preface.

34. *Chronicle-Telegram* (Elyria, OH), February 17, 1919.

35. From a southern perspective, the Ruebush-Kieffer Co. did the same as Rodeheaver, releasing shape note hymnals in round note editions as early as 1891. Perhaps this indicates an early lack of faith in the format's viability. See James R. Goff Jr., *Close Harmony: A History of Southern Gospel* (Chapel Hill: University of North Carolina Press, 2002), 21–23.

36. A similar observation could be made of *The Baptist Standard Hymnal with Responsive Readings*, published in 1924.

37. *Gospel Pearls* was released several years before Rodeheaver bought the Praise Publishing and Hall-Mack catalogs, but our total reflects all of the songs of the eventual Rodeheaver Hall-Mack Co.

38. A close comparison shows that many of the *Gospel Pearls* plates were exactly the same as used in the *Gospel Songs and Hymns/Awakening Hymns* project, immediately identified by Rodeheaver's metronome markings at the top of each song, an unusual practice at the time.

39. Bruce Howe (vice president, Rodeheaver Music Co.), interview with Kevin Mungons, June 20, 2006, Winona Lake, Indiana.

40. Of the many conflicting accounts of the song's origin, the most authoritative is likely the author's own: George Bennard, *The Story of the Old Rugged Cross* (Albion, MI: The Bennard Music Company, 1930). See also C. D. Davenport, "The Real Story Behind 'The Old Rugged Cross,'" *Christian Herald* (April 1981), 22–24.

41. Bruce Howe interview, June 20, 2006. The material in this section is based on Howe's interview, supplemented with various industry trade journals.

42. William J. Kirkpatrick to Charles Gabriel, published in *Gospel Choir* (June 1921), 25.

43. "Rodeheaver bought out the company to obtain Mr. Sanville's services"; see "G. W. Sanville Is Dead at 78, Hymn Expert," *Camden (NJ) Courier-Post*, October 26, 1957, 4. Also see the brief news item in "Gospel Music Catalog," 1917, 15.

44. Isaac M. Mack to Joseph M. Rodeheaver, November 14, 1938, Rodeheaver Collection, Winona Lake.

45. Rodeheaver continued to make smaller acquisitions in the 1940s, including Harry W. Vom Bruch's gospel songs and the catalog of the Norman Clayton Publishing Co.

46. The publishers who agreed on the 1918 pricing structure included the Rodeheaver Co., Hope Publishing Co., Glad Tidings (operated by E. O. Excell), Meyer and Brother, and Lorenz Publishing. Several smaller publishers quickly adopted the same prices. See the anecdotal reference to this in a later letter, Francis G. Kingsbury (with Henry Date) to Homer Rodeheaver, October 1, 1919, Hope Publishing Co. Archives, Carol Stream, Illinois.

47. Ibid.

48. Ibid.

49. Details are summarized from organizational minutes, "Annual Meeting of the Members of the Church and Sunday School Music Publishers Association," 1925–75, Hope Publishing Archives, Carol Stream, Illinois. The organizational name was eventually simplified to Church Music Publishers Association, abbreviated as CMPA throughout.

50. Practically speaking, they excluded the Bible Institute Colportage Association (Moody Bible Institute).

51. See "Annual Meeting," 1925–1940. Hope Publishing Archives, Carol Stream, Illinois. This point was confirmed in our interviews with Bruce Howe (Rodeheaver Co.) and Donald Hustad (Hope Publishing).

52. Homer Rodeheaver to Hope Publishing Co. and E. O. Excell Co., May 22, 1928, Hope Archives.

53. Arthur L. Stevenson, *The Story of Southern Hymnology* (Salem, VA: Arthur L. Stevenson, 1931), 129–30.

54. See the brief history of ASCAP's music licensing model in Chong Hyun Christie Byun, *The Economics of the Popular Music Industry* (New York: Palgrave MacMillan, 2016), 44–49.

55. Membership information from *ASCAP Biographical Dictionary*, Daniel I. McNamera, ed. (New York: Thomas Y. Crowell, 1948). Though ASCAP was founded in 1914, it apparently did not have a printed directory until this first edition in 1948, which lists the year each songwriter joined.

56. Annual Meeting of the Church and Sunday School Publishers Association, June 29–30, 1933, Hope Archives.

57. George W. Sanville to G. Herbert Shorney, May 3, 1938, including statement of 1937 ASCAP revenue. Hope Archives.

58. Sanville to Shorney, May 3, 1938. ASCAP determined a publisher's royalty share through a complicated point system. The CMPA members agreed to share their royalty figures with each other, but the method used to determine the royalties is less clear.

59. Throughout the 1940s, ASCAP granted the Rodeheaver Co. regular increases through the publisher point system, though ASCAP remained famously opaque about how, exactly, the increases were calculated. See "ASCAP Ups Religious Pub," *Billboard*, May 27, 1944, 14.

60. B. D. Ackley to Ina Duly Ogdon, February 14, 1955, Rodeheaver Collection, Winona Lake.

61. B. D. Ackley to Ina Duly Ogdon, February 17, 1955, Rodeheaver Collection, Winona Lake.

62. It would be difficult to estimate how much money Ina Duley Ogdon lost by refusing to join ASCAP, but the amount likely exceeded $25,000.

63. Thomas Kane, *Winona Booklet* (Winona Lake, IN: Winona Assembly and Schools, 1906), 10.

64. Ibid.

65. In addition to *Winona Booklet*, see Thomas Kane, "A Christian Altruistic Object Lesson," *The Christian Evangelist*, March 3, 1904, 293; "What We Owe and the Results of Paying It," *The Assembly Herald*, January 1906, 136–37; and "Winona," *The Advance*, May 31, 1906, 706.

66. F. A. Behymer, "Homer and His Horn Still Going Strong," *St. Louis Post Dispatch*, September 20, 1944, 3D.

CHAPTER 5. NEW TECHNOLOGY TO PROMOTE AN OLD STORY

1. "Imperial Songrecord," *Rodeheaver Musical News*, Spring 1918, 18. Rodeheaver's name and the performer's name (Brewster or Bob Matthews) were prominently featured in advertising and product labels, along with assurances that the performances were authentic examples of tabernacle music.

2. Lester A. Weinrott, "Play That Player Piano," *Chicago History* (Summer 1974), 79.

3. "The Truth at Last," *Music Trade Review*, March 30, 1918, 41.

4. "Imperial Songrecord," 18.

5. "Splendid New Edison Talent on Blue Amberol Records—July List," *Edison Phonograph Monthly* (May 1914), 68.

6. David N. Lewis has generously shared his research with the authors, including his "Homer Rodeheaver Chronological Discography," where he lists Rodeheaver's "Brighten" versions including Victor (1915), Columbia (1916), Emerson (1916), Vocalion (1920), Rainbow (1920), Vocalion (1922), Claxtonola (1922), Gennett (1922), Champion (1922), Okeh (1925), Victor (1925), Columbia (1926), Rainbow (1927), and Rainbow (1948).

7. Billy Sunday Chorus led by Homer Rodeheaver, "Sail On," Bob Matthews and George Brewster, pianos, Victor 18322-B, matrix 19997–2, recorded in New York City, June 11, 1917, 78 r.p.m.; "America," Victor 18322-A, matrix 19999–1. Also see Harry O. Sooy, "Memoir of My Career at Victor Talking Machine Company," unpublished typewritten memoir, Hagley Museum and Library, Wilmington, Delaware, 64. As engineer for the sessions, Sooy called the chorus "wonderful" but "the results of the records were only fair."

8. See Lewis, "Chronological Discography," which lists Victor (1920), Rainbow (1920), Gennett (1922), Champion (1922), Columbia (1924), Okeh (1925), Victor (1925), Montgomery Ward (1925), and Gramophone (1925).

9. Rodeheaver, Homer A. *Twenty Years with Billy Sunday* (Winona Lake, IN: Rodeheaver Hall-Mack Co., 1936), 77.

10. Allan Sutton, *A Phonograph in Every Home: The Evolution of the American Recording Industry, 1900–19* (Mainspring Press, 2011), 258. Tim Brooks made a similar observation about the "wishful thinking" of million-seller claims for individual recordings of the period. See *Lost Sounds: Blacks and the Birth of the Recording Industry 1890–1919* (Urbana: University of Illinois Press, 2004), 143.

11. "Expect Capacity Crowd when Billy Talks Here Tomorrow; Towns on Route to Greet Him," *Trenton Evening News*, August 24, 1916, 1.

12. "Rody's Sister in Auto Smash," *Richmond (IN) Item*, July 4, 1922, 10.

13. See the biographical information in "Death of Lt. Lynn D. Merrill," *Air Service News Letter*, September 16, 1921, 7. Some military records give his name as Linn Merrill.

14. "Two Dead in Aeroplane Accident, *Warsaw (IN) Daily Times*, Friday August 26, 1921, 1. Numerous papers reported the incident, including *Fort Wayne Journal-Gazette*, August 26, 1921, 1, 6; *Chicago Tribune*, August 26, 1921, 1.

15. Ibid.

16. Ibid.

17. "Seen and Heard about Richmond," *Richmond (IN) Item*, January 28, 1923, 4.

18. Ibid.

19. See Robert L. Hilliard and Michael C. Keith, *The Broadcast Century and Beyond: A Biography of American Broadcasting*, 5th ed.(Burlington, MA: Focal Press, 2010), 21. The claims of KDKA were rooted in the aggressive promotional efforts of their parent company, Westinghouse Electric. Plausible counterclaims as the "first" radio station can be made for KQW in San Jose, WWJ in Detroit, or others.

20. "Radio Service," *Pittsburgh Daily Post*, December 10, 1921, 7.

21. "Billy Enjoys First Program by Radio; Listens in His Room," *Richmond (IN) Palladium-Item*, April 27, 1922, 1. The station proved to be a short-lived experiment; the *Palladium* operated WOZ from May 12, 1921, to July 1, 1923.

22. Billy Sunday made a few guest appearances but never had his own radio show, though several radio sources perpetuate a claim that he hosted the *Back Home Hour*, such as Harrison Summers, *A Thirty-year History of Programs Carried on National Radio Networks in the United States, 1926–1956* (New York, Arno Press, 1971), 17. The actual host of "Back Home Hour" was Paul Rader, a Sunday protégé.

23. Ridley Wills, "Men Stand Up When Billy Sunday Asks Their Pledges," *Commercial Appeal (Memphis, TN)*, February 16, 1925, 1–2.

24. "Billy Sunday Shifts from the Sawdust Trails to the Wave Lengths," *New York Times*, October 28, 1934.

25. "Billy Sunday's Songster on WHT Tonight," *Chicago Tribune*, October 30, 1925, 68; see numerous mentions in the *Chicago Tribune* "Church Services" column, 1925–1929.

26. See the *Chicago Tribune*'s "Today's Radio Programs," 1924–1929.

27. WLS program schedules called it "The Rodeheaver Hour" or generically listed it as "Rodeheaver program" or "Rodeheaver quartet," starting in October 1925 and continuing through 1929, in what was intended as a once-a-month format. Rodeheaver's travel schedule continued to interrupt his local radio schedule.

28. "First Nationwide Christmas Carol Sing by Radio This Year," *Arlington Heights (IL) Herald*, December 6, 1929, 1.

29. "Christmas Carol Sing" in *WLS Family Album* (Chicago: Agricultural Broadcasting Co., 1930), 11; "Radio Business Gives Farm Belt Relief," *Chicago Tribune*, December 29, 1929, 4. WLS joined what would become known as the NBC Blue Network, which became the platform for its long-running National Farm Dance show.

30. *Sociability Songs for Community, Home, School* (Chicago: Rodeheaver Co., 1928).

31. George F. Givens, "Radio Gossip," *Elmira (NY) Star-Gazette*, December 1, 1930, 18. Also see "Last Minute Program Announcements," *What's on the Air*, January 1931, 45.

32. "Bits of Broadcast," *Muncie (IN) Star Press*, February 1, 1931, 13.

33. Anne Campbell (words) and B. D. Ackley (music), "There's a Rainbow Shining Somewhere" (Chicago: Rodeheaver Music Co., 1930; © 1930 Curb Word Music (ASCAP); all rights administered by WC Music Corp.).

34. For the period between the two world wars, the online *Discography of American Historical Recordings* lists more than 200 popular and jazz songs with Rainbow themes.

35. Stamps Quartet, "Give the World a Smile" with piano, recorded in Atlanta, GA, October 20, 1927, Victor 21072, matrix BVE-40316, 78 r.p.m.

36. George F. Givens, "Radio Gossip," *Elmira (NY) Star-Gazette*, April 18, 1931, 14.

37. The show name may have been inspired by one of Rodeheaver's favorite poets, James Whitcomb Riley, who had a home in Winona Lake and wrote his *Neighborly Poems* in 1891.

38. One transcription recording of "Neighborly Songs and Poems" is known to exist; Collection of J. David Goldin, Newtown, CT.

39. *Billy Sunday Funeral* (New York: Loizeaux Brothers, 1939).

40. Rodeheaver, *Twenty Years*, 9–10.

41. Though Rodeheaver was a competent writer, he likely had help from his longtime publicity agent, Thomas T. Frankenberg, who previously attracted Helen Sunday's ire by publishing an unauthorized biography of Billy Sunday.

42. Rodeheaver, *Twenty Years*, 79–80.

43. John Philip Sousa, "The Menace of Mechanical Music," *Appleton's* 8 (1906), 278–84.

44. T. S. Eliot, "London Letter," *The Dial*, November 1922.

45. Eliot, ever the obscurantist, refers to a point made by W. H. R. Rivers in *Essays on the Depopulation of Melanesia* (1922), where the Australian people group lost interest in their own tribal life because of colonial interruptions from developed nations—reportedly amusing themselves to death with the white man's gramophone.

46. Charles Winifred Douglas, *Church Music in History and Practice: Studies in the Praise of God* (New York: Charles Scribner's Sons, 1937), 256.

47. Charles Winfred Douglas, ed., *The Kyrial or Ordinary of the Mass with the Plainsong Melodies* (New York: H. W. Gray, 1933), iv.

48. Earl Enyeart Harper, "Progress in Church Music," *Northwestern University Bulletin* 30, no. 22 (January 27, 1930), 5.

49. Torrey Johnson and Robert Cook, *Reaching Youth for Christ* (Chicago: Moody Press, 1944), 35–36.

50. Rodeheaver, *Twenty Years*, 83.

51. Jim Ramsburg, *Network Radio Ratings, 1932–1953: A History of Prime-Time Programs through the Ratings of Nielsen, Crossley, and Hooper* (Jefferson, N.C.: McFarland & Co., 2012), 58–59. Rodeheaver's program is slightly misnamed as "Come, Let's Sing." For its time slot, the show came in second to Beauty Box Theater with a 7.2 share. Top-rated shows such as *The Burns & Allen Show* and *Fred Allen's Town Hall Tonight* achieved a 20 share.

52. "Everybody's Singing," *Santa Anna (CA) Register*, October 30, 1936, 12.

53. Ibid. Rodeheaver's comments about pop songs (performance music) vs. communal songs are interesting and can be taken as an extension of his ideas about "singable" gospel songs for congregational singing.

54. Homer Rodeheaver, "There's a Song in Your Heart," *Radio Guide*, October 24, 1936, 4, 16.

55. "Behind the Scenes: Radio Takes Up the Old Community Sing Idea," *New York Times*, August 2, 1936, 10.

56. John Dunning, *On the Air: The Encyclopedia of Old-Time Radio* (New York: Oxford University Press, 1998), 174. The program ran from September 6, 1936, to August 29, 1937. Dunning's encyclopedia makes no mention of Rodeheaver or earlier community sing programs.

57. The Hired Man [pseud.], "The Old Hayloft," *Stand By*, July 25, 1936, 15. The magazine, produced by *Prairie Farmer*, promoted WLS radio programs and personalities.

58. "Looking for Something Outstanding?" (display ad), *Sponsor*, April 1, 1949, 67. The program was to be syndicated by Spire Productions (3640 Lake Shore Drive, Chicago), but never went into production.

59. "Everybody's Singing," *Santa Anna (CA) Register*, October 30, 1936, 12.

60. Rodeheaver, *Twenty Years*, 83.

61. "'Sidewalks of New York' in Times Square Movietone," *Music Trade Review*, November 3, 1928, 17. The 1928 campaign marked the first sustained use of film in a presidential election. Meanwhile, Louis B. Mayer of MGM had worked with the Republicans to produce a fawning biopic of Herbert Hoover, *Master of Emergencies*.

62. "Politics Takes to Sound Films and Makes 'em Stump Speakers," *Exhibitors Herald and Moving Picture World*, October 27, 1928, 22.

63. "Billy Sunday Comes to the City Today for Political Talk," *Newport News (VA) Daily Press*, October 26, 1928, 1.

64. See the filmography in Edwin M. Bradley, *The First Hollywood Sound Shorts, 1926–1931* (Jefferson, NC: McFarland & Co., 2005); also listed in Roy Liebman, *Vitaphone Films: A Catalogue of the Features and Shorts* (Jefferson, NC: McFarland & Co., 2005). The first of five Vitaphone releases is "Original Songs" with Lynn Cowan ("Master of Ceremonies and Song Writer"), Vitaphone 2245, December 27, 1927, 1 reel. All songs by Cowan, including "Cross Roads," "I'm Down in Buenos Aries," and "Way Out West in Hollywood."

65. "Homer Rodeheaver in Community Singing," unreleased short film produced by Fox Movietone, July 1928, 15 min., 16 mm. Rodeheaver Collection of Morgan Library, Winona Lake.

66. *Fox Movietone News* 1, no. 40, released week of September 5, 1928. See "Rader, Sunday to Speak," *Indianapolis News*, August 4, 1928, 24; "Movietones at Winona Lake," *Jackson County (IN) Banner*, August 29, 1928, 10; "Films, Talkies and Stage Act Comprise Bill," *Los Angeles Times*, September 7, 1928, 27. A print of this film has not been located.

67. Letter quoted in "Rodeheaver Sings Here April 11, Is Still with Evangelist Sunday," *Elmira Star-Gazette*, March 26, 1930, 20.

68. Bruce Howe, interviewed by Kevin Mungons, Winona Lake, IN, June 26, 2006. The Museum of Winona History later made digital transfers of all the known Rodeheaver films.

NOTES TO CHAPTER 5

69. Calia Altstartler and Jennie Ree (words) and Homer A. Rodeheaver (music), "We Want Teddy" (Chicago: Rodeheaver Co., 1912).

70. "Two Years Ago and Now," *Cawker City (KS) Ledger*, December 16, 1920, 2.

71. "Mrs. Hoover's Day Crowded," *Los Angeles Times*, December 25, 1931, 2.

72. "Roosevelt Defends His Farm," *Chicago Tribune*, December 10, 1935, 1.

73. "Out There They Cheered in Indiana," *Harrisburg (PA) Telegraph*, August 20, 1940, 9.

74. "First Lady Dashes on Holiday Rounds," *New York Times*, December 25, 1940, 22. Perhaps the Roosevelt invitation came through Secretary of State Cordell Hull, an old friend of Rodeheaver's from the Spanish-American War (Hull was captain of Company H of the 4th Tennessee Regiment, where Rodeheaver served as bandsman). Rodeheaver played Santa Claus for events hosted by Eleanor Roosevelt between 1936 and 1940.

75. "Evangelism by Radio," *Radio Age* (August 1923), 13.

76. "Church Service Put on Screen," *Los Angeles Times*, December 9, 1931, 10.

77. "Sunday Declined $200,000 Movie Job," *New York Times*, May 14, 1917, 18.

78. Ibid. Sunday was not opposed to movie attendance per se and recommended them as a morally superior alternative to saloons and live theater.

79. Homer Rodeheaver to Billy Sunday, December 7, 1931, Rodeheaver Collection, Winona Lake. After Sunday declined the offer, Rodeheaver recruited Rev. Daniel Poling, pastor of the Marble Collegiate Church in New York.

80. Ibid.

81. "Church Service Put on Screen," *Los Angeles Times*, December 9, 1931, 10. See also "Church Service Film Stirs Controversy," *New York Times*, December 8, 1931; "'Canned Church Service' Film Praised, Censured," *Ithaca (NY) Journal*, December 17, 1931, 11; "RCA Photophone Recording Complete Sunday Evening Church Series," *International Photographer* (January 1932), 22.

82. "Church Service Put on Screen," 10.

83. "News from the Dailies," *Variety* (December 15, 1931), 36; "Church Talkies," *Time* (December 21, 1931), 44. A print of the RCA Photophone film has never been located.

84. For a review of community singing on film, see Esther M. Morgan-Ellis, "Sing-Along Films in the Sound Era" in *Everybody Sing: Community Singing in the American Picture Palace* (Athens: University of Georgia Press), 208–24.

85. *Rainbow Shining Somewhere* (1952), Cordell Fray, 15 min, 16 mm. Features Audrey Meier (piano) and the Phil Kerr Harmony Chorus. Rodeheaver leads songs and plays "Brighten the Corner" on trombone; *Then Jesus Came* (1952), Cordell Fray, 15 min, 16 mm. Features Audrey Meier (piano) and the Phil Kerr Harmony Chorus. Rodeheaver leads songs and plays "In the Garden" on trombone. 16 mm. Rodeheaver Collection of Morgan Library, Winona Lake.

86. Homer Rodeheaver Here to Make Film," *Los Angeles Times*, September 26, 1951, 2. See also Dorothy C. Haskins, "Homer Rodeheaver: America's Foremost Musical Evangelist," *The Lighted Pathway*, January 1955, 8–9.

87. *Homer Rodeheaver Screen Test*, Westminster Films, July 1954, 15 min., 16 mm. Rodeheaver Collection of Morgan Library, Winona Lake.

88. William E. Brusseau, interview with Kevin Mungons, June 22, 2006.

89. *Twenty Years with Billy Sunday* (1956), Westminster Films, 35 min, 16 mm. A revised shooting script is in the Papers of J. Palmer Muntz, Collection 108, Billy Graham Center Archives, Wheaton, Illinois.

90. Brusseau interview. More than fifty years later, the incident clearly pained Brusseau, who declined to name the parties in the dispute.

91. J. Palmer Muntz to Kenneth W. Ogden (a seminary student working as distribution manager at Westminster Films), May 11, 1956, Papers of J. Palmer Muntz, Collection 108, Billy Graham Center Archives, Wheaton, Illinois.

92. William E. Brusseau to J. Palmer Muntz, May 22, 1956, Papers of J. Palmer Muntz, Collection 108, Billy Graham Center Archives, Wheaton, Illinois.

93. In the last months of her life she allowed a recording to be transcribed into a book: Helen Sunday, *"Ma" Sunday Still Speaks* (Winona Lake, IN: Winona Lake Christian Assembly, 1957). Though she saved comparatively few of her own papers, Helen Sunday methodically saved her husband's correspondence, business arrangements, scrapbooks, and photos. These were archived as the William "Billy" and Helen "Ma" Sunday Collection at Morgan Library Archives and Special Collections, Grace College, Winona Lake, Indiana.

94. William G. McLoughlin Jr., *Billy Sunday Was His Real Name* (Chicago: University of Chicago Press, 1955).

95. Irvin S. (Kris) Yeaworth III interview with Kevin Mungons, June 5, 2018. The original negative and outtakes reel for *Twenty Years with Billy Sunday* is missing and thought to have been destroyed in a flood at the Yeaworth property. Several extant prints to *The Billy Sunday Story* (including the Rodeheaver monologues) still exist; see the Rodeheaver Collection at Morgan Library Archives and Special Collections, Grace College, Winona Lake, Indiana.

96. Mark Katz discusses the effects of portability in *Capturing Sound: How Technology Has Changed Music* (Berkeley: University of California Press, 2010), 17–21. He describes five other traits of recorded music: tangibility, visibility, repeatability, temporality, and receptivity. See similar conclusions in Greg Milner, *Perfecting Sound Forever: An Aural History of Recorded Music* (New York: Faber and Faber, 2009), and Robert Philip, *Performing Music in the Age of Recording* (New Haven: Yale University Press, 2004).

CHAPTER 6. THE MISSION OF RAINBOW RECORDS

1. This chapter builds on earlier studies, including Bob Olson, "Homer Rodeheaver: Pioneer of Sacred Records," *Victor and 78 Journal* (Autumn 1998), 36–43; and Thomas Henry Porter, "Homer Alvan Rodeheaver: Evangelistic Musician and Publisher" (DEd diss., New Orleans Baptist Theological Seminary, 1981), 123–40. In particular, we are indebted to colleague David N. Lewis for his article "The Rainbow Records Discography, 1920–1926," *Association for Recorded Sound Collections Journal* 39:1 (2008), 41–79; Lewis also shared his ongoing research, including a pre-publication copy of his "Homer Rodeheaver Chronological Discography" and an unpublished update of his ARSC discography: David N. Lewis and Mike Montgomery, "Rodeheaver Record Company Discography, 1920–1929 (Revised)" unpublished discography, September 2015.

2. The Song Directors Conference ran from August 14 to August 28, 1920, the second year of its operation in Winona Lake. See Rodeheaver's report in the *Gospel Choir*, August 1920, 26.

3. "Rody Heads Music Company," *Syracuse (NY) Herald*, November 18, 1920, 11. The article feels a bit like a rumor and does not actually name any local investors.

4. The entries are dated September and October 1920. If Rodeheaver's brothers were also investors, they are not listed in the pocket planner, which was not a full financial statement. Saxe and Hay also accompanied Biederwolf and Rodeheaver on their 1923–24 world tour. If there were other minority partners early on, Rodeheaver had bought them out by 1930, when the companies were entirely family owned.

5. *Gospel Choir*, November 1920, 3.

6. "Rainbow Records" (display ad), *Gospel Choir*, December 1920, 27.

7. Vaughan Quartet, "Couldn't Hear Nobody Pray," Cincinnati, Ohio, March–April 1923, Vaughan, numbered by matrix (311), 78 r.p.m.; also "Steal Away," numbered by matrix (313). Both of these selections were re-recorded at Gennett studios on November 6, 1924, for which the documentation is clear.

8. Tony Russell, *Country Music Records: A Discography, 1921–1942* (New York: Oxford University Press, 2004), 7.

9. See Lewis and Montgomery, "Rodeheaver Record Company Discography (Revised)," 13–14; Charles K. Wolfe, *The Vaughan Quartets: Original 1927–1947 Recordings*, liner notes to TFS-110, Murfreesboro: Tennessee Folklore Society, 1992. See also the handwritten discography notes in the Charles Wolfe Papers, Center for Popular Music, Middle Tennessee State University.

10. Adlai Loudy, "A Brief History of My Early Life and Ministry," *Bible Student's Notebook*, July 28, 1917, 5484–88; "Reverend Adlai Loudy" (obituary), *Palm Beach (FL) Post*, December 28, 1984, 34.

11. "Rev. Lowdy Is the Samson of the Age," *Winona (MS) Times*, May 11, 1923, 8. Loudy's name was frequently misspelled as *Lowdy* or even *Loudly*.

12. "Homer A. Rodeheaver's Page," *Gospel Choir* (June 1921), 27.

13. Loudy, "A Brief History," 5486. When Adlai Loudy died in 1984, he was the last surviving musician from Rodeheaver's 1920 recording sessions.

14. See Homer Rodeheaver's annual Pocket Planners, 1923–1927, Rodeheaver Collection, Winona Lake. By 1926, his income returned to $37,701, but even at its lowest point during the economic downturn ($21,569 in 1922), the value in today's dollars is more than $300,000.

15. "The Book of Rodeheaver Gospel Music," 59.

16. Homer Rodeheaver, "A Practical Dream," *Rodeheaver's Musical News* (1920), 8. A nearly identical column also ran in the *Gospel Choir*, August 1920, 6.

17. Ibid.

18. Ibid.

19. Ibid.

20. George Sanville, sales letter from the Rodeheaver Co. Philadelphia office, April 1921. Author's collection.

21. The Rodeheaver Record Co. filed a trademark for the label design on March 5, 1921. The application noted that the logo was used on records beginning Oct. 1, 1920 (likely the release date of the first recordings). See Allan Sutton, *American Record Companies and Producers, 1888–1950* (Denver, CO: Mainspring Press, 2018), 437.

22. Rodeheaver had no connection to the 1975 Rainbow label owned by the Henry Hadaway Organisation in England (who later sued Aaron Sixx for co-opting the name Rainbow Record Productions), or the Rainbow label owned by Rainbow Sound Studios, of Nottingham. Those who have actually seen Hadaway's obscure Rainbow label (with its naked lady logo) are unlikely to confuse his work with Rodeheaver's.

23. *Gospel Choir* (March 1921), 7; "Mr. Forkel Promoted," *Northwestern Christian Advocate*, January 5, 1921, 71.

24. "Homer A. Rodeheaver's Page," *Gospel Choir* (June 1921), 27.

25. Ibid.

26. David N. Lewis, "The Rainbow Records Discography," 60–62.

27. His theory is at least plausible; in 1920, there were only a handful of record companies that did custom jobs. See Wolfe, *Vaughan Quartets*.

28. Lewis and Montgomery, "Rodeheaver Record Company Discography (Revised)," 13–14. There are no known ledgers or studio cards for the 1921 Vaughan sessions with Rodeheaver. Surprisingly little is mentioned in *Vaughan's Family Visitor*, a company periodical published 1912–1986, but many of the issues for 1921–22 have not been located.

29. "Hustling for Trade in Cincinnati and Securing It," *Talking Machine World*, May 15, 1921, 127–28.

30. "Homer Rodeheaver Will Make Records at Shillito's" (display ad), *Cincinnati Enquirer*, April 24, 1921, 15; "Hustling for Trade," 127–28. The Sunday-Rodeheaver revival meetings ran from March 6 to May 1, 1921; the session date was April 25, 1921.

31. Rodeheaver does not actually list Gillingham as the Cincinnati session engineer, but his participation seems to be the best way to reconcile the timeline.

32. Interestingly, the Rainbow ads in late 1920 and early 1921 listed a recording laboratory in Winona Lake, but by the middle of 1921, the ads had dropped the mention of a recording laboratory (see 1920 and 1921 issues of the *Gospel Choir*).

33. "Homer A. Rodeheaver's Page," *Gospel Choir* (June 1921), 27.

34. Ibid. After remaking some of the 1920 issues, Rodeheaver assigned the new material to the old catalog numbers, a decision that would stymie discographers for many years until David Lewis unraveled the sequence of remade sides; see "The Rainbow Records Discography," 60–62.

35. Peter W. Dykema et al., eds., *18 Songs for Community Singing* (Boston: Birchard, 1913).

36. "Drink to Me Only with Thine Eyes" and "Flow Gently, Sweet Afton" cornet and band (Victor house band), recorded in Camden, New Jersey, October 19, 1916, Victor 18177, matrix B-18564, 78 r.p.m.

37. "Americanization through Music" (display ad), *Primary Education* (December 1919), 680.

38. "Make Your School a Community Builder" (display ad), *School and Community* (December 1921), 439.

39. "Joins Rodeheaver Forces," *Talking Machine World* (June 15, 1921), 109.

NOTES TO CHAPTER 6

40. *The Book of Rodeheaver Gospel Music* (company catalog), (Chicago: Rodeheaver Co., 1923), 59.

41. Ibid.

42. Ratcliff became known as The Man in White and edited England's most popular collection of community song; see Thomas P. Ratcliff, ed., *News Chronicle Song Book* (London: News-Chronicle Publications Dept., 1930). Ratcliff's collection included a Rodeheaver-like mix of community songs, spirituals, English sea shanties, children's songs, and hymns.

43. *Vaughan's Concert Quartet Book for Male Voices* (Lawrenceville, TN: James D. Vaughan Publishing, 1921). According to U.S. Copyright records, Vaughan applied for a copyright on March 1, 1921.

44. "Homer A. Rodeheaver's Page," *Gospel Choir*, June 1921, 5.

45. Ibid.

46. Stella Vaughan, Kieffer's wife, later reported that Vaughan's Winona Lake quartet consisted of J. E. Wheeler, M. D. McWhorter, Adlai Loudy, and Herman Walker (though Kieffer was present and apparently singing as well). See Stella B. Vaughan, "History of the James D. Vaughan Publishing Company," Installment IV, *Vaughan's Family Visitor* 49 (August 1960), 6. In their subsequent research, Wolfe and Goff treated this as confirmation that the same lineup sang on the first Vaughan recordings.

47. Stella B. Vaughan, "History of the James D. Vaughan Publishing Company," 6.

48. In the ensuing issues of the *Gospel Choir* and *Rodeheaver Musical News*, Rodeheaver and Parley Zartman reported on the 1921 conference and plans for the next summer, but made no mention of the accident.

49. "Rainbow Records in New York," *Talking Machine World* (October 15, 1921), 34.

50. "Rodeheaver Record Co. Activities," *Talking Machine World* (November 15, 1921), 34. The building is now known as the Pakula Building.

51. Ibid. Our account here reconciles the Rodeheaver timeline with all known reports from trade journals, *Gospel Choir*, and contemporary news accounts. It seems best to conclude that Rodeheaver owned (only) one recording outfit and moved it to various locations. Further, the only known engineers are L. E. Gillingham, Thomas P. Ratcliff, and C. R. Johnston, all of whom lived in New York and traveled to Winona Lake or Chicago (Forkel was the Chicago office manager, not an engineer).

52. "Homer A. Rodeheaver's Page," *Gospel Choir*, June 1921, 5.

53. "Rodeheaver Record Co. Activities."

54. Tim Brooks, "High Drama in the Record Industry: Columbia Records, 1901–1934," *ARSC Journal* 33:1 (Spring 2002).

55. "Our Recording Laboratory," *The Book of Rodeheaver Gospel Music*, 64.

56. Rodeheaver did not operate the only custom label in Chicago during the early 1920s. Orlando Marsh Laboratories released custom recordings on Autograph, Electra, and custom labels. Researchers are still exploring the relationship between Rodeheaver and Marsh, the electrical-era pioneer who recorded for many labels. Marsh's early matrix numbers appear to have some relationship to Rodeheaver's, and it seems likely that Marsh recorded for Rodeheaver. We are grateful to Richard Raichelson for sharing research from his forthcoming book on Orlando Marsh. See also Allan Sutton, *American Record Companies and Producers, 1888–1950* (Denver: Mainspring Press, 2018), 306–8.

57. "Our Recording Laboratory," 64. See also "From Our Chicago Headquarters," *Talking Machine World*, November 15, 1921, 123–24. Recordings cited in this section are from the authors' personal collection, the Lewis-Montgomery collection, and the auction catalogs of Kurt Nauck.

58. "New Rainbow Distributor," *Talking Machine World* (January 15, 1922), 1, 80.

59. "New Rainbow Distributor," 114.

60. Homer Rodeheaver, *Gospel Choir*, November 1921, 5.

61. William Howland Kenney, *Recorded Music in American Life: The Phonograph and Popular Memory, 1890–1945* (New York: Oxford University Press, 1999); see the discussion about "foreign" records, 65–87; "race" records, 109–134; and "hillbilly" records, 135–57. Also see David Brackett, *Categorizing Sound: Genre and Twentieth Century Popular Music* (Oakland: University of California Press, 2016), 115–21.

62. This is the approach of Kyle Stewart Barnett, "Cultural Production and Genre Formation in the U.S. Recording Industry, 1920–1935," PhD diss., University of Texas at Austin, 2006, 2. For a somewhat different approach that considers race as the primary factor, see Karl Hagsrom Miller, *Segregating Sound: Inventing Fold and Pop Music in the Age of Jim Crow* (Duram, N.C.: Duke University Press), 2010.

63. "Homer Rodeheaver's Page," *Gospel Choir* (November 1921), 5.

64. Ibid.

65. Arthur H. Foster, "Records of Religious Numbers and Old-Time Ballads Having a Sales Vogue," *Talking Machine World*, July 15, 1922, 6.

66. Ibid. For those who study the family of southern roots music, the writer's comments are especially interesting—essentially equating "old standard hymns" and "old ballads" as the same genre.

67. Homer Rodeheaver, spoken word, "The Mission of Rainbow Records," recorded in New York, October 28, 1924, Rainbow 9059, 78 r.p.m.

68. Ibid.

69. Homer Rodeheaver to John S. MacDonald, November 4, 1925, Rodeheaver Collection, Winona Lake. MacDonald had recorded under the name "Harry Macdonough" and sang with the Edison/Haydn quartet and then became an executive at Victor and later at Columbia.

70. Shea recorded for Singspiration from 1947 to 1950, having met Smith when both worked at WMBI. Smith had also been Billy Graham's roommate at Wheaton.

71. Homer Rodeheaver, spoken word, "Merry Christmas from Homer Rodeheaver," with Ruth Rodeheaver Thomas, soprano, and Paul Mickelson, organ, recorded in Winona Lake, Indiana, Rainbow 1955-A/B, matrix F8-oH-8855-1, 78 r.p.m. Note: after his final Rainbow Christmas recording, Rodeheaver recorded a few more times for International Sacred Recordings (see David N. Lewis, "Homer Rodeheaver Chronological Discography").

CHAPTER 7. SPIRITUALS AND MINSTRELSY

1. Joseph N. Rodeheaver, "The Negro Spiritual," 5. Undated manuscript, six typewritten pages with handwritten emendations. Courtesy Rodeheaver Family Archive, Thomas Rodeheaver and Barbara Rodeheaver Fong.

2. Homer Rodeheaver, *Singing Black* (Chicago: Rodeheaver Co., 1936), 9. Early in his life, Rodeheaver referred to these songs as *spirituals, jubilee songs,* or *plantation songs.* By the time of the Harlem Renaissance, Rodeheaver had adopted the commonly used *Negro spirituals.* Throughout the book we use *spirituals* in reference to this African American song heritage.

3. For a concise history of the folk spiritual and a summary of various origin theories, see Sandra Jean Graham, *Spirituals and the Birth of the Black Entertainment Industry* (Urbana: University of Illinois Press, 2018), 1–13.

4. Dena J. Epstein, "Black Spirituals: Their Emergence into Public Knowledge," *Black Music Research Journal,* vol. 10, no. 1 (Spring 1990), 58–64. By "public knowledge" Epstein was referring to *white* awareness (with deliberate irony), as well as the second generation of Blacks who had less understanding of their shared history.

5. See the summaries in Dale Cockrell, *Demons of Disorder: Early Blackface Minstrels and Their World* (New York: Cambridge University Press, 1997), 140–62; Larry Starr and Christopher Waterman, *American Popular Music: From Minstrelsy to MP3,* 5th ed. (New York: Oxford University Press, 2017).

6. See Lynn Abbott and Doug Seroff, *Out of Sight: The Rise of African American Popular Music, 1889–1895* (Jackson: University Press of Mississippi, 2003), and *Ragged but Right: Black Traveling Shows, 'Coon Songs,' and the Dark Pathways to Blues and Jazz* (Jackson: University Press of Mississippi, 2007).

7. From two parallel Scripture passages, Ephesians 5:19 and Colossians 3:16 (the traditional English translation of the Greek text).

8. The view of "three distinct song genres" was prevalent among Protestants of Rodeheaver's era, but this textual interpretation has fallen out of favor, with many theologians describing "psalms, hymns, and spiritual songs" as literary parallelism, three ways to describe the same thing.

9. William Francis Allen, Charles Pickard Ware, and Lucy McKim Garrison, *Slave Songs of the United States* (New York: A. Simpson & Co., 1867). The compilers carefully transcribed melody and text and then added remarkably detailed notes on their sources. As such, *Slave Songs* is the seminal early text for documenting folk spirituals.

10. For an account of the Jubilee Singers' seminal 1871 tour, see Gustavus D. Pike, *The Jubilee Singers and Their Campaign for Twenty Thousand Dollars* (Boston: Lee and Shepard, 1873). The *Jubilee* name was a nod to the biblical year of Jubilee (Leviticus 25:8–13), when slaves were freed.

11. Graham, *Spirituals and the Birth,* 119.

12. Eric Lott, *Love & Theft: Blackface Minstrelsy & the American Working Class,* 20th Anniversary Edition (New York: Oxford University Press, 2013), 4.

13. Allen et al., *Slave Songs of the United States,* i.

14. John Mason Brown, "Songs of the Slave," *Lippincott's Magazine,* December 1868, 618.

15. Gustavus D. Pike, *The Jubilee Singers and Their Campaign for Twenty Thousand Dollars,* 108.

16. Thomas Wentworth Higginson, "Negro Spirituals," *The Atlantic,* June 1867, 693–94. His term caught on slowly but was commonly accepted during Rodeheaver's era.

17. Theodore Seward, "Preface to the Music" in Gustavus D. Pike, *The Jubilee Singers and Their Campaign for Twenty Thousand Dollars* (Boston: Lee and Shepard, 1873), 163.

18. James Weldon Johnson, *The Book of American Negro Spirituals* (New York: Viking Press, 1925), 20.

19. Scholarly consensus affirms that spirituals were "capable of communicating on more than one level of meaning." See Albert J. Raboteau, *Slave Religion: The "Invisible Institution" in the Antebellum South* (New York: Oxford University Press, 1978, rev. 2004), 249.

20. See the summary in John White, "Veiled Testimony: Negro Spirituals and the Slave Experience," *Journal of American Studies* 17:2 (August 1983).

21. E. Franklin Frazier, *The Negro Church in America* (New York: Schocken Books, 1964), 12–13. See also Jon Michael Spencer (now Yahya Jongintaba), *Re-Searching Black Music* (Knoxville: University of Tennessee Press, 1996).

22. See the discussions of *South before the War* in Graham, *Spirituals and the Birth*, 218–19; and Tim Brooks, *Lost Sounds: Blacks and the Birth of the Recording Industry 1890–1919* (Urbana: University of Illinois Press, 2004), 96.

23. "Keep Movin'," Standard Quartette (H. C. Williams, Ed DeMoss, R. L. Scott, William Cottrell), 1894, Columbia (unnumbered), cylinder; reissued on *Lost Sounds: Blacks and the Birth of the Recording Industry*, Archeophone Records, 2005.

24. *South before the War* featured "few if any real spirituals"; see Graham, *Spirituals and the Birth*, 219.

25. Ibid., "The Minstrel Show Gets Religion," 125–43.

26. Tim Brooks, "'Might Take One Disc of This Trash as a Novelty': Early Recordings by the Fisk Jubilee Singers and the Popularization of 'Negro Folk Music,'" *American Music* 18:3 (Autumn 2000). For the early recordings of the Fisk Jubilee Quartet, see *There Breathes a Hope: The Legacy of John Work II and His Fisk Jubilee Quartet, 1909–1916*. Archeophone ARCH 5020, CD. 2010.

27. Tim Brooks, *Lost Sounds: Blacks and the Birth of the Recording Industry 1890–1919* (Urbana: University of Illinois Press, 2004), 192–215.

28. Homer Rodeheaver, recitation, "When Malindy Sings," recorded in New York, September 12, 1913, matrix C-13771-1, (rejected take).

29. Homer Rodeheaver, *Twenty Years with Billy Sunday* (Nashville, TN: Cokesbury Press, 1936), 49. It is difficult to pinpoint when, exactly, Rodeheaver began his concerts at Black churches, which were rarely covered by newspapers.

30. Ibid., 50.

31. Homer Rodeheaver and Virginia Asher (vocal duet), "Heab'n" with Prince's Orchestra, recorded in New York, May 1916, Columbia A-3559, matrix 78431, 78 r.p.m.; also "Some of These Days," Columbia A-3559, matrix 78432.

32. John B. Herbert, ed., *Rodeheaver Collection for Male Voices* (Chicago: The Rodeheaver Co., 1916), n.p., inside front cover. The subtitle describes the collection as "old familiar hymns, newly arranged; secular songs; Plantation melodies; Prohibition songs and special selections." The book was marketed as Rodeheaver's first collection of spirituals in *Rodeheaver's Musical News* (Winter 1917).

33. Homer Rodeheaver, *The Practical Song Director* (Chicago: The Rodeheaver Co., 1925), 2–3.

NOTES TO CHAPTER 7

34. Homer Rodeheaver, *Plantation Melodies* (Chicago: Rodeheaver Co., 1918). For a profile of J. B. Herbert and discussion of the project, see Charles H. Gabriel, "Dr. J. B. Herbert, Musician-Author," *Rodeheaver Musical News* (Spring 1917), 1.

35. The Methodist minister Marshall W. Taylor published *A Collection of Revival Hymns and Plantation Melodies* in 1883, aimed at Black congregations in the Methodist Episcopal Church. See also John Nelson Clark Coggin, *Plantation Melodies and Spiritual Songs* (Philadelphia: n.p., 1913); *National Jubilee Melodies* (Nashville, TN: National Baptist Publication Board, ca. 1915).

36. The ten songs share nearly identical lyrics, melody, and harmonic structure. In a few cases, the Rodeheaver edition changed the meter from 2/4 to 4/4 and gave chords a different voicing; Rodeheaver also changed the song structure so that the verses were presented first and then the chorus—*Jubilee Songs* usually printed the chorus first.

37. Homer Rodeheaver, *Plantation Melodies*, n.p., inside front cover.

38. Rodeheaver, *Practical Song Director*, 4.

39. Turner H. Wiseman to W. E. B. Du Bois, August 26, 1923. W. E. B. Du Bois Papers (MS 312). Special Collections and University Archives, University of Massachusetts Amherst Libraries.

40. Ibid.

41. See *Plantation Melodies* (1918), *Rodeheaver's Negro Spirituals* (1923), *Southland Spirituals* (1936), *Negro Spirituals and Folk Songs* (1939), *Sixty-Two Southland Spirituals* (1946).

42. See *Sociability Songs* (1928) and *Neighborly Songs and Poems* (1932).

43. James Weldon Johnson (words) and J. Rosamond Johnson (music), "Lift Ev'ry Voice and Sing," *Sixty Two Southland Spirituals* (Winona Lake: Rodeheaver Hall-Mack Co., 1946), 1.

44. Thomas Kane, *Winona Booklet* (Winona Lake, IN: Winona Assembly and Schools, 1906), 10. See chapter 4 for a further explanation of Winona Lake's altruistic ideals.

45. Kane, *Winona Booklet*, 10. Also see several articles on the same theme by Thomas Kane, "A Christian Altruistic Object Lesson," *Christian Evangelist*, March 3, 1904, 293; "What We Owe and the Results of Paying It," *Assembly Herald*, January 1906, 136–37; and "Winona," *The Advance*, May 31, 1906, 706.

46. "Business: Rotarians," *Time*, July 2, 1928.

47. "Rodeheaver Helped Popularize Spirituals," *Wilkes-Barre Record*, May 31, 1928.

48. Interestingly, Rodeheaver's name is nowhere present in the brief history of spirituals written by Johnson, *Book of American Negro Spirituals*, 48–49.

49. Henry Louis Gates, *Stony the Road: Reconstruction, White Supremacy, and the Rise of Jim Crow* (New York: Penguin Press, 2019), 80.

50. Rodeheaver, *The Practical Song Director*, 2–3.

51. Discography of American Historical Recordings, s.v. "T. H. Wiseman (vocalist: bass vocal)," adp.library.ucsb.edu/index.php/talent/detail/41017/Wiseman_T.H.vocalist_bass_vocal.

52. The full group consisted of A. C. Brogdon, tenor; Henry Allen, second tenor; J. C. Eubanks, baritone; and Wiseman, bass; plus Carrie Brewster, soprano; and Mrs. S. E. Hancock, contralto.

53. On the record label, Rainbow erroneously printed the song title as "Hard Tryin.'"

54. Advertisement for Paramount Records, "Be Uplifted by These Sacred Records." *Chicago Defender*, December 22, 1923.

55. Wiseman to Du Bois, August 26, 1923.

56. Brooks, *Lost Sounds*, 95, 201, 402.

57. Rick Kennedy, *Jelly Roll, Bix, and Hoagy: Gennett Studios and the Birth of Recorded Jazz* (Bloomington: University of Indiana Press, 1994), 73.

58. Homer Rodeheaver, baritone, with the Jackson College Jubilee Singers, Frederick Hall, director, "Little David, Play on Your Harp," recorded in Richmond, Indiana, between July and October 1926, Rainbow 1129-B (matrix 12567), 78 r.p.m.

59. Wiseman Sextet with Homer Rodeheaver (spoken word introduction), "Lord, I Can't Stay Away," unaccompanied, 1083-B, recorded in Chicago, by September 1923, Rainbow 1083-B, matrix 6057-B°-9-S-10, 78 r.p.m. Also released as Paramount 12076 and Herwin 92009.

60. Brooks, *Lost Sounds*, 213.

61. John Wesley Work, *Folk Song of the American Negro* (Nashville, TN: Fisk University Press, 1915), 92.

62. Allen et al., *Slave Songs of the United States*, ix.

63. Alice Mabel Bacon, "Work and Methods of the Hampton Folk-Lore Society," *Journal of American Folklore*, vol. 11, no. 40 (January–March, 1898), 20. On Pullen's views, see Terry Miller, "A Myth in the Making: Willie Ruff, Black Gospel and an Imagined Gaelic Scottish Origin," *Ethnomusicology Forum* 18:2 (November 2009), 243–59; and Nancy Love Graham, "The DNA of African American Spirituals and the Rehabilitation of George Pullen Jackson," PhD diss., Oxford University, 2015.

64. W. E. B. Du Bois, "Of the Sorrow Songs," *Souls of Black Folk* (Chicago: A. C. McClurg & Co., 1903), 253.

65. Wiseman to Du Bois, August 26, 1923.

66. Regina Dolan, "Negro Spirituals and American Culture," *Interracial Review* 31 (April 1958), 63–66.

67. "Athletic X," *Ohio Wesleyan Transcript* (Delaware, Ohio), May 18, 1904, 482–83. "Delaware's Dandy Darkies" (May 12, 1904), the concert program.

68. "Entire Audience of Negroes Hits Trail Saturday Evening under Negro Pastor's Urging," *Atlanta Constitution*, December 9, 1917, 16.

69. "Rather Took the Wind out of Matthews' Sails," *Watertown (NY) Re-Union*, April 13, 1918.

70. Homer Rodeheaver, *Worth While Poems* (Chicago: Rodeheaver Co., 1916); Homer Rodeheaver, *More Worth While Poems* (Chicago: Rodeheaver Co., 1929).

71. Homer Rodeheaver, *F'r Instance: 450 Choice Selections of Anecdotes and Illustrations for Public Speakers* (Winona Lake: Rodeheaver Hall-Mack Co., 1949).

72. T. C. Johnson (words) and Charles H. Gabriel (music), "I Draws De Line Right Dar." *Fillmore's Prohibition Songs: A Collection of Songs for the Prohibition Campaign, Patriotic Services, and All Meetings in the Interest of Reform* (Cincinnati: Fillmore Brothers, 1903), 129.

73. Homer Rodeheaver, baritone vocal solo, "De Brewer's Big Hosses," Victor Orchestra and Metropolitan Quartet, recorded in Camden, New Jersey, September 12, 1913, Victor 17455, matrix 13774–2, 78 r.p.m.

74. H. S. Taylor (words) and J. B. Herbert (music), "De Brewer's Big Hosses," *The Live Wire* (Chicago: Rodeheaver Co., 1914).

75. Charles H. Gabriel (words) and Homer Rodeheaver (music), *Old Black Sam: A Vision of Slavery Days* (Chicago: Rodeheaver Co., 1912).

76. Edward H. Bonekemper III, *The Myth of the Lost Cause: Why the South Fought the Civil War and Why the North Won* (Washington, DC: Regnery History, 2015), 11.

77. Homer E. [*sic*] Rodeheaver, "With My Trombone in France," *Association Men* (March 1919), 526–27.

78. See Randall Kennedy, *Nigger: The Strange Career of a Troublesome Word* (New York: Pantheon, 2002). For an early critique, see Clifton Johnson, "There Are Only Niggers in the South," *Seattle Republican*, October 14, 1904, 5.

79. Sterling A. Brown, "Negro Character as Seen by White Authors," *Journal of Negro Education* 2:2 (April 1933), 179. See the commentary in Gates Jr., *Stony the Road*, 93–94.

80. As one example (of many), the white novelist Carl Van Vechten wrote sympathetically about Black life in Harlem—but inexplicably titled his book *Nigger Heaven*. See the summary in Kennedy, *Nigger*, 53–54, 128–30.

81. We use *dialect* as an historical term representing Black southern vernacular as depicted in the minstrelsy era. Walt Wolfram has traced the shifting labels used by scholars of social dialectology, starting with the now-obsolete *Nonstandard Negro Dialect* and moving to terms such as *Black English, Ebonics, African-American Vernacular English*, and the currently popular *African-American English* or *African-American Language*. See Mike Vuolo, "Is Black English a Dialect or a Language?" transcription of a podcast interview with Walt Wolfram et al., www.slate.com/articles/podcasts/lexicon_valley.html, February 2012.

82. Charles Gabriel (words and music), "Where Am De Chil'ren?" song #47 in *Plantation Melodies*. Originally published as sheet music by the St. Louis–based Balmer & Weber (1882). Lyrics reprinted in Gabriel's collection of poetry, *The Slighted Stranger* (Chicago: Rodeheaver Co., 1915), 247.

83. Paul Laurence Dunbar (words) and Will M. Marion (music), "Who Dat Say Chicken in Dis Crowd" (New York: M. Witmark & Sons, 1898). A hit song from the vaudeville show *Summer Nights*, organized by the impresario Edward E. Rice, where a Black cast performed for a whites-only audience. For a summary of Dunbar's life, see Lilian S. Robinson and Greg Robinson, "Paul Laurence Dunbar: A Credit to His Race?" *African American Review* 41:2 (2007), 215–25.

84. For Dunbar, his literary device fit into a broad literary tradition—he also experimented with Irish, German, and Western regional dialects. See Michael Cohen, "Paul Laurence Dunbar and the Genres of Dialect," *African American Review* 41:2 (2007), 247–57.

85. James Weldon Johnson, *The Book of American Negro Poetry* (New York: Harcourt, Brace and Company, 1922), xxxiii, xxxv.

86. Cohen, "Genres of Dialect," 264–65.

87. Usually attributed to George P. Krapp in *The English Language in America*, vol. 1 (New York: Century Co., 1925), 228.

88. This version of the text taken from Paul Laurence Dunbar, *When Malindy Sings*, with photographs by the Hampton Institute Camera Club, decorations by Margaret Armstrong

(New York: Dodd, Mead, 1903). The poem had been published by numerous newspapers as early as 1896.

89. Oscar Brown Jr., "When Malindy Sings," music by Oscar Brown Jr., *Between Heaven and Hell*, Columbia CL1774, 1962; Abbey Lincoln, "When Malindy Sings," music by Oscar Brown Jr., *Straight Ahead*, Candid Stereo 9015, 33 1/3 r.p.m. 1961; Maya Angelou, spoken word recitation, "When Malindy Sings," words by Paul Laurence Dunbar, *Coming Home to the Spirit*, Glide Memorial UMC GCD-4103–2, 33 1/3 r.p.m., 1961.

90. Dunbar, *When Malindy Sings*.

91. Lina Cavalieri, "When Malindy Sings," recorded January–September 1910, New York, Columbia A5224, matrix 30379–3, 78 r.p.m.

92. Homer Rodeheaver, spoken word recitation, "When Malindy Sings," recorded in Camden, New Jersey, February 26, 1916, Victor 35545-B, matrix 13771–2, 78 r.p.m. Rodeheaver had previously recorded the recitation at a 1913 Victor session, but the take was rejected. He recorded later versions with Rainbow/Gennett (1921), Rainbow (1922), International Records (1955), Westminster Films (1955).

93. "New Records for Your Talking Machine," *Times* (Shreveport, LA), July 3, 1916.

94. Edward Margolies, *Native Sons: A Critical Study of Twentieth Century Black American Authors* (Philadelphia: Lippincott, 1968), 29; also see the summary in Lillian S. Robinson and Greg Robinson, "Paul Laurence Dunbar," 219–21.

95. *Negro Spirituals and Folk Songs*, arr. Frederick Hall (Winona Lake: Rodeheaver Hall-Mack Co., 1939), 3.

96. We found no record of any Rodeheaver blackface performances between his 1904 student performance and his 1955 blackface film. It seems likely that his final revival was motivated by his own nostalgia.

97. The three films were *Miracles through Song: "Heartaches," Miracles through Song: "Somebody Cares,"* and *Miracles through Song: "When Malindy Sings."* William E. Brusseau, producer and director, filmed in Pasadena, California, Westminster Films, 1955.

98. Graham, *Spirituals*, 218–19; Brooks, *Lost Sounds*, 96; see also the *South before the War* Company Papers in the Music Library of Yale University.

99. Carl Wittke, *Tambo and Bones: A History of the American Minstrel Stage* (Durham, NC: Duke University Press, 1930). Sounding a lot like Rodeheaver and sharing the same ethos, Wittke offers warm memories of his own blackface performances as a student at Ohio State University (which he intends as a respectful homage). See also Constance Rourke, *American Humor: A Study of the National Character* (New York: New York Review of Books, 1931), 70–90.

100. Charles Musser, "Why Did Negroes Love Al Jolson and *The Jazz Singer*? Melodrama, Blackface and Cosmopolitan Theatrical Culture," *Film History* 23:2 (2011), 196–222.

101. William J. Walls, "What about Amos 'n' Andy?," *Abbott's Monthly* (December 1930), 38–40, 72–74; Herbert B. Alexander, "Negro Opinion Regarding Amos and Andy," *Sociology and Social Research* 16 (March 1932), 345–54; Melvin Patrick Ely, *The Adventures of Amos 'n' Andy: A Social History of an American Phenomenon* (New York: Free Press, 1991).

102. Douglass, who was licensed to preach by the African Methodist Episcopal Church, called minstrel performers "the filthy scum of white society, who have stolen from us a com-

plexion denied to them by nature, in which to make money, and pander to the corrupt taste of their white fellow-citizens." Frederick Douglass, "The Hutchinson Family—Hunkerism," *North Star (Rochester, NY)*, October 27, 1848.

103. See the summary of Garrison in Ibram X. Kendi, *Stamped from the Beginning: The Definitive History of Racist Ideas in America* (New York: Nation Books, 2016), 170–72.

104. Starting in the mid-1950s, many scholars explored the racist roots of minstrelsy. See Ralph Ellison, "Change the Joke and Slip the Yoke" (1958) in *The Collected Essays of Ralph Ellison*, John Callahan, ed. (New York: Modern Library, 1995); Leroy Jones, *Blues People: The Negro Experience in White America and the Music That Developed from It* (New York: William Morrow, 1963); Eileen Southern, *The Music of Black Americans: A History* (New York: W. W. Norton, 1971), 100–4; Nathan Huggins, *Harlem Renaissance* (New York: Oxford University Press, 1971).

105. In addition to Bing Crosby and costar Marjorie Reynolds, the entire band is in blackface and dressed in the same sort of plantation costumes that Rodeheaver would use in *Malindy*.

106. Space does not allow for an analysis of scholarly opinion after Rodeheaver's era. See the summary in Eric Lott, *Love & Theft*. Recent work tends to explore minstrelsy from socioeconomic, post-Freudian, and gendered perspectives, but these works also begin by affirming the racist subtext inherent in all blackface.

107. Joseph N. Rodeheaver, "The Negro Spiritual," 5.

108. Homer Rodeheaver, arr. J. B. Herbert, *Rodeheaver's Negro Spirituals* (Chicago: Rodeheaver Co., 1923), n.p. inside front cover.

CHAPTER 8. JIM CROW REVIVALISM MEETS THE KLAN

1. John Reed, "Back of Billy Sunday," *Metropolitan* (May 1915), 12. The Richmond proposal was forged in a "secret session" of Richmond's ministerial association, marked by "serious dissention" and 13 votes against the Sunday meetings, which nevertheless passed by majority vote. See "Scherer Resigns as Treasurer of Union," *Richmond (VA) Times-Dispatch*, February 15, 1915, 5. The news account does not detail the exact reasons for the dissention, but the segregation issue seems to be a likely subtext.

2. Helen Sunday to William McLoughlin Jr., quoted in *Billy Sunday Was His Real Name* (Chicago: University of Chicago Press, 1955), 273.

3. "Ministers Wrath," *Richmond (VA) Planet*, January 25, 1919, 2. In this section, narrative details of the 1919 Richmond revival (January 12–March 2, 1919) are from contemporary news accounts published in the *Richmond Times-Dispatch*, the *Richmond News Leader*, and the Black-owned *Richmond Planet*. See also Samuel C. Shepherd Jr., *Avenues of Faith: Shaping the Urban Religious Culture of Richmond, Virginia, 1900–1929* (Tuscaloosa: University of Alabama Press, 2001), 62–64.

4. John Mitchell, Jr., "Billy Sunday and the Colored Folks," *Richmond (VA) Planet*, January 18, 1919, 5.

5. "Evangelist Preaches to 15,000 in Auditorium," *Richmond (VA) Times-Dispatch*, January 13, 1919, 1.

NOTES TO CHAPTER 8

6. "The Ministers Conference," *Richmond (VA) Planet*, February 8, 1919, 2.

7. "Negroes and the Sunday Meetings," *Richmond (VA) Planet*, February 8, 1919, 5.

8. "Billy Sunday Gets Word from Music Director," *Richmond (VA) Dispatch*, January 17, 1919, 1. Prior to Rodeheaver's arrival, the paper had puffed him as equal to Sunday in reputation; see "Rodeheaver Expected Here for Big Campaign," *Richmond (VA) Times-Dispatch*, December 27, 1918, 10.

9. "Rodeheaver Here and Wins Hearts of Sunday Crowd," *Richmond (VA) Times-Dispatch*, January 19, 1919, 1.

10. James A. Bland (words and music), "Carry Me Back to Old Virginny" (Boston: John F. Perry, 1878).

11. Edward H. Bonekemper III, *The Myth of the Lost Cause: Why the South Fought the Civil War and Why the North Won* (Washington, DC: Regnery History, 2015), 1–7.

12. The song's controversial history is too long to recount here. Ray Charles offered one solution when he recorded it in 1982 and rewrote the "darky" lyrics. In 1997, the Virginia legislature eventually relegated its status to "State Song Emeritus."

13. "In Rhode Island and Virginia," *Richmond (VA) Planet*, January 18, 1919, 5.

14. "Chicago Council Is After Ku Klux Klan," *Chicago Tribune*, (January 18, 1923), 2; "Let Klan Robes Go to Hold Jobs at Statehouse," *Chicago Tribune*, (January 18, 1923), 5 (the bill was co-sponsored by Albert J. Roberts, the African American representative from Chicago's south side); David J. Goldberg, "Unmasking the Ku Klux Klan: The Northern Movement against the KKK, 1920–1925," *Journal of American Ethnic History* 15: 4 (Summer, 1996), 32–48; Kenneth T. Jackson, *Ku Klux Klan in the City, 1915–1930* (New York: Oxford University Press, 1967), 93–126.

15. "Protestants Disowning the Ku Klux," *Literary Digest* (November 25, 1922), 33.

16. For a study of official positions on the Klan taken by Protestant denominations, see Robert Moats Miller, "A Note on the Relationship between the Protestant Church and the Revived Ku Klux Klan," *The Journal of Southern History* 22:3 (February–November 1956), 355–368.

17. "M. E. Pastors Vote Against Racial Hostility," *Chicago Tribune* (October 9, 1923), 4.

18. The *Christian Cynosure*, published by the National Christian Association (1868–1983), represented "the Christian movement against the secret lodge system." See also Charles A. Blanchard, *Modern Secret Societies* (Chicago: National Christian Association, 1903, and updated frequently through the eight subsequent editions).

19. Clarence N. Roberts, "The Crusade against Secret Societies and the National Christian Association," *Journal of the Illinois State Historical Society (1908–1984)* 64:4 (1971).

20. Jackson, *Ku Klux Klan in the City*, 97–99.

21. From Matthew 6:1–4, "Take heed that ye do not your alms before men, to be seen of them ... let not thy left hand know what thy right hand doeth: That thine alms may be in secret."

22. "Ku Klux Present," *Yorkville Enquirer* (York, SC), February 22, 1922, 4.

23. "Shavings from the Sawdust Trail at Gospel Tabernacle," *Charleston (SC) Daily Mail*, March 16, 1922.

24. See William McLoughlin Jr., *Billy Sunday Was His Real Name* (Chicago: University of Chicago Press, 1955), 272–275; Lyle W. Dorsett, *Billy Sunday and the Redemption of Urban America* (Grand Rapids: William B. Eerdmans, 1991), 96–98. A more recent analysis is more

critical; see William A. Firstenberger, *In Rare Form: A Pictorial History of Baseball Evangelist Billy Sunday* (Iowa City: University of Iowa Press, 2005), 29–30.

25. William McLoughlin Jr., *Billy Sunday Was His Real Name* (Chicago: University of Chicago Press, 1955), 275. McLoughlin cites a 1952 letter from Helen Sunday; apparently, he was the only biographer to ask her a direct question about the Klan.

26. Having recently uncovered fifty news articles about these Klan visits, from at least nine city-wide revival campaigns, it seems fair to observe how few of the news reports have survived in the Winona Lake collection of Billy Sunday papers (which are full of other clippings from his campaigns). Helen Sunday zealously protected her husband's image and was known to purge embarrassing details.

27. "$200 Presented Billy Sunday by Ku Klux Klan," *Lima (OH) News*, April 9, 1922, 6.

28. "12 Ghost-Like Figures of Ku Klux Klan Create Thrill as They Tiptoe into Tabernacle," *Richmond (IN) Item*, May 16, 1922, 1.

29. "Billy Sunday Preaches to Organization," *Fiery Cross*, January 2, 1925, 2.

30. "Billy Sunday's New Friends," *Coschocton (OH) Tribune and Times-Age*, May 26, 1922, 4.

31. "Billy Sunday Klansman?" *Chicago Defender*, March 25, 1922, 3.

32. "Charles Lewis Fowler" in *Dictionary of North Carolina Biography* vol. 2, Thomas G. Dyer, ed. William S. Powell (Chapel Hill: The University of North Carolina Press, 1986), 231–232. "Forrest Tells Aims of Ku Klux College," *New York Times*, September 12, 1921, 15. "Ku Klux to Build 'Hall of Invisibles,'" *New York Times*, September 19, 1921, 17.

33. "Knoxville Negroes Object to Billy Sunday: Claim Noted Evangelist Is Member of Ku Klux Klan," *Tennessean*, February 1, 1923, 6.

34. See "Ku Klux Klan Officers," Indiana Records, 1925, Collection SC 2419, Indiana Historical Society, Indianapolis, Indiana.

35. Jonathan Newell, "Billy Sunday's 1923 Evangelistic Campaign in Columbia, South Carolina," *Proceedings of the South Carolina Historical Association, 2008* (Columbia, SC: The South Carolina Historical Association, 2008), 47–48.

36. "9,000 Men Stand Up When Billy Sunday Asks Their Pledges," *Commercial Appeal* (Memphis, Tennessee), February 16, 1925, 1–2; also see a similar situation reported in "Pithy Paragraphs Picked from the Sawdust Aisles," *Richmond (IN) Item*, May 18, 1922, 6.

37. "Fine Tribute Paid Klan by Billy Sunday," *Fraternalist* (St. Joseph, MO), March 12, 1925, 6.

38. "If You Don't Want to Go to Heaven, Go to Hell," *Tampa Tribune*, April 3, 1919, 1.

39. "Thousands of Kluxers Hear 'Billy' Sunday, *Shreveport Journal*, March 29, 1924, 13.

40. Francis Grimké, "Billy Sunday's Campaign in Washington, D.C.," *Addresses Mainly Personal and Racial*, vol. 1 in *The Works of Francis J. Grimké*, ed. Carter G. Woodson (Washington, DC: Associated Publishers, 1942), 556, 559. Grimké delivered his address during the 1918 Sunday-Rodeheaver revivals.

41. "Religious Hypocrisy," *Chicago Defender*, June 14, 1919, 20. Though Sunday remained relatively silent on racial issues, others in Winona Lake became increasingly vocal. At the 1927 summer conference, Mrs. W. T. Larimer called on white evangelicals to accept Blacks as social equals who deserved "their rightful place" in the church. See W. T. Larimer, "They of Another Color," *Winona Echoes* (Winona Lake, IN: Victor M. Hatfield, 1927), 147–57.

42. The practice of Klan contrafacta began during the first Klan (late 1860s), when pro-Klan and anti-Klan supporters borrowed tunes like "Carry Me Back to Old Virginny" and "When Johnny Comes Marching Home." See Danny O. Crew, *Ku Klux Klan Sheet Music: An Illustrated Catalogue of Published Music, 1867–2002* (Jefferson, NC: McFarland and Co., 2003), 5–14.

43. William J. Simmons, *Kloran: Knights of the Ku Klux Klan*, 5th ed. (Atlanta, GA: Knights of the Ku Klux Klan, 1916), 3–20.

44. Michael Jacobs, "Co-Opting Christian Chorales: Songs of the Ku Klux Klan," *American Music* 28:3 (Fall 2010), 269.

45. See the list in ibid., 376 n. 5 and. 6.

46. Rev. George Bennard (music) and Alvia O.[tis] DeRee (words), "The Bright Fiery Cross" (Indianapolis, IN: The American, 1923). His "Bright Fiery Cross" sheet music featured a red, white, and blue cover with a large red cross, surrounded by eight hooded Klansmen.

47. Rodeheaver renewed the copyright in 1941; the last copyright holder of "The Old Rugged Cross" was Word Music, Inc., which purchased Rodeheaver's publishing empire in 1969 and held the song's rights until it entered the public domain in 1988.

48. Like several of his songs, "Bright Fiery Cross" is registered under "DE REE (Alvia Ottis)," a misspelling of his middle name. The copyright was registered on March 10, 1923; (A 701580 #8222) in *Catalog of Copyright Entries*, Part 1 [B] Group 2 (1924), 350. DeRee skated around the edges of current copyright law by registering the Klan lyrics as a book, not a song.

49. "100 Percent Americans," male quartet (Criterion Quartet), "The Bright Fiery Cross," recorded on October 18, 1923, KKK Records, KKK 75001, 78 r.p.m. The Criterion Quartet is identified on the Gennett Records session card. Less than a year earlier, the same quartet sang backup to the Rodeheaver-Asher duet of "The Old Rugged Cross," with two different takes released as Rainbow 1015-B and Gennett 4894-A.

50. Roland G. Fryer Jr. and Steven D. Levitt, "Hatred and Profits: Under the Hood of the Ku Klux Klan," *Quarterly Journal of Economics* 127:4, 1924.

51. Michael Jacobs, "Co-Opting Christian Chorales," 368.

52. Rick Kennedy, *Jelly Roll, Bix, and Hoagy: Gennett Records and the Rise of America's Grassroots Music* (Bloomington: University of Indiana Press, 2013), 38–42.

53. Vaughan Quartet, "Wake Up America and Kluck, Kluck, Kluck," recorded around April 14, 1924, Vaughan Record Co., Vaughan 825-A, matrix K-11-A-A°-30-1-4, 78 r.p.m. (The date comes from Gennett ledgers.).

54. The Vaughan Quartet, "Wake Up, America and Kluck, Kluck, Kluck," with Theodore Shaw, piano, recorded April 8, 1924, Richmond, Indiana, Vaughan 825, 78 r.p.m. The song was also published as sheet music; see Walter B. Seale (words and music) and Adgar M. Pace (vocal arrangement), Lawrenceville, TN: James D. Vaughan, 1924. See a discussion of this song (and southern gospel racism) in Douglas Harrison, *Then Sings My Soul: The Culture of Southern Gospel Music* (Urbana, IL: University of Illinois Press, 2012), 96–103.

55. Based on extant recordings. Danny O. Crew, *Ku Klux Klan Sheet Music: An Illustrated Catalogue of Published Music, 1867–2002* (Jefferson, NC: McFarland, 2003), 234–235. See also Kurt Nauck, ed., *Vintage Auction #51* (catalog), (Spring, TX: Nauck's Vintage Records, 2012), 49. All three records were released twice with two different labels, causing confusion for

discographers: the first issue from Scottdale, Pennsylvania (without a K number), and the second issue from "International Music Co." in Buffalo, New York (with K number on the label). The recordings themselves are identical and bear the same matrix numbers, faintly visible under the label as a hand-scratched number.

56. Paul Stone Wight, student enrollment records, Moody Bible Institute, 1915.

57. See various items in the "News" column of *Christian Workers Magazine, 1915–1918*.

58. "Two Weddings Feature Big Klan Rally," *Daily Courier* (Connellsville, PA), July 5, 1924, 1; "15,000 Official Figure on Crowd at Rally of Klan," *Daily Courier* (Connellsville, PA), September 2, 1924, 1.

59. See the succession of articles in *Herald of Gospel Liberty*: "The Ku Klux Klan," August 25, 1921, 802; Rodney W. Roundy, "Growth of the Ku Klux Klan," August 25, 1921, 796; "Two Christian Leaders on the Ku Klux Klan," August 17, 1922, 773; and "Ku Klux Klan Disowned by the Churches," October 26, 1922, 1013.

60. "Scottdale Minister to Go to Buffalo," *Pittsburgh Press*, November 9, 1924, 13. Also see Emerson Hunsberger Loucks, *The Ku Klux Klan in Pennsylvania: A Study in Nativism* (New York: Telegraph Press, 1936), 133 (n. 11). Wight's short-lived International Music Company should not be confused with the company of the same name in New York City, a division of Bourne Music that publishes classical music.

61. [Paul S. Wight], *American Hymns* (Buffalo, NY: International Music Co., c. 1925). Like Wight's new record label, his own name was conspicuously missing from the publication.

62. "Arouse, Oh Klansmen True" (matrix A/85141) and "The Way of the Cross" (matrix 20113-A), sung by the Chicago Male Quartet, International Music Co. (Label Address: 307 People's Bank Building, Buffalo, New York), Special (Rodeheaver Record Co.), K-4, 78 r.p.m.; "Let the Fiery Cross Be Burning" and "Welcome the Klan" (matrix unknown), sung by unknown quartet, K-5. No extant copies of the K-5 recording are known, though it is listed in Wight's *American Hymns* catalog and in Danny O. Crew, *Ku Klux Klan Sheet Music*, 234–235. The Chicago Male Quartet may have been the vaudeville group listed in *Musicians and Allied Artists Directory*, 1925–1926, advertised as "Music for all occasions. Ritual music for all Masonic Bodies, Concerts, Clubs, Churches, Banquets, Funerals." But similar names were shared by several groups, making an exact identification difficult.

63. Homer Rodeheaver and organ, "Hats Off to Old Glory," recorded July–September 1925, International Music Co. (Label Address: 307 People's Bank Building, Buffalo, New York), Special (Rodeheaver Record Co.), 20167-A, matrix 85166R (884–2), 78 r.p.m. It is difficult to precisely date this recording session or identify its original purpose. These two songs are the only known Homer Rodeheaver releases on the Special label; perhaps someone at the Rodeheaver Record Co. sold Wight a rejected or unreleased take.

64. Homer Rodeheaver and unknown orchestra, "The Battle Hymn of the Republic," recorded July–September 1925, International Music Co. (Label Address: 307 People's Bank Building, Buffalo, New York), Special (Rodeheaver Record Co.), 20167-B, matrix 85189R (11019–2), 78 r.p.m.

65. "Turn Down Klan Cash," *Tolerance*, November 26, 1922, 3.

66. In terms of Rodeheaver matrix numbers, this time period extends from roughly matrix 7061 (released on Wallin's Svenska Records) to matrix 9056 (the last Klan recording of Paul S. Wight). See Guido van Rijn and Alex van der Tuuk, *New York Recording Laboratories*

Matrix Series Volume 3: The Rodeheaver, Marsh and 2000 Series (Overveen, The Netherlands: Agram Blues Books, 2013); and David N. Lewis and Mike Montgomery, "Rodeheaver Record Company Discography, 1920–1929 (Revised)," unpublished discography, September 2015. Both discographers summarize what is known of the extant discs, though they vary somewhat on dates and chronology.

67. Edwin H. Forkel worked as Rodeheaver Recording Co. business manager until he left in late 1924 or early 1925 to open an Oak Park real estate office. The session engineer for the Klan recordings remains anonymous. L. E. Gillingham had resigned from Rainbow in 1922 for Nipponophone of Japan. Thomas P. Ratcliff and C. R. "Johnnie" Johnston (both living in New York) did not work on Rainbow sessions after 1922.

68. "Rodeheaver Co. Makes an Announcement Which Should Be of Particular Interest to Singers and Teachers," *Music News* (November 14, 1924), 38.

69. Alvia O. DeRee, "The American Flag," *Selected Poems and Songs* (Indianapolis, IN: DeRee Publishing Co., 1928), 16. DeRee lived a peripatetic life in Indiana, working as a machinist and insurance agent, a Klan member, and the pastor of several Indianapolis congregations: the Pilgrim Holiness Church, then the Church of Re-Creation, and then the self-named DeRee Tabernacle (none of which lasted long or exceeded 100 members).

70. "Firwood Church of Christ," *Wilkes-Barre Times Leader*, November 3, 1928, 6. Wight's preaching text for this topic is unknown. By the mid-1930s, Wight was leading music for Gerald B. Winrod, a radical Kansas evangelist known as the Jayhawk Nazi (for his white supremacy and antisemitism).

71. Homer Rodeheaver, *Singing Black* (Chicago: The Rodeheaver Co., 1936), 10.

72. "Musical Missionary," *Time* (June 29, 1936), 26. "Horn Playing Evangelist Makes Hit with Savages," *Tampa Tribune*, June 28, 1936, 9.

73. "See Moving Pictures of Homer Rodeheaver," *Charleston (WV) Daily Mail*, November 12, 1936, 12. "Claims Africans Like Spirituals," *Daily Times* (New Philadelphia, OH), June 17, 1936, 2. Tom Gullette, "A Line on Liners," *Brooklyn Daily Eagle*, June 16, 1936, 21; "Oddities," *Anniston (AL) Star*, June 16, 1936, 2. Arthur Brisband, "Today," *Lancaster (OH) Eagle-Gazette*, June 18, 1936, 6.

74. Arthur J. Moore, [Eulogy for Homer Rodeheaver], *In Memory of Homer Rodeheaver* (Winona Lake: Rodeheaver Sacred Music Conference, 1956), 2–3.

75. Homer Rodeheaver, *Southland Spirituals* (Chicago: Rodeheaver Co., 1936), n.p., inside front cover.

CHAPTER 9. PRESERVING AND EXPORTING THE GOSPEL SONGS

1. Narrative details are from published news reports (mostly written by Frankenberg); Homer Rodeheaver, "My Trip Abroad," unpublished diary, 1924, Rodeheaver Collection at Morgan Library Archives and Special Collections, Grace College, Winona Lake, Indiana; notes and photographs in Theodore Thomas Frankenberg Collection (MS F853), Special Collections, University of Arkansas Libraries. Most of the Rodeheaver entourage were investors in Rainbow Records, and the trip would extensively promote the new venture.

2. "An Eight Months' Evangelistic Tour," *The Friend*, October 1923, 234.

3. "Notes and Suggestions," *Institute Tie*, December 1908, 334.

4. "Around the World with the Gospel Horn," *Hagerstown (IN) Exponent*, July 3, 1924, 4.

5. Homer Rodeheaver, *The Practical Song Director* (Chicago: Rodeheaver Co., 1925), 1.

6. Narrative details about the Japan visit from published news accounts; Rodeheaver, "My Trip Abroad"; Homer Rodeheaver, "The Story of Ugo Nakada," *Home and School: A Journal of Christian Education* (April 1926), 13. See also the biographical profile of Ugo Nakada at www.eiko-church.com/guide/history/nakata-ugo. The authors are grateful to Yoshio Nakamura for his translation of this website.

7. Homer Rodeheaver to Billy and Helen Sunday, September 29, 1923, William "Billy" and Helen "Ma" Sunday Collection at Morgan Library Archives and Special Collections, Grace College, Winona Lake, Indiana.

8. As an example, Moravian literature often repeats a story about Indians attacking the Moravian settlement in Bethlehem, Pennsylvania, at Christmas, 1755—thwarted by the playing of a trombone ensemble. See Joseph Mortimer Levering, *A History of Bethlehem, Pennsylvania, 1741–1892* (Bethlehem: Times Publishing Company, 1903), 330–31. See also Barbara Mitchell, *Tomahawks and Trombones* (Minneapolis: Carolrhoda Books, 1982).

9. John Jennings Merwin, "The Oriental Missionary Society Holiness Church in Japan, 1910–1983" (DMiss diss., Fuller Theological Seminary, 1983).

10. Likely a reference to Rodeheaver's 1915 recording with Victor or possibly his 1916 recording with Columbia; see David N. Lewis, "Homer Rodeheaver Chronological Discography," unpublished manuscript courtesy of the author.

11. Homer Rodeheaver, "The Story of Ugo Nakada," *Home and School: A Journal of Christian Education* 17: 8 (April 1926), 13.

12. Homer Rodeheaver, vocal solo, "Jesus Loves Me" (Rainbow 500-A), "What a Friend We Have in Jesus" (Rainbow 500-B), "Whiter than the Snow" (Rainbow 501-A), and "Fill Me Now" (Rainbow 501-B); recorded in Chicago between July and October, 1922. Though listed in his Rainbow catalogs during the 1920s, no copies have been found.

13. For instance, see Homer Rodeheaver, *Twenty Years with Billy Sunday* (Nashville, TN: Cokesbury Press, 1936), 86.

14. Homer Rodeheaver, spoken word, "The Mission of Rainbow Records," recorded in New York, October 28, 1924, Rainbow 9059, 78 r.p.m.

15. See the tribute website maintained by Ogikubo Eikou Kyoukai (Ogikubo Glory Church, Suginami, Tokyo), a church cofounded by Nakada: www.eiko-church.com/guide/history/nakata-ugo. Nakada's influence on Holiness hymnody is also explored in William Purinton, "United We Sing: Union Hymnals, Holiness Hymnody, and the Formation of Korean Revivalism (1905–2007)," *Asbury Journal* 66 (2011), 36–56.

16. Ugo Nakada, ed., *A Special Selection of Revival Hymns in Japanese* (Winona Lake, IN: Rodeheaver Hall-Mack Co., 1941).

17. Transcribed from Homer Rodeheaver, spoken word and baritone solo with orchestra, "Brightening the Corner around the World," recorded in New York, October 28, 1924, Rainbow 8089, 78 r.p.m.

18. Homer Rodeheaver, "1923 Pocket Diary," unpublished journal, Rodeheaver Collection, Morgan Library of Grace College, Winona Lake, Indiana.

19. "An Eight Months' Evangelistic Tour," 233–34.

20. "Missionaries to Circle Globe in Religious Drive," *Oakland (CA) Tribune*, September 30, 1923, 34.

21. Robin Brown, "Americanization at Its Best? The Globalization of Jazz" in *Resounding International Relations: On Music, Culture, and Politics*, M. I. Franklin, ed. (New York: Palgrave Macmillan, 2005), 89–109.

22. For a critical analysis of cultural imperialism theory, see John Tomlinson, *Cultural Imperialism: A Critical Introduction* (Baltimore, MD: Johns Hopkins University Press, 1991).

23. See Donald P. Hustad, *Jubilate: Church Music in the Evangelical Tradition* (Carol Stream, IL: Hope Publishing, 1981), 230–33. See also Robin P. Harris "The Great Misconception: Why Music Is Not a Universal Language," ed. James R. Krabill, *Worship and Mission for the Global Church: An Ethnodoxology Handbook* (Pasadena, CA: William Carey Library, 2013), 82–89.

24. As an aside, the authors do not believe the idea of *musical* universals is particularly helpful when discussing the meaning of music. Here it seems better to point out a "universal" characteristic of world cultures around the world, a shared affinity for communal song.

25. Homer Rodeheaver to Aimee Semple McPherson, December 31, 1923, written on board the Kiangsu, enroute to Bangkok, Thailand. Rodeheaver quaintly addresses her as "My dear Mrs. McPherson," despite her 1921 divorce from Harold McPherson. Reprinted in *Bridal Call Foursquare*, April 1923, 23.

26. Aimee Semple McPherson, "The Lord's Doing in Angelus Temple," *Bridal Call Foursquare*, October 1923, 19.

27. See Priscilla Pope-Levison, *Building the Old Time Religion: Women Evangelists in the Progressive Era* (New York: New York University Press, 2014). The idea of a woman *evangelist* was less controversial than may be assumed, a point easily confirmed by a quick perusal of evangelical publications of the era, which frequently reported on women ministering as evangelists, Bible teachers, missionaries, and ministry leaders. This consensus approval should not be confused with evangelical views on women serving in *pastoral ministry*, a matter of ongoing controversy.

28. Helen Sunday interview with William McLoughlin, cited in *Billy Sunday Was His Real Name* (Chicago: University of Chicago Press, 1955), 287.

29. For an extended discussion of Rodeheaver's musical influence on McPherson, see Debra Lee Sonners Stewart, "Music in the Ministry of Evangelist Aimee Semple McPherson," (MA Thesis, California State University, 2006), 145–53, 154–63. The author also documents Rodeheaver's participation in McPherson's early hymnal projects, 217–18.

30. M. L. Stewart, "Angelus Temple of Los Angeles, California," *Bridal Call Foursquare*, August 1923, 21.

31. Homer Rodeheaver, *Twenty Years with Billy Sunday* (Nashville, TN: Cokesbury Press, 1936), 78.

32. "He Must Meet Requirements," *Santa Cruz (CA) Evening News*, June 29, 1926, 8. Rodeheaver seems to meet all of her qualifications except height; his passport listed him at 5 feet, 8½ inches tall.

33. "People," *Time Magazine*, February 24, 1930. The gossip item is written from Semple's point of view, reporting the rumor and then quoting Semple's denial, a distinct "yes, we have no bananas" approach.

34. Matthew Avery Sutton interview with Roberta McPherson Salter, March 16, 2004, Foursquare Heritage Archives. By the time of the rumored relationship, Salter was estranged from her mother and may not have been privy to the exact details of the situation.

35. "Aimee's Next?," *Fresno (CA) Bee*, June 22, 1935, 1.

36. "Homer Denies McPherson Reports," *Hammond (IN) Times*, June 25, 1935, 1.

37. "Homer Denies," 1.

38. Ned McIntosh, "Berlin, Damrosch and Toscanini Are All Forgotten When Brewster and Matthews Begin Fighting Ivories at the Sunday Meetings," *Atlanta Constitution*, November 5, 1917, 4.

39. "The First Jass Band," *Chicago Tribune*, October 19, 1916, 2. A social reformer, Swerling was investigating the club while accompanied by the wives of two Chicago aldermen. In the same article, he described the dancing as "an important aid to commercialized vice."

40. Ibid.

41. A newspaper stenographer transcribed Sunday's New York sermons; see William Darr, "The New York Sermons of Billy Sunday: A Stenographic Record," 21 vols. Papers of William A. and Helen Sunday, Morgan Library of Grace College and Theological Seminary, Winona Lake, Indiana.

42. Wilder Hobson, *American Jazz Music* (New York: W. W. Norton, 1939), 79–80. Interestingly, Hobson moonlighted as a jazz trombonist.

43. Kristen A. McGee discusses this in *Some Liked It Hot: Jazz Women in Film and Television, 1928–1959* (note), 27: "Cultural theorists and writers often inserted the term to elicit a sense of spontaneity and innovation—or conversely to connote something corrupt and contaminated."

44. "The First Jass Band," 2.

45. "Talks to the Pupils," *Wilkes-Barre (PA) Record*, February 27, 1913, 5.

46. "This Is Rodeheaver's Famous Trombone, Which Has Never Played Jazz Music," *Richmond (IN) Palladium-Item*, May 23, 1922, Revival Supplement, 1.

47. "Endeavorers in Big Parade," *Reading (PA) Times*, July 14, 1922, 4.

48. Charles H. Gabriel, *Rodeheaver Musical News*, n.d. (1921), 6. Gabriel's comments were part of a photo caption welcoming E. H. Forkel as the new manager of Rodeheaver Music Co.

49. Charles H. Gabriel, *Gospel Songs and Their Writers* (Chicago: Rodeheaver Co., 1915), 6. Gabriel also warned that ragtime "is extremely precarious for the amateur director to employ."

50. Homer Rodeheaver, *The Practical Song Director* (Chicago: Rodeheaver Music Co., 1925), 4.

51. "Rodeheaver Takes Heavy Swat at So-Called Jazz," *Dayton Herald*, July 23, 1923, 20.

52. Charles H. Gabriel, "Editorial," *The Gospel Choir*, February 1918, 4. At one point, Gabriel Jr. worked as managing editor for *The Gospel Choir*, writing a column about church music around the world. He later produced the first radio episodes of *Sam and Henry* that later became *Amos 'n' Andy*.

53. Tampa Blue Jazz Band (pseud. Joseph Samuel's Jazz Band), "Loose Feet," recorded in New York, January 1923, Okeh 4773, matrix S-71141, 78 r.p.m. See W. A. Firstenberger, "Inventory of Sunday Home," Winona History Center, Winona Lake, Indiana. See also his

discussion in W. A. Firstenberger, *In Rare Form: A Pictorial History of Baseball Evangelist Billy Sunday* (Iowa City: University of Iowa Press, 2005), 65–66.

54. "Lutherans Drop Two Noted Hymns," *New York Times*, October 17, 1928, 4.

55. Earl Enyeart Harper, *Church Music and Worship: A Program for the Church of To-day* (New York: Abington Press, 1924), 107–8.

56. Ibid., 108.

57. Talmage W. Dean, *A Survey of Twentieth Century Protestant Church Music in America* (Nashville, TN: Broadman Press, 1988), 75.

58. Ibid.

59. Ibid.

60. "Brighten the Corner Where You Are," Homer Rodeheaver vocal solo: Victor 17763-B (matrix 15855–1, recorded April 3, 1915); Columbia A-1990, (matrix 36352–2, recorded February 1916); Emerson 7158 (No mx recorded June 1916). As was common in the acoustic era, the actual recording speed varies from the "standard" of 78 r.p.m. (Rodeheaver always recorded the song in E-flat major, a helpful touchpoint when remastering the various versions of "Brighten.")

61. "Brighten the Corner" in Homer Rodeheaver and Charles Gabriel, eds. *Gospel Hymns and Songs* (Chicago: Rodeheaver Co., 1917), no. 22. For the most part, the tempo markings in this hymnal match the tempos of Rodeheaver's recorded performances of the same era.

62. Homer Rodeheaver, "A Billy Sunday Tribute," recording of a service at the Billy Sunday Tabernacle, August 8, 1953; reel-to-reel tape. Billy Graham Center Archives, Wheaton, Illinois.

63. Ella Fitzgerald, vocal solo, "Brighten the Corner" with Ralph Carmichael orchestra and chorus, 1967, Capitol ST 2685, stereo LP. Critics often describe this album—and the Capitol years in general—as the low point in Fitzgerald's recording legacy.

64. The Andrews Sisters, vocal trio, "Brighten the Corner" with Victor Young and Orchestra, recorded in Los Angeles, April 13, 1950, Decca 14539, 78 r.p.m.

65. For instance, the Statesmen Quartet sings "Brighten the Corner" at a brisk 140 b.p.m. on their RCA album *In Gospel Country* (1967).

66. Rodeheaver also published parlor songs that did not have religious themes, such as "My Mother," "A Rainbow on the Cloud," and "My Wonderful Dream." Other examples include Prohibition songs such as "Molly and the Baby" and patriotic songs such as "We're All Uncle Sam's Boys Now," "Columbia's Song," "It's My Flag Too," "The Colors That Will Not Run," and "Should the Stars in Your Service Flag Turn to Gold." Most of these were composed by Charles Gabriel.

67. "Moody and Sankey," *The Nation*, March 9, 1876, 157.

68. This is the essential point of Sandra S. Sizer (Tamar Frankiel), *Gospel Hymns and Social Religion: The Rhetoric of Nineteenth-Century Revivalism* (Philadelphia: Temple University Press, 1978).

69. Helen C. Alexander Maclean and J. Kennedy, *Charles Alexander, a Romance of Song and Soul Winning* (London: Marshall Brothers, 1920), 65.

70. His recorded output included "To My Son/Mother's Love" (Victor 17478), "Meet Mother in the Skies" (Vocalion 15309-B, Brunswick 2920-B), "Tell Mother I'll Be There"

(Brunswick 2920-A, Vocalion 15309-A), "My Mother" (a rejected Victor take), "Me and Pap and Mother" (Rainbow 1010-B.2, Gennett 4882), "The Mother's Love" (Rainbow 1057-B), "My Mother's Prayer" (Rainbow 1057-A); see Lewis, "Chronological Discography."

71. Lizzie DeArmond (words) and B. D. Ackley (music), "Mother's Prayers Have Followed Me," *Great Revival Hymns No. 2* (Chicago: Rodeheaver Music Co., 1913), hymn #129. Between 1913 and 1947, Rodeheaver recorded "Mother's Prayers" nine times for eight different labels; see Lewis, "Chronological Discography."

72. Homer A. Rodeheaver, *Worth While Poems* (Chicago: Rodeheaver Co., 1916); Homer Rodeheaver, *More Worthwhile Poems* (Chicago: Rodeheaver Co., 1929).

73. Homer Rodeheaver, *F'r Instance: A Collection of Jokes and Humorous Stories* (Winona Lake: Rodeheaver Hall-Mack Co., 1949).

74. Charles Gabriel, "Editorial," *The Gospel Choir*, February 1918, 4.

75. "Awakening Songs" (advertisement), *Rodeheaver's Musical News*, Spring 1918, 2.

76. Marvin McKissick, "The Function of Music in American Revivals since 1875," *The Hymn* 9:4 (October 1958), 115.

77. Peter W. Dykema, "Musical Aspects of the Community Music Movement" in *Music Teacher's National Association Proceedings* (Hartford, CT: Music Teacher's National Association, 1922), 56–57.

78. "That Little Chap O' Mine" in *Worth While Poems*, 45.

79. Homer Rodeheaver to M. B. Williams, October 9, 1939, Collection 330, Billy Graham Center Archives; quoting Milan B. Williams (words) and Charlie D. Tillman (music), "Mother's Prayers Have Followed Me," *Finest of the Wheat No. 2* (Chicago: R. R. McCabe & Co., 1894), hymn #84.

CHAPTER 10. FALLING OUT OF STEP AT THE CLOSE OF AN ERA

1. "Two Dead, 9 Hurt in Upstate Crash," *Indianapolis News*, August 3, 1940, 20; "Autoist Burns to Death after Highway Crash," *Chicago Tribune*, August 4, 1940, 16.

2. Ruthella Feaster Rodeheaver (second wife of J. N. Rodeheaver), handwritten memoir, 14. Rodeheaver family collection. Quoted with permission of Barbara Rodeheaver Fong and Thomas Rodeheaver.

3. When the Philadelphia office closed, the music editor C. Austin Miles retired after 43 years, to his Pitman, New Jersey home. Miles began working for the Hall-Mack Co., prior to the merger.

4. Karl Detzer, "Brighten the Corner," *Christian Herald*, April 1939, 16.

5. Though the SDA positioned itself as a Protestant Christian denomination, evangelicals questioned the SDA doctrine of soul sleep and the divine authority claimed by founder Ellen G. White. Rodeheaver's support of SDA musicians came at the same time the denomination's leaders were unsuccessfully trying to position their theology as consistently evangelical. See LeRoy E. Froom et al., *Seventh Day Adventists Answer Questions on Doctrine* (Washington, DC: Review and Herald Publishing Association, 1957).

6. Bert H. Wilhoit, "Personality Traits of Homer Rodeheaver," unpublished memoir given to Alan L. Disbro of Winona Lake, Indiana (September 19, 1991), Rodeheaver Collection at Morgan Library Archives and Special Collections, Grace College, Winona Lake, Indiana.

7. Bob Jones, *Cornbread and Caviar* (Greenville, SC: Bob Jones University Press, 1985), 97.

8. R. G. LeTourneau to Homer Rodeheaver, February 21, 1947, Rodeheaver Collection, Winona Lake.

9. Ibid.

10. Homer Rodeheaver to Helen Sunday, April 14, 1947, William "Billy" and Helen "Ma" Sunday Collection at Morgan Library Archives and Special Collections, Grace College, Winona Lake, Indiana.

11. Ibid.

12. "Directions for Announcers," memo from Walter Carlson to WMBI Winona Lake announcers, 1950, 2.

13. "Record Reviews," *Billboard*, May 6, 1950, 129.

14. "Directions for Announcers," 2.

15. For many references to their early relationship, see the ongoing correspondence between Billy Graham and Homer Rodeheaver, 1951–1955, Collection 580, Billy Graham Library Archives, Charlotte, North Carolina. Also note Rodeheaver's comments during "Hour of Decision Program #86" (a transcript of Rodeheaver leading songs at the 1953 Billy Graham Crusades in Detroit, Michigan), Collection 580, folder 234-22.

16. Torrey Johnson and Robert Cook, *Reaching Youth for Christ* (Chicago: Moody Press, 1944), 36.

17. Cliff and Billie Barrows were passing through Asheville by happenstance; they were scheduled to lead music at a Jack Shuler revival in nearby Statesville, North Carolina, June 20–July 2, 1945.

18. Cliff Barrows, interview by Douglas Yeo, April 1, 2014. Barrows frequently spoke of Rodeheaver's early influence. For additional details, see the Barrows interview by Lois Ferm, March 27, 2001, transcript in Billy Graham Library, Charlotte, North Carolina, Collection 141; the Barrows interview by Kerry Fox, October 10, 1992, transcript in BGL Collection 463. Several other oral histories in the BGL collection discuss Rodeheaver's influence. Also see Mark Jackson (son of Rev. Paul Jackson), interview by Kevin Mungons, September 25, 2012. Mark Jackson was four years younger than Barrows and inherited his First Baptist songleading job when Barrows left for college. Jackson also played trombone.

19. "Shuler-Barrows Revival Is Said Making History," *Statesville (NC) Record and Landmark*, June 26, 1945, 1. The Jack Shuler revival was just a few days after the Ashville meeting with Billy Graham.

20. The narrative details about Rodeheaver and Barrows in Winona Lake are summarized from several interviews: Cliff Barrows, interview by Douglas Yeo, April 1, 2014; Cliff Barrows, interview by Lois Ferm, March 27, 2001, transcript in BGL Collection 141; Cliff Barrows, interview by Kerry Fox, October 10, 1992, transcript in BGL Collection 463. See also Roy McKeown, interview by Lois Ferm, July 13, 1971, transcript in BGL Collection 141.

21. "YFC Leaders' Conference," *Youth for Christ*, July 1945, 10.

22. Homer Rodeheaver, *Twenty Years with Billy Sunday* (Nashville, TN: Cokesbury Press, 1936), 78.

23. J. Palmer Muntz to George Beverly Shea, June 24, 1947, Papers of George Beverly Shea, Collection 541, Billy Graham Center Archives, Wheaton, Illinois.

24. Gladys Priddy, "Vision Youth for Christ on World Scale," *Chicago Tribune*, July 27, 1945, 15. Apparently Rodeheaver caught the Youth for Christ organizers with pirated music more than once. For another incident in Boston, see John Abram Huffman Sr., transcript of interview by Bob Shuster, April 14, 1988, Billy Graham Center Archives, Collection 389.

25. By some coincidence, Rodeheaver's life intersected with two different Al Smiths. Alfred E. Smith was the governor of New York and 1928 presidential candidate. Alfred B. Smith founded Singspiration Music in 1941, a gospel music company and record label.

26. Cliff Barrows, ed., *Singing Youth for Christ* (Winona Lake: Rodeheaver Hall-Mack Co., 1950). Though this was the first YFC songbook project, Rodeheaver had previously printed music for the YFC Memorial Day event at Chicago's Soldier Field, May 30, 1945. See Douglas Fisher, ed., *Choral Selections: Chicagoland Youth for Christ* (Chicago: Rodeheaver Hall-Mack Co., 1945).

27. Shea always credited his mother for bringing Rhea F. Miller's poem to his attention; see George Beverly Shea, *Then Sings My Soul* (New York: Fleming H. Revell, 1968), 47–48; *How Sweet the Sound* (Wheaton: Tyndale House, 2004), 193–98. These accounts do not mention that Miller had already written music for her poem, which Shea had replaced with his own tune and then copyrighted. See the ongoing correspondence between George Beverly Shea and Homer Rhea F. Miller 1936–65: Shea Papers, BGCA Collection 541; and Rhea F. Miller Collection, Nazarene Archives, Lenexa, Kansas.

28. Homer Rodeheaver to George Beverly Shea, May 10, 1945, Shea Papers, BGCA Collection 541.

29. George W. Sanville to George Beverly Shea, September 13, 1946, Shea Papers, BGCA Collection 541. Shea had requested to use "In the Garden," which Sanville considered a fair swap for Rodeheaver's use of "I'd Rather Have Jesus."

30. George Beverly Shea to Rhea F. Miller, October 9, 1944, Shea Papers, BGCA Collection 541. As one indication of the song's early success, Shea sent more than $1,000 in royalties to Miller in 1944–45 (more than $13,000 today).

31. Shea to Sanville, September 26, 1946, Shea Papers, BGCA Collection 541, with Stanville's reply to Shea on September 30, 1946.

32. See the surviving radio script for the May 30, 1950, *Club Time* broadcast, Shea Papers, BGCA Collection 541.

33. W. C. Ling to George Beverly Shea, April 12, 1951, Shea Papers, BGCA Collection 541.

34. Chancel Music was incorporated on February 25, 1955, using Shea's home address in Western Springs, Illinois. Rhea F. Miller eventually sold Shea her copyright for the "I'd Rather Have Jesus" lyrics.

35. "Billy Graham Opens Series of Meetings," *Van Nuys (CA) News*, September 13, 1951, 43. Donald Hustad, organist for the Billy Graham team, made a similar comparison; see "Music in Today's Crusades," *Moody Monthly*, March 1963, 25–27, 82.

36. "Music by 'Wheel' Barrows," *Power*, April 7, 1946, a Sunday School magazine produced by Scripture Press. The standard Barrows bio dropped the cheerleader comparison after the mid-1950s, but for now, it sounded exactly like Rodeheaver's story. Perhaps this is only a coincidence, but the Billy Graham bios often mentioned his early aspirations to play professional baseball, remarkably similar to Billy Sunday's story.

NOTES TO CHAPTER 10

37. Bruce Howe, interview by Kevin Mungons, June 20, 2006, Winona Lake, Indiana. Howe expressed similar sentiments in an interview by Brent Wilcoxson and Bill Firstenberger, November 2, 1999, VHS, Rodeheaver Collection, Winona Lake.

38. For another recollection of her statements, see John Abram Huffman, interview by Bob Shuster, April 14, 1988, BGCA Collection 389.

39. The prayer meeting was "lost" in the sense that it is rarely mentioned in Graham's biographies. See Fred A. Hartley, *Everything by Prayer: Armin Gesswein's Keys to Spirit-Filled Living* (Camp Hill, PA: Christian Publications, Inc., 2003).

40. Cliff Barrows, ed., *Singing Evangelism: Billy Graham Campaign Songs* (Winona Lake, IN: Rodeheaver, Hall-Mack, 1950).

41. Rodeheaver's last appearance at a Graham/Barrows Crusade was likely a Nashville event September 3, 1954. Cliff Barrows, interview by Douglas Yeo, April 1, 2014.

42. "Hour of Decision Program #86" (a transcript of Rodeheaver leading songs at the 1953 Billy Graham Crusades in Detroit, Michigan), BGL Collection 580, folder 234-22.

43. Cliff Barrows, interview by Douglas Yeo, April 1, 2014.

44. William Hickey, "The Genie of the Golden Trombone," *Daily Express* (London), March 22, 1954, 6. See also Stanley High, *Billy Graham: The Personal Story of the Man, His Message, and His Mission* (New York: McGraw-Hill Books, 1956), 180.

45. John Pollock, *The Billy Graham Story*, revised and updated edition (Grand Rapids, MI: Zondervan, 2003), 71. This assessment was repeated by Donald Hustad, interview with Kevin Mungons, March 16, 2013.

46. Cliff Barrows emerges as an interesting figure for further study, though he never considered writing an autobiography and was famously reticent in interviews. His public philosophy of ministry was subsumed through his boss, the man he always called "Bill." Given his status as Rodeheaver's revivalist heir, Barrows merits more attention.

47. "Hour of Decision Program #86."

48. In 1942, Bob Jones College had given Rodeheaver an honorary doctorate in sacred music. See "Song Leader Honored," *Cincinnati Enquirer*, June 8, 1942, 16.

49. A subdivision in Melbourne Beach, Florida, still bears Homer Rodeheaver's name, with streets named Winona and Rody.

50. Harry E. Westbury to Thomas H. Porter, May 12, 1980. Cited in Thomas H. Porter, "Homer Alvin Rodeheaver: Evangelist, Musician and Publisher" (EdD diss., New Orleans Baptist Seminary, 1981), 55.

51. An undated home movie from the early 1940s shows this group on horseback at the Rainbow Ranch property. Rodeheaver Collection, Winona Lake.

52. "Rodeheaver Plans Florida Gospel Center," *Tampa Tribune*, August 15, 1949, 10.

53. Westbury to Porter, 55.

54. "The Proposed Boys Ranch," *Orlando Evening Star*, February 21, 1949, 4.

55. "Boys Swap Unhappy Past for Bright New Future," *Orlando Sentinel*, February 1, 1953, 56. See also William F. McDermott, "Rody and His Rainbows" *Christian Herald* (July 1952), 19-21.

56. "Boys Ranch Project Wins Florida Support," *Orlando Sentinel*, March 4, 1951, 37.

57. Billy Graham, *Just As I Am: The Autobiography of Billy Graham* (San Francisco: Harper Collins, 1997), 43. See also Lois Ferm, "Billy Graham in Florida," *Florida Historical Quarterly* 60 (October 1981), 174–185.

58. Boykin took Graham on a tour of his congressional district at the height of primary season, a visit that felt more like a campaign stop. Boykin later called President Eisenhower and suggested that Graham could subtly help with their campaign to slow down the civil rights movement.

59. Billy Graham to Homer Rodeheaver, April 24, 1953; Homer Rodeheaver to Billy Graham, May 7, 1953, BGL Collection 580, folder 234-22.

60. "Profit and Loss Statement" (1954–55), Rodeheaver Co., unpublished financial report, Rodeheaver Collection, Winona Lake.

61. "Million Is Paid for Rainbow Ranch," *Fort Myers News Press*, July 22, 1954, 10.

62. The foundation continued its support of gospel music preservation and education until James Thomas died in 1980, when the remaining trustee dissolved the foundation and directed most of the money to the Boys Ranch.

63. Bruce Howe, interview by Kevin Mungons, June 20, 2006, Winona Lake, Indiana. See also "Homer A. Rodeheaver Dies," *Warsaw Times-Union*, December 19, 1955, 1.

64. Cliff Barrows, interview by Douglas Yeo, April 1, 2014.

65. Virgil P. Brock (words) and Blanche Kerr Brock (music), "Beyond the Sunset," (Chicago: Rodeheaver Co., 1936; © 1936 Curb Word Music (ASCAP); all rights administered by WC Music Corp.).

66. The meeting occurred on December 10, 1955.

67. B. D. Ackley to George S. Schuler, February 18, 1955, Rodeheaver Collection, Winona Lake (replying to Schuler's letter of January 22, 1955, where Schuler had submitted several songs and asked for Ackley's opinion). B. D. Ackley died in 1958, the last living member of the original Sunday/Rodeheaver revival team.

68. "Word to Acquire Rodeheaver," *Billboard*, September 16, 1969, 88.

69. "30,000 Copyrights Backbone of Co." *Billboard*, October 14, 1972, W-3 (special section).

70. Bob Darden, "Word to Shutter Historic Indiana Distrib Facility," *Billboard*, September 5, 1987, 6, 70.

71. Roland Felts to Oswald J. Smith, November 7, 1969, Rodeheaver Collection, Winona Lake.

72. Earl Page, "Word Expansion Worldwide in Religious and Pop as Well," *Billboard Magazine*, September 7, 1974, 38.

73. "Royalties Received from Top Tunes Fiscal Year 1973–74," Rodeheaver Co., unpublished financial report, Rodeheaver Collection, Winona Lake.

74. Word constructed the 35,000-square-foot facility in 1970, creating warehouse space and moving the company offices from the Westminster Hotel. After the ABC purchase, the facility expanded in 1974 and 1984, eventually reaching 81,400 square feet.

75. Lu Ann Inman, interview by Kevin Mungons, January 11, 2020. As director of copyright and licensing for Warner Chappell Music, she had continued in her role through a long series of corporate transitions.

76. "Estate of James Thomas, Deceased," Public Auction Flyer, June 25, 1980.

77. Howe later donated many of these items to The Winona History Center.

78. "Word Acquires Shea Catalog," *Billboard*, December 18, 1982, 36.

79. Darden, "Word to Shutter," 70.

80. Summarized from ongoing coverage in *Billboard, Publishers Weekly*, and *New York Times*.

81. "Warner Music Group to Acquire Word Entertainment," press release, Warner Media, November 26, 2001.

82. According to Lu Ann Inman, Word Music now owned multiple song catalogs from all three Performance Rights Organizations: two BMI catalogs, two SESAC catalogs, and five ASCAP catalogs (including the Rodeheaver Co. and Chancel Music), a confusing situation that led to their consolidation.

83. Mark Geil, "Music in Recession," *Christianity Today*, June 2, 2009.

84. "Gaylord selling Word Entertainment for $84 million," *Nashville Post* November 26, 2001; David A. Fox, "Judgment Day for Thomas Nelson," *Nashville Post*, June 29, 2000.

85. Nielsen SoundScan began tracking point-of-sale data in 1991. Their initial efforts did not include information from Christian booksellers, a significant market that joined in 1995. See "Christian Albums Chart Gets SoundScan, Bookstores Data," *Billboard*, April 15, 1995, 4, 72.

86. Deborah Evans Price, "Industry Hopes Material & Spiritual Prosperity Will Continue After a Year of 'Remarkable Growth,'" *Billboard*, April 25, 1998, 37.

87. Charles M. Blow, "Swan Songs?," *New York Times*, July 31, 2009, A17.

88. Homer Rodeheaver, *Twenty Years*, 78.

CHAPTER 11. EPILOGUE

1. Rodeheaver was named to the Gospel Music Hall of Fame in 1973. Other Rodeheaver associates were inducted later, including George Bennard (1976), Charles Gabriel (1982), and B. D. Ackley (1991). With the ongoing "hall of fame" proliferation in American music, Rodeheaver was also named to the Southern Gospel Music Association Hall of Fame (2003) and the Christian Music Hall of Fame (2007).

2. Homer Rodeheaver, *Singing Down the Sawdust Trail: The Life Story of Homer A. Rodeheaver*, 6. Undated, unpublished manuscript with handwritten corrections by Rodeheaver, Rodeheaver Collection at Morgan Library Archives and Special Collections, Grace College, Winona Lake, Indiana.

3. Rodeheaver, *Singing Down the Sawdust Trail*, 4.

INDEX

Page numbers in italic refer to illustrations.

"Abide with Me," 153
"A Billy Sunday Tribute," 224
abolitionist movement, 40, 42, 188
Ackley, Alfred H., 139
Ackley, Bentley D.: ASCAP royalties, 111; business partnership with Rodeheaver, 62, 66–67, 70, 78, 91–92, 102, 231, 311n67; critique of new gospel songs, 245–47, 250; friendship with Rodeheaver, 82, 242; as pianist, *81*, 224; on power of music idea, 69–70; rift with Rodeheaver and Sunday, 80–82; on tempo of gospel songs, 224; Winona Lake home, 231
acoustical recording era, 118, 137, 145
Adam Geibel Music Co, 107
"Address to Negroes of America," 158
African Americans. *See* Blacks and Black culture
"A Glad Way Home," 153
A Group of Unusual Negro Spirituals for Choirs and Large Chorus Work, 175
Alexander, Charles, 55–57, 65–67, 69, 77–78, 104, 211, 225, 272n29
All-Day Singings, 4, 153–54
"All Hail the Power," 102

All-Night Sings, 4, 154
"Amazing Grace," 5
"America," 21, 103, 118
American Broadcasting Corporation, 237, 247–49
American Dialect Society, 183
American Missionary Association, 26
American Red Cross, 118
American Society of Composers, Authors, and Publishers (ASCAP), 104–5, 109–11, 238
Ames Quartet, 159
AME Zion Church (Chicago), 188
Amoynese (Xiamenese language), 215
Andrews Sisters, 224
Angelou, Maya, 184
Angelus Temple (Los Angeles), 217–19
Anti-Saloon League, 134
AOL Time Warner, 249
Arizona State University, 6
Armory Park (Toledo), 65–66
Armstrong, John, 41
Asher, Virginia: as a Bible teacher, 31, 80, 218; duets with Rodeheaver, 31, *31*, 86, 118, 122, *122*, 151, 161, 171, 203–4, 300n49
Atlanta Colored Music Festival, 18
"Atlanta Compromise," 20

Atlanta Constitution, 14, 16–17, 29, 34
Atlanta Cotton States and International Exposition, 19
Atlanta Georgian, 22
Atlanta Independent, 14, 190
Atlanta revival campaign (1917), 13–37, 67, 158, 171, 179, 183, 190, 212, 263n1, 264n21
Atlanta University, 26
Atlantic Monthly, 83
"'Aum,' the Sacred Hum of the Universe," 159
Awakening Songs, 28, 103, 200

Bacon, Alice Mabel, 178
Baldwin pianos, 118–19
Baptists, 26, 108, 233
Barrows, Cliff: appearances with Rodeheaver, 139, 163, 239–40; and Billy Graham, 234–36, 239, 246, 308n17; at Rodeheaver's funeral, 245; as a songleader, 139, 163, 235–37; as trombone player, 50, 234–35, 240–41
Bashford, Erma May, 155
Bateman, Walter J., 50
"Battle Hymn of the Republic," 204
Beddoe, Dan, 145
Bellows, George, 84–85, *84*
Bell Telephone Laboratories, 162
Benson, John T., 104
Berle, Milton, 131, 188
Bethel African Methodist Episcopal Church (Columbia, South Carolina), 173
Bethel Jubilee Quartet (Wiseman), 176
"Beyond the Sunset," 245, 248
Bible Institute Colportage Co., 98, 280n50
Biederwolf, William E.: with J. Wilbur Chapman, 54, 56; and denominational cooperation, 233; early meetings with Rodeheaver, 53, 60; evangelistic tours with Rodeheaver, 54–55, 61–63, 73, 270n77; friendship with Billy Sunday, 63; and Interdenominational Association of Evangelists, 54, 75–76; as a model for Billy Sunday, 66; report on Rodeheaver and Georgia Jay, 76; and Rodeheaver hymnals, 54–55, 62, 66; "Simultaneous Campaigns," 56; vaudeville complaints about, 86; and Winona Lake, 54, 56, 61, 112; world tour with Rodeheaver, 88, 210–12
Biglow & Main Co., 97–98, 101, 104
Bilhorn, George, 62
Bilhorn, Peter P., 62, 91–92
Bilhorn Brothers Music Co., 62

Bilhorn-Fischer hymnal, 62
Bilhorn Folding Organ, 62
Billboard, 234, 247, 249
Billy Graham Center Museum of Evangelism, 6
Billy Sunday campaigns with Homer Rodeheaver: Atlanta (1917), 13–37, 67, 158, 171, 179, 183, 190, 212, 263n1, 264n21; Boston (1916), 16–17, 67, 86, 100, 190; Cincinnati (1921), 150–51, 215; Columbia (South Carolina, 1923), 173, 176, 197; Los Angeles (1917), 13, 64; Mt. Holly (New Jersey, 1930), 90, 125; New York (1917), 35, 67, 100, 118, 190; Philadelphia (1915), 56, 67, 77–80, 83–86, 171, 190, 271n6; Richmond (Virginia, 1919), 190–93; Richmond (Indiana, 1922), 122, *122*, 196; Tampa (1919), 197, 217–18; Toledo (1911), 6, 65–67, 69, 83, 262n11, 271n6
"Billy Sunday Songs," 114
"Billy Sunday's Successful Songs," 47
Billy Sunday Story, The, 141, 286n95
Billy Sunday Was His Real Name, 140
Birth of a Nation, The, 21, 141
blaccent, 186
Black churches: in Atlanta, 19–21; in Chicago, 188; choirs, 13, 21, 34; clergy, 19–23, 26, 191–93; hymnals, 4, 24, 36, 103–4, 171–73; in Richmond, Virginia, 191–93; and segregated revival meetings, 14, 190–93; use of Dr. Watts hymns, 21, 23; use of *Gospel Pearls*, 4, 23–24, 36–37, 104, 173; use of gospel songs, 24, 36; use of spirituals, 24–25, 183, 213, 293n35. *See also* names of churches; names of individual clergy
blackface: as "good" and "bad" forms, 186–89, 296n99; in Hollywood films, 188; and minstrelsy, 167–70, 179–82, 297n106; Rodeheaver performances in, 9, 46, 139, 165–66, 179, *187*, 253, 296n96
Black gospel (as a genre), 2, 4–5, 14; Chicago publishers of, 201, 205; golden era of, 4–5, 132; in *Gospel Pearls*, 4, 23–24, 36–37, 103–4, 173; its liturgical function (testimony), 36; performance groups, 132, 245. *See also* gospel songs, *names of individual songs*
Blacks and Black culture: characterizations of music, 4, 9, 11, 24, 26, 30, 32, 167–68; criticisms of blackface, 169, 185, 187–88; and jazz, 220–24; in Jellico, Tennessee, 38, 50–51, *166*,

INDEX

167; racial categories in music, 4–5, 8, 30, 36, 110, 159–60, 176, 252; and ragtime, 220–23; recordings with Rodeheaver, 9, 27, 30, 117, 158, 163, 174, 175–78, 186, 202; Rodeheaver's employment of, 173–75, 178, 183; Rodeheaver's relationship with, 9, 18, 22, 34, 46, 165–66, 166, 171–74, 179–82, 188–89, 209, 253; in Rodeheaver's youth, 39–40, 50–51, 166; Sunday's relationship with, 17–21, 190–92, 195–98. *See also* blackface; dialect; Fisk Jubilee Singers; Ku Klux Klan; minstrelsy; race and racism; spirituals; slaves and slavery; *names of specific ensembles and individuals*

Blackwood Brothers, 156, 164

Blanchard, Charles, 193–94

Bland, James A., 193

"Blest Be the Tie That Binds," 199

Bliss, Philip P., 42

Blue Amberol cylinders, 116–17

"Blue Bells of Scotland," 49

blues: as a music category, 8, 96, 159–60, 167–68, 216; played by Thomas Dorsey, 23; recordings for Rodeheaver Special label, 206–7

Bob Jones College (Bob Jones University), 235, 242, 310n48

"Booze Sermon," 28, 79, 180

Boston Red Sox, 197

Boston revival campaign (1916), 16–17, 67, 86, 100, 190

Boston Symphony Orchestra, 6, 49

Boston University, 45, 155

Boykin, Frank, 243–44, 311n58

Boy Scouts, 195, 205

Boys Town (Omaha, Nebraska), 243

Brewster, George Ashley, 14–15, 21, 23, 30–32, 114–15, 118, 192, 220

"Brighten the Corner Where You Are": as a cheer-up song, 72, 126; compared to ragtime, 73, 220–23; in foreign languages, 215–16, 216; in *Gospel Pearls*, 24; in *Great Revival Hymns No. 2*, 70; lack of theology, 30, 73; and Ina Duley Ogdon, 69, 111; as a Rodeheaver hit song, 69–71, 70, 85, 93; Rodeheaver recordings of, 117, 281n6; as a Rodeheaver trombone solo, 30, 138; tempo of, 223–24

"The Bright Fiery Cross," 9, 195, 199–200, 204, 207

"Bring Them In," 91

Bronfman, Edgar, 249

Brooklyn Dodgers, 46

Brooks, Tim, 157

Brown, John Mason, 169

Brown, Oscar, Jr., 184

Brumbaugh, Martin, 78

Brunswick-Balke-Collender Co. (records), 118

Bryan, Texas, 75

Bryant, Anita, 224

Buck, Dudley, 52

"Bull Moose," 135

Bull Run, 40

Bunny, Bugs, 188

Burleigh, Harry T., 18, 32, 173, 177, 184

Burmese, 215

"Butterfly Kisses," 192

cakewalks, 73, 167, 220

Calumet Sociability Hour, 124–25

Calumet Sociability Hour (radio program), 124–25

Calumet Steel Fence Post Co., 124

Camden, New Jersey, 116

Camden Post-Telegram, 82

Campbell, Lucie, 37

Campbell County, 38, 51, 269n66

Campfire Girls, 124

Candler, Asa G., 243

Cantonese-Bangkok (language), 215

Cantor, Eddie, 187

Capital City Communications, 248

"Capital of Evangelicalism," 98

Carlile, Wilson, 50

Carlisle, Bob, 250

Carlson, Walter, 234, 240

"Carry Me Back to Old Virginny," 192, 300n42

"Casey Jones," 203

Cavalieri, Lina, 185

Celebration Hymnal, The, 249

Champion Records (Gennett), 118

Chancel Music Co., 239, 248, 309n34

Chapman, J. Wilbur, 53–54, 56, 63, 65, 75, 144, 233

Chapman-Alexander Simultaneous Campaign, 77

Chappell & Co. 97

Chautauqua movement, 16, 33, 48, 50, 60, 126, 133, 170, 225, 278n10

315

INDEX

cheer-up songs, 72, 126
Chicago as "Capital of Evangelicalism," 98
Chicago Coliseum, 58
Chicago Concert Co., 126
Chicago Daily News, 75
Chicago Defender, 188, 196, 198
Chicago Fire of 1871, 28, 93
Chicago Gospel Tabernacle, 123, 219
Chicago Mercantile Exchange, 124
Chicago Tribune, 49, 59, 75–76, 193, 220
Chicago YMCA, 62
Chinese-Canton (language), 215
Chinese-Mandarin (language), *216*
Chinese-Swatow (language), 215
Chopin, Frédéric, 181
Christian Church (Disciples of Christ), 203
Christian Cynosure, 193, 298n18
Christian record label, 146–49, 250
Christian Service Songs, 103
Christian Worker's Magazine, 101
Christmas Carol Sing, 124, 135
"The Church in the Wildwood," 153
Church Music Publishers Association (CMPA), 106–10, *109*, 280n49
Church of the Open Door (Los Angeles), 139
Cincinnati revival campaign (1921), 150–51, 215
Civil War, 37–38, 40, 52, 167, 197, 226
Clarke, Edward, 201
Clark University (Atlanta), 21
classical music, 252
Claxtonola Records (Brenard Manufacturing Co.), 118
Cleveland Naps, 66
Club Time Aluminum Choral Singers, 237–38
code switching, 185
Cohan, George M., 87
Cokesbury Hymnal, 108
Coleman, Robert H., 107–8, *109*
Columbia (South Carolina) revival campaign (1923), 173, 176, 197
Columbia Records: community sing records, 150–52; financial losses, 146; negotiations with Rodeheaver, 162; patent dispute with Victor, 145; personal label, 157–58; recording artists, 132, 134; recording technology change, 162; Rodeheaver recordings, 117, 147, 171, 176

"Come, Thou Fount of Every Blessing," 15, 21
Come On, Let's Sing (radio program), *129*, 130, *131*
"Come to Jesus," 184
commercial spirituals, 167, 170, 183
communal singing (revivalism): and Charles Alexander, 55–57, 65–67, 69, 77–78, 104, 211, 225; and Cliff Barrows, 139, 163, 235–37, 240; and commercial recordings, 152–53; contrasted with performance music, 4, 132, 245–46; on film, 133–41; and Ku Klux Klan, 198–201; on radio, 123–27, 130–31, *131*; on records, 146–47, 152–54, 162; repertoire of, 3, 99; in revivals, 57, 129, 223, 239; Rodeheaver's "power of music" and, 11; Rodeheaver's view of, 11, 80, 133, 164, 217, 255; of spirituals, 150, 173–74; and technology, 113–16; and Youth for Christ, 234–35. *See also* community singing movement; songleader
community singing movement: Peter Dykema and, 152, 228–29; in England, 153; on film, 133–36, 158; and Ku Klux Klan, 198–201; positive benefits of, 152; and "power of music," 228; and progressive era music education, 53, 152–53, 228–29; on radio, 130; on Rainbow Records, 152–53; and Rodeheaver, 136, 227. *See also* communal singing (revivalism)
Concert Quartet Book, 153–54
concert spirituals, 167–71, 188
Confederacy, 20, 38, 197
congregational singing. *See* communal singing (revivalism)
Conn, C. G., 49, 119
Conqueror Records (Sears, Roebuck and Co.), 118
Cook, Bob, 234
coon songs, 167–68, 170, 180, 220
copyright law: and ASCAP, 109–11; authorship as a legal concept, 97; copyright infringements, 96–97, 237; Copyright Law of 1909, 93–97, 200, 204; copyright trading in hymnal business, 91–92, 100, 103, 107–8, 237–38; parody songs, 96; record company interpretation of, 238–39. *See also* mechanical license
"Couldn't Hear Nobody Pray," 144, 153
Cowan, Lynn, 134

INDEX

Crawford, Joan, 188
Criterion Quartet, 200–201, 204
Crosby, Bing, 188, 297n105
Crosby, Fanny, 95
Crumit, Frank, 130
cultivated music, 52, 220. *See also* vernacular music
cultural hegemony, 217
cultural imperialism, 217
Curb Records, 249
Curtis JN-4 biplane, 120
Cusic, Don, 154

Daily Express, 240
"Dandy Darkies." *See* "Delaware's Dandy Darkies"
Darr, Bill, 2
Davis, Jefferson, 181
Dean, Talmadge, 223
"De Brewer's Big Hosses Can't Run Over Me," 133–34, 180, *181*, 209
Decca Faith Series, 224
Decca Record, 118, 224
"De Gospel Pass," 170
"Delaware's Dandy Darkies," 46, 52, 179, 187
delegation system, 78–80, 117, 195, 197
Democratic National Committee, 133
DeRee, Alvia Otis, *195*, 199–200, 204, 207, 300n46, 300n48, 302n302
Detroit Tigers, 66
Devotional Melodies, 105
dialect: Black attitudes toward, 32, 183–86; in literature, 183; in music, 25, 32, 169, 177–78, 180–85, *181*; in Rodeheaver jokes, stories, 179–82, 183–85, 187; in Rodeheaver's *Old Black Sam*, 181; as a term, 295n81; in "When Malindy Sings" (film), 184–86, *187*. *See also* Paul Laurence Dunbar; "When Malindy Sings"
Diamond Discs (Edison Records), 29, 116–17, 145
"Dixie," 197
Dolan, Regina, 178
"Don't Leave Me, Daddy," 17
Dorsey, Thomas A., 23–24, 36–37, 103, 188, 251, 264n21
Douglas, Charles Winfred, 128–29
Douglass, Frederick, 188, 296n102
"Down by the Riverside," 172

"Drink to Me Only with Thine Eyes," 152
Dr. Watts hymns, 21, 23
"Dry Bones: The Old Ark's A' Movering," 177
Du Bois, W. E. B.: agnostic beliefs, 26; on Black dialect, 184; friendships with, 32, 35; on gospel songs, 26; on race relations, 19–20; relationship to Atlanta pastors, 20, 26; on spirituals, 21–22, 25–27, 178; T. H. Wiseman letters, 173–74, 176, 178
Dunbar, Paul Laurence: coon songs of, 183–84; critical reaction to, 32, 184–85; dialect poetry, 183–85, 295n; recordings of poetry, 170–71, 184–86, 187. *See also* "When Malindy Sings"
Dye, Gertrude Ackley, 248
Dykema, Peter, 152, 228–29

Ebenezer Baptist Church (Atlanta), 21–23, 36–37
Edison, Thomas, 145–46
Edison cylinders, 116, 141
Edison Records, 116–17, 145–46, 156, 170
Egyptian, 215
Eliot, T. S., 128, 283n45
Elks (Benevolent and Protective Order of), 79, 194
Elmer Gantry, 89
Emerson Records, 117
England's Church Army, 50
Erdman, Charles R., 137
Erwin, Horace, 50
Evangelical Publishing Co, 98
Excell, Edwin O.: business model, 62, 97, 107; and money-making altruism, 112; recordings of, 30, 117; Rodeheaver's relationship with, 91, 97–98, 100–101, 107; song catalog, 55, 62, 69, 97
eye dialect, 184

Famous Hymns, 62
Favorite Songs, 91
Federal Reserve Bank, 146
Federolff, Rose, 80
Felts, Roland, 247, 250
Fenley, William H., 82
Fessmire, Lloyd, 234
Fields, Arthur, 176
Fiery Cross, 9, *195*, 197, 199–200, 202–3, *202*, 204, 207

INDEX

Fifteenth Presbyterian Church (Washington, DC), 198
"Fight, Ames, Fight," 159
Fillmore, Charles M., 225
Fillmore, Henry, 47, 222, 268n41
Fillmore Brothers, 47, 222
film (as a medium): Rodeheaver's use of, 9, 34, 99, 111, 133–41, 164, 187, 208; Billy Sunday's skepticism of, 113, 127; vaudeville use of, 33. *See also* Rodeheaver films
First Baptist Church (Ceres, California), 235
First Congregational Church (Atlanta), 18
Firstenberger, Bill, 222
First Methodist Church (Mishawaka, Indiana), 127
First Methodist Church (Warsaw, Indiana), 209
First Ward Ball (Chicago), 58
Fischer, Fred G., 60–62, 92
Fisher, William Arms, 173
Fisk Jubilee Singers: critical assessment of, 26, 169, 178; recordings of spirituals, 170, 177; Rodeheaver recordings of, 150–51, 177–78; tours by, 168–69, 188, 211; "When Malindy Sings" recording, 184
Fisk University, 150–51
Flanagan, Father Edward J., 243
Florida Bible Institute, 234, 243
"Flow Gently, Sweet Afton," 152
Foley, Red, 224
folklorists, 8–9, 36
folk music and folk songs, 8–9, 18, 27, 36, 50, 183
folk spirituals, 166, 170, 178
Fong, Barbara Rodeheaver (grand-niece), 260
Football Association Challenge Cup, 153
Ford, Tennessee Ernie, 224
Forgotten Depression of 1921, 146
"The Forty-Sixth Psalm," 52
Foster, Stephen, 134, 178, 181
4H Clubs, 79
Fourth Volunteer Regiment Band, 47
Fowler, C. Lewis, 196
Fowler, Wally, 4, 154
Fox Movietone, 134–36
Franconia (Rodeheaver home), 68
Frankel, Harry, 130
Frankenberg, Theodore T., 210, 212

Fraternalist, 197
Fray, Cordell, 138
Frazier, E. Franklin, 170
Freed, Leigh B., 163
Freemasons, 79, 194, 275n80, 275n81
Friends of Seika, 215
F'r Instance: A Collection of Jokes and Humorous Stories, 180, 226
"From Greenland's Icy Mountains," 199
Frost, John D., 194
functional art, 26
fundamentalists, 10, 233, 245

Gabriel, Charles H.: arrangements of spirituals, 24–25, 27, 171; and "Brighten the Corner," 69–72, 70; collaboration with Ina Duley Ogdon, 67, 69; commercial spirituals of, 183; communal singing views, 69–70, 99; comparisons to ragtime and parlor songs, 220–23, 226, 305n49; dialect songs of, 180–83; financial arrangement with Rodeheaver, 67, 81, 95, 100; and "His Eye Is on the Sparrow," 24; and "Old Black Sam," 181–82; reputation of, 24; as Rodeheaver Co. employee, 100; temperance songs of, 180; tempos of gospel songs, 223–24
Gabriel, Charles H., Jr., 305n52
Garrison, William Lloyd, 188
Gates, Henry Louis, 175
Gaylord Entertainment, 249
General Electric Co., 162
Gennett Record Co., 118, 145, 159, 162, 176–77, 201–2, 205
genre formation, 1–5, 8, 29–30, 35–37, 105
genteel tradition, 225
Gilbert, Paul J., 54
Gill, Albert P., 65
Gillette Original Community Sing, The, 131
Gillingham, L. E., 150–51, 156–57, 302n67
"Give the World a Smile," 126
Glad Tidings Publishing Co., 98
Glenwood Ave. Christian Church (Buffalo), 203
"The Glory Song," 71
"God Bless America," 11
"God Knows We're Here to Stay," 203
"God Save the King," 103
Gospel Choir, 125, 151, 156

Gospel Hymns and Sacred Songs (Sankey), 101
Gospel Hymns and Songs (Rodeheaver), 101, 224
Gospel Hymns 1–6 (Sankey), 55
gospel hymns, 3–4, 26, 185, 261n6. See gospel songs
gospel music: and authenticity, 8, 25–27, 36; and "bridge the gap" philosophy, 67, 126, 223, 236, 250; commercial aspects of, 7–9, 28–29, 91–97, 113–15, 235–36; devotional aspects of, 53, 72–73, 96, 111, 226–27, 252; as a functional art, 26; racial segregation and, 8–10; as testimony 10, 27, 36, 225. *See also* Black gospel; northern gospel; southern gospel
Gospel Pearls, 4, 23–24, 36–37, 103–4, 173
Gospel Song Evangelistic Movement, 58, 69, 78, 212
Gospel Song Evangelistic Movement (1908), 58–59, 78
Gospel Songs (Sankey), 28
gospel songs: in Black church worship, 24, 36; cheer up songs, 69–72, 126; criticism of, 28, 72–73, 220–22; critiqued by W. E. B. Du Bois, 26; defined by Rodeheaver, 3, 27, 72; demonstrated on phonographs, 7, 152–53; history of, 3–5, 42, 55–57, 105; jazz influence on, 3, 15, 73, 115, 133, 213–16, 220–23; in mass singing, 68–69; in missionary endeavors, 210–17; "modernism type" (performance music), 245–46; as parlor songs, 224–26, 229; power of music, 11–12, 126, 217, 227–29; ragtime influence on, 3, 15, 213, 220–23; and sentimentalism, 128, 178, 225–29; singability of, 71, 245–46, 284n53; tempo of, 32, 223–24; theological aspects of, 3, 10–11, 73, 233, 226–27; universal appeal of, 14, 202–3, 217; in urban revivalism, 58–90. *See also* gospel music, *names of individual songs and performers*
Grace College and Seminary (Winona Lake), 2, 244
Graham, Billy: business with Rodeheaver, 236–37, 240, 243; compared to Billy Sunday, 239–41; evangelistic team, 163, 234–35, 246; friendship with Rodeheaver, 139, 234–36, 236, 240; and Rodeheaver Boy's Ranch, 243; Rodeheaver support of crusades, 240–41; Youth for Christ and, 235–37, 239. *See also* Cliff Barrows; George Beverly Shea
Graham, Ruth Bell, 244
gramophone, 128, 141, 283n45
Grand Old Opry, 249
Grange (National Grange of the Order of Patrons of Husbandry), 79
"Great Is Thy Faithfulness," 101
Great Revival Hymns, 66
Great Revival Hymns No. 2, 71–72, 85, 103
Green, Oscar W., 158
Griffith, D. W., 21
Grimké, Francis J., 35, 198
Group of Unusual Negro Spirituals for Choirs, A, 175
Grove's Dictionary of Music and Musicians, 3–4
Gullah (dialect), 182

"Hail to the King," 54
Hall, Frederick Douglass, 22, 174, 188
Hall, J. Lincoln, 100
Hall, Wendell, 131
"Hallelujah" (from *Messiah*), 186, 222
"Hallelujah Trombone," 222
Hall-Mack Co., 100, 105, 107, 110. *See also* Rodeheaver Hall-Mack Co.
Hammontree, Homer, 89
Hampton Institute (Virginia), 178
"Hand Down De Robe," 170
Hanley, Frank, 60
"Happy darkey" myth, 170–71, 185, 192–93
"Hard Trials," 176, 293n53
Harlem Renaissance, 34, 173, 182, 184
Harper, Earl, 129, 223
Harringay Arena (London), 240
Harrison, James A., 183
Hawaiian music, 212
Hay, Florence, 143, 210
"Heab'n," 25, 31, 171
heart balm suits, 73–76
"Heav'n," 32, 186
"He Lifted Me," 24
Heller, Eddie, 149
"Help Somebody Today," 72
Henderson, Myrtle, 54–55
Herbert, John B., 55, 63, 171, 173, 180, *181*
Herwin Records, 118
Higginson, Thomas Wentworth, 169
"Higher Ground," 24

INDEX

hillbilly music: as an influence in Rodeheaver's childhood, 9, 166; as a music category, 4, 8, 36, 73, 110, 160, 252
Hillside (Rodeheaver home), 68
"His Eye Is on the Sparrow," 5–6, 24
Hitchcock, John M., 59
Hit-the-Trail Holliday, 87
Hobson, Wilder, 221
Hoffman, Elisha, 91
Hogan, Ernest, 220
Holbrook, Harold F., 50
Holiday Inn, 188
Holland, John, 124
"Home, Sweet Home," 199
Homer Rodeheaver in Community Singing (film), 134
Honore, Lockwood, 76
Hoover, Herbert, 134–35, 284n61
Hoover, J. Edgar, 240
Hope Publishing, 98, 106–7, 110
Hour of Decision, 243
Howe, Bruce, 82, 104, 135, 163, 230, 239, 242, 245, 247–49
Huntinghouse Dancing Academy (Chicago), 159
Hutton, David, 219
hymnal business: copyright trades, 91–93, 100, 103, 107–8, 237–38; and denominational control, 7, 28, 147; importance to Chicago commerce, 98; major companies listed, 98; pricing agreements, 107–8; on Printer's Row (Chicago), 98–102, 231; trade organization for, 106–8; typesetting for, 7, 92, 98, 106; as vertical integration, 7, 92, 97
hymnals, orchestrated, 103
hymnals, shape note, 5, 28, 103, 153, 279n35
Hymns for His Praise, 54
Hymns for His Praise No. 2, 54–55, 62–63
Hymns of His Grace No. 1, 62

"I Do, Don't You?," 23
"I'd Rather Have Jesus," 237–39, 248
"I Draws De Line Right Dar," 180
"If Your Heart Keeps Right," 29, 72, 101, 116
"I Have a Dream," 37
"I Know the Lord," 104
Iliff School of Theology (Denver), 155, 206
"I'm Always Chasing Rainbows," 126

Imperial Player Roll Co., 115
"In Christ There Is No East or West," 37
Inman, Lu Ann, 248
Interdenominational Association of Evangelists, 54, 63, 75
International Holiness Union and Prayer League, 213
International Music Co., 202, 203, 301n60
International Sacred Recordings, 213–14
Inter Ocean, 59
Inter-State Manufacturing Co., 43
"In the Garden," 5, 100, 106, 138, 248
"In the Service of the King," 72
Iowa Soldier's Orphans Home, 226
"I Walk with the King," 116, 171
Ives, Burl, 224

Jackson, George Pullen, 8–9, 262n18
Jackson, Mahalia, 24, 251
Jackson, Rev. Paul, 235
Jackson, Stonewall, 197
Jackson College Jubilee Singers, 165, 174, 176–77
Jackson State College (Mississippi), 22
James D. Vaughan Publishing Co., 164
James D. Vaughan School of Music, 145
Janis, Elsie, 130
Japanese (language), 215, 216
Jay, Georgia, 16, 69, 73–77, 74, 111, 125, 274n73
Jay, Laura, 73–74, 76–77
jazz music: compared to blues, 23; as a corrupting influence, 213; criticism of, 73, 305n43; gospel music compared to, 3, 115, 160–61, 220–24, 237; as a music category, 96, 159–60, 167–68, 211–12, 216–17; recorded by Rodeheaver Records, 206–7; Rodeheaver's view of, 133, 147, 160; in Billy Sunday's record cabinet, 141, 222
Jazz Singer, The, 134
Jellico (Tennessee): and Blacks, 38, 51, 166; coal mines, 43, 51; Kimberly Lumber Company, 53; lynchings, 51, 167; Methodist Church, 125; railroads, 38, 39, 42–43, 51; Rodeheaver Brothers Lumber Company, 51; Rodeheaver home, 51, 269n66; Rodeheaver Manufacturing Company band, 38–39, 39; Yumbert Rodeheaver music store, 39, 51, 94, 99; town band, 38–39, 39
Jemison, David Herbert, 268n44

INDEX

Jenkins, Lourana, 40
"Jesus Is All the World to Me," 222
J. Heath & Co, 159
Jim Crow: influence on record industry, 8; and Rodeheaver's silence, 167; Billy Sunday's segregated meetings, 14, 19, 190–93; and Billy Sunday's silence, 34–35, 84. *See also* Ku Klux Klan; race and racism
J. M. Henson Music Co, 164
Johnson, James Weldon, 32, 169, 173, 177, 184
Johnson, John Rosamond, 173
Johnson, Torrey, 129
Johnston, C. R., 156
Jolson, Al, 16–17, 126, 187
Jones, Charles Price, 37, 103
Jones, Bob, Jr., 82, 233
Joplin, Scott, 220
J. O. Prescott, 162
Joss, Addie, 66
Jubilee Songs, 145 172, 182–83
jubilee-style spirituals, 36. *See also* concert spirituals
"Just as I Am," 199
"Just Outside the Door," 145

Kane, Thomas, 112
Kansas Forward Movement, 60
Kaufman, Irving, 130
Kavanaugh, Thomas, 115
KDKA, 121, 282n19
"Keep Movin'," 170
"Keep the Home Fires Burning," 97
Kenfield, Leroy S., 49
Kim, Perry, 8
Kimberly Lumber Co., 51, 53
King, Alberta Williams, 23, 37
King, Martin Luther, Jr., 23, 37
King, Martin Luther, Sr., 23, 36–37
Kingsbury, Francis G., 106
Kings Mountain Coal Co., 51
Kinney, Florence, 122, *122*
Kirkpatrick, William J., 100, 105
Kiwanis International, 79
Kladd (Klan songleader), 199
"The Klansman and the Rain," 203
Knight, Vic, 130
Knights of Columbus, 79
Knights of Pythias, 79
Knoxville & Ohio Railroad, 38, 43

Korean (language), 215, *216*
Kramer, Worth, 175
Ku Klux Klan: in *Birth of a Nation*, 21; in Chicago, *191*, 193–94; finances of, 201; in Indiana, 20, 197, 201, 207, 302n69; opposition from religious leaders, 193–98; recordings by, 201–4; relationship to local pastors, 193–94; Rodeheaver and Sunday attitudes toward, 20, 194–98, 204–7; Rodeheaver recordings of, 165, 202–7, *202*, *204*, *204*; songs of, 96, 141, 198–203, *204*, 300n42; and Stone Mountain (Georgia), 20, 37, 264n16; use of "The Old Rugged Cross," 9, 96, 165, *195*, 198–204, *202*, *204*, *204*, 207; veneer of respectability, 21, 200, 207; visitations at Sunday meetings, 79, 194–97, 299n26
Kurtz, Ada Turner, 132
KYW, 122–23

Lakeside Building (Chicago), 97–98, 100
Lake Swan Bible Conference (Melrose, Florida), 243
Lamont, Jean, 80
Lancaster Camp Ground (Lancaster, Ohio), 44, *front cover*, 59
Lanier University, 196
"Lassus Trombone," 47, 222, 268n41
Lemon Hill summer conference, 56, 60, 77–78, 132
LeTourneau, Robert G., 233, 236
Lewis, David N., 6, 150
Liberator, The, 188
"Lift Every Voice and Sing," 158, 175
Lillenas, Haldor, 109
Lincoln, Abbey, 184
Lions Clubs, 79
Little Brown Church of the Air, 124
"Little David, Play on Your Harp," 177
Long, Edwin M., 64
"Loose Feet," 222
"Lord, I Can't Stay Away," 177
"The Lord's Prayer" (song), 37, 169
Loren, Sophia, 188
Los Angeles revival campaign (1917), 13, 64
Lorenz, Karl, 109
Lorenz Publishing Co., 107, 110
Los Angeles Times, 137
Lost Cause (southern narrative), 192, 197

INDEX

Lost Prayer Meeting (Winona Lake), 239, 310n39
Loudy, Adlai, 144–45, 153
Louisville & Nashville Railroad, 38, 42
"Love's Old Sweet Song," 134
"The Loyal Boosters," 159
lynching, 51, 167, 198
Lyon & Healy Co., 49, 98, 115

MacDonald, John S., 161–62
Machen, J. Gresham, 72–73
Mack, Irvin H., 100, 109
Mantia, Simone, 30, 49
Martin, Frederick, 145
Martin and Morris Music Co., 201
Martin Band Instrument Co., 159
Maryville College, 57
Mason, Lowell, 3, 42, 55, 147
Masons. *See* Freemasons
Matthews, Bob, 14–15, 21, 23, 30–32, 118, 122, 122, 151, 173, 192
Maulan Aerodrome (France), 120
Mayflower, 41
McCallie Military Academy (Chattanooga), 120
McClurg Building (Chicago), 102, 156, 206
McCracken, Jarrell, 247–48
McIntosh, Ned, 15, 21–22, 31–32
McKendree Centre Chapel Methodist Episcopal Church (Hocking County, Ohio), 40
McLoughlin, William G., Jr., 82, 140
McPherson, Aimee Semple: and gospel songs beliefs, 218; marriages, 218–19; relationship with Rodeheaver, 125, 217–19; Billy Sunday conflict, 125, 218
McPherson, Harold, 218
McRae, Carmen, 24
"Me and Pap and Mother," 306n70
mechanical license (recordings): compulsory, 96, 277n6; and Copyright Law of 1909, 94–96; and Ku Klux Klan, 204. *See also* copyright law
"Meet Mother in the Skies," 306n70
Meier, Audrey, 138
"The Menace of Mechanical Music," 128
Mendelssohn Male Quartet, 126
Meredith, Isaac H., 109
Merrill, Lynn D., 119, 120–21, 155–56

Messiah (by Handel), 215, 222
Methodist Book Concern (Chicago), 67, 100, 149
Methodist Episcopal Church (denomination), 40, 52, 108, 173, 296n102
Methodist Episcopal Church South (denomination), 108
Methodist Hymnal (1935), 107–8
Methodists, 26, 42, 56, 105, 125, 127, 150–51, 173, 176, 193, 208–9, 232–33, 241–42
Metropolitan Opera, 49, 145
Meyer & Brother, 98
Miles, C. Austin, 110, 307n3
Miller, Frances, 80
Miller, Mitch, 138
Miller, Polk, 176
Miller, Rhea F., 237–38, 309n27, 309n30, 309n34
Mills Brothers, 224
minstrelsy: contrast to spirituals, 168–70, 182; development of, 167–68; dialect in, 182–86; influence on Rodeheaver, 179–81, 183, 192; offensive nature of, 187–88, 193, 268n41; as popular entertainment, 32, 224–25, 268n41; Branch Rickey and, 46, 179; Rodeheaver minstrel shows, 46, 179. *See also* blackface
Miracles through Song: "Heartaches" (film), 139
Miracles through Song: "Somebody Cares" (film), 139
Miracles through Song: "When Malindy Sings" (film), 186–87, 187, 296n97
Modesto High School (California), 235
"Molly and the Baby," 133, 306n66
"Money-Making Altruism," 112, 175
Monon Building (Chicago), 93, 100, 102, 156
Montgomery Ward Records, 118
Moody, Dwight L., 28, 42, 53, 55–56, 60, 87, 97, 211, 214, 239
Moody Bible Institute (Chicago), 31, 53, 58, 73, 79, 203, 213, 235, 273n48
Moody-Sankey campaign, 77–78
Moore, Arthur J., 208–9, 243
Moore, Grace, 51–52, 270n69
Moravian trombone choirs, 213, 303n8
Morehouse College, 18, 22
More Worthwhile Poems, 226
Morgan, G. Campbell, 121
Morris Brown College, 18

INDEX

Morton, Jelly Roll, 177, 206
"The Mother's Love," 306n70
mother songs and poems: in revival meetings, 225–26; in Rodeheaver poetry books, 226; Rodeheaver's memories of his mother, 44, 185. *See also names of individual songs and poems*
"Mother's Prayers Have Followed Me," 29, 116, 226, 306n70, 307n71
Mount Memorial building (Rodeheaver property), 154
movies. *See* film; Rodeheaver films
Movietone News, 134–35
Mt. Holly (New Jersey) revival campaign (1930), 90, 125
Muntz, J. Palmer, 140, 236
Musical America, 73
musical universals, 217, 304n24
Music Trade Review, 97, 115
"My Country, 'Tis of Thee," 14
Myers, James A., 184–85
Myers, Mrs. James, 177
"My Mother," 306n66, 306n70
"My Mother's Bible," 229
"My Mother's Prayer," 306n70
"My Old Kentucky Home," 49, 199
"The Mystic City," 201

NAACP, 26, 35, 188
Nakada, Juji, 213–15
Nakada, Ugo, 214–15, *214*
National Association for the Advancement of Colored People (NAACP), 26, 35, 188
National Baptist Convention U.S.A, 103–4
National Baptist Hymnal, 23
National Broadcaster's League, 137
National Christmas Carol Sing, The (radio program), 124
"National Negro Hymn" ("Lift Every Voice"), 175
National Singing Convention, 155
Native American music, 212
Nazarene Publishing House, 108
NBC, 125, 131
Negro Church in America, The, 170
Negro English, 183
Negro Songs, 176, 183
Negro Spirituals (1923), 173
Negro Spirituals and Folk Songs (1939), 175, 185

Negro spirituals. *See* spirituals
Neighborly Songs and Poems (radio program), 126, 283nn37–38
Ness, Ted, 50, 234
Newcomb (Tennessee), 38–39, 43, 45, 51, 166
Newcomb Manufacturing Co., 51
New Jersey Liquor Dealers Association, 82
New Orleans Rhythm Kings, 177
New South, 17–18, 37
New York revival campaign (1917), 35, 67, 100, 118, 190
New York Times, 2, 28, 82, 87, 118, 123, 130, 137, 223
New York Tribune, 87
nigger, niggah (as a racist term), 47, 50, 180–82, 268n41, 295n78. *See also* N-word
Nightingale, Florence, 156
"The Ninety and Nine," 117
Norcross, Marvin, 247
Northern Baptist Seminary (Chicago), 207, 231
northern gospel. *See* white gospel
North New Ireland (language), 215
No True Scotsman argument, 8
novelty songs, 130–31, 180
N-word (euphemism), 182
Nyland, Einar, 8

Ocean Grove Camp Meeting (New Jersey), 105
Odd Fellows, 23, 79, 194
Odell, Joseph H., 83
Ogden, William, 91
Ogdon, Ina Duley, 67, 69, 70, 111
Ogikubo Eikou Kyoukai (Tokyo church), 215
Oh Brother, Where Art Thou, 250
Ohio Wesleyan Transcript, 52
Ohio Wesleyan University, 45–47, 46, 48, 52, 55, 155, 179
Ohio Wesleyan University Cadet Band, 46, 48
Okeh Phonograph Corp., 118, 159, 162
"O Kunde Jag Förtälja," 158
Old Black Sam: A Vision of Slavery Days, 181, 187
"The Old-Fashioned Faith," 116
"The Old Fiery Cross," 199–200, 203, *202*
"Old Folks at Home," 134
Old Fourth Ward (Atlanta), 17, 19

INDEX

"The Old Klansman's Home," 199
"The Old Rugged Cross": and Klan music, 9, 96, 195, 198–200; and Klan recordings, 202–7, *202*, *204*; Rodeheaver copyright of, 104–5, 249, 300n47; as a Rodeheaver hit song, 101, 118, 238, 247–48
Oliver, Jessie, 176
100% Americans (Klan quartet), 201, 300n49
166th Aero Squadron, 120
"Onward, Valiant Klansmen," 199
"Onward Christian Klansmen," 199
"Onward Christian Soldiers," 199
"Onward Ku Klux Klansmen," 199
Orchestra Hall (Chicago), 227
Oriental Mission Society, 214
Original Dixieland Jazz Band, 220
Orlando Evening Star, 243
"O That Will Be Glory," 69

Palmolive Community Sing (radio program), 130, *131*
Panic of 1907, 62
Paramount Records (New York Recording Laboratories), 118, 145, 150, 159, 176, 202, 206–7
parlor songs, 133, 224–26, 229
Patrick Conway's Band, 49
Paul Whiteman Orchestra, 221
Peale, Norman Vincent, 243
Peniel Baptist Church (Palatka, Florida), 243
pentecostalism, 27, 218
Pentecostal Revivalist, The, 218
performance rights, 94, 109, 111
Person, Carrie Booker, 37, 103
Peterson, Albert, 122, *122*
Philadelphia Orchestra, 49
Philadelphia revival campaign (1915), 56, 67, 77–80, 83–86, 171, 190, 271n6
Phil Kerr Harmony Chorus, 138
Phillips, Philip, 65, 211
piano rolls, 29, 94, 114–16, 141, 147, 201
Piano Row (Chicago), 92, 98, 102, 114–15, 206
Pike, Gustavus D., 169, 171–72
Plantation Melodies, 25, 171–73, *172*, 183
plantation spectacle, 170, 186
power of music, 11–12, 127, 217, 227–29, 255
Prairie Farmer, 123
"Praise God from Whom All Blessings Flow," 58
Praise Publishing Co., 100

Prayer Revival of 1858–59 (Philadelphia), 77
"Prepare Ye the Way of the Lord," 54
presentism, 10, 188
Presley, Elvis, 5
Printers' Row (Chicago), 92, 98, 100, 102, 231
Proctor, Henry Hugh, 18–19, 22, 25, 27, 32, 34, 158
Progressive party, 135
Prohibition songs, 133, 180, *181*, 185, 227, 249
Protestant Council of New York City, 245
Protestant denominations, 27, 42, 56, 77–78, 86, 213–15, 223, 232–33, 274n75, 307n5
Protestants: and doctrine, 2, 73, 87, 113, 168, 232–33; and gospel songs, 3, 6, 42, 103, 223; Billy Graham coalition of, 245; and Ku Klux Klan, 20–21, 193–94, 207; missionary outreach, 213; and racial attitudes, 187; and radio, 126; and Rodeheaver hymnals, 102–3, 108; and self-identity, 10; Billy Sunday coalition of, 22, 60, 162
Pryor, Arthur, 30, 49
psalms, hymns, and spiritual songs, 168, 291n8

race and racism: Black minstrel performers and, 167–70; condemnations of N-word, 182, 295n78; Harlem Renaissance and, 34–35; in Jellico, Tennessee, 167; lynching, 51, 167, 198; racial categories in music, 8, 36, 110, 252; racial separation and Booker T. Washington, 19–20; Rodeheaver's silence on, 167; and segregated revival meetings, 14, 190–93; stereotypes in minstrelsy, 168–71; stereotypes in prohibition songs, 180–81; Billy Sunday's silence on, 17, 19, 21, 34–35, 190–93, 197–98. *See also* blackface; Blacks and Black culture; Ku Klux Klan; minstrelsy; slaves and slavery
race music, 8, 36, 110, 252
Rader, Paul, 123, 219, 282n22
radio: and ASCAP, 109–11, 238; and Christian programming, 123; and communal singing, 124, 127, 130–32, 164; and Copyright Law of 1909, 94; negative critiques, 128–30, 141, 162; and Rodeheaver beginnings in, 122, *122*, 124–25; and Rodeheaver recordings, 136–37; Rodeheaver's view of, 99, 123; Rodeheaver's voice and trombone, 129, 132–34; Sunday's view of, 113, 122–23. *See also* Rodeheaver radio programs

324

INDEX

ragtime music: as a category of music, 73, 167, 211–12, 216, 220; as a corrupting influence, 213; and Henry Fillmore, 222, 268n41; gospel songs compared to, 3, 15, 220–24, 226, 237; Billy Sunday's view of, 221
rainbow (trope), 126, 148
Rainbow Point (Rodeheaver home), 121, 135, 210, 230–31, *231*, 242, 245, 248, 253
Rainbow Point with Homer Rodeheaver (radio program), 131
Rainbow Quartet, 145
Rainbow Ranch (Palatka, Florida), 242–44
Rainbow Recording Corporation (Eddie Heller), 149
Rainbow Records: advertising, *119, 149, 151, 158, 204*; and Black groups, 9, 104, 170, 174, *174*, 176–77; competition with other labels, 160–62; and diversity of artists, 8, 158–59; establishment of, 146–49, 163; Klan recordings with, 201–7, *202, 204*; marketing of, *119*, 120–21, *149*, 151, 152–53, 155, *158*, 159, 240; mission of, 96, 142, 161–62; recording engineers, 151, 163; recording studios for, 102, 143, 154, 156; Rodeheaver recordings with, *148, 149*, 176–77, 215; Special label recordings, 157–59, *158*, 202–7, *202, 204*; and Vaughan Records, 144–45, 150
Rainbow Sacred Records (variant name), 148–49
Rainbow Shining Somewhere (film), 138
Ratcliff, Thomas P., 152–53, 157, 289n42
Rayner, Dalheim & Co, 201, 205
RCA Photophone (film), 136–37
Reading Times, 55
Record of Christian Work, 66
Red Cross, 118
Reed, John, 83–86
Reisenweber's Cafe (New York), 220
"Rescue the Perishing," 93
Restoration Movement churches, 108
Revival Hymns, 62, 66
revivalism: compared to vaudeville, 7, 16–17, 33, 86–88; gospel songs and, 59, 69–73, *70*; Billy Graham and, 235, 239–41, 246; and jazz, 220–23; and Ku Klux Klan, 194–98; legacy of, 5–6, 139; Rodeheaver pivot from tabernacle model of, 3, 9, 88–90, 112, 117–18, 146; tabernacle era's decline, 88–90, 112; tabernacle model of, 10, 63–65, 117, 150;

technology impact on, 122. *See also* Protestants; *names of individual revivalists*
Rhodes, Lulu R., 34
Richmond (Indiana) revival campaign (1922), 122, *122*, 196
Richmond (Virginia) revival campaign (1919), 190–93
Richmond Planet, 191–93
Rickey, Branch, 46, 179
Riley, James Whitcomb, 183
Robinson, Jackie, 46, 179
"Rock of Ages," 184
Rodeheaver, Elizabeth "Bettie" P. (stepmother): children, 16, 68, *68*; death, 128; death of son, Jack, 119–21; marriage to Thurman Rodeheaver, 68; as Rodeheaver property manager, 68, 154, 210
Rodeheaver, Erma May Bashford (sister-in-law), 155
Rodeheaver, Frances "Fannie" C. (mother): death, 44, 225, 243; friendship with African Americans, 18, 40, 166; marriage to Thurman Rodeheaver, 40, 43, *43*; mother of Homer Rodeheaver, 42, 44–45, 185, 229, 243
Rodeheaver, Hamon (uncle), 43
Rodeheaver, Homer: appearance fees, 89–90; attitude toward Blacks, 9, 18, 22, 34, 46, 165–66, *166*, 171, 173–74, 179–80, 182, 188–89, 209, 253; as an author, 28, 127, 138, 180, 207–9, 226, 254, 283n41; death, 209, 245; "early adopter" of technology, 7, 10, 37, 113; early meetings with Sunday, 60–61; education, 45–48, *46*, 52–53, 156, 268n44; family origins, 38–42, *41*; fascination with world languages, 215–17, *216*; on gospel music as a congregational idiom, 3, 9–10, 14, 23, 36–37, 99, 132, 284n53; magic tricks, *front cover*, 16, 59, 61, 86; Masonic memberships, 79, 274n80; money-making altruism, 111–12, 175; music as "universal language," 14, 212–13, 214, 216–17; new gospel songs, 28–29, 42, 63, 66–67, 70–73, 78, 96, 101–2, 237, 245; poetry recitations, 126, 171, 185, 226; "power of music," 11–12, 14, 28–29, 67, 72, 126–27, 161, 173, 213, 215, 217, 227–29, 255; as a public speaker, 46; Rainbow Point home (Winona Lake), 121, 135, 210, 230–31, *231*, 242, 245, 248, 253; relationship with brothers, 42, 44, 67, *68*, 99, 155, 231–32, 287n4;

325

Rodeheaver, Homer (*continued*): relationship with Sunday, 1, 27, 124–25, 127; and the Roosevelts, 135–36, *136*, 285n74; as a songwriter, 50, 54, 135, 181–82, 270n78; Spanish American War, 16, 268n39, 285n74; on spirituals as a congregational idiom, 25–26, 150, 173–74; tour to Africa, 49, 127, 207–9, *208*; tribute to the Confederacy, 197; view of inter-faith cooperation, 27–29, 107–8, 232–33; vocal characteristics, 133; voice teachers, 132–33; wealth and philanthropy, 27, 112, 233, 235, 241–44; and women, 55, 73–77, 119, 125, 217–19; as the "World's Greatest Songleader," 228, 234, 254; world tour, 49, 63, 88, 121, 125, 206–7, 210–16, *211*, *214*, *216*; WWI tour of France, 49, 88, 120, 135, 182. *See also* Billy Graham; Ku Klux Klan; minstrelsy; Rainbow records; Rodeheaver films; Rodeheaver Music Co.; Rodeheaver radio programs; Rodeheaver Record Co.; songleader; spirituals; Billy Sunday; Billy Sunday campaigns with Homer Rodeheaver; Helen Sunday; trombone and Rodeheaver; *individual song titles*

Rodeheaver, Isaiah (brother), 42

Rodeheaver, Jackson "Jack" (half-brother): airplane accident and death, *119*, 120–21, 155–56; early years, 16, 68, *68*; future with Rodeheaver Co., 155; relationship with Homer Rodeheaver, 111

Rodeheaver, John Jenkins (uncle): business ventures with Thurman Rodeheaver, 41–43, 51; as church leader, 39, 41–42; Civil War service, 40

Rodeheaver, Joseph Newton (brother): care of Homer Rodeheaver, 44; education, 45, 57, 155; grandchildren (Thomas, Barbara), 260; relationship with Blacks, 166, 188; relationship with brothers, 42, 44, 67, 68, 99, 155, 231–32, 287n4; role with Rodeheaver Company, 105, 155, 231; role with Rodeheaver Record Co., 206–7; teaching positions, 155, 206–7, 231; travel with Homer, 125, 210; wives, 125, 155, 231, 268n42

Rodeheaver, Ruthella Feaster (sister-in-law): assessment of Rodeheaver's Chicago office, 230–31; recollections of Henry Fillmore, 268n42; travel with Homer Rodeheaver, 125

Rodeheaver, Thomas (grand-nephew), 260

Rodeheaver, Thurman Hall (father): brothers, 40–41, 43, 51; business ventures, 41–43, 51, 68; Civil War service, 40, 266n7; death, 40, 52; marriages, 40, 43, 68; views on education, 45

Rodeheaver, Yumbert Parks: auto accident, 119–20, 230; and Church Music Publishers Association, 106–8, *109*; decline and death, 42, 230; early business ventures, 51–52, 94; managing partner in Rodeheaver Co., 67, 80, 99–100, *109*, 111, 155, 206; musical pursuits, 39, *39*, 44, 47, 51, 94; relationship with brothers, 42, 44, 67, *68*, 99, 155, 231–32, 287n4

Rodeheaver Auditorium (Bob Jones University), 242

Rodeheaver Boys Ranch (Palatka, Florida), 138, 244

Rodeheaver Brothers Lumber Co., 51

Rodeheaver Co.: in Chicago, 93, 98, 100, 102, 114, 230; closure of Winona Lake offices, 248–49; corporate acquisitions, 105–7; hymn publishing, 28, 108, 218, 237, 240; market share, 110–11; move to Winona Lake, 230–31; ownership share of Homer Rodeheaver, 244; in Philadelphia, 100, 230; publishing mission, 99, 206; radio program sponsorship, 123; Rodeheaver-Ackley Co. (first corporate name), 62, 66–67, 80–82, 97, 102; Rodeheaver Hall-Mack Co. (final corporate name), 104–6, 138, 247; sale to Word Music, 1–2, 247. *See also* ASCAP; Church Music Publishers Association; Ku Klux Klan; Rodeheaver Record Co.; *names of individual family members*

Rodeheaver films: African trip, *208*, *209*; Fox Movietone, 134–36; *Homer Rodeheaver in Community Singing*, *134*; *Miracles through Song: "Heartaches,"* 139; *Miracles through Song: "Somebody Cares,"* 139; *Miracles through Song: "When Malindy Sings,"* 186–87, *187*, 296n97; *Rainbow Shining Somewhere*, 138; RCA Photophone, 136–37; *The Sidewalks of New York*, 133–36; *Then Jesus Came*, 138; *Twenty Years with Billy Sunday*, 139–41; Westminster Films, 138–41

Rodeheaver Hall-Mack Co. *See* Rodeheaver Co.

Rodeheaver Manufacturing Co., 38, 43

Rodeheaver Music Co. *See* Rodeheaver Co.

INDEX

Rodeheaver radio programs: *Calumet Sociability Hour*, 124–25; *Come On, Let's Sing*, 129, 130, 131; *The National Christmas Carol Sing*, 124; *Neighborly Songs and Poems*, 126, 283nn37–38; *Palmolive Community Sing*, 130, 131; *Rainbow Point with Homer Rodeheaver*, 131; *Rodeheaver Sings*, 114, 125–26; *Worth While Poems*, 126
Rodeheaver Record Co. (as parent company), 143, 148, 156, 206–7
Rodeheaver School of Sacred Music, 244
Rodeheaver Sings (radio program), 114, 125–26
Rodeheaver's Musical News, 147
Roosevelt, Eleanor, 136, *136*, 285n74
Roosevelt, Franklin D., 135–36
Roosevelt, Theodore, 94, 135, 285n69
Root & Cady Co., 93
Rosen, Eleanor H., 159
Rotary International, 79
Rothenhoeffer, Hans David, 40
Ruebush, Ephraim, 5
Runyan, William M., 101–2

Sacred Harp, The, 5
Saenger, Oscar, 133, 155
"Safe in the Arms of Jesus," 143, *148*
"Sail On," 118
Saltar, Sam, 50
Salter, Roberta Semple, 219, 305n34
Sandburg, Carl, 85
Sankey, Ira D.: and Biglow & Main (New York), 97; and Chicago World's Columbian Exposition (1893), 220; compared to Rodeheaver and Cliff Barrows, 239; and *Gospel Hymns 1–6*, 55; and *Gospel Songs*, 28; as a gospel song writer, 3, 42, 97, 225; influence on Rodeheaver, 71–72; musical partner to D. L. Moody, 42, 77–78, 211; Rodeheaver recordings of, 117; as a song-leader and soloist, 53, 65
Sanville, George, 105, 108–11, *109*, 231, 238, 242
sawdust trail, 16, 28, 64, 66, 84, 90, 93, 219, 241
Saxe, Grace, 80, 125, 128, 143, 210, 218, 287n4
"School Days," 159
School of Sacred Music, 232, 244
School of Sacred Music. *See* Song Director's Conference (Winona Lake)
Schuler, George S., 245
Scoville, Charles Reign, 98

Seagle, Oscar, 132
Sears, Roebuck & Co., 123
secret societies, 79, 193–94
Seika no Tomo, 215
Seventh Day Adventist, 232–33, 307n5
shape note hymnals, 5, 28, 103, 153, 279n35
Shea, George Beverly, 163, 235–40, 246, 248, 290n70, 309n27, 309n30, 309n34
Shiller Cafe (Chicago), 220
Shillito's Department Store (Cincinnati), 151, *151*
Shorney, Herbert, 109
"Shoutin' Liza Trombone," 222
Shreveport Journal, 198
Shriners (Ancient Arabic Order of the Nobles of the Mystic Shrine), 79
Siamese (language), 215
Simco Hollow, Ohio, 41
"The Sidewalks of New York," 133–36
Sidewalks of New York, The (film), 133–36
Silvertone Records (Sears, Roebuck, and Co.), 118
Simmons, William J., 20, 196, 201
Simultaneous Campaigns, 56, 60, 77
Sinatra, Frank, 188
"Since Jesus Came into My Heart," 24, 214
Sing Along with Mitch (television show), 138
Singing Black, 27, 31, 36, 207–9
Singing Evangelism: Billy Graham Campaign Songs, 240
Singing Youth for Christ, 237, 240
"Sing Me a Song of Iowa State," 159
Sing Songs of the Southland, Vol. 1–3, 175
Singspiration Record Co., 163
Sixty-Two Southland Spirituals, 175
Skipwith, William H., 192
slavery, 38, 40, 167, 169–70, 176–77, 181, 192, 207
slaves and slavery: in Jellico, Tennessee, 38; myth of happy slaves, 181, 192–93; and Rodeheaver family, 40; as source of the spirituals (Rodeheaver's view), 173, 207–9; Year of Jubilee (biblical reference), 291n10
Slave Songs of the United States, 168–69, 171, 177–78, 182–83, 291n9
Smith, Alfred B. (publisher), 163, 237
Smith, Alfred E. (politician), 133–36
Smith-Spring-Holmes Orchestra, *143*
Sociability Songs for Community, Home, School, 124

INDEX

"Some of These Days," 171,
Song Director's Conference (Winona Lake), 142, 144–45, 151, 153–56, 206–7, 212, 232–34
songleader: Charles Alexander as, 55–57, 65–67, 69, 77–78, 104, 211, 225; in Ku Klux Klan meetings, 199; D. L. Moody's use of, 53; Rodeheaver as, *front cover*, 1, 6, 32, 35, 48, 52–53, 57, 59; Rodeheaver's Uncle John as, 41–42; Rodeheaver training next generation of, 212–15, 214, 227; and the trombone, 30, 50, 132. *See also* communal singing (revivalism); Song Director's Conference (Winona Lake); *names of individual songleaders*
"Song of the Sunbeams," 72
Songrecord piano rolls, 115
Songs for Service, 100–101
Songs of the Great Salvation, 101
Souls of Black Folk, The, 26
Soundscan technology, 249–50
Sousa, John Philip, 49, 128
South before the War, 170
Southern, Eileen, 11
Southern Baptists, 108, 243
southern gospel: as a genre, 2, 4–5, 14; golden era of, 4–5, 132; music publishers, 164; performers, 224, 251; recordings of, 4, 132; Rodeheaver's view of, 14; and James D. Vaughan, 4. *See also* gospel songs; *names of individual songs*
southern music, 8, 36, 252
Southland Spirituals, 175, 208
South Loop (Chicago), 230
souvenir sales (revival tabernacle), 27–28, 92
Spanish-American War, 47, 176, 285n74
Special label (Rodeheaver Records Co.), 157–59, *158*, 202–7, *202*, *204*. *See also* Rainbow Records
A Special Selection of Revival Hymns in Japanese, 215
special tabernacle edition (of hymnals), 28, 103
Spelman College (Atlanta), 18
spirituals: authenticity debate, 8, 25, 32, 37, 150, 168, 177–79, 183–84, 262n16; commercial spirituals, 167, 170, 183; compared with minstrelsy, 167–69, 184, 188; concert spirituals, 167, 170; dialect in, 32, 182–85; folk spirituals, 166, 170, 178; in Gospel Pearls, 4, 23, 103–4, 173; meaning of, 22, 26–27, 169–70, 2929n19; origin of, 8–9, 167–68, 173, 207–9; plantation spectacle (faux spirituals), 170, 181, 183; preservation of, 24; Rodeheaver performances of, 31, 117, 133, 171, 208; Rodeheaver publications of, 24–27, 25, 165, 171–75, *172*, 183, 185; Rodeheaver recordings of, 22, 171, 174, 176–78, 186, 205; in Rodeheaver's childhood, 18, 39–40, 50, 166, 168, 171; Rodeheaver view of, 31, 36, 50, 150, 166, 168, 174, 189, 252; stylistic controversies, 25–26, 178, 185, 212; as worship music, 24, 32, 173. *See also* Blacks and Black Culture; Fisk Jubilee Singers; Wiseman Sextet; *names of individual spirituals*
Stamps, Virgil O., 145
Stamps Quartet, 126, 164
Standard Publishing Co., 108
Standard Quartet, 170
Starr Piano Co., 145
"The Star-Spangled Banner," 254
Statesmen Quartet, 164, 306n65
"Steal Away," 144, 153
Steger Building (Chicago), 102
Stephenson, David C., 20, 207
Stover, F. R., 79–80
Straight, Charlie, 115
Stuart, Jeb, 197
Studebaker Theater (Chicago), 177
"The Stuttering Klansman," 203
substitutionary atonement (theology), 3, 113, 233
Sunday, Billy: accusations of Klan membership, 196–97; and B. D. Ackley, 80–82; ambivalence about film, 134–38, 285n78; ambivalence about radio, 113, 122–23, 282n22; comparison to Billy Graham, 239, 309n36; and Blacks, 17–18, 180; criticism of, 82–86, 84, 180, 198; and decline of tabernacle revivalism, 87–90; dress and deportment, 15, 33, 65, 89; as an early fundamentalist, 10; early meetings with Rodeheaver, 60–61; ethical questions, 75–76; final campaign with Rodeheaver, 90; financial arrangement with Rodeheaver, 63, 92; financial model, 16, 27, 71, 83; and Fred G. Fischer, 61; and Klan offerings, 194–97, 205,

299n26; and Aimee Semple McPherson, 217–18; and media, 14, 78; offerings, 66, 68, 85, 118; personal wealth, 66, 68, 83, 140; and prohibition, 180, *181*; relationship with Rodeheaver, 1, 27, 124–25, 127; relationship with W. E. Biederwolf, 63, 75–76; revival team (Sunday party), 13, 28, 78–80, 82, 88, 103, 122, 125, 275n84; sermons, 14, 65, 180, 228; silence on Jim Crow, 17, 19, 21, 34–35, 190–93, 197–98; souvenir stands, 27–28, 63, 67, 92, 204; special meetings for Blacks, 17, 20, 34; tabernacles, 19, 37, 63–65, 80, 116, 118, 224; as "vaudeville revivalist," 16, 86–87, 113; view of ragtime and jazz, 221, 222. *See also* Billy Sunday campaigns with Homer Rodeheaver; Helen Sunday; *names of coworkers*

Sunday, Billy, Jr., 68, 119
Sunday, George, 80
Sunday, Helen: as gatekeeper for Billy Sunday, 83, 88–89, 125, 127, 140, 283n41, 286n93, 299n26; relationship with Rodeheaver, 89, 125, 127, 135, 137, 233, 235; role in Sunday Party, 34, 79; view of Ku Klux Klan, 190, 193–94, 299n26. *See also* Billy Sunday campaigns with Homer Rodeheaver
Sunday School Board of the Methodist Episcopal South, 108
Sunday School songs: of William Bradbury, 3; in Hall-Mack catalog, 105; of William J. Kirkpatrick, 100; in Rodeheaver's childhood, 44; "Sunday School circuit" (vaudeville), 87
Sunday School Times, 66
Sutton, Allan, 118
Swerling, Joseph, 220–21
"Swing Low, Sweet Chariot," 21, 169, 184
Syracuse Herald, 143

Tabernacle Publishing Co., 98, 107
Tagalog (language), 215
"Take My Hand, Precious Lord," 23–24, 199
talkie films, 134, 138, 141, 162
Talking Machine World, 116, 152, 156, 159–60
Talley, Joe, 50
Tampa Bay Casino, 197
Tampa Blue Jazz Band, 222
Tampa revival campaign (1919), 197, 217–18

Tampa Times, 218
"Tell Mother I'll Be There," 225, 306n70
temperance movement, 42, 195, 264n12
temperance songs, 55, 180, *181*
tempo of gospel songs, 223–24
Tenyo Maru, 88
Tharpe, Sister Rosetta, 24
"That Little Chap 'O Mine," 228
"Then I'll Take Off My Mask," 203
"Then Jesus Came," 240
Then Jesus Came (film), 138
"There's a Rainbow Round My Shoulder," 126
"There's a Rainbow Shining Somewhere," 114, 126
Thind, Bhagat Singh, 159
Thomas, James, 128, 231, 247–48
Thomas, Ruth Rodeheaver (half-sister): early years, 16, 68, *68*; education, 155; hostess for Homer Rodeheaver, 231; musical pursuits with Homer Rodeheaver, 117, 142, *148*, 155; sale of Rodeheaver Hall-Mack Co., 247; wife of James Thomas, 128, 231, 246
Thomas Nelson Co., 249
Thompson, William Hale, 123
"Throw Out the Lifeline," 93
Tidwell, Mark J., 266n3
Tigner, Marcy, 50
Time (magazine), 49, 137, 175, 208, 219
Times-Dispatch, 192
Tindley, Charles A., 37, 103
Tin Pan Alley: and ASCAP, 109; and Copyright Law of 1909, 95; marketing similar to gospel publishers, 7, 28–29, 117; Rodeheaver's avoidance of, 130, 133; song plugging of, 71; and Billy Sunday parody, 82–83
Tokyo Bible Institute, 214
Toledo Blade, 66
Toledo Mud Hens, 65–66
Toledo revival campaign (1911), 6, 65–67, 69, 83, 262n11, 271n6
Tolerance, 193, 196, 205
"To My Son/Mother's Love," 306n70
Tongues of Fire, 214
Torrey, R. A., 53, 55–56, 62, 67, 211
Torrey-Alexander choir, 56
Torrey-Alexander revival campaigns, 55–56, 77–78
Towner, Daniel B., 42, 53, 58, 62, 65, 97, 101–2

Treaty of Paris, 47
Triumphant Service Songs, 103
trombone: Cliff Barrows leading singing with, 50, 234–35, 240–41, 246; Christian evangelists playing, 30, 50, 234, 308n18; comparison of Rodeheaver and Pryor playing, 49; Henry Fillmore composing for and playing, 47, 222, 268n42; Leroy Kenfield, 30; Simone Mantia, 30; Aimee Semple McPherson's requirement, 219; Arthur Pryor, 30, 49; role in Sunday meetings, 86; Gardell Simons, 30
trombone and Rodeheaver: acquires first, 47–48, 268n44; in Africa, 49, 208–9; in bands, 16, 46, 48; brand endorsements, 49, 119; criticism of playing, 49, 233–34; in Dead Sea, 49; in France, 49; goals in playing, 49–50; instruments used, *front cover*, *1*, *13*, *35*, *46*, *48*, *49*, *59*, *81*, *122*, *149*, *211*, *236*, *251*; leading singing with, 1, 30, 35, 47, 48, 54, 251; as personal brand, 6, 30, 48, 132; plays, 7, 14, 24, 47, 49, 54, 56, 61, 64; recordings made, 117, 132, 138, 142, *148*; repertoire played, 30, 49, 117, 197, 221, 285n85; "Reverend Trombone" nickname, 6–7, 269n57; Will Rogers's view of, 50
trombone and songleading, 20, 234–35
trombone choir (Moravian), 213, 221, 303n8
Trotter, Mel, 154, 240
Tullar-Meredith Co., 107–8
Turpin, Thomas, 220
Twain, Mark, 183
Twenty Years with Billy Sunday (book), 118, 127, 139, 283n41
Twenty Years with Billy Sunday (film), 139–41
two-step marches, 220

Union Furnace, Ohio, 40, *41*, 42
Union Tabernacle; Or, Movable Tent Church, 64
United Daughters of the Confederacy, 20
United Lutheran Church in America, 223
universal language (music), 212–13

Variety, 137
vaudeville: acts, 16–17, 134, 170, 220–21; comparisons to Rodeheaver, 15–16, 86–87; comparison to revivalism, 7, 16–17, 33, 86–88; and coon songs, 167; and parlor songs, 224–25; and spirituals, 177; and Billy Sunday, 116, 86–87, 113

Vaughan, James D., 4, 103–4, 145, 153–54, 164
Vaughan, Keiffer, 156
Vaughan, Stella, 156
Vaughan Quartet, 144, 153, 155–56, 201–2
Vaughan Record Co., 144–45, 150, 202
Vaughan's Concert Quartet Book for Male Voices, 153–54
Venable, Samuel Hoyt, 20–21
verbal blackface, 186
vernacular music, 1, 3, 52, 159, 216, 220, 224–25. *See also* cultivated music
Victor Talking Machine Co: as a "big three" label, 147; and communal singing records, 152–53; early jazz sessions, 220; "first" country sessions, 8; Fisk Jubilee sessions, 170–71; and lateral cut discs, 145; RCA Victor pressings, 163; Rodeheaver recordings for, 116–18, 126, 142–44, 176, 180; Rodeheaver's dissatisfaction with, 162; and George Beverly Shea, 238–39
Vitaphone (sound film system), 134
Vocalion Records, 117

WABC-Columbia, 130
"Wake Up, America, and Kluck, Kluck, Kluck," 201, 300n54
Walls, William J., 188
Walnut Street Baptist Church (Waterloo, Iowa), 128
Walton, Robert A., 52–53
warm-up songs, 71, 224
Warner Music Group, 249
Washington, Booker T., 19
Washington Boulevard Methodist Church (Oak Park, Illinois), 149–50
Waters, Ethel, 24
WEAF, 125
Weisberger, Bernard, 87
"We'll Be Waiting When You Come Back Home," 96–97
Wembley Stadium (London), 153
Wesley, Charles, 39
Wesley, John, 39
Westbury, Harry, 242–43
Western Association of Writers (Winona Lake), 183
Western Pennsylvania Christian Missionary Society, 203
Westminster Choir, 137
Westminster Films, 138, 140

INDEX

Westminster Hotel (Winona Lake), 154, 230–31, 235, 239
West Virginia Infantry Volunteers, 40
Wheaton College, 6, 193
"When Billy Sunday Comes to Town," 82
"When Johnny Comes Marching Home," 300n42
"When Malindy Sings," 139, 171, 184–86
"Where Am De Chil'ren?," 183
White, George L., 168–69
"White Christmas," 188
white gospel (as a genre), 4–5, 14, 26, 36, 177, 181
white spirituals (southern folk songs), 8–9
"Who Dat Say Chicken in Dis Crowd," 183–84
WHT, 123
Wight, Paul Stone, 199–200, 202–7, 202
Williams, Adam D., 19, 21–23
Williams, Milan B., 64
Williamson, John Finley, 137
William Street Methodist Episcopal Church (Delaware, Ohio), 52
Willkie, Wendell, 135–36
"Will the Circle Be Unbroken," 5
Wilson, Woodrow, 135
Wings Over Jordan Favorite Spirituals of 1939, 175
Winona Assembly and Summer School Association (1895–1915), 112
Winona Lake Bible Conference (general), 54, 119, 120–21, 134–35, 230, 233–34
Winona Lake Christian Assembly (1939–1988), 140, 210, 232–33
Winona Lake: criticism of, 72; Grace College, 2, 244; Interdenominational Association of Evangelists (IAE) meetings, 54, 218, 270n76; Lost Prayer Meeting (Billy Graham), 239; and "Money-Making Altruism," 112, 175; Rainbow Point (final Rodeheaver home), 131, 210, 231, 232, 245; Rodeheaver Co. headquarters, 2, 98, 230–31, 247–48; Rodeheaver homes, 16, 68, 68; Rodeheaver philanthropy to, 242, 244; Rodeheaver property ownership, 68, 68, 139, 154, 230; Rodeheaver recording studio, 142–44, 151, 155–57, 161, 163, 205; Billy Sunday home, 68, 127. *See also* Song Director's Conference; Youth for Christ
Wisconsin Chair Factory (Port Washington, Wisconsin), 145
Wiseman, Turner H., 173–74, 176, 178, 183, 188
Wiseman Quartet and Sextet, 104, 165, 174, 176–78
WLS, 123–24, 131, 282n4
WLS National Barn Dance, 124
WMAQ, 137
WMBI, 233–34, 237
WMC, 123
"The Wonder of It All," 239
Word Music Co., 2, 247–49
Work, John Wesley, Jr., 170, 177
World's Columbian Exposition of 1893, 220
Worth While Poems (book), 126, 180, 226
Worth While Poems (radio program), 126
WOZ, 122, 122, 282n21
Wurlitzer Co., 49, 119

Yale Divinity School, 18–19
Yeaworth, Irvin S. (Shorty), 140–41
Yeo, Douglas, 6
"Yes, the Klan Has No Catholics," 199
"Yes, We Have No Bananas," 199
YFC choruses, 237
YMCA, 33–34, 49, 62, 80
"You Must Come in at the Door," 186
Young, Cy, 66
Youth for Christ (YFC): and Billy Graham, 234–35; music of, 129, 236–37, 240, 245, 250; purpose statement, 235–36; Rodeheaver involvement with, 139, 236–37, 241–42; and Winona Lake, 139, 163, 235–37, 239

Zion Travelers, 178, 186
"Zip Coon," 169

KEVIN MUNGONS is a Chicago-based writer and editor. As backlist curator and editor for Moody Publishers, he champions content from 125 years of book publishing. He has worked as editorial director for nonprofit organizations, and continues to help authors and organizations tell their story. A longtime church musician, he researches and writes about gospel music, early recordings, and radio.

DOUGLAS YEO has received acclaim as a teacher, author, and performing artist. Following his long career as bass trombonist of the Boston Symphony (1985–2012), he was professor of trombone at Arizona State University and now teaches at Wheaton College (Illinois). A graduate of Wheaton College and New York University, he is the author of five books and dozens of articles. He has performed, presented master classes, and held residencies on five continents. He received the International Trombone Association's highest honor, the ITA Award, in 2014. His ongoing research interests include the intersection of music with faith, and musical instruments both ancient and modern. Visit him online at yeodoug.com and thelasttrombone.com.

MUSIC IN AMERICAN LIFE

Only a Miner: Studies in Recorded Coal-Mining Songs   *Archie Green*
Great Day Coming: Folk Music and the American Left   *R. Serge Denisoff*
John Philip Sousa: A Descriptive Catalog of His Works   *Paul E. Bierley*
The Hell-Bound Train: A Cowboy Songbook   *Glenn Ohrlin*
Oh, Didn't He Ramble: The Life Story of Lee Collins, as Told to Mary Collins
    Edited by *Frank J. Gillis and John W. Miner*
American Labor Songs of the Nineteenth Century   *Philip S. Foner*
Stars of Country Music: Uncle Dave Macon to Johnny Rodriguez   Edited by *Bill C. Malone and Judith McCulloh*
Git Along, Little Dogies: Songs and Songmakers of the American West   *John I. White*
A Texas-Mexican *Cancionero*: Folksongs of the Lower Border   *Américo Paredes*
San Antonio Rose: The Life and Music of Bob Wills   *Charles R. Townsend*
Early Downhome Blues: A Musical and Cultural Analysis   *Jeff Todd Titon*
An Ives Celebration: Papers and Panels of the Charles Ives Centennial Festival-Conference   Edited by *H. Wiley Hitchcock and Vivian Perlis*
Sinful Tunes and Spirituals: Black Folk Music to the Civil War   *Dena J. Epstein*
Joe Scott, the Woodsman-Songmaker   *Edward D. Ives*
Jimmie Rodgers: The Life and Times of America's Blue Yodeler   *Nolan Porterfield*
Early American Music Engraving and Printing: A History of Music Publishing in America from 1787 to 1825, with Commentary on Earlier and Later Practices   *Richard J. Wolfe*
Sing a Sad Song: The Life of Hank Williams   *Roger M. Williams*
Long Steel Rail: The Railroad in American Folksong   *Norm Cohen*
Resources of American Music History: A Directory of Source Materials from Colonial Times to World War II   *D. W. Krummel, Jean Geil, Doris J. Dyen, and Deane L. Root*
Tenement Songs: The Popular Music of the Jewish Immigrants   *Mark Slobin*
Ozark Folksongs   *Vance Randolph; edited and abridged by Norm Cohen*
Oscar Sonneck and American Music   Edited by *William Lichtenwanger*
Bluegrass Breakdown: The Making of the Old Southern Sound   *Robert Cantwell*
Bluegrass: A History   *Neil V. Rosenberg*
Music at the White House: A History of the American Spirit   *Elise K. Kirk*
Red River Blues: The Blues Tradition in the Southeast   *Bruce Bastin*
Good Friends and Bad Enemies: Robert Winslow Gordon and the Study of American Folksong   *Debora Kodish*
Fiddlin' Georgia Crazy: Fiddlin' John Carson, His Real World, and the World of His Songs   *Gene Wiggins*
America's Music: From the Pilgrims to the Present (rev. 3d ed.)   *Gilbert Chase*
Secular Music in Colonial Annapolis: The Tuesday Club, 1745–56   *John Barry Talley*
Bibliographical Handbook of American Music   *D. W. Krummel*
Goin' to Kansas City   *Nathan W. Pearson Jr.*
"Susanna," "Jeanie," and "The Old Folks at Home": The Songs of Stephen C. Foster from His Time to Ours (2d ed.)   *William W. Austin*
Songprints: The Musical Experience of Five Shoshone Women   *Judith Vander*

"Happy in the Service of the Lord": Afro-American Gospel Quartets in Memphis
    Kip Lornell
Paul Hindemith in the United States   *Luther Noss*
"My Song Is My Weapon": People's Songs, American Communism, and the Politics of
    Culture, 1930–50   *Robbie Lieberman*
Chosen Voices: The Story of the American Cantorate   *Mark Slobin*
Theodore Thomas: America's Conductor and Builder of Orchestras, 1835–1905   *Ezra Schabas*
"The Whorehouse Bells Were Ringing" and Other Songs Cowboys Sing
    Collected and Edited by Guy Logsdon
Crazeology: The Autobiography of a Chicago Jazzman   *Bud Freeman,
    as Told to Robert Wolf*
Discoursing Sweet Music: Brass Bands and Community Life in Turn-of-the-Century
    Pennsylvania   *Kenneth Kreitner*
Mormonism and Music: A History   *Michael Hicks*
Voices of the Jazz Age: Profiles of Eight Vintage Jazzmen   *Chip Deffaa*
Pickin' on Peachtree: A History of Country Music in Atlanta, Georgia   *Wayne W. Daniel*
Bitter Music: Collected Journals, Essays, Introductions, and Librettos   *Harry Partch;
    edited by Thomas McGeary*
Ethnic Music on Records: A Discography of Ethnic Recordings Produced in the United States,
    1893 to 1942   *Richard K. Spottswood*
Downhome Blues Lyrics: An Anthology from the Post–World War II Era   *Jeff Todd Titon*
Ellington: The Early Years   *Mark Tucker*
Chicago Soul   *Robert Pruter*
That Half-Barbaric Twang: The Banjo in American Popular Culture   *Karen Linn*
Hot Man: The Life of Art Hodes   *Art Hodes and Chadwick Hansen*
The Erotic Muse: American Bawdy Songs (2d ed.)   *Ed Cray*
Barrio Rhythm: Mexican American Music in Los Angeles   *Steven Loza*
The Creation of Jazz: Music, Race, and Culture in Urban America   *Burton W. Peretti*
Charles Martin Loeffler: A Life Apart in Music   *Ellen Knight*
Club Date Musicians: Playing the New York Party Circuit   *Bruce A. MacLeod*
Opera on the Road: Traveling Opera Troupes in the United States, 1825–60
    Katherine K. Preston
The Stonemans: An Appalachian Family and the Music That Shaped Their Lives
    Ivan M. Tribe
Transforming Tradition: Folk Music Revivals Examined   *Edited by Neil V. Rosenberg*
The Crooked Stovepipe: Athapaskan Fiddle Music and Square Dancing in Northeast Alaska
    and Northwest Canada   *Craig Mishler*
Traveling the High Way Home: Ralph Stanley and the World of Traditional Bluegrass
    Music   *John Wright*
Carl Ruggles: Composer, Painter, and Storyteller   *Marilyn Ziffrin*
Never without a Song: The Years and Songs of Jennie Devlin, 1865–1952
    Katharine D. Newman
The Hank Snow Story   *Hank Snow, with Jack Ownbey and Bob Burris*
Milton Brown and the Founding of Western Swing   *Cary Ginell,
    with special assistance from Roy Lee Brown*

Santiago de Murcia's "Códice Saldívar No. 4": A Treasury of Secular Guitar Music from
    Baroque Mexico   *Craig H. Russell*
The Sound of the Dove: Singing in Appalachian Primitive Baptist Churches
    Beverly Bush Patterson
Heartland Excursions: Ethnomusicological Reflections on Schools of Music   *Bruno Nettl*
Doowop: The Chicago Scene   *Robert Pruter*
Blue Rhythms: Six Lives in Rhythm and Blues   *Chip Deffaa*
Shoshone Ghost Dance Religion: Poetry Songs and Great Basin Context   *Judith Vander*
Go Cat Go! Rockabilly Music and Its Makers   *Craig Morrison*
'Twas Only an Irishman's Dream: The Image of Ireland and the Irish in American Popular
    Song Lyrics, 1800–1920   *William H. A. Williams*
Democracy at the Opera: Music, Theater, and Culture in New York City, 1815–60
    Karen Ahlquist
Fred Waring and the Pennsylvanians   *Virginia Waring*
Woody, Cisco, and Me: Seamen Three in the Merchant Marine   *Jim Longhi*
Behind the Burnt Cork Mask: Early Blackface Minstrelsy and Antebellum American Popular
    Culture   *William J. Mahar*
Going to Cincinnati: A History of the Blues in the Queen City   *Steven C. Tracy*
Pistol Packin' Mama: Aunt Molly Jackson and the Politics of Folksong   *Shelly Romalis*
Sixties Rock: Garage, Psychedelic, and Other Satisfactions   *Michael Hicks*
The Late Great Johnny Ace and the Transition from R&B to Rock 'n' Roll   *James M. Salem*
Tito Puente and the Making of Latin Music   *Steven Loza*
Juilliard: A History   *Andrea Olmstead*
Understanding Charles Seeger, Pioneer in American Musicology   *Edited by Bell Yung
    and Helen Rees*
Mountains of Music: West Virginia Traditional Music from *Goldenseal*   *Edited by John Lilly*
Alice Tully: An Intimate Portrait   *Albert Fuller*
A Blues Life   *Henry Townsend, as told to Bill Greensmith*
Long Steel Rail: The Railroad in American Folksong (2d ed.)   *Norm Cohen*
The Golden Age of Gospel   *Text by Horace Clarence Boyer;
    photography by Lloyd Yearwood*
Aaron Copland: The Life and Work of an Uncommon Man   *Howard Pollack*
Louis Moreau Gottschalk   *S. Frederick Starr*
Race, Rock, and Elvis   *Michael T. Bertrand*
Theremin: Ether Music and Espionage   *Albert Glinsky*
Poetry and Violence: The Ballad Tradition of Mexico's Costa Chica   *John H. McDowell*
The Bill Monroe Reader   *Edited by Tom Ewing*
Music in Lubavitcher Life   *Ellen Koskoff*
Zarzuela: Spanish Operetta, American Stage   *Janet L. Sturman*
Bluegrass Odyssey: A Documentary in Pictures and Words, 1966–86   *Carl Fleischhauer
    and Neil V. Rosenberg*
That Old-Time Rock & Roll: A Chronicle of an Era, 1954–63   *Richard Aquila*
Labor's Troubadour   *Joe Glazer*
American Opera   *Elise K. Kirk*

Don't Get above Your Raisin': Country Music and the Southern Working Class
   Bill C. Malone
John Alden Carpenter: A Chicago Composer   Howard Pollack
Heartbeat of the People: Music and Dance of the Northern Pow-wow   Tara Browner
My Lord, What a Morning: An Autobiography   Marian Anderson
Marian Anderson: A Singer's Journey   Allan Keiler
Charles Ives Remembered: An Oral History   Vivian Perlis
Henry Cowell, Bohemian   Michael Hicks
Rap Music and Street Consciousness   Cheryl L. Keyes
Louis Prima   Garry Boulard
Marian McPartland's Jazz World: All in Good Time   Marian McPartland
Robert Johnson: Lost and Found   Barry Lee Pearson and Bill McCulloch
Bound for America: Three British Composers   Nicholas Temperley
Lost Sounds: Blacks and the Birth of the Recording Industry, 1890–1919   Tim Brooks
Burn, Baby! BURN! The Autobiography of Magnificent Montague   Magnificent Montague
   with Bob Baker
Way Up North in Dixie: A Black Family's Claim to the Confederate Anthem
   Howard L. Sacks and Judith Rose Sacks
The Bluegrass Reader   Edited by Thomas Goldsmith
Colin McPhee: Composer in Two Worlds   Carol J. Oja
Robert Johnson, Mythmaking, and Contemporary American Culture   Patricia R. Schroeder
Composing a World: Lou Harrison, Musical Wayfarer   Leta E. Miller and Fredric Lieberman
Fritz Reiner, Maestro and Martinet   Kenneth Morgan
That Toddlin' Town: Chicago's White Dance Bands and Orchestras, 1900–1950
   Charles A. Sengstock Jr.
Dewey and Elvis: The Life and Times of a Rock 'n' Roll Deejay   Louis Cantor
Come Hither to Go Yonder: Playing Bluegrass with Bill Monroe   Bob Black
Chicago Blues: Portraits and Stories   David Whiteis
The Incredible Band of John Philip Sousa   Paul E. Bierley
"Maximum Clarity" and Other Writings on Music   Ben Johnston, edited by Bob Gilmore
Staging Tradition: John Lair and Sarah Gertrude Knott   Michael Ann Williams
Homegrown Music: Discovering Bluegrass   Stephanie P. Ledgin
Tales of a Theatrical Guru   Danny Newman
The Music of Bill Monroe   Neil V. Rosenberg and Charles K. Wolfe
Pressing On: The Roni Stoneman Story   Roni Stoneman, as told to Ellen Wright
Together Let Us Sweetly Live   Jonathan C. David, with photographs by Richard Holloway
Live Fast, Love Hard: The Faron Young Story   Diane Diekman
Air Castle of the South: WSM Radio and the Making of Music City   Craig P. Havighurst
Traveling Home: Sacred Harp Singing and American Pluralism   Kiri Miller
Where Did Our Love Go? The Rise and Fall of the Motown Sound   Nelson George
Lonesome Cowgirls and Honky-Tonk Angels: The Women of Barn Dance Radio
   Kristine M. McCusker
California Polyphony: Ethnic Voices, Musical Crossroads   Mina Yang
The Never-Ending Revival: Rounder Records and the Folk Alliance   Michael F. Scully
Sing It Pretty: A Memoir   Bess Lomax Hawes

Working Girl Blues: The Life and Music of Hazel Dickens   *Hazel Dickens and Bill C. Malone*
Charles Ives Reconsidered   *Gayle Sherwood Magee*
The Hayloft Gang: The Story of the National Barn Dance   *Edited by Chad Berry*
Country Music Humorists and Comedians   *Loyal Jones*
Record Makers and Breakers: Voices of the Independent Rock 'n' Roll Pioneers   *John Broven*
Music of the First Nations: Tradition and Innovation in Native North America
    Edited by Tara Browner
Cafe Society: The Wrong Place for the Right People   *Barney Josephson,*
    with Terry Trilling-Josephson
George Gershwin: An Intimate Portrait   *Walter Rimler*
Life Flows On in Endless Song: Folk Songs and American History   *Robert V. Wells*
I Feel a Song Coming On: The Life of Jimmy McHugh   *Alyn Shipton*
King of the Queen City: The Story of King Records   *Jon Hartley Fox*
Long Lost Blues: Popular Blues in America, 1850–1920   *Peter C. Muir*
Hard Luck Blues: Roots Music Photographs from the Great Depression   *Rich Remsberg*
Restless Giant: The Life and Times of Jean Aberbach and Hill and Range Songs
    Bar Biszick-Lockwood
Champagne Charlie and Pretty Jemima: Variety Theater in the Nineteenth Century
    Gillian M. Rodger
Sacred Steel: Inside an African American Steel Guitar Tradition   *Robert L. Stone*
Gone to the Country: The New Lost City Ramblers and the Folk Music Revival   *Ray Allen*
The Makers of the Sacred Harp   *David Warren Steel with Richard H. Hulan*
Woody Guthrie, American Radical   *Will Kaufman*
George Szell: A Life of Music   *Michael Charry*
Bean Blossom: The Brown County Jamboree and Bill Monroe's Bluegrass Festivals
    Thomas A. Adler
Crowe on the Banjo: The Music Life of J. D. Crowe   *Marty Godbey*
Twentieth Century Drifter: The Life of Marty Robbins   *Diane Diekman*
Henry Mancini: Reinventing Film Music   *John Caps*
The Beautiful Music All Around Us: Field Recordings and the American Experience   *Stephen Wade*
Then Sings My Soul: The Culture of Southern Gospel Music   *Douglas Harrison*
The Accordion in the Americas: Klezmer, Polka, Tango, Zydeco, and More!
    Edited by Helena Simonett
Bluegrass Bluesman: A Memoir   *Josh Graves, edited by Fred Bartenstein*
One Woman in a Hundred: Edna Phillips and the Philadelphia Orchestra   *Mary Sue Welsh*
The Great Orchestrator: Arthur Judson and American Arts Management   *James M. Doering*
Charles Ives in the Mirror: American Histories of an Iconic Composer   *David C. Paul*
Southern Soul-Blues   *David Whiteis*
Sweet Air: Modernism, Regionalism, and American Popular Song   *Edward P. Comentale*
Pretty Good for a Girl: Women in Bluegrass   *Murphy Hicks Henry*
Sweet Dreams: The World of Patsy Cline   *Warren R. Hofstra*
William Sidney Mount and the Creolization of American Culture   *Christopher J. Smith*
Bird: The Life and Music of Charlie Parker   *Chuck Haddix*
Making the March King: John Philip Sousa's Washington Years, 1854–1893   *Patrick Warfield*

In It for the Long Run   *Jim Rooney*
Pioneers of the Blues Revival   *Steve Cushing*
Roots of the Revival: American and British Folk Music in the 1950s   *Ronald D. Cohen and Rachel Clare Donaldson*
Blues All Day Long: The Jimmy Rogers Story   *Wayne Everett Goins*
Yankee Twang: Country and Western Music in New England   *Clifford R. Murphy*
The Music of the Stanley Brothers   *Gary B. Reid*
Hawaiian Music in Motion: Mariners, Missionaries, and Minstrels   *James Revell Carr*
Sounds of the New Deal: The Federal Music Project in the West   *Peter Gough*
The Mormon Tabernacle Choir: A Biography   *Michael Hicks*
The Man That Got Away: The Life and Songs of Harold Arlen   *Walter Rimler*
A City Called Heaven: Chicago and the Birth of Gospel Music   *Robert M. Marovich*
Blues Unlimited: Essential Interviews from the Original Blues Magazine   *Edited by Bill Greensmith, Mike Rowe, and Mark Camarigg*
Hoedowns, Reels, and Frolics: Roots and Branches of Southern Appalachian Dance   *Phil Jamison*
Fannie Bloomfield-Zeisler: The Life and Times of a Piano Virtuoso   *Beth Abelson Macleod*
Cybersonic Arts: Adventures in American New Music   *Gordon Mumma, edited with commentary by Michelle Fillion*
The Magic of Beverly Sills   *Nancy Guy*
Waiting for Buddy Guy   *Alan Harper*
Harry T. Burleigh: From the Spiritual to the Harlem Renaissance   *Jean E. Snyder*
Music in the Age of Anxiety: American Music in the Fifties   *James Wierzbicki*
Jazzing: New York City's Unseen Scene   *Thomas H. Greenland*
A Cole Porter Companion   *Edited by Don M. Randel, Matthew Shaftel, and Susan Forscher Weiss*
Foggy Mountain Troubadour: The Life and Music of Curly Seckler   *Penny Parsons*
Blue Rhythm Fantasy: Big Band Jazz Arranging in the Swing Era   *John Wriggle*
Bill Clifton: America's Bluegrass Ambassador to the World   *Bill C. Malone*
Chinatown Opera Theater in North America   *Nancy Yunhwa Rao*
The Elocutionists: Women, Music, and the Spoken Word   *Marian Wilson Kimber*
May Irwin: Singing, Shouting, and the Shadow of Minstrelsy   *Sharon Ammen*
Peggy Seeger: A Life of Music, Love, and Politics   *Jean R. Freedman*
Charles Ives's *Concord*: Essays after a Sonata   *Kyle Gann*
Don't Give Your Heart to a Rambler: My Life with Jimmy Martin, the King of Bluegrass   *Barbara Martin Stephens*
Libby Larsen: Composing an American Life   *Denise Von Glahn*
George Szell's Reign: Behind the Scenes with the Cleveland Orchestra   *Marcia Hansen Kraus*
Just One of the Boys: Female-to-Male Cross-Dressing on the American Variety Stage   *Gillian M. Rodger*
Spirituals and the Birth of a Black Entertainment Industry   *Sandra Jean Graham*
Right to the Juke Joint: A Personal History of American Music   *Patrick B. Mullen*
Bluegrass Generation: A Memoir   *Neil V. Rosenberg*
Pioneers of the Blues Revival, Expanded Second Edition   *Steve Cushing*

Banjo Roots and Branches   *Edited by Robert Winans*
Bill Monroe: The Life and Music of the Blue Grass Man   *Tom Ewing*
Dixie Dewdrop: The Uncle Dave Macon Story   *Michael D. Doubler*
Los Romeros: Royal Family of the Spanish Guitar   *Walter Aaron Clark*
Transforming Women's Education: Liberal Arts and Music in Female Seminaries
  Jewel A. Smith
Rethinking American Music   *Edited by Tara Browner and Thomas L. Riis*
Leonard Bernstein and the Language of Jazz   *Katherine Baber*
Dancing Revolution: Bodies, Space, and Sound in American Cultural History
  Christopher J. Smith
Peggy Glanville-Hicks: Composer and Critic   *Suzanne Robinson*
Mormons, Musical Theater, and Belonging in America   *Jake Johnson*
Blues Legacy: Tradition and Innovation in Chicago   *David Whiteis*
Blues Before Sunrise 2: Interviews from the Chicago Scene   *Steve Cushing*
The Cashaway Psalmody: Transatlantic Religion and Music in Colonial Carolina
  Stephen A. Marini
Earl Scruggs and Foggy Mountain Breakdown: The Making of an American Classic
  Thomas Goldsmith
A Guru's Journey: Pandit Chitresh Das and Indian Classical Dance in Diaspora
  Sarah Morelli
Unsettled Scores: Politics, Hollywood, and the Film Music of Aaron Copland and
  Hanns Eisler   *Sally Bick*
Hillbilly Maidens, Okies, and Cowgirls: Women's Country Music, 1930–1960
  Stephanie Vander Wel
Always the Queen: The Denise LaSalle Story   *Denise LaSalle with David Whiteis*
Artful Noise: Percussion Literature in the Twentieth Century   *Thomas Siwe*
The Heart of a Woman: The Life and Music of Florence B. Price   *Rae Linda Brown,
  edited by Guthrie P. Ramsey Jr.*
When Sunday Comes: Gospel Music in the Soul and Hip-Hop Eras   *Claudrena N. Harold*
The Lady Swings: Memoirs of a Jazz Drummer   *Dottie Dodgion and Wayne Enstice*
Industrial Strength Bluegrass: Southwestern Ohio's Musical Legacy
  Edited by Fred Bartenstein and Curtis W. Ellison
Soul on Soul: The Life and Music of Mary Lou Williams   *Tammy L. Kernodle*
Unbinding Gentility: Women Making Music in the Nineteenth-Century South
  Candace Bailey
Punks in Peoria: Making a Scene in the American Heartland   *Jonathan Wright
  and Dawson Barrett*
Homer Rodeheaver and the Rise of the Gospel Music Industry   *Kevin Mungons
  and Douglas Yeo*

The University of Illinois Press
is a founding member of the
Association of University Presses.

University of Illinois Press
1325 South Oak Street
Champaign, IL 61820-6903
www.press.uillinois.edu

Printed by Printforce, United Kingdom